Hang 'Em High

ALSO BY BOB HERZBERG
AND FROM MCFARLAND

*The Left Side of the Screen:
Communist and Left-Wing Ideology
in Hollywood, 1929–2009* (2011)

*Savages and Saints: The Changing Image
of American Indians in Westerns* (2008)

*The FBI and the Movies: A History
of the Bureau on Screen and Behind
the Scenes in Hollywood* (2007)

Shooting Scripts: From Pulp Western to Film (2005)

Hang 'Em High

Law and Disorder in Western Films and Literature

BOB HERZBERG

McFarland & Company, Inc., Publishers
Jefferson, North Carolina, and London

LIBRARY OF CONGRESS CATALOGUING-IN-PUBLICATION DATA

Herzberg, Bob, 1956–
Hang 'em high : law and disorder in western films and
literature / Bob Herzberg.
    pages cm
Includes bibliographical references and index.

ISBN 978-0-7864-6838-6
softcover : acid free paper ∞

1. Western films—United States—History and criticism.
2. American fiction—Film adaptations.   3. Film adaptations—History
and criticism.   4. West (U.S.)—In motion pictures.   5. West (U.S.)—
    In literature.   6. Motion pictures and history.   I. Title.
    PN1995.9.W4H44 2013   791.43'6278—dc23   2013026677

BRITISH LIBRARY CATALOGUING DATA ARE AVAILABLE

© 2013 Bob Herzberg. All rights reserved

*No part of this book may be reproduced or transmitted in any form
or by any means, electronic or mechanical, including photocopying
or recording, or by any information storage and retrieval system,
without permission in writing from the publisher.*

Cover photograph: Clint Eastwood in *Hang 'Em High*, 1968,
directed by Ted Post (United Artists/Photofest)

Manufactured in the United States of America

*McFarland & Company, Inc., Publishers
Box 611, Jefferson, North Carolina 28640
www.mcfarlandpub.com*

To my nephew, Mike:
When you were a little boy, you kept
begging me to pick you up and spin you around.
Today, you're a city councilman.
I can't help but think there's a connection somewhere...

Acknowledgments

I'd like to thank those individuals and organizations that have helped me immeasurably in my work on this book.

My thanks to the Margaret Herrick Library in Beverly Hills who provided me with oodles of studio correspondence, production files, budget sheets, pressbooks, synopses, original screen treatments and letters to and from the Production Code Administration. I'm particularly grateful to them for information on the Paramount films *The Tin Star* and *Nevada Smith*, as well as the classic westerns *The Man from Colorado* and *Silver Lode*. All of this much-needed help came from the polite and hard-working folks at the library's Special Collections Desk, as well as administrators Barbara Hall, Jenny Romero and Linda Harris Mehr who helped me in choosing the right files to research.

I'd like to thank the incredible Ned Comstock, who gave me the original synopsis and press copy for *No Name on the Bullet* from the Universal Collection at the University of Southern California's Cinema Arts Library. In years past, Ned has helped me find the rarest of the rare, or the equivalent of the Dead Sea Scrolls of Hollywood studio files, to help with my research. Many thanks, my friend.

I'd also like to thank Sandra Day Lee and Jonathon Auxier, director and curator, respectively, of the Warner Brothers Archives of the School of Cinematic Arts at the University of Southern California. These two people have always been helpful and, as an added bonus, I got a chance to visit one of the most beautiful college campuses I've ever seen. Not that a beautiful environment is always mandatory for a researcher, but when you're a high school dropout like me, you become easily impressed by all that fresh-cut campus grass and that obligatory fountain they always build in the middle of it.

I also thank my amazingly still-loyal friends who, thanks to my Facebook posts and many a drunken night at some sleazy dive, know more about the planned book than I do myself. And I salute my wonderful family who had invited me to many a special occasion or celebration of some kind, only to be rudely told that the New Hemingway is working on a project that will set the literary world on its ear — or ears — and that I haven't got time to attend some time-killing trifle like a wedding or a funeral. Folks, I apologize for my usual self-involvement and I promise it won't happen again until I finish this next one...

Most of all, I'd like to thank Colleen, my beautiful wife of 16 years and lover of the 10 years before that. She has read and reread my work, proofread and re-proofread it, and, as a movie buff extraordinaire, offered sharp, inciteful criticism. She was never a western fan, and she tells me that it was through my influence that she started to appreciate this underrated art form. Her love, her loyalty, and her cooking have sustained me through these many years, and I will cherish her always. I especially applaud her patience and fortitude in seeing, yet again, westerns that we had already seen many years before, and especially my unwanted commentary on a certain film's production background and historical accuracy, or lack of it. Let this be a warning: Never sit next to a person like me in your neighborhood movie house or in front of a DVD player in your home!

I certainly hope that this book helps renew interest in many of the films I've chosen to discuss. Abuse of the law and the God-given right to due process in the old west is a subject the Hollywood westerns and pulp novels have used again and again. For the most part, however, duly appointed lawmen have always won out over hired gunmen, mob rule and those who rode the vengeance trail.

There are those who say that the western never gave us a message. I disagree. In their own way, these films and novels emphasized the triumph of our Constitution and our Bill of Rights.

For a free nation, you can't get a better message than that...

Table of Contents

Acknowledgments	vii
Introduction	1
1. Mistrials: 1929–1939 — The Depression, the Talkies and Manipulation of the Law in the Old West	5
2. International Hangmen: 1940–1949 — War in the Present and Totalitarian Behavior in the Old West	35
3. Chaos: 1950–1955 — The Cold War, HUAC and Mob Rule in the Old West	63
4. Badge-Toters: 1956–1959 — Reaffirming the Rule of Law in the Old West	115
5. Deadly Force: 1960–1969 — Riding the Vengeance Trail as War Breaks Out at Home and Abroad	155
6. Bloodbath: 1970–1976 — Vietnam, Race Riots and Abuse of the Law in the Old West	188
7. Reload: 1977–1992 — American Cynicism and Revisionist Western History	217
8. Back Trail: 1993–2013 — The Last Twenty Years	238
Chapter Notes	243
Bibliography	247
Index	251

Introduction

"We've got the bastards. Well, what are we waiting for? Let them swing, I say!"
— Farnley, member of the lynch mob. *The Ox-Bow Incident*

The above statement encapsulated in a nutshell the worst of frontier justice in the old west. The Twentieth Century–Fox film of 1943 would never touch the heavy ideology or darkness of the novel, not to mention the above salty language; but the book accurately brought home to twentieth century audiences the horrors of mob rule and mockery of due process, and consequently, the repudiation of our Bill of Rights and the rejection of our Constitution. And it was not as if such horrors were committed only in the primitive environment of the 19th century west, where horses were the primary mode of transportation and county sheriffs could be hundreds of miles away. South of the Mason-Dixon line, and in many cases north of it, lynching of American citizens of a certain skin color was still going on, many times sanctioned by local, state and in some cases, federal law enforcement.

Western novels and films were written, not merely as two-fisted action-packed adventures, but as moral statements backing our American system — the rights of the individual, the pursuit of justice, the adherence to due process of the law, and the repudiation of mob rule and ethnic discrimination. The fact that those in power in the old west didn't always act as reputably or as wisely as they did in the western novel or film did nothing to lessen those ideals. The west was "the new country." Its towns were not as populous as the big cities of the east, nor did it have an entrenched criminal justice system; yet, in far too many cases, it was a place where corruption and political chicanery were already established. In many ways, then, the test of democracy truly began in the regions west of the Mississippi where lawmen were few and far between, where Indians still held sway and the perpetuation of race war continued unabated, where an uncontrollable mob could actually storm a jail and overpower a lawman, something that would be unthinkable in New York or Chicago.

The struggle for democracy and equal justice under the law were not always issues that occupied the usual cowboy hero, but it was there. It was there smoldering beneath the surface as he romanced the comely heroine, whether she was the rancher's daughter or the cute young schoolmarm; it was there as the hero cared for and even carried on long conversations with his horse (which we presume were one-sided); it was there as he got himself involved in some God-forsaken range war between territorial combatants of incredible ignorance and short-sidedness; it was there as he sought to prove the innocence of a falsely accused man and find the real culprit, who was usually named Pecos or Cactus or some other similarly slandered piece of vegetation.

In the following pages, you'll read about the pursuit of justice in the old west, and how it was depicted in western novels and Hollywood films as compared to the actual frontier reality; how the western myth was created to reinforce our American democracy and its promotion of the rule of law; the fascinating world of the western writer and the almost limitless variations that he used to promote the myth; and the production background of these western films, some of which were made from those novels, that emphasized American justice over mob rule and vigilantism.

The issues were sometimes far more complicated than the old stereotype of the clean, upstanding hero and the always dressed-in-black villain. The western hero didn't always consider that he was upholding our American way of life; the villain certainly didn't think of himself as some kind of frontier fascist; and the law, which, in reality, was capable of giving the wrong parties a way to avoid punishment, indeed could be an ass. In the interim, the hero confronted issues of his own besides fighting mob rule; and a major preoccupation for some of them was justice vs. revenge. In *Unforgiven*, a crooked lawman fails to pursue men who have assaulted a prostitute, and her co-workers hire Clint Eastwood's gentle farmer (with a past) to settle the score. Unlike the films of previous decades, we find that this time, the meek will not inherit the Earth.

In a Columbia B called *Across the Sierras* (which had nothing to do with the Sierras), Wild Bill Elliott (an underrated performer) prevents the lynching of Richard Fiske, telling the would-be lynchers that if they have a legitimate complaint, to take it to the sheriff. After anti-lynching "A" melodramas like *Fury*, *They Won't Forget* and *You Only Live Once*, circumventing due process was considered un–American and anti-democratic; the ideology deeply influenced the western, both As and Bs.

I will discuss classic westerns like *The Virginian*, the novel, and the film version of it made at the dawn of the talkies, and go up to the era of *Unforgiven* and the remake of *True Grit*, when the western film seemed to be on the wane. I'll also discuss those writers whose works were the basis of some of these films: Lauran Paine, Lewis B. Patten, Will C. Brown, Owen Wister, Walter Van Tilberg Clark, Elmore Leonard, Oakley Hall, Max Brand, Borden Chase, Emerson Hough, Conrad Richter, Tom Blackburn and Thomas McGuane. Though their novels or film treatments didn't always make it to the screen in their original form, these men deeply influenced the genre, reinforcing it and blessing it with their own unique and distinctive variations of the myth.

Some of the films discussed will be the first version of *The Virginian* and both versions of *Destry Rides Again*, as well as their source novels; *The Ox-Bow Incident* and its source novel; *Silver Lode, No Name on the Bullet, Hang 'Em High, The Oklahoma Kid, The Tin Star, Firecreek, Death of a Gunfighter, Vigilante Terror, Tom Horn, Riding Shotgun, Woman They Almost Lynched, Unforgiven, Jack Slade* (and the real-life gunfighter who inspired the film), *Along the Great Divide, Warlock, The Naked Spur, Rage at Dawn* and more. In all of these films, issues of extreme justice are brought up, as well as the rejection of due process. Yet in most of these westerns, made as they were before the cynical 1970s, American justice wins out.

In this work, I will quote from studio files, Production Code correspondence, newspaper reviews of the day, the novels that some of these films are based on, and the observations of some film historians who have their own take on these works. As an avid reader of westerns and a member of the Western Writers of America (and an Easterner yet!), I've attained a healthy respect for the efforts of the western author and how he has, in his own way, influenced our culture. The Ernest Haycoxes and Luke Shorts have not merely given readers a thrill; they were authentic documentarians who have celebrated our Americanism, repudiating the greed of the various Bosses of the Valley who sought to steal land from more-deserving folks and used violence to attain their ends.

It's good to know that the western gave us decency and due process; equality over inequality; success stories based on hard work, not privilege; all those things that are the antithesis of the vengeance trail and the rioting mobs, the warrior culture and thought control. Sure, many westerns were based on myth, with the stories clashing sharply with historical reality. At times, they perpetuated stereotype over fact, depicted compassionate authority figures over systemized corruption, failed to differentiate between "hostiles" and peaceful Native-American tribes, as well as ignoring its vast culture, and kept all its heroes persistently white, male and Christian.

The cowboy hero was usually too uneducated to verbalize the benefits of the Constitution or the Bill of Rights, or even the Magna Carta, but in his own slowly comprehending, yet two-fisted, quick-draw way, that was *exactly* what he ended up fighting for. There is an appropriate line from Universal's 1960 western *Seven Ways from Sundown* (based on Clair Huffaker's novel), when two ruffians want to take killer Jim Flood (Barry Sullivan) from the custody of Texas Ranger Seven Jones (Audie Murphy) in order to lynch him. When one asks Jones whether he understands Oklahoma law, Flood wryly answers for him, "No, but he upholds it anyway...." It is a line that is a coda for any screen character played by war hero Audie Murphy, as well as a line that fits the traditional cowboy hero who follows the rule of law.

In the following pages, you'll read how Hollywood (including its Production Code Office) and the publishing industry helped fashion the western into a unique art form that promoted the social-political agenda of a free, democratic America and exported the image to the world; and how our history was at times twisted and altered to fit the myth, and how the myth became so powerful, it reaffirmed our unique American identity.

The old west created the all-too-real phrase "Judge Colt and His Jury of Six." But six-gun justice was not always the order of the day, just as modern-day police officers are not supposed to open fire unless physically threatened. Unlike the myth, westerners had far more restraint than the above quote would imply.

We are a nation of laws, and in this country, murder is rarely, if ever, a social-political act. As the western makes a tentative comeback (again!) thanks to a box office smash like the remake of *True Grit*, we find that the values of the pursuit of justice that is so much a part of the old west can still entertain an America that now has Blackberries, MP3s and Facebook.

In the trailer for the Wild Bill Elliott "B" of 1953, *Vigilante Terror*, the narrator proclaims how one man fought an uphill battle against "the rule of gun and rope!"

The popularity of the western novels and films that came out of America proved beyond a shadow of a doubt that the brave defender of justice may have been fighting his battles alone onscreen, but off-screen, he had the approval of millions.

1

Mistrials: 1929–1939
The Depression, the Talkies
and Manipulation of the Law
in the Old West

"Out of whose hands do they take the law?"— *Molly Stark Wood*

In 1890, the federal government declared the frontier closed.

The following year saw the first published work from a young man who would give birth to a new literary genre that would permanently mythologize all that happened on that very same frontier.

Born in Germantown, Pennsylvania, on July 14, 1860, Owen Wister was the son of Owen Jones Wister, a wealthy physician, and Sarah Butler Wister, the aristocratic daughter of British actress Fanny Kemble. Financially well off, they were able to send their son to the best schools in England and Switzerland. As if that wasn't prestigious enough, young Owen was also educated at St. Paul's School in Concord, New Hampshire, and Harvard University. It was at Harvard that he became close friends with a man who also made a tremendous impact in his chosen field, Theodore Roosevelt.

With a famous actress as his grandmother and his own mother a pianist of some note, Owen developed a fondness for the arts and, after graduation from Harvard in 1882, went to a Paris conservatory to pursue a career in music. However, after two years, the homesick young man returned to America to begin a career in New York as a bank clerk. Perhaps due to his physical ailments, the intense pressure of working in New York's financial community, or the crowds and the frenetic activity of the city itself, Wister suffered a nervous breakdown. However, good friends came to his rescue. A Republican from the east who was thrilled to be out in the west, Theodore Roosevelt influenced the young man from Pennsylvania to go west to recuperate. In 1885, Wister traveled to Wyoming where the clear western air and amiable folks he met rejuvenated him. He also fell in love with the west. At the urging of his friend Teddy, he wrote articles and short pieces on his impressions of the west. In 1891, one year after the government declared the closing of the frontier, his short story "Hank's Woman" was published in *Harper's*.

But short stories and sketches on the west didn't pay the bills. Perhaps with some influence from his parents, he enrolled at Harvard Law School and became an attorney in 1888. Though he had his own office in the Francis Rawle Law Firm in Philadelphia and was now financially prosperous, the young man still felt unfulfilled. Mired in legal paperwork in the east, his heart was really somewhere west of the Mississippi.

Again, thanks to the influence of his pal Teddy, Owen's journals and notes became the basis of his fiction. He was already a published author; now, with the the Johnson County War which had torn apart his beloved Wyoming settling back into the dustbin of history, the young attorney decided to give the nation his own take on the conflict. In Wyoming, he had met folks he believed were decent and friendly and he admired their ways. To Wister, these men and women of the west didn't have any airs, didn't treat him much differently than they had anyone else, and indeed, recognized a kindred spirit (even if he was a "dude").

The Johnson County War had made headlines across the country in the spring of 1892. It pitted the powerful cattle barons and their paid lackeys (including lawmen, yellow journalists, sellout politicians and even the governor), against the homesteaders and small ranchers. Spreading to Natrona and Converse Countys, the Johnson County War took its toll on those settlers who defied the cattle barons of the Wyoming Stock Growers Association. To the homesteader, the organization's killing of innocent people had little to do with the problem of "rustlers," but everything to do with power and greed for territory. There *were* rustlers, no doubt, but both their power and numbers were grossly inflated by the WSGA, with the cattle interests assigning these thieves the same power and influence they themselves obviously had.

As Wister recuperated in Wyoming during the 1880s, the war had not reached the flashpoint yet. However, it would have been virtually impossible for the young ex-banker *not* to have met and become friendly with members of the Wyoming Stock Growers Association. Dressed in fancy western suits, topped by sharply cut Stetsons, dining sumptuously on roast pheasant, served with the finest silverware on brand-new china, and drinking the finest wines west of the Pecos, the cattle barons must have cut impressive figures to the intelligent but culturally naïve young man. Their bountiful lands, rich with grass, full of thousands of head of cattle which spread across the beautiful plains of Wyoming, would have dazzled any Easterner, even a well-bred child of privilege. It was quite possible that Wister saw these men as the anointed cultural elite who were in the same social status and who possessed the same driving ambition as his bourgeoisie parents back east. Indeed, many of the author's accumulated correspondence still existing today are letters written between 1912 and 1915 between himself, Dr. Charles B. Penrose and the members of the WSGA, particularly one of its most infuriating apologists, Association trouble-shooter W.C. Irvine.

Wister sought more of a creative outlet than writing short stories about the west. It's quite possible that the young attorney-author decided to show his gratitude to the movers and shakers of the west who were getting a bad rap.

In 1902, Wister wrote *The Virginian: The Horseman of the Plains*. Decades before Clint Eastwood popularized the Man with No Name, Wister created the myth of the strong, silent cowboy, a nameless ranch hand from Virginia referred to by its eastern narrator as either "the Virginian" or "the southerner." In this sprawling novel (a little over 400 pages, depending on edition), Wister never directly comments on the Johnson County War. Instead, he focuses on building up his strong, non-intellectual hero, a man of few words whose native smarts have nothing to do with book learning or schooling, but plenty to do with his ties to the land. He meets and falls in love with a schoolmarm from Vermont, Molly Stark Wood. At first resisting his rustic charms, she nevertheless tutors this "primitve" in the classics, lending him volumes of Shakespeare and other literary giants. Soon, the southerner's native cowboy wisdom gets to the cute but cloistered intellectual babe; as the story goes on for many years and she gets to know the west, as well as her handsome riding partner, their roles will be reversed, with the "pupil" teaching the easterner a thing or two about love and justice, the western way.

By personalizing his characters, by having the story told sympathetically by its also nameless eastern narrator, Wister almost puts us in the place of its central character, as well as the other inhabitants of Medicine Bow like Judge Henry and his wife, and even Molly, who starts to understand (up to a point) the west itself. However, the creation of this intellectual schoolmarm has more of a background than most critics of the time noticed. In 1898, Wister married his cousin Mary Channing, a highly intelligent young woman who was an educator. An active member of the Philadelphia Board of Education and one of the founding members of the Civic Board of Philadelphia, Mary was a dedicated and impassioned defender of women's rights. Family and friends soon got to calling her by her nickname: Molly. This explains why Wister's narrator at first refers to the schoolmarm character as "Mary," but then calls her "Molly" for the rest of the book; it's a little inconsistent, but not to the loving husband who wrote it. Jon Tuska would write rather viciously that Wister was a "curious, neurotic man," and claimed that the author "seems to falter in his understanding of basic human relationships." It's not certain whether Tuska knew that Wister had six children with Mary and remained a faithful husband until her tragic death (in childbirth) in 1913, fifteen years after their wedding. Her death affected him so much that the broken-hearted author abandoned work on his novel *Romney* and rarely returned to writing fiction again. It sounds like Wister knew a great deal about human relationships, including its pain.

However, the boom is usually lowered on the late nineteenth-early twentieth century author when the plot of *The Virginian* takes on the important issues of due process and the use of the death penalty. Throughout the novel, the Virginian has two albatrosses: the all-dressed-in-black villain Trampas, and (the Virginian's) best friend, Steve. Trampas is an arrogant bully, cattle rustler and murderer; and Steve is the Virginian's busom buddy who throws in his lot with Trampas and joins him on his raids. Warned by the Virginian to break with Trampas and quit cattle-rustling, Steve is caught with other rustlers by a posse (led by the Virginian) and, friendship or no friendship, hanged along with the others.

This aspect of the plot was the most controversial element in what some, a century later, would refer to as "a bunch of clichés," "fantasies" and "the mythologizing of the west." Wister's own mother called her son's book "episodic," with sequences dedicated to the adventures of a rambunctious hen, as well as the Virginian's hokey speech to a group of people at a railroad station, frankly ridiculous. However, when the Virginian presides over the hanging of his best friend, anti-death penalty writers in the twentieth century went ballistic.

Jon Tuska wrote in his *The Filming of the West*: "On the frontier, loyalty counted for much more than some murky vision of abstract justice which seems to preoccupy Wister's hero. The blood lust for capital punishment obsessed Wister, who was its staunch advocate."[1] Yet in his analysis of the novel, Tuska wrote that he found "eastern values superimposed on the west, as they are in the novel, inappropriate."[2]

Published in 1902, the novel was a bestseller before that phrase came into use. In 1908, it became a hit Broadway play co-written by Wister and playwright Kirk La Shelle. Silent star Dustin Farnum played the lead, and after he left the play to do a film, the role was taken over by William S. Hart. Fancying himself a bonafide expert on the west, the actor (from Newburgh, New York), chastised Wister for having Steve hanged by his best friend. As he said in an interview with writer John Scheets years later:

> In the first place, the foreman [the Virginian] would have refused flat-footed to trail his friend, and the ranchers would have respected him for it. And if he had led them to his friend and they had found his friend, he would have done it for a reason. He would have stepped to his friend's side and said: "Well, gentlemen, I have done my duty and brought you here, but if you hang him, you've got to hang me too! And we ain't neither of us strong for being hung while we've got our guns on."[3]

The neurotic actor, who had his own problems with human relationships, seems to have created a scenario straight out of one of his own silent westerns.

In his biography of Hart, author Ronald L. Davis wrote, "Hart's reading of the code of the West is arguable, and he grew more unqualified in his pronouncements on western ways as his connection with the frontier became more public. 'The truth of the West meant more to me than a job and always will,' Hart said."[4]

In the novel, Molly argues with the judge's wife about the Virginian's lynching of his best friend, with pro– and anti–death penalty opinions being thrown back and forth. However, the schoolmarm is only accepting of this western way of life when the Judge himself explains things to her. At times, Judge Henry compares the hangings to racial persecution in another part of the country: "For in all sincerity, I see no likeness in principle whatever between burning Southern Negroes in public and hanging Wyoming horse thieves in private. We do not torture our criminals when we lynch them. We do not invite spectators to enjoy their death agony.... We execute our criminals by the swiftest means, and in the quietest way." Public or private, quiet or not, mob rule is further legitimized by the Judge:

> [I]n Wyoming, the law has been letting our cattle thieves go for two years. We are in a very bad way, and we are trying to make that way a little better until civilization can reach us. The courts, or rather the juries, into whose hands we have put the law, are not dealing with the law. They are imitation hands made for show, with no life in them, no grip. They cannot hold a cattle thief. And so when your ordinary citizen sees this, and sees that he has placed justice in a dead hand, he must take justice back into his own hands.... Call this primitive, if you will, but so far from being a *defiance* of the law, it is an *assertion* of it — the most basic asserton of self-governing men.

Molly is still not swayed by the judge, even when Wister makes him sound reasonable in his arguments and sincere in his beliefs. As he finishes his speech, the judge hopes that one day, they'll all do without war or capital punishment. In the meantime, however, "[T]hey are none of them so terrible as unchecked theft and murder would be."

This kind of thinking infuriated leftist writer Herbert Mitgang, who wrote in the *New York Times* issue of December 2, 1989 "The 1902 novel, ancestor of the classic western, turned out to be not only corny and flag-waving but also intolerant and reactionary by today's standards. The story includes sentimental lectures on Americanism that sound like a jingoist speech from Theodore Roosevelt, to whom the book is dedicated." In his own analysis of the lynching in his appropriately titled book on western novels turned into films, *The Wister Trace*, Loren D. Estleman wrote "Lesser artists, seething with democratic outrage, have sought to press contemporary eastern values on a period and a society that Wister knew too well to attempt to influence. The reader, like the (eastern) narrator, is forever on the outside looking in."[5]

Ultimately, Molly suppresses her outrage over the lynching. Before the great debate

DOWN THE HATCH (1929). Richard Arlen shares a drink with Gary Cooper in the first talkie version of *The Virginian*. All film versions of Owen Wister's classic tale, including this one, retained the novel's controversial pro-lynching philosophy.

over the death penalty, the Virginian had been ambushed and wounded by Trampas and saved by the compassionate Molly, who then brought him back to the judge's house to recuperate. During that time, her love for him grew.

Soon, with the Virginian back in town and in good health, Trampas picks the Virginian's wedding day to Molly as the appropriate time to tell the southerner, "Get out of town by sundown." Molly begs the Virginian to run away with her, but a true Man of the West doesn't do such things, even when his schoolmarm sweetie threatens to break off with him if he goes to meet the black-clad villain in the street. Since a man's gotta do what a man's gotta do (or, for that matter, "There are some things a man can't ride around"), the Virginian goes out in the street and meets Trampas. Realizing that Shorty, a poor little cowboy who also stole cattle, was shot in the back by Trampas, the Virginian makes sure that he cannot be approached by anyone except from the front.

In sharp contrast to the thousands of gunfights in both pulp and literary westerns for the past 120 years, Wister's showdown, the first published version of this classic western situation, is a model of restraint:

> A wind seemed to blow his [the Virginian's] sleeve off his arm. He replied to it, and saw Trampas fall forward. He saw Trampas raise his arm from the ground and fall again. Then he lay there, still. A little smoke was rising from the pistol on the ground. He looked at his own, and saw the smoke flowing upward out of it.
> "I expect that's all," he said aloud.

Seeing that her love has survived his fateful encounter with Trampas, the tearful Molly promptly forgets her threat to leave him and rushes into his arms. After their wedding and subsequent honeymoon in the mountains, the happy couple prospers, with the Virginian using his smarts to become an entrepreneur and his wife giving birth to many children in the growing community of Medicine Bow.

Eternally grateful for having put their town on the map, Medicine Bow, Wyoming, would erect a statue to Wister. Though the eastern-born writer would never again write any fiction to match the phenomenal popularity of *The Virginian*, he was still a much-respected man of letters, publishing many volumes of history and even more novels. The widower and father of six (who never remarried) never lacked for family or friends, including Theodore Roosevelt and other giants of politics and literature. *The Virginian* was filmed several times, with the author (and his children) profitting greatly from movie sales of the novel. His heirs also later profited from the Universal TV series.

The Virginian is still a classic of American literature, written by a sensitive, intelligent and highly complicated man who, in real life, was the opposite of "bloodthirsty."

Yet the question remains: Did our hero have to resort to lynch law to prove his point?

The story of the 1929 movie *The Virginian* begins in the town of Medicine Bow, Wyoming, in the 1880s. A tall, lanky, nameless young southerner referred to as the Virginian (Gary Cooper) and other drovers from Judge Henry's outfit are bringing cattle through town. The Virginian runs into his old pal Steve (Paramount contract star Richard Arlen, a man who would always return to the studio even up to the A.C. Lyles westerns of the 1960s). Their first meeting would bring laughs to audiences today, with both actors straining mightily with their phony western accents as they affectionately call each other assorted endearing names like "horse thief" and "side-winder." Cooper's forced, twangy accent is awful. He is no Virginian, despite having the up-and-coming western star and native Virginian Randolph Scott as his dialogue coach (they would remain friends for the next three decades).

In the saloon, the two men are offering a senorita a drink when the black-clad Trampas (Walter Huston) horns in. When Trampas starts to call the Virginian a name, the southerner pulls his gun and says the now-classic line, "If you want to call me that, *smile!*" Schoolmarm Molly Stark Wood (Mary Brian) arrives in town and, seeing a cow supposedly running towards her, panics and flees until she is literally swept off her feet by the Virginian. Soon, thanks to Steve, she finds that the cow is harmless and chastises her "rescuer." This begins their friendly rivalry for the girl. In the novel, Molly is practically a prisoner in a stagecoach driven at high speed by a drunken stage driver. After it ends up in a lake, the Virginian, on his horse, pulls her out and ferries her over to the riverbank, but the panicked girl doesn't even bother to thank him; however, the cowboy *does* keep her dropped handkerchief as a memento.

Warned by the Virginian not to steal cattle, Steve is caught by his best friend and his posse. Reluctantly, the Virginian is forced to hang Steve and the two men he is caught with (Trampas beat a hasty retreat). Later, after the Virginian is dry-gulched by Trampas, his horse, belonging to the judge, automatically brings the wounded man back to the jurist's ranch. While still nursing him, Molly is horrified when she learns that the man she's lovingly tending to has hanged his best friend. This begins an interesting argument between Molly and the judge's wife which turns into a shouting match. It also gives us a line of dialogue that is historically inaccurate. During her impassioned argument with Mrs. Henry, Molly claims that her grandfather fought Indians in the Cherry Valley Massacre during the Revolutionary War when in reality her grandfather couldn't possibly have been born yet.

The film dispenses with the sober, yet firm defense of rope justice by Judge Henry that's in the book.

The day comes when the Virginian and Molly are to be wed. However, Trampas, accompanied by his men, tells the Virginian to get out of town. Despite Molly's threat to leave him, the Virginian goes to the showdown and kills Trampas, causing the schoolmarm to take him back. They unite in the dusty street of Medicine Bow as the film ends.

A skilled and versatile actor, Huston looks quite ridiculous in his black duds. Cooper, who was at his most expressive during his 1930s Paramount years, gets better as the film progresses; but Mary Brian is undoubtedly the best actor in the film. Not having to worry about her accent, she is quite moving in her role as the confused schoolmarm; not only is she torn between her "sophisticated" eastern ways and the ways of the rough-hewn Virginian, but she's totally convincing in her revulsion at old west capital punishment.

Paramount remade *The Virginian* in 1946, starring Joel McCrea. In his *The Filming of the West*, Jon Tuska made this outrageous comment: "Of all the Virginians—Dustin Farnum, Kenneth Harlan, Gary Cooper—Joel McCrea seemed the most natural in hanging his best friend."[6]

A year after *The Virginian*'s release, MGM produced the first all-talking movie on the life story of a famous old west icon, a young hellion who died at the age of 21. The talkies were indeed starting off with a bang....

"His gun wouldn't fire ... and mine would."— *Billy the Kid*

The story of Henry McCarty Antrim, aka Billy the Kid, is one that is steeped in the debate on the role of justice (otherwise known as "the Unwritten Law") vs. the rule of law (or due process as dictated by the Constitution and the Bill of Rights).

A young Irish-American ruffian from New York's Hell's Kitchen, Henry became a world-famous icon of young outlawry in the last year of his short life. The west was populated by "Kid" outlaws, but they were mostly two-bit punks who robbed and killed, hardly caring one way or the other why they did the deed. With Billy, there always seemed to be a reason behind *why* he did his misdeeds, or at least that is what we get from the movies' conception of him; and I believe *that* is why he's better remembered today than all the others. Billy *was* a robber and a murderer, no doubt; but he was also a product of the times and the terrain. In Lincoln County, New Mexico Territory, he was appointed a "regulator," sworn to bring the Murphy-Dolan gang to justice. After the murder of his benefactor John H. Tunstall, Billy's methods of going after the perpetrators weren't exactly within the letter of the law, but the ordinary westerner (and later those in the east) thrilled to his take-no-prisoners style. His daring escape from the Lincoln County Jail and his murder of the bullying and arrogant deputy Bob Ollinger cemented the legend. When the infamous Santa Fe Ring oppressed the citizens of the territory and then hid behind a self-serving veil of the law, Billy struck back, indirectly exposing the uncomfortable alliance between the Ring and the territory's elite. When promised amnesty and then lied to, Billy continued the outlaw life rather than surrender and get the hangman's noose. In an odd way, he almost lived that famous credo of the Hollywood JD film: "Live fast, die young, and leave a good-looking corpse...."

A silent film had been made by the small Vitagraph company way back in 1911, *Billy the Kid*. It's lost forever, so it is impossible to know exactly what their take on the young outlaw was (Billy was shot dead by Sheriff Pat Garrett just 30 years before the film's release).

On October 18, 1930, MGM released its own version of the legend, *Billy the Kid*.

Alabama-born Johnny Mack Brown was an MGM leading man usually cast in the studio's society films; that is, until MGM got Clark Gable from Warners and started to build him up, effectively swiping parts from the former college football star. Brown had dark hair (not blonde hair like Billy) and at 26 he was too old to play the young outlaw who was shot dead at 21. He was never a very good actor; the role and the film ended up pointing the way towards a future in the field of B westerns where versatile acting was not needed.

Based on Walter Noble Burns' rather ridiculous book on Billy's exploits which emphasized the myth, not the reality, the film was directed by the talented King Vidor. In all the Billy the Kid films, Hollywood blatantly ignored the outlaw's New York upbringing and this film is no exception. Billy Bonney (an obvious alias) just springs up in the west with no eastern past at all. We are also told, ad nauseam, that Billy started killing when some drunken lout manhandled Billy's attractive mom. This was also nonsense. After marrying army veteran William Antrim, Catherine McCarty took Billy west where she eventually owned her own laundry and even speculated in property; she ended up purchasing some choice real estate in the Midwest and in Silver City, New Mexico. She was also a consumptive, and the tuberculosis that filled her lungs caused her to die rather painfully on September 16, 1874, when Billy was 18 years old.

In the film, Billy is pursued by best friend Pat Garrett (the cliché of the hero-outlaw pursued by his pal is another enduring footnote in the Billy the Kid legend). Played by MGM contract star Wallace Beery, Garrett might look and sound drunk, but the actor's performance effectively removes the *real* Garrett's pomposity and lack of humor. Billy is also seeing the pretty Claire Randall (Kay Johnson), another repudiation of historical accuracy (Billy was partial to Latinas).

Middle-aged actor Wynston Standing plays John Tunstall, the studio unwittingly inaugurating a permanent tradition in Billy the Kid films in which the Englishman who took Billy in hand is considered a wise father-figure to the wild youngster. And few would look at the historical reality that tells us that Tunstall was all of 24 years old at the time he was murdered by the Murphy-Dolan crowd. More like a big brother to Billy, Tunstall was an ambitious Englishman, having come to Lincoln County by way of British Columbia. Rather naively, he hoped to start a mercantile business in the territory and get an army contract with nearby Fort Stanton. However, without any political contacts, and up against the Murphy-Dolan goliath, the Englishman was playing a losing hand. His death at the hands of the Ring's gunmen was not unexpected. However, Hollywood would continue to cast middle-aged actors as Tunstall; this, added to the myth that Billy's first kill came about by the assault on his mother, made the outlaw more sympathetic by the twin motivation of avenging the outrages perpetrated on one real parent and one surrogate.

The company hired Sophie Poe, the widow of John Poe (one of Pat Garrett's deputies who was active in the pursuit of the Kid), as the film's technical advisor. After witnessing scene after scene which brought far too much sympathy to Billy, Mrs. Poe had had enough. Pulling over King Vidor, she bitterly complained, "Sir, I knew that little buck-toothed killer, and he wasn't the way you're making him at all!" "Mrs. Poe," replied the future director of *The Fountainhead*, "I understand your feelings, but this is what the people want."[7] After Vidor informed his bosses of her complaints, the studio unceremoniously fired the old woman and hired a new technical advisor, William S. Hart.

If the studio wanted to emphasize the fantasy over the reality, they couldn't have done any better than hire the long-past-his-prime Hart. An eternal cowboy in his own mind and self-proclaimed expert on the west, Hart was ridiculously lionized by certain film historians for bringing "reality" to the western. However, according to his latest biographer, Ronald L. Davis, "[Hart] viewed life through the eyes of an actor steeped in nineteenth-century melodrama and was steadfast in his allegiance to Victorian virtues. His 'real' West on film came more from appearances and trappings than complex characterizations or discerning social commentary."[8] Routinely laughed at by the real cowboys who worked on his films, Hart would make pronouncements on all subjects dealing with the west, when the pompous actor had absolutely no idea what he was talking about.

Hart's introduction to the film company was obviously planned by the actor to take full visual impact of the entrance of a self-involved and vain legend. While filming a scene in the desert, the cast and crew became aware of a rider in the distance, appearing as if he were a lone sentinel of the west, coming closer and closer until they discovered it was that icon of the prairie, William S. Hart![9]

Johnny Mack Brown was always proud of his friendship with Hart, and studio publicity made much of the old actor's donating to the film the actual guns used by Billy. However, very few at the time questioned how Hart came upon these guns, or questioned their authenticity.

Brown also followed Hart's advice *vis-à-vis* the gun battles in the picture. As the actor remembered, the silent screen star told him, "Diminish your target, and keep your heart as far away as you can from an enemy's bullet."[10] Not even the aging Wyatt Earp or Bat Masterson (both of whom died in the late 1920s) ever claimed that, in order to survive a gunfight, a cowboy had to cover his chest and ridiculously bob and weave while he was attempting to accurately fire his pistol.

Nevertheless, with the firing of Mrs. Poe and the hiring of the revisionist Hart, the film glosses over the moral dilemma of Billy's private vendetta against the Murphy-Dolan crowd, presenting his deeds in a sympathetic light. It also highlights the friendship between Garrett and Billy, with the tragic foreshadowing of the Kid's impending death seen as almost a variation of Hart's clichéd good-badman role in his own films. However, Billy's death at the hands of Pat Garrett (he dies in the lawman's arms) would only be seen in European theaters. In the American version, Garrett allows Billy and his Anglo sweetie to escape across the border, even after the outlaw has cold-bloodedly (if somewhat justifiably) murdered all his enemies.

Shot on location in Gallup, New Mexico, the Grand Canyon and Southern California, *Billy the Kid* was also blessed with the wonders of 70mm wide-screen process (think CinemaScope in the early 1930s). John Wayne's *The Big Trail* was also shot in this process. However, the nation's exhibitors, already having converted their theaters to sound films, balked at the expense of having to do it all over again for the dubious widescreen process. Even when *Billy the Kid* was shot simultaneously in 35mm, this "narrower" print couldn't help but keep everyone in long shot, and robbed the actors of desperately needed close-ups. Both films inevitably failed at the box office.

Though the film tanked, MGM would tackle the Billy the Kid story in another 11 years, during the days of the Production Code, making the Kid even *more* sympathetic. The myth perpetuated by Burns, Hart, Brown and Vidor would be the blueprint steadfastly adhered to in all subsequent portrayals of the Kid for the next half-century. In each of these films, western justice, that is, the kind dealt out by angel of vengeance Billy Bonney, though not encouraged, was understandable; and through their greed and machinations within the law, Billy's enemies were most definitely portrayed as villains.

However, there would be one major difference: Under the dictates of the Production

Code, Billy had to die. There would be no William S. Hart–like saccharine endings in which Garrett allowed the Kid and his girl to escape across the border (with the possible exception of *The Outlaw*, a Howard Hughes–produced freak show that had little to do with the real Billy the Kid, much less good taste). From 1941 onward, Billy would die for taking the law into his own hands, this time in the American version as well as the European.

It wouldn't be until Emilio Estevez portrayed the gunsel as a giggling little psychopath in 1988's *Young Guns* that Billy would be depicted more darkly (though the audience *still* rooted for him to kill off the film's super-capitalist bad guys).

As the Depression took hold, the ambiguities of American law, especially the democratic concept of trial-by-jury, with its less-than-perfect outcomes, became a recurrent theme in the American western. One particular novel written by a giant of the pulp western became the basis for another parable on the imperfections of old west justice.

However, when the novel was filmed by Universal in 1932, it starred a man who had brought immense popularity to the genre in the 1920s. In fact, his on-screen reputation as a two-fisted hellion almost took all the attention away from the original story....

"He a ridin', fightin' fool!"— *stagecoach passenger*

Originally serialized as *Twelve Peers* in the February 1, 1930, issue of *Western Story* magazine (one of the many "slicks" of the era), the property became the novel *Destry Rides Again* on August 22 of that year. It was a massive bestseller at a time when jobs were practically nonexistent. Much of its popularity was because the story was a fantasy escape from the times, as well as the fact that it was written by a giant of western literature, Max Brand.

His real name was Frederick Faust. Born in Northern California, he detested everything about the west, and he seemed to have contempt for actual western history. His publishers wanted him to go on publicity junkets where he would camp with real cowboys, or join them on the cattle trail; Faust reluctantly did these, but then cut his trips short by days and ran back to the comforts of the "civilized" east. He hated the cowboys, whose salty talk, sweat-stained clothes and working-class ethics revolted the high-toned and elitist writer. His many volumes of poetry barely sold enough to pay the rent, and critics routinely scoffed at his efforts, but when he wrote about men like Destry and Silvertip, he could do no wrong.

Destry Rides Again, despite its many clichés, actually tries for something different. Its central figure is Harrison Destry, a two-fisted, liquor-guzzling, straight-shootin' buckaroo who wouldn't have lasted five minutes in the real west. Practically everyone he meets he rubs the wrong way; this is because Harry says whatever he thinks to everyone's face, regardless of whose feelings he hurts or how brazen he sounds. He seems to think he's being honest and plain-spoken when in reality he's a tactless bully. Not surprisingly, his blunt talk to the town's leading citizens angers them, but since the insults are coming from a ridin', fightin' hellion like Destry, his targets are forced to swallow their pride and take it. (In the novel, the town is called Wham.) The only person whom Destry likes is tomboyish ranch gal Charlotte Dangerfield. However, since she's a tomboy, Brand has the other characters rather maliciously refer to her as "Charlie."

Another person he's supposedly on friendly terms with is a respected middle-class citizen named Bent. Destry used to beat the snot of his pal when they were boys; the hate-filled Bent never forgot this.

A man is shot dead in the streets. Since Destry is such an obnoxious bore, and since his best friend is plotting to destroy him, guess who's going to be framed for murder? He is brought before a jury of, not his peers, but his verbal victims, and the verdict is a predictable "guilty!" The former swaggering hellion addresses the jury by sneering at their being his "peers" and calls them twelve "half-bred pups," a slander on half-bred pups. Then the two-fisted roustabout declares, "When my ten years has come up, I'm gonna call on all of these here, and if they ain't in, I'm gonna leave my callin' card anyway!"

Here, Brand impugns the very American system of trial by jury by implying that a prejudicial jury of twelve can get away with sending an innocent man to prison. Not many pulps of the time had this subplot, nor this rather radical interpretation of a miscarriage of justice. Usually in the fiction of the day, juries were fooled into believing the hero was guilty of the crimes the villain had actually committed; twelve guys who hated the hero's guts seated on an American jury was a new one for the pulp western.

Here, even the author's usual clichés were influenced by the pessimism of the nation's crippling Depression. In *Destry Rides Again*, the two-fisted, blunt-speaking hero can dish it out in a saloon brawl or on a dusty trail, but he doesn't stand a chance against the sharp-suited boys who work the back rooms with big cigars in their maws and gold-plated watches in their vests; in other words, an old west version of the bourgeoisie power brokers who got us into the Depression in the first place.

When Destry is released and returns to Wham, the Whamians are shocked to see the once-swaggering hellion now reduced to a scared, timid little rabbit. The explanation is that prison has psychologically damaged him, so his former enemies are now brave enough to mercilessly bully and taunt him. However, when challenged, Destry surprises his enemies by gunning them down — and doing it justifiably since his opponents started the fight and drew first. Yet Brand actually freaks us out after one justifiable gundown when he has Destry give a truly insane laugh.

It turns out that Destry is shamming; the dumber-than-a-sack-of-hair hellion has finally wised up. He is using his alleged cowardice to draw the bullying villains into a gunfight he knows he will win; his revenge is draped in the cloth of justifiable self-defense. In other words, the moral of the story seems to be: When dealing with those power brokers who hide behind respectability and twist the law to their own ends, don't show your true face, but instead play mind games with them until the final showdown.

In the novel, there is a subplot about a boy who admires Destry. The kid's father is a liar and a braggart, and obviously doesn't have the sterling qualities of the ex-jailbird. At the book's climax, Destry's arch enemy Bent tries to gun down his former tormentor. Brand now puts our hero on the receiving end of the gunfire, and the old hellraiser sees that the Way of the Gun has only led to misery. After Bent is vanquished, Destry settles down with Charlie, and it is heavily implied that Destry and his tomboyish cutie will adopt the boy, despite that fact that the kid *already* has parents.

With the Depression hitting the nation in October 1929, the studios cut back their production of westerns. In quick succession, Fox got rid of both Tom Mix and Buck Jones; MGM released the overrated Tim McCoy; First National dumped Ken Maynard; and it would be a few years before Paramount would return to the production of their Zane Grey series. It was thought that the pessimistic times weren't conducive to the sunny optimism of an old west tale. Only two studios continued to produce westerns with any kind of consistency: Universal and Mascot.

Mascot put a new twist on the western by "modernizing" it. Cowboys were still chasing outlaws on trusted steeds and romancing the rancher's daughter, but now the stories actually included automobiles and airplanes. Now the Virginian, told to "get out of town by sundown," could book the next flight out of Medicine Bow. When Mascot merged with Monogram, Victory Pictures and other "little" independents into Republic Pictures in 1935 the new studio continued the trend of the "modern western." Therefore, Gene Autry and Roy Rogers' films had automobiles and planes.

After Fox cut loose their biggest star, Tom Mix, the actor made a few westerns for Joseph Kennedy's FBO Pictures (later to become RKO) and returned to live appearances in circuses (he had once been a trick rider for the legendary Miller 101 Wild West Show). It would not be an exaggeration to say that Mix was the defining superstar of his day. He roughly pulled the western away from the clichéd, heavy-breathing Victorian morality plays of William S. Hart and made them far more fun and exciting. On the down side, he also made them more childish and fantastic. Though his cowboy garb was more or less modest on screen, off-screen he dressed like a fashion plate. His characters also wore leather gloves and there were rare times when he wore two guns, something cowboys just didn't do (*one gun was taxing enough on your hip*). However, to his credit, his villains were rarely killed; and when he did use a gun, if at all, it was to wing an opponent, not kill him. With his child audience in mind, Mix brought a spirit of fun and excitement to the western. It's no surprise that several of his works were film versions of action-packed novels by Max Brand and Zane Grey, emphasizing the mythic, escapist elements of the genre.

After Universal bought the rights to *Destry Rides Again*, studio head Carl Laemmle Sr. insisted on the casting of Mix. Laemmle had faith in the western, continuing the studio's output with As, Bs and serials, like *The Indians Are Coming!* (It is said that Laemmle didn't much care what his scenarists wrote, as long as, he insisted in his thick German-Jewish accent, "The Indians are *comink*!") In time, the feisty Laemmle would sign Ken Maynard, Hoot Gibson and Buck Jones to the studio as well.

Destry Rides Again was Mix's first talking film. In his publicity, studio flacks painted Tom as an adventurer who had fought alongside Pancho Villa and served in everything from the Boer War to Theodore Roosevelt's Rough Riders; a man who was a straight-shootin', gunfightin' terror of the plains who also used to be a sheriff, and was personally responsible for making the early twentieth century west safe for women, children and small dogs.

Yet our two-fisted film star hellion was petrified of the microphone....

Trained by Universal's top acting coaches in the then-new field of delivering lines to a microphone, Mix reluctantly made *Destry Rides Again* his first talkie. Though appearing stiff and uncomfortable at times, Mix's bigger-than-life presence and ability to handle action scenes carried the day. In homage to the superstar playing him, Destry's first name was now *Tom*. As the movie begins, we see a cowboy riding out of the hills. It is definitely *not* Max Brand's Destry, but an irrepressible force of nature named Tom Mix. Here, the star's cult of personality clearly grabs the story in its big leather-gloved hands and doesn't let go until **The End** flashes across the screen.

A group of children who apparently happen to be Tom Mix fans are waiting for their hero to ride down and visit them, which our star is more than willing to do. He puts on a shooting exhibition for them, demonstrating for these innocent children a rather frightening validation of the gun culture then popular in the 1930s.

Cut to a stagecoach where we have the wonderful Zasu Pitts as a temperance leaguer meeting another passenger who's a bartender. Said bartender knows that if the stagecoach is held up, the outlaws will have to deal with the stage line's co-owner, Tom Destry. "Why, he's a ridin', fightin' fool!" the barman puffs. (*The Fightin' Fool* is the title of another cliché-ridden Brand western of the day containing elements of silliness.) Needless to say, when outlaws hired by Brant (not "Bent," and played by Earle Foxe) try to hold up the stage, Destry rides down from the hills and kicks some outlaw butt. In this film, the novel's Destry is elevated to co-owner of a stage line, using his guns and fists in the pursuit of justice. In fact, because the hero is played by the redoubtable Mix, the villains have an almost indescribable terror of Destry that is far greater than in the book.

Because Destry is a crimp in his plans, Brant and the crooked sheriff (Stanley Fields) decide to frame the fightin' fool for murder. Two cowpokes pretend to have a fistfight and Destry intervenes; one of them then pulls Destry's gun and kills the other cowpoke (who, we assume, was happy to give his life in the knowledge that Destry will go to jail for his murder). Universal executive Stanley Bergermann, with Tom Mix's total approval, had scenarist Richard Schayer change the plot from a crooked jury consisting of Destry's enemies sending him to prison to having the bad guys masquerade as witnesses to the crime so they could give false testimony. Therefore, trial by jury is not impugned; Destry's enemies are working from outside the system and bearing false witness. This time, Destry's threat is delivered not to the jury, but to the lying witnesses who framed him. Still, Charlotte (not "Charlie," and played by Claudia Dell) will wait for him. (For the film version, Charlotte totally loses her tomboyishness and runs around in dresses most of the time.)

When Destry is released (certainly not after ten years), he feigns a cough, telling Charlotte that prison has made him a broken man. When the villains hear this, they are laying for Tom, hoping to bully him mercilessly. But as Destry is about to approach town, he tells his horse Tony (excellently played by Tony Jr.) that he hopes his "act" will work. It was obvious that the filmmakers didn't want Mix's legion of children fans in the audience to think that their hero was "yellow" for even a moment, and he tips his hand to the audience way before the novel's Destry did. Of course, the villains go to the saloon and are thrown out through the doors, beaten up or shot to pieces. When Tom catches up to the sheriff at Charlotte's house and tries to make him confess, a bullet comes through a window and kills him. This was one of the first times this cliché was used in talkies.

Finally making one of the villains confess that Brant set him up, Destry confronts his erstwhile "friend." Because Mix was then 51 and had survived a life-threatening bout with peritonitis months before filming, longtime Mix cameraman Daniel Clark rather ridiculously speeds up the fight, making it unintentionally funny. With Brant and the bad guys defeated, Destry ends up with Charlotte.

The April 16, 1932 issue of *Harrison's Reports*, though panning Claudia Dell's performance, called the reproduction of Tom's voice "excellent."[11]

In the immediate future, the icon that was Tom Mix would ride through assorted twists in life's trail; divorce, a new wife (his last), paying back alimony to four women, being sued by his own daughter, lawsuits, IRS troubles, various painful injuries on film and in live performances (Mix rarely used stuntmen), and losing all his money in a circus venture—and then came his final, fatal drive on Highway 80 between Tucson and Florence, Arizona. When he missed a detour and his Cord roadster flipped over, causing him to die of a broken neck, it was already 1940, a year that found the world in flames. Villains like Hitler and Stalin were making the duplicitous Chester Bent look like an amateur. Two years later, war correspondent Max Brand, the author of *Destry Rides Again*, was killed by a shrapnel blast in Italy. The year 1940 saw the publication of Walter Van Tilburg Clark's *The Ox-Bow Incident*, a powerful cry against the lynch-mob mentality of Nazi Germany and the other totalitarian powers of Europe and Asia.

However, Universal Pictures wasn't through just yet with Brand's classic tale. So when

Hitler and Stalin decided to carve up Europe between them and the Imperial Japanese Army continued their conquest of Asia, the studio again revived the character of Destry, making him unrecognizable from the Tom Mix version. However, thanks to this remake, western justice now took on global significance.

With the exception of the occasional A Western (like Cecil B. DeMille's over-the-top *The Plainsman*), the genre was mired in movies with running times of barely 70 minutes. And though the films of Buck Jones, Ken Maynard and new musical western star Gene Autry could hardly be called major social statements, the messages in their films remained All-American: lynchings and mob rule were wrong, private vendettas must be sublimated to the rule of law and fair play, and justice, not revenge, must win out.

But what if there were a certain region of the country where those in charge of the law were corrupt; now arrogant victors, they would exploit a conquered people and make their crooked shenanigans all seem legal. Despite the fact that said people had a culture steeped in racism and aristocratic arrogance was (to the filmmakers) beside the point; they were the victims of injustice, period.

And so, on August 12, 1938, a full three months before Kristallnacht, Paramount released a film that twisted the facts about a certain period in our history, making racial aggressors look like victims and portraying those who sought the death of Jim Crow as the villains....

"I'm an American. I don't need an emperor to give me land." — *Kirk Jordan*

Emerson Hough was born on June 28, 1857, in Newton, Iowa. A toddler during the Civil War, young Emerson was raised by loving parents, and had the added blessing of being a child from the victorious North, as well as coming from a region that never saw war (though the young men of Iowa fought valiantly in several of the Union's major battles). After his graduation from the University of Iowa in 1880 with a degree in philosophy, Hough moved to White Oaks, New Mexico, and became a newspaperman. Returning to the Midwest in 1886, he became a journeyman reporter for papers in Ohio, Kansas and his native Iowa. An avid outdoorsman who enjoyed hunting and fishing, he wrote dozens of articles about camping and outdoor life; in 1889, he was a feature writer for *Forest & Stream*, later to become *Field & Stream*, and was even an "outdoor" columnist for *The Saturday Evening Post*. He was impressed with the many places he saw, so it was not a surprise when the budding journalist started writing adventure stories. As time went on, his stories evolved into tales of the old west, making him one of the few authors of the genre to write about a period he had actually lived through, instead of the usual twentieth century western author writing from the viewpoint of a more "politically enlightened" (and industrialized) era. And so, having grown up at a time when the Indian was still seen as a menace to white civilization (unlike those authors raised in the twentieth century who never experienced the Indian Wars), Hough made them the stubborn impediments to progress in his *The Covered Wagon*.

His stories and novels accentuated the cowboy and trail hand as heroes who contributed to the building of the nation. Again, unlike the western author of the twentieth century, Hough had met these men and got to know them well. Having personally witnessed the massacre of the buffalo in Yellowstone in 1893, he became a staunch conservationist, and became friendly with fellow westerner and future president, Theodore Roosevelt.

There were other relationships and connections Hough had made during his time out west that the author probably didn't want made public. While in New Mexico Territory, he had become friendly with the region's movers and shakers. Shortly after the murders of prosecutor Albert Fountain and his son Henry (when the attorney was going after political boss Albert B. Fall and the crooked Santa Fe Ring), Hough's friend, Sheriff Pat Garrett, wanted to go after the murderers. Not long after Garrett testified against Fall at his trial, the former lawman was shot dead in 1908. When the territory's new attorney general, James M. Hervey, wanted to help finance an investigation into Garrett's murder, it was Hough who cautioned him "Jimmie, I know that outfit around the Organ Mountains, and Garrett got killed trying to find out who killed [Albert] Fountain, and you will get killed trying to find out who killed Garrett. I advise you to let it alone."[12]

Hough lived to see the nation grow from a barely settled country that considered his own beloved Iowa the "western frontier" to one that became a major player on the world stage. During World War I, the now 60-year-old Hough served in the U.S. Army Intelligence Division, eventually rising to the rank of captain. During that hectic time, he returned to his western past and gave us his two most famous novels, both of which were filmed as silents by Paramount, *The Covered Wagon* and *North of '36*. The latter work, published years before *Gone with the Wind*, lacked the tragic dimensions of the Margaret Mitchell bestseller (which in itself was a "moonlight and magnolia" apologia for Confederate arrogance and which perpetuated racist stereotypes). However, its portrayal of the South, while lacking the purposeful brainwashing that Mitchell infused in her work, still saw the plight of the white southerner as one that wasn't necessarily of his making. The novel's plot bears this out.

At the Del Sol ranch in Texas, the tempestuous Taisie Lockart (whose father had died and left her the ranch) and her ranch hands face a world where the Southern rebellion has gone bust. Evil carpetbagger Marvin Fletcher would like to seize Taisie's ranch; as a state treasurer, he and his fellow carpetbaggers have been looting the state till and preventing funds from going to poor Texans. To pay the northerners' enormous taxes and save the ranch, Taisie will have to drive her cattle to Abilene, Kansas. Riding to the proverbial rescue is her old flame Dan McMasters; Dan had joined the Union during the war, a little sticking point in their relationship that Taisie hasn't forgotten. However, she is forced to have McMasters, an experienced cattleman, drive her cattle to Abilene, a trip that she will join him on. But hold your horses! Or cattle. It seems that McMasters is actually a secret government agent assigned to investigate the evil carpetbaggers, with a major target of his probe being the contemptible Fletcher. Before the final fadeout, Fletcher and the other anti-southern bigots will be defeated, and Taisie will join Dan in Washington D.C. and become the wife of a mid-nineteenth century spook.

Drowning in Victorian era contrivances, this work is the unsubtle depiction of the different factions during the post–Civil War period. The southerner is to be sympathized with; however, unlike Margaret Mitchell's later work, not all northerners were to be considered evil. In fact, the ending, where McMasters' Union army veteran winds up with Southern belle Taisie implies an end to bitterness and recriminations and the start of reunification. Just as Taisie must forget her own bitterness against Dan and the North, so the South must unite with the rest of the nation again. There would be no burning of Atlanta in Hough's novel; the villains were carpetbaggers who were exploiting the South. Unfortunately, though there were such reprobates who sought to enrich themselves on the backs of southerners, the work ignores the efforts of sincere Radical Republicans who wanted to end postwar exploitation and the racist treatment of blacks.

Paramount filmed the novel twice, first as a silent with Jack Holt as McMasters, then under the title *The Conquering Horde* in 1931, with Richard Arlen as McMasters and Fay Wray as Taisie. By 1938, in the wake of the phenomenal bestselling success of Mitchell's *Gone with the Wind*, Paramount again returned to the novel they had owned for many years, feeling that the public was ready for another Civil War story.

And so, on August 12, the studio released *The Texans*. Hough did not live to see the film versions of *North of '36*, having died on April 30, 1923, just a few weeks after Paramount's March 16 premiere of the film version of his *The Covered Wagon* in New York City.

The scenarists for this new version were Bertram Millhauser (whose best work was the Basil Rathbone-Sherlock Holmes films in the forties), novelist and playwright William Wister Haines, and writer-director Paul Sloane. Millhauser and Sloane had been writing forgettable silent films since World War I, and Haines was certainly no slouch at writing programmers either. The director was James Hogan, a B movie helmsman then primarily known for directing Paramount's double-feature Bulldog Drummond series. The hiring of these men seemed to signal an obvious lack of trust in Hough's material; one does wonder what a DeMille (whose works usually reeked of Victorian era melodramatics and hysterical overacting) would have done with Hough's tale. Yet one must give the scenarists and the director credit for this: Their film made light of new realities in the international scene. Unlike the silent films based on Hough's story, the 1938 version would make an urgent plea for all Americans to stick together as war clouds gathered elsewhere.

As our story begins, titles are scrolling up the screen declaring what point of view will be brought before audiences *vis-a-vis* its portrayal of the South: "The south was ruled as a conquered enemy. Northern politicians wallowed in an orgy of power—of plunder by organized mobs—of tribute and tyranny and death."

Our story begins at the port of Indianola, Texas, where victorious bluecoats and their southern white helpers are loading captured southern property onto riverboats to take the "spoils" back up north. The propaganda here is blatant, with the director also pointedly showing us, in long shot, a fat black soldier, a bottle in his hand, shoving an old southern woman and a Confederate officer out of his way, a big smile on his face. When a piano is stamped Confiscated Rebel Property, black Union soldiers are among those bluecoats enjoying the scene.

Trying to drive her wagon through the Union blockade of the town is Ivy Preston (top-billed Joan Bennett), who is apparently carrying crates of rifles marked Farm Implements. When Rebel soldier Kirk Jordan (Randolph Scott in the last film on his Paramount contract) sees that her wagon is in danger of being searched, he prods the Reb soldiers into singing "Dixie," a song the fat Union sergeant in charge calls seditious. After this scene, director Hogan again gives us a brief shot of black Union soldiers standing to the side smoking and relaxing, an inference that they are enjoying the southerners' plight (as well as perpetuating the stereotype of laziness).

When Ivy gratefully allows Kirk to board her wagon, she reveals her plans. The smuggled guns are to be put in the hands of returning southern troops, soon to be backed by the Emperor Maximilian, who will join the Rebs with French and Mexican troops and wipe out the Union. To her dismay, she finds that Jordan is not only sick of fighting, but that he actually sympathizes with the Yankees, many of whom he believes are not as bad as the ones guarding the dock. Scott is excellent here, as he sadly wonders about the sight of "French and Mexican troops fighting against the United States."

In this brief scene, the scenarists are already conjuring up the horror of a foreign aggressor laying waste to our nation; in 1938, with the country still suffering from the

Depression and half the world rapidly going totalitarian, such a scenario seemed a distinct possiblity.

The "civil administrator" of the town (fancy word for carpetbagger) is Isaiah Middlebrack (Robert Barrat) who alerts the sergeant at the docks that a Reb spy is shipping guns in crates marked farm implements. Then Middlebrack shows us an incredibly sharp picture for 1865 of Robert Cummings in a Reb uniform. Again, Hogan and his screenwriters (with apparently no complaint from Paramount) are favoring their white southern audience with some blatant propaganda. The director shows the sergeant with his feet up while eating a sandwich, while black soldiers are clearly seen in the background sitting on barrels doing absolutely nothing.

Out in the woods, Ivy hooks up with her Reb spy boyfriend Alan Sanford (Cummings), whose assistant is another Paramount contract player, the up-and-coming Richard Denning. Back in town, the cute gunrunner is physically manhandled by Middlebrack in his office and accused of sending guns to "the enemy," but she is saved by the arrival of her grandma (appropriately called Granna and played by May Robson) and her aging pal Chuckawalla (a total waste of Walter Brennan). Bitterly, Granna spreads the pro–Southern revisionism a little *too* thick as she spits out, "You and your plundering, murderous Reconstruction!"

Again, a form of government that would have ended southern racism for all time and finally granted victimized African-Americans long-overdue civil rights is plainly seen in this film as evil. At the time the film was made, Jim Crow laws were still the order of the day down south, and the insane lynchings of African-Americans continued without letup, the lynching parties themselves always getting away with their crimes. It certainly called into question which side here was really "plundering" and "murderous."

After this fight, Jordan grabs Ivy and takes her out of town. When she maintains that southerners died in a good cause, Jordan says, "No, they didn't. They died so a lot of crazy galoots could go fight for a little tin emperor — against their own country...."

Dan McMasters is a Federal agent in Hough's novel; Hogan and his screenwriters turned his character into a southerner (and played by a southerner, though not a Texan, as the studio claimed in its PR). In *The Texans*, Kirk Jordan may be a loyal Reb, but it is obvious that, like Dan McMasters, he is also the voice of the future, looking for a day when all Americans can be united. To him, the South is now one with the North, and it's his sincere belief that a foreign dictatorship looking to exploit the divisions among Americans is not to be trusted. In 1938, with both fascists and communists seeking to divide and conquer, Jordan seems to be talking from the perspective of a much later time than 1865.

Meanwhile, at the failing Boca Grande Ranch (which was the Del Sol Ranch in the novel), Ivy, Granna and Chuckawalla are reunited with their ranch hands, who have decided to stay out of loyalty to their cute boss. However, riding to their rescue is Jordan and his partner Cal (Raymond Hatton). Jordan offers Ivy the chance to have her cattle driven up north to Abilene where the Union will pay them plenty for their beef, but Ivy is against any scheme which will benefit the North, even if it saves her own ranch.

That night, Middlebrack and some bluecoats arrive and the overseer arrogantly announces that Ivy will have to pay crippling taxes, or else he will seize the ranch and its cattle. Suddenly realizing that her best way to get some much-needed cash is to have Jordan drive the cattle up north, she and Granna get Middlebrack so drunk, the carpetbagger passes out. Effortlessly, the entire crew sneaks past the sleeping Yankees, who are led by the fair-minded Lieutenant Nichols (Harvey Stephens). Ivy's plan is simple. They're to drive the cattle across the Rio Grande into Mexico, then recross the Rio and travel to Abilene; this is to be done despite the fact that Middlebrack, along with Nichols and his men, will be hot on their trail. Simple!

The scenes of cattle crossing the Rio Grande are impressive and most unusual for a B maven like Hogan. Once the entire crew crosses over into Mexico, Nichols and his men, on the American side of the Rio, about-face. Now free from pursuit, Jordan and Ivy argue about the destination of the cattle, with the embittered Rebel woman insisting that they take the cattle to Mexico City because General Jo Shelby and his men need them. When Ivy claims that "Shelby's army means freedom" (apparently, "freedom" for whites only), Jordan wisely retorts, "With Maximilian ruling us!" Here, the cattle drover fully realizes that in order to secure a dictator's help, the bargain will come with totalitarian strings attached; and what Ivy calls "freedom" will only result in America's enslavement. When Jordan tries to have her friends change her mind, he is told how stubborn she is, with Chuckawalla delivering the usual sexist line of the grizzled sidekick: "Women are like horses. Some'll take to rawhide and some won't."

Their Mexican ranch hand arrives to announce that Senora Ivy has changed her mind and that the cattle are instead going to Abilene. By way of explanation, Hogan cuts to Ivy obviously referring to Jordan as a "Yankee boy" as she childishly hits a box with a switch. Suddenly this stubborn, proud, fanatically loyal Rebel woman, after all her pro–Southern speeches and treasonable actions, in what amounts to less than two minutes' screen time, changes her mind because Jordan's words about the nation being united finally got to her? Or was it the usual movie cliché that a stubborn, strong-willed woman will always sell out her beliefs as soon as a handsome guy asks her to?

As the trek continues, Ivy and Jordan's relationship is still built on ideological arguments, but the melting has begun. When Granna calls Jordan a good boy, Ivy's sarcastic reply could be seen as a coda for Randolph Scott's screen image: "*Too* good. And *always* right!"

Meanwhile, at the state capitol in Austin, Middlebrack, along with Nichols and his commanding officer General Corbett (Richard Tucker), pay a visit to the Radical Republicans running the state. It is *not* a flattering portrait. Hogan's camera pans from a framed picture of George Washington to a Reconstruction official leaning back in his chair, a bottle in his hand, fast asleep; another official is stuffing his face with a sandwich; another man has booze dripping down his chin as he's making a pronouncement; and all of them are righteous and arrogant about dictating their orders to the South "for their own good." After one of these men complains about lack of cooperation from the army, the general replies, "Gentleman, I protest the use of the United States Army for private vengeance and legalized swindling!" Switching gears again, the scenarists wisely portray the army leadership as against these crooked officials, even if the portrayal of the Reconstruction itself is horribly distorted to present the South as the victims. The scene is almost a realization of Jordan's contention that all Yankees are not bad (the depiction of the Union officers). Still, the propaganda is plain, if not downright cartoonish: Those who wish to change the South's ways (like for instance, its racism) are greedy, glutinous drunks who have no right to dictate terms to anyone.

Ironically, this scene almost reminds one of D.W. Griffith's portrayal of Reconstruction officials, as well as African-Americans, in his *Birth of a Nation* (1915). This extra-long silent melodrama is still considered a classic of film, but it is a violently racist one as well; the pathetic ravings of a racist Southern author (Thomas F. Dixon, Jr.) and the renowned helmsman himself (who contributed to the photoplay) masquerading as art. Besides the predictable disparaging portrait of Radical Republicans, Griffith shows us what he thinks will happen when their supposedly pro-black agenda is realized. Midway through the film, there is a scene showing Congress populated by African-Americans who are either drunk, fast asleep, have their bare feet up on their desks, or are constantly gnawing on fried chicken legs. In the Paramount film of 1938, this stereotype is now switched to the white northern officials who are trying to punish the South.

Meanwhile, our merry band of good ol' boys (and ladies) are traveling through a blinding, wind-swept blizzard. (You might wonder why everyone in the caravan is clad in furry winter coats and scarves when none of these folks had any inkling that they'd be going on this trip at all). Since they are now back on American soil, Middlebrack, along with a reluctant Nichols and his men, pursues the southerners. Out in the middle of the prairie, the group is attacked by the Indians (Hogan and the scenarists don't say which tribe), when Ivy and Sanford refuse to pay passage through with one of their steers. During the attack, it looks like the end for the southerners until the Union cavalry arrives in the nick of time. During the fight, Middlebrack is tomahawked by Cal.

Finally, the whole bunch gets to Abilene. Leading the cattle into town as he sits next to Ivy on their wagon, Jordan declares his love for her and gives the would-be traitor a big kiss. Quitting the outfit, Jordan tells Cal that they'll leave town. Ironically, this scene is also the last one Randolph Scott would ever appear in under his long-term contract with Paramount, his sad but determined comment "Never again" carrying an interesting meaning beyond just the character's state of mind. Scott was on his way to much bigger things in the western genre, and his screen persona would grow far beyond his early Paramount vehicles.

However, Ivy has changed her spots. When Sanford wants her to support him in starting a new secret organization called the Ku Klux Klan, a group of ex–Confederates "who meet at night and wear masks," she pooh-poohs him with "How childish!" When he asks her what she means, she responds with a line that finally shows that democracy has finally taken hold of her: "This is America! We govern by laws, not by night-riding!"

Then, seeing Jordan and Cal walking off, she runs after them and grabs the tall man's arm, announcing that she has "some trapping to do, but I won't take long!"

Certainly, one can see by the poor writing in this film just *why* Scott, who was fast becoming a good judge of what would work for him, did not care to renew his association with the studio. Throughout the film, a character's motivations change within the blink of an eye. Though engaged to Sanford and wanting the South to rise again, at the end of the film, without any actual change that we can see, Ivy condemns him as a boy always "playing soldier" and suddenly becomes a believer in federal law and due process. Though it is implied that she has seen the light because of Jordan, we really don't get a clear picture of this either.

Jordan goes from a poor ex-soldier who wears ill-fittting clothes to becoming a cattleman in record time. How did this happen? Who got him this position? The film's scenarists fail to answer this question. During the Indian attack and the cavalry's rescue, Middlebrack is murdered by Cal, a fact the cattle driver practically admits to Nichols, but the lieutenant does nothing. He doesn't even put him under arrest.

The film also takes conflicting stands on hot-button issues. It is a blatant apology for the South, and by extension, its racism and even the rebellion itself. However at the end, Sanford's wish to form the KKK is ridiculed by Ivy, who calls the idea of men meeting at night and wearing masks "childish." The Klan is seen as an entity not adhering to the rules of democratic law, yet the filmmakers' visual portrayal of African-American soldiers at the beginning of the film went right along KKK lines, showing them as lazy and clearly enjoying the South's plight. (Griffith also had this imagery in *Birth of a Nation*.) Also, when Ivy proclaims that America is a nation of laws, which half of the nation is she talking about? Though it is obvious that she means the entire country, now reunited, would be ruled by law, remember that Jim Crow *was* the law in the South at the time and for a century afterward.

Poorly written and, in many ways, poorly acted (with the possible exception of Randolph Scott), *The Texans* addressed issues of postwar law and order in a defeated Texas, condemning those who exploit the South, yet also embracing reunification with the North. At the same time, its hero becomes a spokesman for democracy and powerfully warns the audiences of 1938 of the dangers of foreign aggression. Night-riding is not condemned as much as it is scolded; and the plight of African-Americans trapped in a racist South is never once addressed. In fact, despite the traditional western film's reliance on scenes of lynching, in reality, the lion's share of these atrocities actually took place down south, and African-Americans were the prime victims.

As the world moved closer to war, screenwriters would use episodes of history to return to the Robin Hood theme of the outlaw who is really a hero, as well as portray the forces of law and order as the real villains. In 1939, Warner Brothers attained the height of miscasting by putting their number one gangster in a western. Then they compounded this blunder by casting their number two gangster opposite him....

> "This [a gun] is the only law that I know is worth a hoot in this part of the country. The *only* law."— *Jim Kincaid aka the Oklahoma Kid*

A good many years before the craven Jack Warner sold out his screenwriters and other left-leaning personnel to HUAC, he and his brothers had welcomed Communist and liberal artists all through the Depression era and the war years. Will Hays and Joseph Breen's Production Code office would dampen some of the studio writers' more controversial plots, but one cannot fault the efforts of these men to, at least, try to liven up some tired old genres by taking them in new directions. One of Warners' favorite ploys was to attack a sacred American cow and then, midway through the film, back off from any controversy and turn it into some conventional melodrama (such as *Bordertown, Taxi* and *They Drive By Night*, to name a few). Their biggest male star, James Cagney, was far more left-leaning in the Depression era than he would care to admit after he became a conservative in the postwar years (his highly *un*informative autobiography, *Cagney by Cagney*, never once mentions his leftist past).

However, in September 1938, the actor starred in this left-leaning oater which powerfully commented on the difference between accepted capitalist law and the stigma of outlaw anarchy, blurring the line between those people whom we are taught to accept as success stories and those whom we are taught to condemn as outcasts. Cagney had no problem with the screenplay, written and rewritten by no less than six different scenarists. Shot in black and white as compared with the studio's other big western to be released in 1939, the Technicolor *Dodge City* with Errol Flynn, *The Oklahoma Kid* made up in leftist dogma what it lacked in visuals and production mounting (the Flynn film was directed by the great Michael Curtiz, whereas Cagney's production was directed by the less-inventive Lloyd Bacon).

President Grover Cleveland expresses his desire *not* to take Oklahoma's Cherokee Strip from the Indians and open it to white settlement, but he has decided to go by the "will of the people," meaning all those juicy votes. This means that the Indians are to receive "appropriation money," payment for their land. In reality, the Indians would have little use for white man's money until the twentieth century when they learned to play the capitalist game like white men. At the time, the money meant little to a people for the loss of their lands and the demise of their culture.

Soon we cut to a stagecoach carrying said Indian appropriation money as it rumbles right into an ambush set up by Whip McCord (Humphrey Bogart) and his gang members Doolin (Edward Pawley), Handley (future blacklister Ward Bond), Curley (Lew Harvey), and Indian Jack (underrated character actor Trevor Bardette). Suddenly appearing on the hill to thwart the robbery, William S. Hart–style, is the New York–accented Oklahoma Kid (Cagney). Actually, as the scene progresses amidst all the loud gunfire, it turns out that Kid is *not* thwarting the robbery, but actually robbing the robbers.

Later, at a saloon in town, McCord notices that the Kid just placed a bet with newly minted Indian money from the stage holdup. The battle lines are now drawn. Just before the Land Rush starts, the Kid meets Jane Hardwick (one of the three gorgeous Lane sisters, Rosemary) and her stuffy lawman boyfriend, Ned Kincaid (Harvey Stephens, the straight-as-an-arrow lieutenant from *The Texans*). Soon it will be revealed that the Oklahoma Kid is actually Jim Kincaid, Ned's brother, and the son of the upright John Kincaid (Hugh Sothern)! Obviously, the screenplay implies, a righteous upbringing does not prevent a black sheep from becoming an infamous outlaw.

Meanwhile, out on the Strip, McCord and his thugs have beaten others to a nice portion of real estate and hammered their stakes in the ground (those who beat the "official" group set to ride for the land were called Sooners, a name that, to this day, is used by one of the state's basketball teams). McCord informs Ned and John Kincaid that he is going to start a town, which, of course, will include gambling, larceny and murder. ("You take care of their virtues and I'll take care of their vices," McCord informs them.) In this film, the spread of capitalism means rampant crime and corruption; to the leftist screenwriters, the start of a business doesn't mean something that will benefit the community, but something that will be a means to their destruction. Later, Judge Hardwick (Donald Crisp) will call McCord and his gang a "closed corporation of closed mouths," the scenarists using the magic buzzwords "closed corporation" that has nothing to do with the old west. In this film, those who use capitalism (and, by extension, what passes for respectability in America) are actually villains like McCord and his men; those who favor rebellion and anarchy (like the Kid) are the *real* good-guys.

Certainly Cagney was not anyone's idea of a "kid" outlaw. At one point, Hardwick mentions that he just had a "very interesting conversation with this young man." By this time, the Warner screenwriters were well-aware of Cagney's vanity; in film after film, various characters would refer to him as a "young man." As late as 1950, when a 52-year-old Cagney filmed *Kiss Tomorrow Goodbye*, the actor's character would be referred to as "young man" and also unrealistically romance *two* women in their twenties. When Donald Crisp said his line in 1938, the "young man" was already pushing 40.

Meanwhile, as Kincaid presses for law and order to fight McCord's machine, the black-suited, New York–accented thug has no intention of letting the do-gooder live. When Kincaid threatens to have McCord hanged, the gang boss promises to have *Kincaid* hanged instead, and do it "by his [Kincaid's] own law and order." Before you can say "Here's lookin'

PUBLIC ENEMY GOES WEST: Sheriff Wade Boteler (left) arrests the New York–accented James Cagney as Donald Crisp (right) helps disarm him in *The Oklahoma Kid* (1939). In this picture, the two-fisted outlaw is the good guy and those who twist the law to their own advantage are the villains.

at you, kid," Kincaid is framed for a killing done by McCord's men and unceremoniously thrown in jail where he is soon visited by his supposedly no-good son, Jim (the Kid). The Kid insists on breaking his father out of jail but John stubbornly insists on staying, claiming that the decent principles of law and order will eventually set him free. During the visit, deputies overhear that the Kid is Kincaid's son. After the Kid leaves town, McCord whips up mob frenzy with this information and, led by McCord's men, they break into the jail and hang Kincaid from the building's balcony. The Kid rides into town and sees his father still hanging there (Bacon just shows the beginnings of a rope, not the swinging body).

Earlier, McCord had planned to have his own crooked jurist sentence Kincaid to the rope. To get the honest Hardwick out of the way, a phony letter is sent to him so that he would leave town; however, he is brought back by the Kid ("I'm now working for law and justice," he unconvincingly says while stopping Hardwick's stage at gunpoint). When Hardwick returns, it prompts McCord to form the lynching party. Just as in *Destry Rides Again* (the Stewart version), a crooked judge is set to railroad someone, but when the good guys use an honest judge or send for a federal magistrate (a representative of the government, and always portrayed in these films as morally pure and virtually incorruptible), the villains are provoked to take drastic action. Predictably, the innocent Wash is shot dead in *Destry Rides Again*; in *The Oklahoma Kid*, John Kincaid is lynched. In both films, these actions galvanize the hero to fight back.

After the lynching, while Hardwick insists on wiring the territorial judge, the Kid plans to go after McCord's men, all the while complaining that by-the-book law and order are useless against a man like McCord. Even when his daughter begs him to stop the Kid from his quest for vengeance, Hardwick replies that he's not sure he has a right to stop him and even admits to cheering him on. Again, the film practically promotes the Kid's use of violent action to right wrongs ahead of the supposed twists and loopholes of American law that allow a McCord to get away with his crimes.

However, the Kid's idea of vengeance apparently adheres strictly to Production Code standards. Three of the four men he's after always draw first, thus allowing him to gun them down legally (as well as morally), this despite the fact that he pretends to turn away from them, baiting them to draw. With the fourth man, Doolin, the Kid tracks him into the desert and, instead of killing him, brings him back to confess that McCord incited the lynching. Using this info, Ned goes to McCord's saloon to make the arrest but is shot by the gang leader. When the Kid arrives, he and McCord get into a huge, slam-bang fight in the empty saloon which allows Bacon liberal use of Warners' stuntmen. (At the time this scene was shot, *both* Cagney and Bogart were pushing forty.) Staircases are demolished, wooden chairs and tables are smashed and Warners' punch sound effects are used frequently and often. McCord grabs a gun and is about to drill the Kid, but the gang boss is killed by the dying Ned.

At fadeout, the now honest Kid is allowed to settle down with the judge's daughter. Again, those who think that they can follow the righteous, old-fashioned idea of law and order against a prairie fascist like McCord, are punished by being killed; those who follow the way of rebellious anarchy (like the Kid) and fight their own way, live in the end and get the girl. Judge Hardwick is obviously allowed to live because he harbors no snotty airs and accepts the Kid on his own terms; those who are judgmental (like Ned) get blasted.

In an interoffice memo to producer Sam Bischoff, dated July 11, 1938, scenarist Norman Reilly Raine wrote:

> Either of the above-mentioned angles [injustices done to the Indians over the land question and building up a civilization on the plains], if properly developed, might make a "Big" story—a "Picture with a Message," of some social or historical significance; but if straight entertainment is sufficient it is contained in the present script. It is a plain, straightforward, fast-moving and exciting story of an adventurous kid moving outside the law, but pitting himself against even more criminal and vicious lawbreakers in defense of his father. It is sharply personal; and an effort to inject larger issues or to give it more important status would, in my opinion, weaken the Kid's story without attaining the other, unless it was a complete rewrite ... and this would probably mean a totally new story.[13]

Raine wisely insists on focusing on the Kid's "personal story," and not for the studio to make a western "with a message." It is obvious that the original script had far more socio-political comment than the finished version; this is verified by Hal B. Wallis' memos to Sam Bischoff and director Lloyd Bacon. In one particular memo to Bischoff, dated October 24, a month after filming commenced, the producer wrote: "Remember that you were going to have Duff [Warren Duff, one of the writers] go through the entire script and work on the speeches, the dialogue particularly, with a view to eliminating all of those inane, pointless, silly speeches."[14]

Typically, the Warner honcho found fault with the playing of the lead character by his usually tempestuous star, as he did when he wrote to Bacon on October 20: "Somehow or other, Cagney grinning all through these scenes doesn't particularly characterize him as the happy-go-lucky, dashing bandit of the early days—it just doesn't come off, so let's play it for straight drama."[15]

Despite Wallis' claim about the "happy-go-lucky dashing bandit of the early days," a figure that never existed outside of poorly written pulp westerns and the movies, it was obvious that the producer was once again trying to rein in his star and his indulgences. In the same memo, Wallis points out that Cagney had also tried to grin his way through *Angels with Dirty Faces* until he (Wallis) ordered the actor to do retakes and be grimmer and more hard-bitten. "Everyone will tell you that the picture was helped tremendously by so doing," Wallis claimed, correctly as it turned out.

However, in a *New York Times* review of March 12, 1939, Frank Nugent's opinions did not jibe with Wallis'. After referring to Bogart's appearance in the film ("Another authentic westerner—from Tenth Avenue!"), Nugent wrote:

> There is something entirely disarming about the way he [Cagney] has tackled horse opera, not pretending to be anything but New York's James Cagney all dressed up for a dude ranch. He cheerfully pranks through every outrageous assignment his script writers [sic] and directors have given him ... Mr. Cagney doesn't urge you to believe him for a second; he's just enjoying himself and, if you want to trail along, so much the better for you.[16]

Commenting on the film's social comment (even *after* Wallis' insistence on cutting speeches), Howard Barnes, in his *New York Herald Tribune* review of March 11, 1939, wrote:

> If you listen carefully, you may hear some phrases [delivered by Mr. Cagney] which would seem to suggest that this westward migration [the Oklahoma land rush] involved the robbing of Indians and a good deal of trickery on the part of those sturdy pioneers who are best known on the screen these days as Empire Builders. Take it from me, though, *The Oklahoma Kid* has next to no social significance and gets by as entertainment simply because Mr. Cagney and his assisting players make it a rousing horse opera.[17]

While pointing out that any social commentary in the film was quickly suppressed by its entertainment value, Barnes also mentioned that Cagney's "Tenth Avenue accent and occasional gestures make his impersonation of a Tulsa outlaw highly anachronistic, [but] as far as I am concerned, this is eminently correct." Disagreeing with Barnes was *Variety*, which called the actor's performance "unbelievable," and said that he played the part "without variation of his Hell's Kitchen manner."[18] Unlike Bogart, who thought it was all junk anyway and took the bad reviews in stride, Cagney was infuriated by them. Instead of addressing the incongruity of using his Yorkville accent in a western, the actor whined that no one noticed how well he was sitting his horse (Cagney owned several on his farm at the time).

Critics were certainly not known for praising how well actors in westerns were sitting their horses; still, when it was released on March 11, 1939, *The Oklahoma Kid* was a box office smash which helped take the western in new, and occasionally subversive, directions.

After a decade of the B westerns dominated by Buck Jones, Gene Autry and Hopalong Cassidy, the big-budget western was making a comeback thanks to John Ford's *Stagecoach*. By the end of the year, another A western would be released, though this one would make pointed comments about the times in which it was made....

"No one sets themselves up above the law around here!"— *Tom Destry*

In 1938, the world was in pretty bad shape. Mirroring the persecution felt by the Jews of Germany and elsewhere, much of it would soon be in turmoil. Meeting little resistance, Hitler's armies marched into the Sudentenland and Austria. After a pact had been signed in Munich between British Prime Minister Neville Chamberlain and the German government, the pompous Englishman declared the agreement "a peace for our times," thereby sacrificing Czechoslovakia to the National Socialists.

LAW-DOG WHISPERER. Mischa Auer (left) gives James Stewart some urgent news as Marlene Dietrich eavesdrops in *Destry Rides Again*. Unlike the Tom Mix version, this 1939 remake compared Destry's reluctance to use guns to pre-war appeasement.

Released two and a half months after the beginning of World War II, *Destry Rides Again* was certainly timely. Its production commenced a mere six days after Nazi tanks crossed the west Polish border (September 7, 1939) and one week before Soviet tanks rolled across its eastern frontier. Both totalitarian nations were honoring the conquerers' bargain they had made according to the "secret protocols" buried within the infamous Nazi-Soviet Pact they had cheerfully signed in August of that year. If anything, the invasion of Poland, coming as it did on the heels of Franco's successful fascist rebellion in Spain and Japanese aggression in the Pacific, proved beyond a shadow of a doubt that dictatorships didn't play by democratic rules.

Yet one might ask what the words "dictatorship," "democracy," or "appeasement" have to do with your basic cliché-ridden shoot-'em-up? Or what Max Brand's beloved Destry character had to do with some Nazi goose-stepping his way across Europe?

Our story begins in the hellraising frontier madhouse called Bottleneck. Director George Marshall, a helmsman who had been directing since silent days with hundreds of films to his credit, opens the film with a literal bang. Right after the Universal Pictures satellite spins, his camera settles on a Bottleneck signpost that is quickly riddled with bullets as the opening credits come on. It is a wonderfully audacious way to start a western and perfectly fits the bawdy, anything-goes atmosphere of a wild west town. The casting of its leading lady is also symbolic of the radical departure this 1939 version would make from Brand's novel. In the book, Charlotte Dangerfield is the *only* female character of any significance;

in this version from producer Joe Pasternak, the tomboyish frontier babe is rudely shoved aside by the character of Frenchy, an over-the-top German-accented temptress who is as wild as the men in her saloon and sings up a storm to boot. She was played by an actress-singer who was herself larger than life, Marlene Dietrich. Rumor has it that Universal wanted Paulette Goddard, recently in the hit *The Women*, but Pasternak claimed that he had always wanted Dietrich for the role — as well as for himself. Apparently, he only got her for the role. The singer's last few bombs for Paramount got her labeled "box office poison." Her over-the-top performance as the all–American wildcat Frenchy (try to imagine just *why* she's named that) with a strong German accent revived her career.

A poor farmer is upstairs in saloon boss Kent's (Brian Donlevy) office playing poker with him and his henchmen (Warren Hymer, Allen Jenkins) and the crooked mayor Hiram Slade (Samuel S. Hinds) when Frenchy just happens to spill a drink on the farmer's lap, throwing his winning hand into disarray. After he finds that his ace has been replaced by a deuce, the farmer calls them all cheats until he is pistol-whipped and thrown into the street. To prevent a killing, Marshal Keogh (Joe King) goes up to Kent's office to protest and, after a gunshot, is never seen again.

Rather cruelly, Kent and Mayor Slade choose pathetic town drunk Washington "Wash" Dimsdale (the overacting Charles Winninger) as the new sheriff. Taking the badge seriously, he sends for Tom Destry (James Stewart), presumably a two-fisted hellion like his late father. When he arrives on the stage, however, he is holding a woman's parasol and birdcage for Janice Tyndell (Irene Hervey), to the amusement of Kent's gang and the painful disappointment of Wash.

After Destry enters the saloon, Kent tries to confiscate his guns and learns that the shy cowpoke never wears any. Apparently, the new deputy is a man who doesn't carry guns because of his own father having been shot in the back while wearing them.

Now, after all these scenes of western mirth and amiability, comes the film's most violent scene: the Catfight. When Russian émigré Boris Stavrogin (Mischa Auer) loses his pants in a crooked game with Frenchy, his feisty wife Lily Belle Callahan (the pretty 33-year-old Una Merkel, made to look prissy and severe with her hair up in a bun and wearing the usual frontier gingham dress) confronts her. When Frenchy tells Lily that her husband would rather "be cheated by me than married to you," the risqué implication of that line couldn't be any plainer. During the fight, director Marshall cunningly puts cheering cowboys in the forefront of the shots to partially block the women as they violently pull hair and roll all over the saloon's dirty floor. Some film historians say that Dietrich and Merkel let the stuntwomen keep their pay, then enthusiastically did the fight themselves. And certainly the fight *looks* improvised, as everyone claims, though one wonders if the two actresses were actually faking it when they went at each other. On the IMDb website is a claim that Merkel was furious when she realized that Dietrich was *really* fighting and responded in kind. Jimmy Stewart said that he vastly enjoyed dumping the bucket of water on them and that Marshall would have him do it to them again and again in retakes. This was not to mention him doing it to them *again* for a *Life* magazine photo spread.[19]

When a rowdy shoots up the street, Destry, a man who quotes books and stories like any twentieth century pseudo-intellectual at a stuffy wine-and-cheese party, borrows the miscreant's guns and puts on a shooting display that shocks everyone. After saying that one can have fun with the "toys" (not weapons), he turns serious and threatens the rowdy with jail. It is the first indication that Destry is nobody's fool, and Stewart appropriately plays the book-loving deputy with an edge; though he pretends to be a peaceful lamb, by his facial expressions and reactions to others, the actor conveys that there is a genuine rage under the supposedly calm surface. Almost reflecting the doppleganger motif of Brand's gunslinger, Stewart successfully portrays both sides of Destry's complicated personality; using the lamb character to lull thugs like Kent and his gang into a false sense of security and then the "lion" to uphold the law when it really matters. His punch to Janice's brother Jack (the up-and-coming Jack Carson), when the cowpoke implies that the deputy has a more-than-friendly relationship with Frenchy, shows the character's righteousness that has nothing to do with conning Kent.

Kent and his gang are trying to cheat farmers out of their land and take over the valley. The mustachioed bad-guy also runs Bottleneck as his own little Reichstag, where the citizenry is scared to death to mention the late Sheriff Keogh when Destry starts asking the usual embarrassing questions. Kent has effectively turned this wild western hamlet into a sagebrush fascist state where only the strong rule; and the "untermensch" like the pathetic Wash are driven to booze, and hardworking farmers are cheated and pushed off their land by crooked card sharps and phony deed claims (Munich Pacts?). Within the atmosphere of this prairie New Order, subterfuge is needed, and disclosure is out of the question. Tom Destry fully realizes this, and so he poses as the mild-mannered fool.

Things come to a head when he arrests Gyp Watson (Warren Hymer) for Keogh's murder. Kent is not worried, however, because the corrupt Mayor Slade will preside over Gyp's trial, guaranteeing an acquittal. Again, as in every totalitarian state, the verdict is predetermined and a servant of the regime will never be indicted for his crimes (just as the Nazi thugs who murdered Jews and burned their homes and synagogues during Kristallnacht were never arrested). However, when Destry wires for a federal judge, Kent takes action.

Throughout the film, Destry has flirted with the tempestuous Frenchy in her boudoir (that is, between her rendition of classic Dietrich standards). Through it all, he realizes that she is probably good at heart, and tries to get her to get involved in the Resistance movement against Kent. One night, as she keeps Destry in her room, Gyp is freed from jail and Wash is shot in the back. After the old man dies in Destry's arms (and we have to see Winninger overacting shamelessly), the lawman heads towards his hotel room as the music surges. He leaves the hotel now wearing his father's guns. The mask is off for all to see; lamb has now become lion.

Worried for Destry's safety, Frenchy begs the town's "proper" women, including her wrestling opponent Lily Belle, to help Destry by storming Kent's saloon. The same solution to rampant sin and lawlessness was offered in William S. Hart's pretentious, pseudo-allegorical *Hell's Hinges* in 1916. However, screenwriters Felix Jackson, Gertrude Purcell and Henry Myers sprinkle the drama with liberal doses of bawdy humor, as well as making a barbed comment on sexism. When Jack Tyndell and the farmers attack the saloon and Kent and his gang fight back, the town's bustle-wearing women come between them, with both sides calling for them to get out of the way. Safe in the knowledge that western chivalry will not allow even the villains to shoot at them, the women burst into the saloon with oversized clubs and frying pans. Mayor Slade and the Watson brothers get clobbered rather than shot to pieces.

During the battle, Destry has apparently embraced his inner guerrilla. Before you know it, the formerly gun-hating lawman is now tossing fuse-burning bombs through Kent's saloon window. What book did he get *that* from? During the subsequent riot, Kent is stalking Destry with a rifle. He fires just as Frenchy runs into Destry's arms and takes the bullet. Destry quickly guns down Kent, and the German-accented saloon tart with the

French name dies in the lawman's arms. At the end, Destry is telling the gorgeous Janice another one of his endless stories, this time about marriage, though there is nothing in the film thus far that even implies that the two ever became that close. It is obviously a device to have Destry end up with a "good girl," not a slut like Frenchy. This is the reverse of Universal's later 1952 western *The Lawless Breed*, scripted by communist Bernard Gordon, in which saloon gal Julie Adams evolves into a loving wife, and the hero's neurotic, uppercrust prairie girl fiancée (played with appropriate snobbery by B queen Mary Castle) gets killed off halfway through the film. It's a good picture, but as an accurate film biography of psycho gunman John Wesley Hardin, it's awful.

Frank Nugent, in his *New York Times* review of November 30, praised Pasternak for changing the images of the stars of *Destry Rides Again*:

> With a sweep of his Hungarian fist, he has taken Marlene Dietrich off her high horse and placed her in a horse opera and has converted James Stewart ... into the hard-hitting son of an old sagebrush sheriff. Such epics as Max Brandt's [sic] tale of the coming of law and order to the frontier town of Bottleneck have been told often enough before. What sets this one off from its fellows, converts it into a jaunty and amusing chronicle is the novelty of finding Dietrich and Stewart in it and playing it as wisely as if their names were Mr. and Mrs. Hoot Gibson.[20]

Then Nugent focuses on the scene that stands out among all the mayhem, one that Max Brand had never even written:

> The scene that really counts, though, is the catfight between Miss Dietrich's Frenchy and Una Merkel's Mrs. Callahan. We thought the battle between Paulette Goddard and Rosalind Russell in *The Women* was an eye-opener; now we realize it was just shadow-clawing. For the real thing, with no holds barred and full access to chairs, tables, glasses, bottles, water buckets and as much hair as may be conveniently snatched from the opponent's scalp, we give you not *The Women*, but two women who fight it out in the Bloody Gulch over a pair of Mischa Auer's pants.[21]

Universal had wanted to remake the Tom Mix "B" for years, this time on an "A" budget, with "A" stars and an "A" screenplay. By 1939, Carl Laemmle, who had been a big fan of Mix, was long gone. The new regime had no intention of imitating the sometimes laughable cult of personality that was the main feature of the Mix version; it turned Brand's seedy and uncouth Harrison Destry into the clean-cut, two-fisted "fightin' fool" who co-owned a stage line. By the time Felix Jackson, Gertrude Purcell and Henry Myers wrote their screenplay, the tragic Mix was a has-been traveling the roadways of America from one fleabag circus to another. Pasternak had a major star in mind for the role of Tom Destry, and quickly contacted Gary Cooper to see if he was interested in the role; however, he turned it down. This is too bad, since the shyness inherent in this new incarnation of Destry would have fit the laconic Cooper perfectly.

According to James Stewart, Jackson's original treatment retained the subplot of vengeance that was in Brand's novel. After modestly saying he was hired because he came "cheaper than Coop," Stewart explained:

> Coop was to have played a man who rides into town looking to avenge the death of his father. When Pasternak got me, he didn't think I could play a part like that so he made my character someone who becomes a deputy in this wide-open town, but someone who doesn't believe in wearing a gun. But finally he does put on his gun.... And that kind of paved the way for *Shane*, I always felt. And that idea kind of appealed to me. I thought that this made for a different kind of western.[22]

However, in Brand's novel, Destry is *not* avenging his father; he's going after the men on a tainted jury who falsely sentenced him to prison. Yet Stewart's claim about Jackson's

HAIRSTYLES BY MARLENE. Marlene Dietrich pulls Una Merkel's hair in the classic catfight from *Destry Rides Again* (1939). The most famous scene in the film, it is *not* in Max Brand's original novel or the Tom Mix version.

treatment makes sense in another way: In the finished film, we are told that Tom Destry's father had been shot in the back while performing his duties as sheriff. After Purcell and Myers collaborated with Jackson on the screenplay, they would keep Destry's father as a martyr figure, but make the reasons Junior comes to Bottleneck less personal. Instead, the old man's death would be used by the son to illustrate the folly of wearing guns.

In the novel, after leaving prison, Destry pretends to be a coward to draw the villains into confrontations that he knows he will win — and legally too. In the Stewart film, as played by the intense actor, Destry pretends to be far more innocent than he is in order to entrap the villains and indict them legally. Yet the screenplay remains ambivalent enough to suggest something else. Early on, Destry rejects the use of guns because of his father being shot in the back. Is he *really* against the use of guns outside of shooting at inanimate objects, or is he your standard cowboy hellion masquerading as a milquetoast? The climactic scene where Destry becomes a bomb-throwing warrior on horseback certainly implies that he's a lot more violent than even your usual western lawman, since they rarely threw explosives at the bad guys (and with such pinpoint accuracy too).

Reportedly, before accepting the role of Frenchy, Dietrich asked one of her then-lovers, author Erich Maria Remarque (who wrote the anti-war *All Quiet on the Western Front*), if the film would make her more American, and if it did, "Can I do more against the Nazis?" Remarque answered, "Of course!"[23] The singer-actress detested the Nazis, and became their implacable enemy from then on, generously giving her time to entertain U.S. troops in the war zones of Europe. She was also smart enough to see that the film's subtext (a group of peace-loving people forced to fight for their homeland against a ruthless enemy) pertained to the current international situation.

Certainly, as the world was going to hell, the plot elements within *Destry Rides Again* only reinforced its standing as a cinematic oddity. Unconventional for a western, it gave us a cowboy hero who never wore a gun; instead he quoted book passages and basically talked the villains to death. In this film, women, usually passive and helpless in the genre, were strong and aggressive; instead of a *mano-a-mano* fistfight between hero and villain, it had a female slugfest to end them all; its climax would have the town's *women*, rather than a posse of men, storm the villains' saloon. Filmed two years before Pearl Harbor, *Destry Rides Again* powerfully demonstrated that you can't sweet-talk your way out of a conflict with the forces of evil.

Now with Nazis and Bolsheviks sweeping across Europe and Asia, Universal Pictures took Max Brand's tale of a man who used dissembling and subterfuge in his quest for vengeance and turned it into a full-blown sagebrush advertisement for an Arsenal of Democracy. As the war years beckoned, and Hollywood gave us films that were blatantly anti–Nazi and anti–Japanese, the western attacked fascism by having their 19th century tales euphemistically comment on the present-day crisis. In Universal's *Deep in the Heart of Texas* starring B western stars Johnny Mack Brown and Tex Ritter (one of our greatest singers as well), Brown's father (played by William Farnum) keeps postwar Texas as his own private fascist state, and fights to keep it out of the Union. When Brown announces, "Texas will never follow a dictator," those in the audience were well aware of which dictators he was talking about. At the end, dying of a bullet wound given him by one of his own men, the now-reformed old man insists on taking the allegiance to the United States of America before he expires.

Led by government representative Ritter, the good guys attack the villains' stronghold and insure that Texas will become part of a democracy (though the irony will have a group of black people, obviously separated from the whites, cheering the flag of the state that still legalized lynchings). The violent storming of the villains' compound is the same climax as *Destry Rides Again*, though without the bustle-wearing women.

If anything, these films showed that when a fascist-like state enforces unjust laws, due process is *not* an option. Like Cagney's Oklahoma Kid or the new gunslinging Destry would find out, only force of arms, not law books or pseudo-intellectual discourse, will ever rid the world of dictators

.

2

International Hangmen: 1940–1949
War in the Present and Totalitarian Behavior in the Old West

> "You can rest assured that in this court a horse thief always gets a fair trial before he's hung." —*Judge Roy Bean*

Out of all the famous (and infamous) figures of the old west, one of the more baffling is Judge Roy Bean. Though everyone seems to be in agreement that the eccentric jurist never went to law school a day in his cantankerous life, there is some controversy whether he was truly sincere in his sometimes off-the-wall rulings, or whether he was a closet sadist who just liked making those hapless souls who appeared before him dance (sometimes on air).

Born in Mason County, Kentucky, in 1823 (some say 1825), Roy Bean sought to escape his ol' Kentucky home for a life of adventure. At the tender age of 15 (or maybe 17), he joined his brother Sam for a trek out west. After the two joined a wagon train headed into New Mexico Territory, Roy crossed the border and set up a trading post in Chihuahua, Mexico. However, all was not rosy during his south-of-the-border stay and within a few years, the future judge found himself fleeing back across the border with the Rurales hot on his tail. It seems that the adventurous young Kentuckian had killed a man, though who exactly and why is rather vague. He would escape to Southern California, where another brother, Joshua, became the first mayor of San Diego. It's not known whether it was here in his brother's "bailiwick" that the future judge observed the joys and responsibilities of judicial power, though it soon became apparent, especially by that killing, that Roy Bean was *not* a nice young man.

With his brother casting a sizable shadow on the town's law establishment, the future jurist gambled with abandon, drank like a fish, shamelessly bragged of his prowess with both guns and fists, and encouraged the ignoble sport of cockfighting—which, of course, he bet on. Under the influence of brother Joshua, Roy was appointed as a lieutenant of the state militia—a dangerous move considering his younger sibling's penchant for trouble. Predictably, in 1852, the result of his shameless posturing about his pistol prowess got the future judge into a duel where he wounded a man. Though put under arrest, Roy was able to escape; but his days as a privileged member of the town's elite were over when Joshua was killed by a rival in a love triangle. Without his brother's protection, Roy fled back to New Mexico Territory, where his brother Sam had become a sheriff.

It was certainly obvious by now that Roy liked having the protection of siblings in important posts, and he openly sought to insulate himself against the harshness of frontier life (and accountability for his crimes, petty or otherwise) behind a cloak of immutable legality. Roy would be a bartender in his brother's saloon and, when federal troops weren't looking, he smuggled guns from Mexico to the beleagured Confederate army. After the war's end, Roy got married for the first time (as far as we know) in San Antonio on October 28, 1866, to Virginia Chavez; he was 43, she was 15. They had four children, including a boy named Sam (named after his brother), another named Roy Jr., two girls (Laura and Zulema) and an adopted son named John.

Despite his familial responsibilies, Roy Bean the Crook was never very far away. It is said that he supported his family during the postwar years by selling stolen firewood and watered-down milk. In fact, in order to increase profits and stretch out his milk supply, he would add creek water to it. When cheated customers confronted him with the bizarre sight of minnows swimming in their milk, Bean's reaction was worthy of Walter Brennan: "By Gobs! I'll have to stop them cows from drinkin' out of the creek."[1]

In 1880, fleeing Virginia and the children, as well as San Antonio lawmen, Bean ended up in a truly one-horse town called Vinegaroon in Pecos County (now Val Verde County), not far from El Paso. In 1882, the Galveston, Harrisburg & San Antonio Railroad wanted to link the state capital with El Paso; between those two points were 530 miles of desert. It was in Vinegaroon that Roy Bean opened a saloon (actually a tent with a long plank laid across two old barrels which served as a bar) and served railroad workers, though it was said that the future judge was his own best customer. With the nearest courtroom literally a week's ride away (this was *Texas*, not Rhode island), Pecos County Commissioners needed local law enforcement. Somehow, they had heard of Roy Bean, garrulous friend to the railroad workers who dispensed sage advice and tall tales with his rotgut whiskey. Instinctively aware that such a character should never be trusted with a badge and a loaded firearm, county officials instead appointed him justice of the peace for Precinct #6, Pecos County, Texas. It was not recorded what his reaction was to the appointment, or whether he was sober when he heard it.

Now an official representative of the county, Bean moved north to a small tent city not far from the railroad tracks then being laid and opened another saloon (Bean made sure he was never further than an arm's length from booze at any time). And it was here in this insignificant little tent city that a myth about the man was created. Apparently, despite the legend that Roy Bean named his little burgh after British actress Lillian Langtry (real name, Emilie LeBreton), this town was *already* named Langtry in honor of railroad boss George Langtry (some say he was a foreman for a work crew, others say he was an engineer).

It was somewhere around this time that the novice judge became inexplicably infatuated with the British actress whom he'd never met, renaming his saloon the Jersey Lillie (which was sometimes how the actress was billed), hanging her picture on the wall behind him and singing her praises to cowpokes who'd never heard of her. He also dispensed justice in a firm but black-humored manner. It was said that one of the little ways he cowed the accused was by keeping a tame bear tied up outside the Jersey Lillie. It is uncertain how he got hold of the animal, who probably never hurt a fly. He was also known to short-change railroad passengers, telling his tall tales and causing them to linger at his bar until they were forced to run for the departing train without receiving their change. Another variation of this chicanery had irritated passengers angrily demanding their change in the middle of one of his stories; this caused Bean to fine them for "disturbing the peace," the fine being the exact amount of change the customer was supposed to receive.

Bean served "ice cold beer" and billed himself as "the Law West of the Pecos." His bizarre rulings would have gotten him laughed out of any court in the world. When an Irish track worker was accused of murdering a Chinese man, the killer's friends threatened to destroy the Jersey Lillie if he was found guilty. Scanning the pages of an old law book he probably didn't understand, the judge rapped on his table with the butt of a pistol and finally gave his ruling: "Gentlemen, I find the law very explicit on murdering your fellow man, but there's nothing here about killing a Chinaman. Case dismissed."[2]

Fining people for all manner of indiscretions (and, of course, keeping much of the proceeds), Roy Bean also made sure that he gained a reputation as a hanging judge. However, though he threatened to hang hundreds of men who had the misfortune to appear before him, Roy Bean never actually hanged anyone. Perhaps he had heard of the reputation of Judge Isaac Parker, the Fort Smith, Arkansas, jurist who *did* hang 88 men, and wanted to build on that image. Either way, the irascible Bean sometimes surprised folks when he would help them out financially (it is said that he would buy medicine for poor and sick people in and around Langtry). He also made sure that all court costs and the assistance of local deputies were paid out of his own pocket; therefore, county commissioners had no cause to ever remove him since he didn't cost the county treasury one dime. In fact, it seemed that Roy Bean, former crook and murderer, now granted full legal powers by the county, was just what Langtry, Texas, needed. For better or worse, he *was* the Law West of the Pecos from 1882 to 1902.

As time went on and the railroad brought more people to his "bailiwick," the sudden influx of civilization changed things for the old roustabout. His son, Sam, was killed in a gunfight in nearby Del Rio (it's uncertain exactly when). Then, on March 19, 1903, after a night of heavy drinking in Del Rio, Bean returned home at 10:03 A.M. Twelve hours later, Judge Roy Bean was dead. There were those who claim that the old jurist had lost his will to live, with his son dead and the town's sudden industrialization worrying him (he supposedly went on his final drinking binge because a power plant was being built on the banks of the Pecos River). He had complained bitterly that old men like him were being left behind.

What he did leave behind, however, was an indelible image. Predictably, Bean became a yardstick for judicial corruption, the small-time judge who fined someone $16, and when they gave him $20, he would suddenly raise the fine by four dollars ("That's my rulin'!" he would exclaim). Yet he was also someone who was needed on the frontier to lay down a set of rules to follow, even if he himself was not a sterling example of morality. Indeed, Roy Bean, and others like him, symbolized the duality of American law: the crook and the man of integrity, the con artist who protected the public from even *bigger* con artists, a man who probably meant well even as he picked your pocket; and finally, the man who threatened the death penalty on the accused, but didn't have the heart to go through with it. It was even said that Bean was smart enough to see right away that some of the men before him were just penniless drifters and he actually "allowed" them to escape.

History will probably see him for what he was, a crook who "switched sides" and worked hard to uphold an image of legal fairness and due process, even as he pocketed the difference. In the old west, the badman sometimes became the good guy—and vice versa. Considering his character, that of a dishonest man who eventually sought to do right by his community, Bean will always be remembered for representing both the good and the bad in the legal system of the American frontier.

And that's my rulin'....

> After careful and reasonable consideration, I regret to advise you that the character, Cole Hardin, is still inadequate and unsatisfactory for me, in my opinion, as is the story....[3]

This was film icon Gary Cooper on the latest script offered him by Samuel Goldwyn. Realizing full well that the screenplay threw all the good lines and bits of business to the alleged supporting actor, and well aware of his own growing stardom ("Like you, I have a position to uphold.... My professional standing has been jeopardized from the beginning."[4]), "Coop" was ready for a major rebellion against the man whom legend has it actually said, "Include me out." But Sam Goldwyn didn't get to be Sam Goldwyn by just changing his name (though that was part of it); he insisted on Cooper honoring his contractual obligations.

At the time, Cooper was Hollywood's highest paid star, and its most popular (alongside Gable). He was honoring non-exclusive contracts with both Paramount and Goldwyn Studios, with a Warner Brothers contract being waved at him by year's end. The Montana-born icon was not lying when he said he had a certain position to uphold. He would even receive a Best Actor Oscar in less than two years. However, there was no escaping the facts; the role of a cowboy drifter, no matter how honest, strong and upright, was not going to overwhelm the actor playing the plum role of Judge Roy Bean, especially if the actor was a two-time Oscar winning scene-stealer named Walter Brennan.

With Goldwyn putting pressure on the actor, Coop wrote the producer that he'd reluctantly do the film, but that the experience had "irreparably damaged" their professional relationship. Apparently, it didn't, since Cooper would star in Howard Hawks' *Ball of Fire*, produced by Goldwyn, the following year.

The Westerner would have fine production mounting (an estimated $2,000,000 budget), and a major director, William Wyler. And to appease Cooper, the script was expanded so that his role would be equal to that of the Judge. This explains why the film has an unprecedented *six* screenwriters. Supposedly based on a treatment by Stuart N. Lake, the screenplay was eventually credited to Jo Swerling and pulp western author Niven Busch (who wrote the novel *Duel in the Sun*). It was Busch who rewrote Sterling's screenplay, creating the character of drifter Cole Hardin; but also helping beef up the script were such writers as W.R. Burnett, Oscar LaFarge and Lillian Hellman. Busch would later comment on Lake's treatment: "There was really only a slim tracing of story and no character for Cooper at all."[5]

Nevertheless, threatened with a breach of contract lawsuit by Goldwyn, Cooper had no choice but to embrace the role of Cole Hardin and hope that he would survive opposite his good friend Brennan (the actor ultimately supported Cooper in five of his films).

Our story begins in Langtry, Texas, at the Vinegaroon saloon, heaquarters and unofficial courthouse of Judge Roy Bean (Brennan). Surrounded by pictures of British actress Lillian Langtry, as well as a motley crew of low-life trash, the judge either sentences strangers to outrageous fines or, in the case of alleged horse thieves, strings 'em up. Despite his slovenly appearance and sleazy hangers-on, Bean is a major power-broker and entrepreneur in the territory, a portrayal which couldn't be further from the truth. Siding with the cattle interests (whom we never actually see) against the farmers and homesteaders, the judge has his saloon gang initiate a reign of terror on these poor families. Unfortunately, Goldwyn's army of screenwriters failed to consider that Texas never had any homesteaders to begin with. They were a republic until joining the union, a time when they achieved full statehood. Therefore, Texas never had territorial status, nor did the government own land for homesteaders to file on (unlike the territories in the west). Still, one does wonder why the screenwriters cast the underhanded but likable Bean as the film's main villain.

When drifter Cole Hardin (Cooper) wanders into Langtry, he is arrested and brought before Bean's "court" for horse-stealing. Hardin says that the horse was sold to him by another man, but he knows his number is up until he notices the many pictures of Lillian Langtry hanging behind Bean. Talking fast (well, as fast as Cooper talks anyway), Hardin cons the judge into believing that the cowpoke had actually met and befriended the British actress, a tall tale that softens the judge's stance on hanging him. When the *real* horse thief (former B cowbow hero Tom Tyler) shows up in the Vinegaroon, Hardin knocks the man down and almost gets a bullet in the back for it until Bean shoots the thief dead. It seems that Hardin's moxie, his proving that he was not a horse thief, his alleged friendship with "Miss Lily" and the fact that he could match the judge's imbibing drop for drop win the cowpoke admiration from the old jurist.

This idyllic relationship is interrupted by frontier realities. Bean's murderous henchmen attack the homesteaders and try to run off what cattle they have (two of the young homesteaders are Dana Andrews and, making his movie debut, Forrest Tucker). Befriending Jane Ellen Matthews (Doris Davenport), the daughter of the homesteaders' leader, Hardin comes to know these people and sees how wrong Bean is to try and chase them off. After Jane Ellen's father is run down by a gang led by Chickenfoot (the versatile Paul Hurst), Harper and some men try to storm the Vinegaroon and shoot Bean, but they are stopped by Hardin. Lke the fair-thinking, straight-shootin' cowpokes of old, from George O'Brien to Hoot Gibson, Hardin is there to keep the two sides apart and prevent any killing.

Ultimately, Cole's sympathy with the homesteaders causes him to go to San Antonio and get himself deputized to go after Bean. Now a fully sanctioned representative of the law, Hardin will be empowered to arrest his "friend." A pro–law and order man off-screen as well, Cooper liked playing the hero who enforced the law and fought for justice even when his character was *not* officially a lawman (as in *Dallas*, *Vera Cruz*, *Along Came Jones*, and in its most powerful incarnation, *Man of the West*). People forget that one of his most famous roles, Marshal Will Kane in *High Noon*, was one of the rare times Cooper actually played an officially sanctioned lawman from the start of the film; yet there would be numerous times he would play the reluctant cowboy who fought for law and order without benefit of a badge.

Realizing that Bean was traveling north to see Miss Lily in one of her engagements, Hardin shows up in the theater (Bean has bought up all the seats and is the only one in the theater). As he sits in the front row in his rather pathetic, moth-eaten Confederate uniform, the judge is shocked to see the curtain rise on, not a beautiful British actress, but a tall Montana-accented cowboy wearing a deputy's star.

Not seeing Miss Lily, Bean starts shooting at his former friend and Hardin returns fire. After hitting Bean, Hardin is forced to carry the dying judge over to Langtry's dressing room. The stage star (played by another Lily, actress Lillian Bond) finally meets her admirer, but the old judge dies moments after he enters the room. Wyler excels in this scene. As we see Langtry from Bean's point of view, the scene slowly fades to black; the beautiful Miss Lily is the last thing the old man sees before he dies.

Of course, Bean never met Lillian Langtry and he was not shot and killed in the 1880s; he lived until 1903 and died after a night of heavy drinking (the man was either 80 or 82 when he went on his final bender). Langtry visited the town allegedly named after her several months after her admirer's death.

There were other discrepancies. Ideologically, had there actually been homesteaders in West Texas, Bean probably would have sided with *them* rather than the cattlemen (though he would have known where his bread was buttered as well and not crossed them). And no cowpoke or anyone else had ever gone after Bean.

YEP. The iconic Gary Cooper in *The Westerner* (1940). Though taking a backseat to Walter Brennan's Judge Roy Bean, the Montana–born actor made his presence felt in a less showy role.

However, the film's central performance almost makes one forget the historical inaccuracies. Brennan never lets you forget the evil cutthroat beneath the slimy, slightly comical exterior, and his judge's naivete is ably balanced by cold-bloodedness, as when he tells the homesteaders that the only thing they'll be building is their own coffins, something the real Bean never said.

On location (eight miles outside Tucson, Arizona), according to one crew member, there would be snow and ice on the ground at night, yet the temperature would rise by midday and the crew "would bake." According to screenwriter Niven Busch, Cooper was certainly no pretender at knowing the west: "If I was stuck [in the screenplay] I ran down to Cooper's dressing room and he would put me right. Cooper was such a fund of information about the west."[6]

Though the screenplay was cobbled together, Wyler tried to focus on the camaraderie between Bean and Hardin. As he said on the film's release, "There isn't anything at stake, not even the heroine's life, or the father's mortgage."[7] Unfortunately, the director seems to have forgotten about Bean's men terrorizing the homesteaders and their having trampled the heroine's father to death, among other atrocities. Of course, the various scenarists switching the film's tone from comedy to melodrama and back again didn't help matters by not finding some unifying theme to the story. Wyler shot the film in November 1939, then shot added scenes in February 1940 (which was when the film was supposed to be released). Goldwyn ultimately released the film in September, with premieres in Dallas and Fort Worth.

In his *New York Times* review of October 25, Bosley Crowther lauded Cooper as an "exceedingly modest fellow" for performing his thankless role and then letting Brennan take the picture away from him. However, the critic slammed the film for switching back and forth between being a character study and an old-fashioned cattlemen vs. homesteaders

COURT'S IN SESSION. Walter Brennan as the real-life Judge Roy Bean and Gary Cooper as the fictional Cole Hardin in *The Westerner* (1940). The Samuel Goldwyn production turned the judge into a likable, but evil land-grabber.

story. Still, praising the performances of the two leads, he wrote, "[Brennan's] clean-cut characterization of the leather-skinned but sentimental judge is one of the finest exhibits of acting seen on the screen in some time. And Mr. Cooper, too, is up to his usual standard of understated perfection."[8]

Indeed, despite Coop's "understated perfection," Brennan reaped the rewards. When he won his third Oscar in the Best Supporting Actor category, Brennan wasn't the only one in the audience who was shocked. An audible gasp rose when presenter Wallace Beery announced his name.

Judge Roy Bean would eventually be played on TV by Edgar Buchanan in the mid–1950s (appropriate casting there); and in 1972 by, of all people, Paul Newman (*total* miscasting there). The judge would appear as an ugly and vindictive gargoyle in the over-the-top performance of Victor Jory in Audie Murphy's last film, the appropriately named *A Time for Dying*; and a Bean-like judge would be depicted as a wily villain (played by John McIntire) in Anthony Mann's *The Far Country*. And though the judge seemed like good material for the western film and TV show, remember that it was the old jurist's almost comic ability to cheat stuffed-shirt tourists and pompous asses that made him appealing, not his alleged ability to hang felons. Judge Isaac Parker *was* a hanging judge, yet this old jurist, far more principled than bloodthirsty, did *not* get his own TV series, and barely made it to the movies (and certainly not as a positive character, unless you consider Pat Hingle's role as a Parker clone in *Hang 'Em High*). When *The Westerner* was released in the autumn of 1940, World War II had already started, and Bean's alleged penchant for hanging horse thieves and sidewinders suddenly took a backseat to worldwide carnage. Ironically, the film's release would coincide with the publication of a literary work that commented rather directly on the old west's supposedly neurotic need to hang people.

However, unlike Walter Brennan's black-humored performance as Judge Roy Bean, this landmark novel didn't find anything funny about a hanging....

> "We're the cocks of the dung-heap, all right; the bullies of the globe."
> —Gerald Tetley

In the fall of 1940, as the world was first absorbing the full meaning of the word *blitzkrieg*, Random House in New York published *The Ox-Bow Incident*, an indictment of lynch mobs written by a mild-mannered educator at the University of Nevada named Walter Van Tilburg Clark.

In the October 12, 1940, issue of *The New Yorker*, Clifton Fadiman referred to *The Ox-Bow Incident* as his "unwavering choice for the year's finest first novel." After claiming that the book has "many of the elements of the old-fashioned horse opera — monosyllabic cowpunchers, cattle rustlers, a Mae Western leading lady, barroom brawls, shootings, lynchings [and] a villainous Mexican," it "bears about the same relation to an ordinary western that *The Maltese Falcon* does to a detective story."[9]

Certainly, part of Fadiman's claim must be taken in the context of a writer whose generation was used to seeing a certain type of western product, both on screen and in book and story form; that is, the usual cliché-ridden shoot 'em up with all the usual noncontroversial and escapist plot elements fully intact. In other words, Fadiman was implying that *The Ox-Bow Incident* was as old-hat as any book written by Max Brand or Zane Grey. Indeed, the first part of the sentence calls into question whether the esteemed critic actually read the book. The "cowpunchers and cattle rustlers" are more spoken about rather than actually seen; not *one* scene in the novel actually takes place on the range, nor is any cattle thief actually seen in the entire book. The "Mae Western leading lady," if you want to call her that, is a former saloon gal and the girlfriend of one of the protagonists, Gil Carter; her prospective beau is some dandified dude from Frisco, and her appearances are fleeting and *not* instrumental to the plot. The "barroom brawl" is quick and barely lasts half a page, distinctly different from the long and laborious decriptions of barroom brawls in Louis L'Amour's works. The "shootings" is really only one act in which a drunken stage driver wings Gil's buddy, Art Croft, by accident. As for the "villainous Mexican," the fellow is actually one of the victims of the lynching; and though the man is definitely underhanded and on the wrong side of the law, "villainous Mexican" does not properly describe him.

However, Fadiman *does* have the "lynching" part right.

In fairness to the critic, it's not as if he went on to put this literary classic into a narrow cliché-ridden box; in fact, he went on to praise the novel further:

> *The Ox-Bow Incident* is not so much a story about a violent happening as a mature, unpitying examination of what causes men to love violence and to transgress justice. What lends the book an unusual touch — almost a touch of genius — is the way in which everything that is important in it revolves around the most profound moral issues and is presented only in terms of the tensest melodrama. Each of the characters — there are a score of them and they are realized with over-elaborate precision — bears a special relation to the problems of violence, from the sadistic Tetley to Davies, the saint manqué. But none of them figures merely as a spokesman for an idea

or even a feeling; each one, you sense, is a whole life of which only a facet is presented in this particular episode.[10]

Fadiman's description is accurate here. Clark's writing style is infinitesimally specific. The characters are so full of detail one can almost envision the pores of their skin. Every, and I mean *every*, character in the book is introduced with a full biographical background and complete physical description; no one says a word without their faces also registering some kind of meaningful look; no one walks down the street or mounts his horse without making a silent statement about the evils of lynching. In other words, though one has a more-than-perfect description of what's going on and where these people are congregating, the book is painfully overwritten.

Again, one must disagree with Fadiman as to these people *not* being types. Despite the letter-perfect descriptions of these characters and their milieu, these people are *exactly* that. The message that lynching is evil is laid on with sledgehammer subtlety; Tetley, Deputy Mapes and the other folks who are pro-lynching are depicted as either sadists or dysfunctional losers with their own personal axes to grind; even one old woman is a bloodthirsty monster who hopes that the men will be hanged. However, perhaps to demonstrate the weakness of those who perceive themselves to be righteous, Clark fares no better with those few who are against the lynchings: the guilt-ridden (and endlessly tiresome) storekeeper Davies, and Tetley's deeply disturbed son Gerald.

In fact, midway through the book, Clark, the quiet and bookish teacher at the University of Nevada, allows Gerald to vent his neurotic spleen on Croft for many pages. In an effort to be friendly to Tetley's alienated "weakling" son during the pursuit, Croft initiates a conversation with him, to his regret. Gerald's rather depressing worldview is a hateful little diatribe which slams both men and women (to Gerald, women are "sneaks," whereas men are just "bullies") and he makes the assumption that everybody on the planet wants to dominate everyone else (in 1940, this might not have been too far from the truth). It is not too far-fetched to assume that the annoyingly whining Gerald might be a spokesman for the mild-mannered author who created him. A good example of Gerald's endless spiel: "All any of us really want anymore is power. We'd buck the pack if we dared. We don't, so we use it; we trick it to help us in our own little killings. We've mastered the horses and cattle. Now we want to master each other, make cattle of men. Kill them to feed ourselves. The smaller the pack, the more we get."

Again, when Clark wrote these words in 1940, his comments about men seeking to "master each other" and making "cattle of men" took on far more urgency as concentration camps and gulags dominated half the globe and apathy and appeasement seemed to dominate the other half.

The book is narrated by cowboy Art Croft. Though one gets the impression that he is as ignorant as the rest of the townsfolk, his meticulously drawn descriptions of the people around him, as well as the surrounding countryside, implies that this simple cowpoke had taken a course in English literature and creative writing from Harvard — or perhaps the University of Nevada. (I love when authors give us simple, not-too-bright central characters whose first-person narrations make them sound like Steinbeck or Hemingway.)

The novel is ponderous despite its very serious subject matter. After one rather simple-minded youngster reports on the "murder" of the rancher to the townsfolk (including the rancher's friend, the vindictive Farnley), most of the first half of the book is spent with the hastily formed posse milling around the street in front of Canby's saloon as they wait for Major Tetley to leave his southern-style mansion and lead them. As one can tell, the book drowns in talk, much of it being savage verbal portraits of the posse members (and one rather fat, sociopathic woman apparently) as they share their less-than-impartial feelings about the lynchings. Storekeeper Davies wants everyone to wait for the fair-minded sheriff (who's out of town), or at least the town's pompous judge, but the people's bloodlust won't allow them to wait even a moment — except perhaps for Tetley to get his butt out of the house. Unlike the film version, Carter and Croft are not necessarily against the lynching; they're just less bloodthirsty than everyone else (except for Davies, who, you get the impression, wouldn't step on a roach without agonizing about it for weeks). When Tetley finally does arrive, practically yanking along his neurotic son Gerald behind him, the long-awaited pursuit is finally underway! This, of course, means that the endless talk will now be continued on horseback.

When the posse finally finds the three men camped far out on the trail (in Ox-Bow Valley), one of them, a young man named Martin, is in possession of some cattle he just purchased, but he foolishly doesn't have of a bill of sale. In the west, such a stupid act is considered suicide if the buyer is caught by a group of ignorant folks who think that he might have stolen them — which is exactly what the situation is here. The second victim, a rather pathetic and simple old man named Harvey, blathers on endlessly. Only the Mexican, a cool-headed fellow named Martinez (and an expert knife-thrower to boot), shows some brains. He's smart enough to pretend not to know English (that is, at first); and his contempt for these racist, bloodthirsty Anglos is not without good reason.

When the lynching does finally happen, it is almost anti-climactic; a tragedy without melodrama, an injustice performed as an afterthought. The real melodrama occurs when Gerald attempts to commit suicide by diving off a cliff into the river; the whiny young man is saved by Croft and others. Then the posse runs into the sheriff, who informs them that, though some cattle were stolen, no one was ever killed. *Oops*!

When Croft is back in town recuperating from his accidental bullet wound, he is rudely visited by Davies, who wakes him up and then continues Gerald's whining. During this endless discourse on the horrors of lynching, the old storekeeper finally gets to the point and blurts out that young Gerald hanged himself from a crossbeam in a barn. After Davies wrings his hands for another hour, bartender Canby arrives to announce that *Major Tetley* has just committed suicide by running himself through with his own sword. Davies is now whimpering like a kicked puppy and Croft has to send Canby after the old man to stop *him* from committing suicide too! If Clark was indeed attacking fascist powers like the Japanese for their tyranny, apparently he admired their penchant for hara-kiri.

Clark went on to write *The Track of the Cat*, the autobiographical *The City of Trembling Leaves* and a volume of stories and poems. Despite the movie sale of two of his works, he would never "go Hollywood;" he remained basically a teacher and citizen of his native Nevada (his father was president of the University of Nevada). He died in the early 1970s, a time when the Vietcong gave Southeast Asia a new version of "lynch law."

Considered a classic for its time by the critics and snatched up by an eager reading public, *The Ox-Bow Incident* was purchased by Darryl F. Zanuck's Twentieth Century–Fox studios shortly after its publication. Ironically, the man who authorized the studio's purchase was soon to become the project's greatest enemy....

> ...*The Ox-Bow Incident,* a story of mob violence and its dreadful consequences, had been a flop. In spite of its significance and its dramatic value, our records show that it failed to pay its way. In fact, its pulling power was less than that of a Laurel & Hardy comedy we made about the same time.[11]

This was Darryl F. Zanuck in a long letter to Jack Warner, dated February 15, 1944, on the feasibility of making an "important picture" like *Wilson* as compared to an escapist film which always pulled in the audience. Here, the head of Twentieth Century–Fox was using the film version of Clark's novel as an example of just how "profitable" movies with message really were.

In the movie, two cowpokes, Gil Carter (Henry Fonda) and Art Croft (Harry Morgan), who had spent months out on the winter range, ride into a small town in Nevada in 1885 full of piss and vinegar. Stopping at Darby's (not Canby's) saloon, and merely for the hell of it (not the drunken poker game in the novel), Carter starts beating and stomping obnoxious loudmouth Farnley (communist actor Marc Lawrence) until Darby (Victor Kilian) knocks him out cold with a bottle. Before the dustup, there was idle bar talk about the town's rustler problem; by the time Carter revives, the tow-headed youth Green (East Side Kid Billy Benedict) rides in and tells the townsmen that a rancher named Kincaid was shot in the head and his cattle stolen.

With the sheriff (Willard Robertson) out of town, the power-hungry Deputy Mapes (Dick Rich) and the vindictive Farnley form a mob which ultimately consists of the town's most dysfunctional, bloodthirsty losers. They include the incredibly dislikable Smith (Paul Hurst), old Jenny Grier (Oscar-winner Jane Darwell), and various other examples of rope-happy, blithering idiots. The pompous Judge Tyler (Matt Briggs) tries to make a speech (apparently the quiet Kincaid is *now* one of his good friends) and insists on waiting for the sheriff, a suggestion contemptuously spurned by the arrogant Farnley. In the novel, it is *Clark* who has endless contempt for the jurist. As written by the author, Tyler *never* stops blathering, and when he tries to dissuade the mob, it is not because he believes in law and order, but because he obviously likes to hear himself make pronouncements (as well as the fact that the mob is trespassing on his jurisdiction).

Since most fascistic mobs need a strong leader with far more brains and charisma than the thuggish Mapes or the vindictive Farnley, former Confederate Major Tetley (Frank Conroy, complete with rebel gray outfit and campaign hat) is enlisted to show them the way. He also brings along his reluctant offspring Gerald (William Eythe), who's far less whiny here than in the novel. On the side of the Quality of Mercy are storekeeper Davies (again, far less whiny, and played with great dignity by character actor Harry Davenport) and the Reverend Sparks (the film's only African-American actor, Leigh Whipper). Though the obnoxious Smith goads Sparks into joining, the wise reverend knows that he is being ribbed and decides that, even though he is against the lynching, he *should* go anyway. As Wellman has the powerful humming of a Negro spiritual playing quietly on the soundtrack, Sparks agrees to go, if only to read the words of the Bible over the dead outlaws. Wellman imbues the scene with powerful understatement; unsaid in this sequence is the irony of a black man joining a lynch mob, not because of any bloodlust, but because of compassion for, and obvious identification with, the men who are going to be lynched.

Screenwriter Lamar Trotti cuts out several ranchers joining the posse, as well as a racist, mentally challenged young man named Gus who has contempt for Sparks and all other "Negroes." Actually, Gus *does* appear briefly in the film near the beginning; he is played by the tragic Rondo Hatton. However, like Billy Benedict's errand boy, he completely disappears once the mob goes on its journey, but amazingly reappears in Darby's after the lynchings are done. Where were Gus and Green all that time?

Trotti's screenplay keeps the wounding of Croft, as well as Carter's awkward meeting with Rose on the halted night stage. (Rose is played by B actress Mary Beth Hughes, ridiculously given third billing, way ahead of sidekick Harry Morgan.) But Trotti cuts out the endless gloom and blind darkness that the mob has to ride through in the middle of the night. In fact, not only is the night ride in the novel realistically pitch black, but the hunt takes place in the dead of winter, during a snowstorm, with the lightly dressed posse members feeling the biting cold. In the film, though the characters are dressed in heavier coats, there isn't one snowflake on the obvious soundstage set depicting the Ox-Bow Valley (in the novel, Croft generously offers the freezing Sparks his coat). To boost Henry Fonda's star status, many of Croft's lines in the novel are given to Carter in the film, including his conversation with Sparks.

Soon, the mob finds three men asleep at a campfire; they are Martin (Dana Andrews), Harvey (John Ford's older brother Francis), and Juan Martinez (Anthony Quinn). Martin and the others are caught with cattle without a bill of sale, an act of prairie suicide if accosted by a rope-hungry mob like this one. Twenty-five years later in *Hang 'Em High*, Clint Eastwood's Jed Cooper makes a variation of this mistake when he shows Ed Begley and his lynch mob a bill of sale written by the thief and murderer who sold him the stolen cattle.

As in the novel, the angry but frightened Martin is not afraid to cry before his persecutors, with Tetley slams him for acting "like a woman." Later, the arrogant ex–Reb will insult his own offspring with "I will not have a woman for a son," when Gerald flinches from his dad's order to whip the horses out from under the men wearing nooses.

Tetley's sadistic, prolonged questioning of the accused men (in the book) is shortened for the film (which runs at a B movie length of one hour and fourteen minutes). Still, successfully transferred to the screen is Harvey's feeble-mindedness, as well as Juan's obvious contempt for this racist mob. Oozing endless charisma, future superstar Quinn almost blows away everyone else on the set. By just gazing insolently at his accusers and reacting with "No sabe," as well as a private little smirk or two, the actor lets us see that Martinez may be a crook, but he is also so much smarter than the ignorant bigots surrounding him. When he attempts an escape, even though the mob fires at him repeatedly, he is only grazed in the leg. Apparently, when deadly force is actually needed, these rope-carrying clowns are useless; they can only kill a man when he is helplessly mounted on a horse with a noose around his neck. After he removes the bullet from his leg, Juan accurately tosses the blade at the vindictive Farnley's feet. Again, without hitting us over the head, Wellman makes a searing point that this particular minority figure is certainly a far more talented and resourceful individual than the bigots around him. By the 1950s, now a well-deserving Oscar-winner, Quinn would make a series of westerns in which his charismatic Latino is the *hero*. But, these were Bs not considered worthy of major budgets or co-stars. By 1958, the actor would reunite with Henry Fonda on another parable about the abuse of law and order, the film version of Oakley Hall's novel *Warlock*.

When a vote is taken whether to lynch the three men, only seven posse members show them mercy, including Carter, Croft and Davies (apparently, Sparks' vote doesn't count)—not enough to stop the executions.

Finally, at dawn, after Martin has written a letter to his wife, the three men are hanged. When Gerald refuses to whip one of the horses, he gets clobbered by his own father for his squeamishness. After the hangings, the posse is met out on the trail by the sheriff, who informs them that Kincaid was only wounded and is very much alive. After ripping the deputy star off Mapes' shirt, the angry lawman threatens to indict all those involved in a way that Clark's sheriff *doesn't* in the book. In fact, in the novel, the sheriff, though righteously angry, doesn't decide to prosecute, and instead, some in the posse are actually invited

NECKTIE PARTY. No actor appeared in more anti-lynching films than the great Henry Fonda. Here, his cowpoke defies the vindictive Major Tetley (Frank Conroy) in *The Ox-Bow Incident* (1943). Paul E. Burns stands with noose; Leigh Whipper (in black shirt and suspenders) is in background.

to join him in his hunt for the rustlers who are still on the loose. This is certainly a far more realistic occurrence (remember, these men are his friends) than the implication of indictments in the film, a line that was obviously insisted upon by PCA head Joseph Breen.

After the now guilt-ridden posse members (and one homely woman) return to town, Tetley is verbally indicted by his son in a way he wouldn't have the nerve to do in the book (PCA moralizing again). As Gerald calls him everything he can think of from outside the locked house, Tetley enters his study and then closes the door. After a moment, we hear a gunshot. But then, Wellman actually blunders here; right after the shot, *someone* starts to open the study door, then the scene quickly cuts outside to Gerald. Did Tetley miss? Did he just "wing" himself and he was opening the study door to enlist Gerald's help to stem the bleeding? *Who* was opening that study door? (Apparently, in both novel and film, there is no Mrs. Tetley.) Amazingly, Wellman keeps the scene in and never re-shot it.

At Darby's, Carter reads aloud Martin's letter that was never read aloud in the book, an anticlimax if there ever was one. At curtain, when Croft asks Carter where they are heading, the now-compassionate cowpoke replies that they (meaning he) will look after Martin's wife and kid, a Breen-induced happy ending that Clark never would have come up with.

Though the film's box office was weak, critics took note of the film's power. In his *New York Times* review of May 10, 1943, Bosley Crowther raved:

William Wellman has directed the picture with a realism that is as sharp and cold as a knife from a script by Lamar Trotti which is beautifully brief with situations and words. And an all-around excellent cast has played the film brilliantly. The manner in which Mr. Wellman has studied his characters is a lesson in close-up art. And the terror which he has packed in that night "trial," with the ruthless lynchers glowering around a mountain fire while the doomed men face their fate in pitiful misery, is drama at its cruel and cynical best.[12]

After praising Dana Andrews for "a heart-wringing performance," and acknowledging good work by the rest of the cast, Crowther notes that "Frank Conroy's performance of the demagogue (all rigged out in a Confederate officer's uniform) imparts to it a perceptive significance which is good to keep in mind." At the time the esteemed critic wrote these words, the South was continuing the tradition of Confederate racism with its unrestrained lynchings of African-Americans.

In an ironic foreshadowing of the way Zanuck would see the film, Crowther ends his review with, "*The Ox-Bow Incident* is not a picture which will brighten or cheer your day. But it is one which, for sheer, stark drama, is currently hard to beat."[13]

Unfortunately, the film tanked. Both Fonda and Wellman, who deeply believed in it, were forced by Zanuck to do films they held in contempt (for Fonda it was *The Immortal Sergeant*; for Wellman, it was *Thunderbirds*).

In *Young Mr. Lincoln* (1939), Fonda stops a lynch mob with wit, humor and honesty, telling them that folks sometimes do things in a group that they would never have done by themselves, almost a harbinger of his defiance of mob rule in the Wellman film. However, in 1943, as Germany was ridding the world of its so-called "racial inferiors," *The Ox-Bow Incident* depicted a far darker terrain than that shown in Ford's film; in the Ox-Bow Valley, the Fonda character would have no homespun wit or sage humor to use against these prairie fascists. Realistically outnumbered and outgunned, good guys Gil Carter and Art Croft can do nothing but stand by helplessly as three men are murdered for their status as lesser beings by their persecutors.

Nineteen forty-six was the first full year that the world was at peace. Over at MGM, a place where musical escapism was the order of the day, the studio decided to cast two of their contract stars in a western. However, unlike the usual shoot 'em up, this one would be based on a classic of rural literature. It was the story of a cattle baron who made his own law and the nephew who witnessed the changes in the land around them.

Unfortunately, they didn't make what you'd call the greatest choice in hiring a director....

"First to go had been Lutie Brewton, then the sea of grass..."—*Hal Brewton*

"Spencer Tracy, Cattle baron ... ruthless, rugged! Katharine Hepburn, fiery ... fascinating gal from St. Louis! Robert Walker, gun-shooting and gambling fool! Melvyn Douglas. He knew women! Soft words. Soft looks!"[14]

The quote above was the tagline for MGM's big western spectacular of 1947, *The Sea of Grass*, without a doubt one of the least memorable films in a year Hollywood would prefer to forget. At the time, the industry's box office was starting its postwar decline before hitting rock bottom during the 1950s, the era of television; the U.S. Supreme Court ruled that the studios' ownership of their own movie theaters was a violation of anti-trust laws; and it was the first year of the HUAC hearings into Communist infiltration into the motion picture industry. In the late spring of 1946, mighty MGM, which had bought the rights to Conrad Richter's 1936 frontier novelette *The Sea of Grass*, decided to act as if nothing was amiss in the film capital when they put the story before the cameras.

An underrated literary classic (like other Richter works), the short book told the story in the first-person by the young man, Hal Brewton, nephew of the powerful cattleman Jim Brewton, as he witnesses the changes in the land with the encroachment of the homesteaders (some immigrant and some native) who flocked to the west in the post–Civil War years to grab up land. The Homesteaders Act of 1868 allowed a family of homesteaders to settle on 160 acres of government land and, after five years, own it by "proving up" on the land (meaning digging ditches and wells for irrigation and farming the soil). Though the group was technically called "homesteaders," cattlemen who grabbed all the land before they did had other names for them, the cleanest one being nesters.

In the novel, teenage Hal is living with his uncle, Colonel James B. Brewton. Hal is living a lively, carefree existence as the blood kin of the most powerful man in New Mexico Territory, and residing in a huge spread surrounded by sprawling waves of high grass. His and his uncle's world is turned upside-down by the arrival of the woman he is to marry, Lutie Cameron, and the far-less romantic arrival of the nesters.

After meeting Hal, Lutie insists on walking all over the countryside and getting to know it down to the last blade of grass, sea and all. This also includes a visit to a family of nesters; in fact, her friendliness and lively personality, which has her playing with the nesters' children, totally wins them over. Then, as soon as she announces that she's to be the wife of Col. Jim Brewton, the nesters give her the biggest freeze since the Wyoming blizzard of '76.

Soon, it is heard that the old colonel is back in town at the local courthouse. It seems that two of Brewton's cowhands had shot and wounded one of the nesters for homesteading a little too close to the colonel's cow pastures, and they now face justice. When Hal and Lutie arrive at the courthouse, they are just in time to see Jim Brewton arrive and witness the total respect that everyone, including the judge, has for this vibrant and powerful figure. Towering over six feet in height, with black eyes and black hair, bobbing his head constantly as if he was a bucking, wild stallion, or a bull ready for battle, Jim Brewton is, as recorded by the breathless and admiring Hal, God in a long, gray broadcloth coat and high leather boots who picks up the land in his massive hands and makes it bend to his will. Impressed by the great man's very presence, the judge, an old friend, rules the defendants not guilty.

This angers the attorney fighting for the nesters' rights, a blonde-haired young man named Brice Chamberlain. Between the lines here, Hal points out that this first introduction to Brewton on his own turf impresses Lutie, but he also lets us know that she is also taken by the young and handsome prosecuting attorney as well. As Hal leaves the courthouse with Lutie, they ignore the body of the nester who had filed charges against Brewton's men now dead in the back of a buckboard with a sheet over him (Brewton's ranch hands apparently work fast).

Hal is sent east to medical school. Of course, the young man would've much preferred to stay west with his rough 'n' tough uncle and be a cowboy; he attributes his forced evacuation to the east and the hated "academy" to Lutie's evil influence (this, despite the fact that he is obviously charmed by her himself). In the coming years, the colonel proves himself to be a true cattleman by banging out several heifers himself. They are named Jimmy, Sarah Jane and Brock, the last a boy with a head full of mysterious blonde hair, an odd trait since he looks nothing like his siblings or the dark-haired Jim Brewton.

As the nesters continue their advance, building crude shacks and lean-tos, their oxen and cattle devouring the sacred sea of grass on Brewtonland and snatching some of the colonel's cattle in order to feed their families, something more personal is happening in the

Brewton household. After living in Brewtonland for several years as the lady of the house and giving birth to three children, Lutie suddenly wants out.

As Hal starts to notice, rumors are spreading that Jim Brewton's wife is also the mistress of the ambitious prosecuting attorney, Brice Chamberlain. In fact, the go-getting young man (who apparently knows the president personally) has wrangled himself an appointment as the district's new federal judge. When the nesters file suit after suit against Brewton and his men, the new judge swings the case in their favor with hardly the bat of an eye. In this way, the young hotshot gets even with Brewton for losing to him so many times in the past.

As Lutie is brought by the resentful Hal to the same train station she had arrived at years before, the townspeople are watching closely, waiting for her lover Brice Chamberlain to discreetly board the train with her. To Lutie's horror, she finds that the new judge is letting her travel alone (apparently, there was some court "business" he had to attend to). With the homewrecker openly ditching the married woman in front of the whole town, Lutie is now forced to go east and fend for herself; she is too proud to turn around and beg Brewton's forgiveness.

In the intervening years, no one knows just what happened to Lutie. However, the ambitious Chamberlain, whose power in the territory now rivals his hated enemy Brewton, continues to gradually confiscate the old colonel's land for the government, which, of course, he then turns over to the nesters.

After returning to New Mexico, Hal, now a full-fledged doctor, expresses his contempt for the newcomers as his uncle arrives in the courtroom to answer another lawsuit:

> And now these people who had waited for the West to be safe and the pioneering done were barking and snapping around my uncle's legs like a pack of dogs. They had him fairly surrounded, were raising their paws on him here and tearing out a piece of him there. But after I watched him seat himself again in the old, fearless, unconquerable way, without so much as a glance at the nesters behind him, I knew that although he had lost his case, they didn't have him down.

However, God's justice is at hand (or at least this is what Hal says). A drought arrives, and as time passes, the experienced cattlemen are able to catch the rain to use it for their own grasslands as the fumbling nesters watch their own crops dry up and perish. (Hal never quite explains just *how* the cattlemen "catch the rain," but the passage definitely implies that God has put His money in beef futures.) With their crops and stock dying, many of the nesters flee the territory, giving Jim Brewton a kind of belated victory. Again, the pro-cattlemen Hal implies that when the lives of these poor people are ruined, it is all God's Will.

Hal had always seen the two brothers get into vicious tumble-around fights when they were boys, with the dark-haired Jimmy battling the unusually blonde-haired Brock, and was always surprised at their animosity. Finally one day, when some saloon punk watching the two brothers fight says he'd bet on "the Chamberlain kid," it suddenly hits the rather dense new doctor that one of his cousins is a heifer from a different herd.

Years later, the three Brewton children grow up; Sarah Jane is a devout, church-going, piano-playing young woman (playing tunes on the piano originally bought by Lutie, and never gotten rid of); Jimmy is a dark-haired young man who resembles his father, the colonel: and Brock becomes a charming gadabout, part-gambler, part-hellion, part John Cassavetes in *Saddle the Wind*.

Now a young man, Brock cuts a charming but dangerous figure around town. He's seen riding with a half-breed Indian nester as his girlfriend (a sure sign of evil and degradation, according to Richter), he romances (or something more than that) saloon gals and gambles and is just a selfish, vain, self-serving bastard — a chip off his old man, the federal judge. After Brock shoots a saloon lowlife named Dutch Charley, the principled Jim Brewton wants him to turn himself in, an act of decency the young hellion balks at. Brock quickly flees the territory, and soon Hal is reading that the young roustabout is wanted for robberies and murder throughout the west. Whether the stories are true or not, Richter lets us figure it out.

A sheriff's posse surrounds a cabin where a wounded Brock is holding them off. Brice Chamberlain is alerted to the boy's plight; however, like his ditching of Lutie, the judge suddenly finds some important courtroom business to attend to and does not bother to show up as his offspring is about to die. Then, Jim Brewton rides into the area; ignoring Brock's warnings not to come any closer, the old man enters the cabin and talks Brock into putting down his gun. But it is too late; the young man dies. The colonel is at Brock's funeral; predictably, Chamberlain *isn't*.

After 15 years, Lutie returns. Despite the poor timing, it seems that the still-lively Lutie is just what is needed, as the old man, sympathetic to what she might have been through all those years, gladly takes her back.

Born in Pennsylvania, Conrad Richter was raised in a family of ministers. The young man was set for the same occupation until he turned black sheep and decided on writing as a career. When he and his wife moved to New Mexico in 1928, he was enthralled with the land. From then on, he would be a writer of rural tales and, despite such occasional X-rated plot elements as Lutie sleeping with Brice Chamberlain, the moralist and clergyman that was in his blood always came to the fore. As one can tell from *The Sea of Grass*, nowhere in the novel does the dignified Jim Brewton grab his ol' Betsy, ride to town and blow Brice Chamberlain off the map; after years of having homesteaders murdered by his men, the old colonel is "punished" when his great love, Lutie Cameron, abandons him, and when his land is eaten away by the encroaching nesters. Take note that Brice Chamberlain, despite his power and influence (essentially becoming what Brewton was, though far more of a backstabber and cutthroat), does *not* have a wife or family throughout the entire book; he is, as he deserves to be, eternally alone. Brock's stature as a loose cannon is predictable because he is the "spawn" of a corrupt man; and it is his own misbehavior which finally brings him down. The nesters, who would have been seen as victims in any clichéd pulp western, are far more vindictive here; their greed for Brewton's land and their contempt for him is brought home to us by the obviously biased Hal (who seems to forget that his uncle's ranch hands, on *his* orders, were having them murdered). Though it is obvious that Richter portrays the big landowner as a man of dignity and principle, it is equally obvious that he doesn't sympathize with the poor souls trying to start a new life on territory that is actually free government land. It's certainly a far more intelligent and complicated portrayal of the cattlemen-homesteader wars than western authors had shown, with both sides seen in more ambiguous terms; but what also stands out is Richter's portrayal of the nesters' champion, Brice Chamberlain. For if we see that the crusading prosecutor–federal judge is also power-hungry and a home-wrecker, riding on the coattails of the homesteaders to ensure his appointment as a powerful jurist, then what is Richter saying about the rights of the people that this scoundrel is supposedly fighting for? Again, by portraying the idealist as a bastard, Richter is refreshingly avoiding the clichés of a Louis L'Amour or Frank Gruber. Still, Richter's allegiances to the big cattlemen is a bit obvious. Like Lutie and Hal as they ignore the dead nester in the back of the buckboard, the moralistic author doesn't dwell on the corpses of the men Brewton has had killed, or the families whose lives his men have ruined.

As MGM prepared to film this western, with the material containing more soap opera than gunplay, it hired an ex-communist director who envisioned a sprawling western melodrama whose characters' passions were never dwarfed by the scope and power of the land in which the tale was set.

It didn't exactly turn out that way....

A lady from St. Louis named Lutie Cameron (played by the always mannered Katharine Hepburn) arrives in New Mexico territory to marry powerful cattle baron Jim Brewton (the inimitable Spencer Tracy). Two of Brewton's hands are being tried in court for having shot and wounded homesteader Andy Boggs (underrated character actor Trevor Bardette). Prosecuting the case is Brice Chamberlain (Melvyn Douglas), much older and far less blonde than the young handsome sharpie of the novel. At Brewton's appearance in court, the biased judge (another western pro, Robert Barrat) throws out Boggs' case, absolving the two shooters.

Unlike the book's Chamberlain, the movie's Chamberlain is totally devoid of any duplicity, outside of his desire for a married woman; and the film has made Hal Brewton, the book's narrator, totally disappear. This second change is a blow to the film that Elia Kazan did not bother to mention in his own self-serving autobiography. Without Hal's mostly sympathetic commentary (despite his own pro–Brewton bias), the audience becomes oddly detached from the events on-screen and is forced to view these characters from a distance. Consequently, when the married Lutie has Chamberlain's child and then leaves Jim Brewton, the audience feels absolutely nothing.

In the intervening years, Brock has become a swaggering young hellion (played by the talented but swaggering young hellion actor, Robert Walker) who likes both a drink and a wench. Since everyone in town knows that he's the son of the newly appointed federal judge Brice Chamberlain, Brock is needled about his birth by gambler Dutch Charlie (Douglas Fowley) during a game of stud poker. When Charlie draws, Brock shoots him dead. Unlike the book, *this* Brock seems to have enough principle *not* to tell the colonel just why he shot Charlie.

Later, Brock is trapped in an abandoned nester's shack by a posse and soon dies of his wounds. Right after this, Lutie returns just in time for the funeral. She is reunited with the colonel and happiness returns to Brewtonland.

The film has several flaws, most of which the screenplay (by western screenwriter Marguerite Roberts and Vincent Lawrence) fails to address. (Lawrence allegedly wrote the screenplay at Fox; when MGM got hold of the property for Tracy and Hepburn, Roberts rewrote it.) For instance, midway through the film, Lutie's great lover, Chamberlain, seems to disappear and is inexplicably gone for much of the second half. In an effort to punish the alcoholic Walker for his many on-set rages and tardiness, MGM demoted him by giving him the small role of the grownup Brock. Though the tragic actor is excellent in the part, the screenplay doesn't exploit the fact that Walker could have gone much further with it had he been given more time on screen. Lutie also disappears at the midpoint; and you'd think the screenplay would have answered that burning question as to what she'd been doing with herself during those fifteen years. In the book, Hal only speculates, but we never know for sure just *what* she was doing in all that time; here, the screenwriters miss a golden opportunity to finally tell us how Lutie survived.

In the book, Colonel Jim Brewton is portrayed as a tough, powerful force of nature; a strong, steady, ornery, unbroken horse, if you will. Roberts and Lawrence, perhaps reflecting Hal's own bias towards his uncle, made the onscreen cattle baron more sinned against than sinner. Though a benign tyrant, he is more victim than dictator; and we are decidedly *not* on Lutie's side when she tries to stop the colonel from giving the vindictive nesters a break. This lack of fire in Brewton might also be Tracy's fault; the veteran actor, suffering from his own alcoholism, underplays to the point of walking through the part.

Marguerite Roberts was an author and scenarist who liked writing parts for some of Hollywood's greatest tough-guy actors. Though good at writing crime thrillers and mysteries, she excelled in the western. Part of this insight might have come from her pedigree. As she explained years later, "I was weaned on stories about gunfighters and their doings, and I know all the lingo too. My grandfather came west as far as Colorado [she was born in Greeley in 1905] by covered wagon. He was a sheriff in the state's wildest days."[15]

GUESS WHO'S COMING TO DINNER. The wonderful Spencer Tracy as the ruthless cattle baron opposite his off-screen paramour Katharine Hepburn as his bride and ideological opponent in *The Sea of Grass* (1947). The film suffered from director Elia Kazan's contempt for the western genre.

As a contract scenarist for MGM, she wrote for Gable, Taylor and Tracy. Unfortunately, the talented Roberts was blacklisted in 1952. After her blacklist ended ten years later, she wrote screenplays for John Wayne, Charlton Heston and Dean Martin. Ironically, though she had been a Communist, her screenplay for *The Sea of Grass* bestows much sympathy on tough-minded capitalist Jim Brewton. Lacking the hysteria of more renowned Party members like John Howard Lawson and her fellow Coloradoan, Dalton Trumbo, Roberts had too much love for the western to let it be buried under Marxist dogma.

Unfortunately, the film's helmsman would display no such love for the genre.

After his successful directorial film debut with Fox's *A Tree Grows in Brooklyn*, Elia Kazan utilized the non-exclusive clause in his contract with Darryl F. Zanuck and went to work for MGM on *The Sea of Grass*. Impressed by what others said about the book (I don't know if he read it himself), the Broadway-oriented Kazan envisioned the film version as a thinking man's Western, a statement that already revealed his contempt for the genre (as if westerns were made just for idiots).

Predictably, when producer Pandro S. Berman enthusiastically informed Kazan that he had an enormous amount of stock footage of prairie grassland to use for back projection, Kazan was appalled. He wanted to shoot on location. The director also claimed that Katharine Hepburn had 22 dresses made for her, something we do *not* see in the finished film. After seeing the horses to be used for the production, Kazan claimed that he told the

THE WRONG KEY. The tragic Robert Walker as the "bad seed" son of cattle baron Spencer Tracy (center) in *The Sea of Grass* (1947); Phyllis Thaxter looks on. The MGM film dispenses with the novel's point of view as narrated by the cattleman's loyal nephew.

MGM wranglers that the horses used in the story should be thinner and not as well-fed; as if audiences were *really* going to care about the horses' weight rather than the action on-screen. According to Kazan, the wranglers gave him a long, blank stare. At another point, the helmsman claimed that Hepburn purposely praised Tracy after every take to undercut any criticism he might have of the aging actor's scenes.[16]

In his autobiography, Kazan harshly criticized MGM set director Cedric Gibbons. Claiming that Gibbons had enormous power at the studio, Kazan wrote that the designer had the sets already built and had the back projection of New Mexico backgrounds done without telling him or seeking his approval. "Cedric Gibbons, who laid down the law in everything, made the sets too grand, and the costumes were too pretty ... and then there was the policy of 'star treatment' to which I was entirely opposed."[17] This is an interesting comment from a man who helped make Marlon Brando and James Dean household names.

Shot between May and August of 1946 on an estimated budget of $3,600,000, *The Sea of Grass* was held up from release until February 1947. Despite the efforts of all concerned (excepting, that is, its obviously disenchanted director), the film lost money. It opened at New York's Radio City Music Hall on the 27th with an accompanying stage act consisting of tenor Robert Marshall, high-wire performer Harold Barnes, the Corps de Ballet and an equine named Pansy the Horse.

It's not known whether Pansy looked well-fed while appearing before his adoring public....

In 1948, Columbia Pictures would release a western which made another powerful statement about those in official positions who abused their power. This film would feature a central character who executed those he perceived as felons while hiding his own prejudices behind a cloak of judicial propriety. Not since *The Ox-Bow Incident* would those in authority look more menacing....

> "There's only one way to stop you! And that's to take the power of life and death away from you!"—*Federal Marshal Del Stewart*

By mid–1945, most of America's soldiers had returned home. And though many of these men returned in body, thousands of them did not return in spirit. "Post-traumatic stress," a term that was unknown then, plagued these men upon their return and would stay with them, more or less, till the end of their days. The federal government, running the hospitals that housed far too many of these wounded men, did what they could to repair their bodies, but ultimately did little to repair their psyches. Thinking that tons of bandages and a spot of surgery would fix up our boys and make them upright and productive members of American society again, our government totally ignored the scars they *couldn't* see. As if that wasn't enough, the American soldier who had risked his life to make the world free would have a tough time readjusting himself to working in a society that was (on the surface anyway) at peace; that is, when there were jobs to be had. Many veterans had been promised positions by enthusiastic employers who got carried away with their own patriotic fervor, yet many a returning soldier would have his hopes for a decent job dashed when their calls were not returned. Tormented by their own demons, these war-ravaged men had come home from one war, only to find themselves fighting another, as an uncomprehending society looked the other way.

On October 9, a little over five months after General Dwight D. Eisenhower declared "mission accomplished," an 11-page outline for a western novel arrived in the offices of the Louis Shurr Agency, one of Hollywood's biggest literary agencies. By the 29th, the outline was evaluated by its staff, and then on December 1 it was received by Warner Brothers' story department. Titled *The Man from Colorado*, the outline was cut to 9½ pages when it was evaluated by Warner proofreaders as possible film material. Though the author had been a screenwriter of minor B films, he was just starting to make a name for himself as a writer of pulp westerns and mysteries: Borden Chase.

His prologue for the outline goes straight to the heart of the story, and in its simple language, it grabs us right away and doesn't let go:

> The urge to destroy—to kill, is an inbred thing. The heritage of every animal that walks the earth. Control of this urge is, perhaps, the greatest accomplishment of Man. The desire is there, but from infancy he is taught to control it. We MUST control it or we put him away in a cell and shut him off from the rest of civilization with iron bars.
> Then comes war. The teachings of a million years are swept away. Man is taught to kill, encouraged to kill. For a time, the control is lifted. Or rather, it is relaxed. For even in the mass killing that comes with war, certain specific rules or controls are imposed upon the fighters.
> Our story deals with the aftermath of war and the problems it presents in this respect.[18]

For those who are familiar with Chase's later classic Hollywood westerns, including *Red River* (originally a short story, then expanded into a novel), one might be surprised on the direction the author takes in his story. At no time in his prologue does he specify a time frame; his character "Man" is not inhabiting a specific period in history; he is neither a fighter in the Civil War, nor the recent World War, he is just a species following certain rules that separate him from other animals who kill. It is a fascinating beginning to a story that comments on how war changes peaceful men forever. Chase sets his story at the time of the Civil War. Owen Devereaux is a commander of a New York Volunteer Cavalry Regiment that has been active in containing Confederate partisan activity. Devereaux is a well-born New Yorker who was an attorney prior to the War. His second-in-command is Del Stewart, "a Westerner, and the son of a famous scout." In the closing days of the War, Stewart and Devereaux find a group of Reb soldiers bivouacked at the foot of a hill. After the two split: "[W]e go with Stewart to see him doing a workmanlike job of killing. Caught up in the excitement, it is with reluctance he accepts the offer of surrender by the Confederates and learns that these men feel they are fighting a lost cause."[19]

Upon finding his commanding officer, Stewart also finds that a massacre has taken place; "Once again, Devereaux has shot his way out of an ambush and left a mound of dead men to tell the story." However, in the next passage, Chase bitterly comments on the accolades awaiting Devereaux, as well as other men who have earned the title of Hero:

> Another medal is to be added to the long list of decorations that are already his. It means the Civil War's greatest hero will again be decorated by President Lincoln. That night and for many nights, the men of his troop will boast and drink toasts to their comrades.[20]

However, as Del walks among the bodies, admiring "the perfection of his commander's work," he finds a half-buried white flag. The Rebs were planning to surrender. Here, Stewart and Devereaux stare at each other and, when the second-in-command asks about the white flag, his superior merely laughs and says that the use of the flag was "a Confederate trick." Del believes him, but has his doubts. He thinks back to when Devereaux prevented the escape of six Confederate prisoners by killing them. But the killings his superior has committed are far too many to be called coincidence. And now Chase makes a telling comparison with murderers in the twentieth century: "Were it today, Stewart might have suspected that his commander was a psychopathic killer."[21]

The war is over and the two are at the New York Armory celebrating their victory; as Chase puts it, "Society is out in force. Ancient heroes bedecked with medals, ladies in silks—all the trappings and finery that make such occasions so very colorful." Prominent among the upper crusters is Catherine Van Pelt (of the New York Van Pelts), "the belle of the occasion." Though she is fond of Del, it is common knowledge that her other boyfriend, Devereaux, will propose to her. However, Stewart, deeply troubled by what he knows about his commander, bluntly tells Cathy *not* to marry the war hero, a remark that causes Devereaux to challenge his second-in-command to a duel. However, Stewart sees no point in fighting a duel with "a national hero—the Sergeant York of the Civil War," and declines the duel. This act causes him to lose face with his men "to whom Devereaux is a God."[22]

Then the scene switches to Cripple Creek in Colorado Territory, where Devereaux the war hero is appointed federal judge. Already renowned as a "hanging judge," when his marshal is unable to track down outlaws, Devereaux goes out and gets the felon personally; this results in "more notches on his gun and additional acclaim as a hero." Here, Chase idly surmises that Devereaux is a deadly gunfighter because of the fact that he always knows he is going to kill: "Premeditated murder makes him seconds faster on the draw." Observing Devereaux's cult of personality from afar is former regimental surgeon Dr. Morriman. Seen as an eccentric by the men in his outift, the medico has apparently pioneered the field of psychiatry. After visiting Devereaux in Cripple Creek while on his way to his home in Peaceful Valley, California (Chase says that this will be recognized as the San Fernando Valley), the doctor cites several postwar cases to his host and closely watches his reaction.

Also in Cripple Creek is Del Stewart. Again, Chase makes a comment on our returning combat veterans; however, he adds to his synopsis a subplot with undercurrents of class conflict:

> All wars follow a pattern and in Stewart we meet the prototype of the present-day maladjusted soldier. A round peg in a square hole, he has drifted back to his native territory and is serving as a guard on the wagon teams that freight machinery to the mines. Cold, methodical, and blunt — he kills for pay to protect the investment of Eastern capital.[23]

While having a drink in the local saloon, Del is recognized by severals soldiers who call him a coward and start a fight. This forces Del, who has apparently become an efficient killer on his own, to kill to defend himself. Now the talk of the territory, Del becomes a hunted man. When Cathy, now Mrs. Devereaux, makes a sympathetic comment about Del, the judge straps on his guns and goes looking for his rival. Lodged in the local jail, Del is visited several times by the compassionate Cathy and a sympathetic Dr. Morriman, who has been writing about the judge to his friend in Washington, the surgeon general. Realizing that Owen has already tried the case in his own mind, Cathy and the doctor help Del escape, though he is wounded in the attempt. While in hiding, Morriman removes the bullet and Cathy "learns to love the man she is nursing back to life." After Del's complete recovery, Cathy is forced to return to her husband. (To save face with the town, Owen claimed that Del kidnapped her.)

Strapping on his guns yet again, Devereaux goes after Del and finds him, not realizing that in the past year his quarry has been practicing his draw and is now faster than ever. After the gunsmoke clears, Devereaux lies dying, but, as Chase explains, "He wanted to kill Stewart, but even as he loses, he wins. From now to eternity, Stewart is an outcast. A killer."[24]

Still a wanted man, and now the killer of a federal judge, Del somehow makes it to Peaceful Valley and finds, to his great joy, not only his friend, Dr. Morriman, but the beautiful Cathy waiting for him.

In a letter to Jack Warner, dated December 5, Joseph I. Breen wrote that a "suitable screenplay" could be made of the material, though he had one proviso: "[I]t should be made quite clear that when Devereaux's wife is taking care of Stewart, there should be no indication of illicit sex or any physical love between the two."[25]

Not trusting such heavy psychological material, Jack Warner took a pass, eventually selling the treatment to Columbia. (It would be another two years before, finally acknowledging the popularity of film noir, Warners would make its first "psychological" western, *Pursued*, starring Robert Mitchum.) In a letter to Columbia president Harry Cohn, dated May 7, 1946, Breen cautioned the studio boss on the new script. There was to be no "wanton slaughter on the part of the Colonel in the war period," cut the officer's killings to the "very minimum necessary," "the montage should not show any hangings or killings," and, predictably, there was to be "absolutely no indication of any illicit sex between Del and Cathy."[26] On December 9, Breen gave Cohn this memorable warning about one particular action on page 36: "Please avoid any undue brutality in this killing scene."[27] He also insisted that shots of men with nooses around their necks be cut, along with shots of hanging bodies; and, of course, the dance hall girls were to wear something more than just "spangles."

When Cohn finally had the new script before the cameras, there were several changes. Owen is no longer a former New York lawyer; Cathy had now become Caroline and she has no Big Apple ties; Stewart is not the son of a renowned scout; Dr. Morriman is now a civilian, as well as Owen's uncle (and he's lost his psychiatry background; he's now just a regular country doctor); the roles of the enlisted men in Stewart and Devereaux's company have been enlarged and have a major part in the story; Stewart is no longer considered a coward and, in fact, Devereaux appoints him as his federal marshal; and though the story is still set in Colorado, the town is no longer called Cripple Creek.

William Holden, signed to non-exclusive contracts with both Paramount and Columbia, would play the heroic Del Stewart. Looking for a handsome leading man who could hold his own against Holden, the studio ultimately cast the actor's off-screen friend Glenn Ford. At first, the Canadian actor hesitated. Then, realizing what John Barrymore had said about how good it was to play a villain, and also at the urging of his then-wife Eleanor Powell, Ford signed on. At this point, things were about to get a little weird. Columbia director Charles Vidor wanted to break his contract with the studio and sign with, of all people, Warner Brothers; and so the helmsman sued Harry Cohn in Los Angeles Civil Court for the incredibly shocking crime of cursing at him too much.

The whole thing was a farce. Though Owen Devereaux was not presiding, the case was a victory for Cohn as he had several of his employees (the ones that he usually cursed at), including Glenn Ford, testify that their boss was a model of decorum and that Vidor was himself a crude, filthy-mouthed bully. In a typical example of Cohn's gratitude for his favorable testimony, Ford was cast in *The Man from Colorado* with Charles Vidor as his director. Needless to say, the helmsman treated the actor horribly until Cohn, realizing that the conflict was holding up the shoot, replaced Vidor with contract director Henry Levin (an amiable helmsman who would still be with Columbia when they put out the Matt Helm series in the mid–1960s).

Union troops are surrounding a platoon of Rebs in Jacob's Gorge in Colorado Territory. Looking through his field glass, Colonel Owen Devereaux (Ford) sees that the Confederates are waving a white flag. Devereaux orders the Rebs to be decimated with cannon fire. After the carnage, the colonel's second-in-command, Captain Del Stewart (Holden), surveys the area and finds a crumpled white flag. However, in a surprise move, the young officer kicks the flag into a hole and buries it, covering up for his friend. In his tent, Devereaux writes in his diary that he believes he's going insane. Though Devereaux refers to the two men as "a team," Del has retained his humanity whereas Devereaux has become a spit-and-polish martinet. After the news comes that the war is over, the men celebrate wildly. When the colonel catches his sergeant, Jericho Howard (the wonderful James Millican), drinking too much, he orders him put under arrest.

Back in town, Devereaux , Del and the men are regarded as heroes. Jericho's younger brother Johnny (Jerome Courtland) is bitter that his big brother can't share in the glory. The owner of the Great Star Mining Company, Big Ed Carter (always playing rich men, Ray Collins), nominates Devereaux for federal judge, a position he accepts only if Del becomes his federal marshal. Taking the advice of Devereaux's uncle Dr. Meriam (the ubiquitous Edgar Buchanan) to be near his friend and prevent him from killing, Del accepts the job. To top off his good fortune, Devereaux will marry Caroline Emmet (Ellen Drew), the girl both he and Del have always loved. Suddenly, out on the street, the Reb major who survived the destruction at Jacob's Gorge appears and is about to shoot Devereaux; the colonel takes advantage of the Reb's tiredness, grabs the gun and pumps two bullets into him. Originally, the scene had Devereaux empty the gun into him, but Joseph Breen insisted that the colonel fire no more than *two* bullets. (Glenn Ford actually cocks the pistol's hammer for the second shot, a historically accurate move since there were no double-action firearms during the Civil War. Showing hair-triggered firearms during the Civil War period is another blatant historical inaccuarcy which plagues far too many Hollywood westerns.)

Unfortunately, Devereaux's dictatorial ways in the army have remained with him.

When Carter steals the gold claims of the men in Devereaux and Del's company, even to the point of having his goons beat them up and throw them off their own property, Devereaux unreasonably rules against them and *for* the mining company. Meanwhile, Jericho has escaped and soon heads an outlaw gang. When a posse is formed, Devereaux breaks his own promise not to strap on a gun and goes with Del to hunt for Jericho. Ultimately, Devereaux takes out his wrath on the one man the posse did capture and orders him hanged.

Just before his wedding to Caroline, Devereaux is warned by Del *not* to marry her, and then calls him sick, a remark that causes the judge to punch out his friend. After the nuptials, Caroline finds that her hubby becomes even more high-strung, especially after she rather tactlessly keeps asking why Del isn't around. When Jericho kills a man guarding the mining company's payroll (veteran western baddie Ian MacDonald), he drops a gun which he had rather stupidly carved the initials "J.H." on it. Interpreting the initials to denote "Johnny Howard" instead of Jericho, Devereaux orders the young man's arrest. (During a visit to Owen's home, Johnny had tactlessly called the judge "crazy," a word that, as we quickly see, sets him off.) Now in jail, Johnny refuses to squeal on his big brother. Knowing that Johnny is innocent, Del warns Devereaux not to hang Johnny, and then rides out and tracks down Jericho, making the outlaw return with him. The two are horrified to discover that Devereaux has purposely defied his marshal's orders and hanged the young man. Del breaks with Devereaux once and for all and, years before *High Noon*, pulls off his badge and tosses it to the ground.

Del joins Jericho's gang. When Owen is about to hang more men who are at odds with Carter, a covered wagon arrives with the gang and the men are rescued. Though the original script has Del shooting at Devereaux's men, Breen insisted that Del "not do any shooting in this scene since he is your sympathetic lead." Consequently, Del is reduced from shooter to just driving the wagon.

When Del is tricked into giving himself up, he is rescued by Caroline and Dr. Meriam and they hide out with Jericho's gang. Pushed to the limit by Carter over the robberies, as well as the town's awareness that his wife has run off with his former best friend (Devereaux claims that she was kidnapped), the tormented man orders that the district where the outlaws are hiding be burned to the ground. (Apparently, the little town can only be gotten to by one tiny bridge, a little far-fetched to say the least.)

During the burning, everyone is forced to flee right into Devereaux's arms, including the outlaw gang. Only Del, Caroline, Jericho and Dr. Meriam are still in the burning town. Prodded to the point of hysteria by Carter, who tactlessly calls the jurist "crazy," Devereaux rides across the bridge himself to get his enemies. When he finds them, he wounds Jericho and is about to murder Del. Then the outlaw attacks him with the constantly rolled-up chain he's had with him since he was arrested for drinking on duty. Devereaux and Jericho, murderous judge and murderous outlaw, are both crushed beneath a falling building wall.

At the end, with Devereaux's diary in hand, Del is going to Washington to do right by his fellow ex-soldiers who have been cheated by Carter. Chances are that Washington would probably side with the mining company.

All the actors are excellent, but credit Glenn Ford for giving a superb performance, one that provides the tormented Devereaux with far more sympathy than the character had in either Chase's original, or the screenplay by Robert Hardy Andrews and Ben Maddow. Ford's Owen Devereaux is a stiff ramrod officer who carries himself with ultra-rigid military bearing, even as a civilian. Tightly controlled in manner, gesture and feelings, he usually explodes when people call him "crazy." Even when Devereaux discards an object, whether it's a rifle, an empty pistol or even a piece of paper, he flings it away with such fury that one has little doubt that such a man could discard human beings in the same rough manner. Unlike the Owen of Chase's treatment, who goes out to kill his enemies, the Owen of the film can't help himself, and Ford, though playing a villainous character, does allow

A DRIVEN FORD. Deputy Ben Corbett is restrained by a psychotic Glenn Ford in *The Man from Colorado* (1948). Here, the Canadian actor portrays a Civil War veteran who can't stop killing — even when he's appointed a federal judge.

his humanity to come out once in a while. The character is pushed and pressured from all sides; his wife still pines for his best friend; Danny Howard and the other ex-soldiers interrupt his dinner and the young man ends the incursion by calling him "crazy"; instead of treading softly around Devereaux, Del roughly orders him *not* to hang Johnny, definitely the wrong approach; and Carter keeps pressuring him to act against the outlaws, while also rubbing it in Devereaux's face that his wife ran off with his best friend.

Robert Hardy Andrews was a prolific screenwriter going back to the early talkie era, and his output ranged from gangster movies to westerns to social commentary. However, his screenwriting partner for this project would have his own cinematic output heavily dictated by the friends he kept. Ben Maddow was a member of the Communist Party, and his work always carried with it the usually veiled attack on American institutions. Maddow was a frequent collaborator of John Huston, and in the coming years, he did the screenplays for *The Asphalt Jungle* and *The Unforgiven*. However, behind the liberal helmsman's back, Maddow would refer to him as "an intellectual amateur."[28]

After his blacklist, Maddow continued to work on screenplays, but without credit. Though he would stubbornly deny it years later, he ratted on his friends to HUAC in 1958, just so he could "get out of the dark" (as fellow blacklistee Walter Bernstein put it)[29] and get his name onscreen again.

However, in 1947, years before his blacklist, Maddow's anti-capitalist and, at times, anti–American slant is all over the script of *The Man from Colorado*. Added to the obvious canard that a much-admired American war hero is in reality a psychotic murderer, there is the biased portrayal of Carter and his mining company, symbols of capitalist success, as nothing more than thugs in respectable positions. Though one does admire a script that, by euphemism, tries to highlight the problems of returning soldiers who have had their property and rights taken away from them, Maddow divides their problems distinctly along class lines. Devereaux, the high-ranking officer, comes home a psychotic killer; the enlisted men who have experienced the hardships of battle every bit as much as their commander, are "working class" and they have no psychological problems whatsoever. They are considered *economic* victims due to the capitalist system, not murderers like the autocratic Devereaux. Therefore, since they're fighting what the screenplay depicts as a capitalist exploiter, they have a God-given right to become outlaws. (When Communist screenwriters wrote western scripts, it was a sure thing that the portrayal of outlaws would be romanticized to the point of absurdity.)

During the war, Communist screenwriters, ordered by the Party to write pro-war and pro–American scripts (the USSR was under attack and needed American help in fighting Hitler), refrained from attacking American institutions, including its armed forces. However, once the war was over and the Soviet Union didn't need us any more, the Party quickly switched gears and had their screenwriters write scripts that were *anti*war. Predictably, this message promoting peace was meant for democratic nations only; no such antiwar films were *ever* produced for Russian audiences which showed an equally disparaging portrait of the Red Army. With this new propaganda, the American soldier, particularly its officer corps, would be attacked by leftists screenwriters with relish. In the later Eurowestern *Custer of the West*, written by Communist screenwriters Bernard Gordon and Julien Zimet, there is some dialogue about a cowardly officer fleeing a battle "with his back to the enemy"; the official report on the incident is blocked and the dead officer is instead rewarded with a posthumous medal. This contemptible assertion that the heroism of the American soldier has always been based on a lie is first played up in *The Man from Colorado*.

Certainly, Maddow's adherence to following the Party line *vis-à-vis* the unflattering portrayal of American soldiers, was indirectly picked up by, of all people, Joseph Breen. Again, in his list of deletions from Maddow and Andrews' script, he insisted on cutting a line uttered by an angry Del: "'War's nothing but legal murder anyhow' will undoubtedly offend people since it conveys the idea that all men who fought in the last war are murderers. We must ask that this line be changed."[30]

Maddow (and the Party) apparently forgot that the men they were now calling "murderers" helped save the Soviet Union's bacon just three years before.

Critics certainly had no problem with the film. In the November 18, 1948, *Hollywood Reporter*, the unnamed reviewer wrote: "A good story, a thrilling production, fine performances and dynamic direction; these are the elements merged in *The Man from Colorado* to make the super western the major box office entry from Columbia."[31] The reviewer also justly praised the "deft characterization of James Millican."

On the same day, *Variety* called it a "tense western melodrama" that will "unquestionably shake loose a shower of shekels.... Scripting by Robert Andrews and Ben Maddow of the exciting Borden Chase original is a model for galloper concocters."[32]

In the coming years, the "galloper concocters" would branch out into other fields. At the dawn of the new decade, the western reached its Golden Age before television milked whatever qualities it had and helped start its thirty-year decline. During this golden period, the depiction of old west justice would darken considerably. With the eventual breaking of the Production Code, the folks who populated the west got meaner and more vindictive. It was as if everyone took a cue from Owen Devereaux and used a rope to pronounce sentence on the accused before the charges were even read.

As the Cold War grew hotter and fear of nuclear annihilation reached its zenith, it was no surprise that American movie audiences, seeking to escape the tensions of the mid–twentieth century, would instead find their nineteenth century forebears making a rush to judgment....

3

Chaos: 1950–1955
The Cold War, HUAC, and
Mob Rule in the Old West

> "A gun, like any other source of power, is a force for either good or evil, being neither in itself, but dependent upon those who possess it."
> —from the prologue of *Colt .45*

As one can tell by the above quote, it is not the weapon itself which matters in a fight, but the man behind it. In other words, violence is perfectly okay, as long as only the good guys are using it.

On May 27, 1950, Warner Brothers released *Colt .45*, just weeks before the release of Universal-International's *Winchester '73*, directed by Anthony Mann (both films have the name of a firearm company and a two-digit number in their titles). They were released at the height of the Cold War, as Communist spies were stealing our A-bomb secrets and the detonation of a Soviet H-bomb was on the horizon. Therefore, just as the western compared the Indian wars of the past to the more contemporary Red Menace, the genre euphemistically compared advances in 19th century weaponry to the ultimate weapon of the mid-twentieth century. However, there was one major difference: Neither of the above mentioned films condemned the use of this new firepower, but they took pains to distinguish between the good and evil individuals who possessed them. In fact, a Warner Brothers press release emphasized the need of keeping a new weapon "out of the hands of the wrong element — Indians and bandits in the Colt days, Russians and the Iron Curtain now."[1]

The film's basic theme went right over the heads of the Production Code Office. It was the violence that the weapons wrought, not the weapons themselves, they were concerned about. In a letter to Jack Warner, dated August 17, 1949, Joseph I. Breen wrote: "The unacceptability of this story lies in the wholesale wanton slaughter of human beings described in the script. There is a completely excessive amount of killing throughout this story which will have to be drastically reduced if we are able to approve the finished script."[2]

In the same year as this letter, Warners had released *White Heat* with James Cagney. A box office smash which returned Cagney to the gangster genre that made him famous, *White Heat* was also controversial for its seemingly mindless violence. Despite the film's numerous scenes of shootings, clubbings, punches, and other assorted acts of physical assault, the film was granted a seal by the Production Code office. This was because the screenplay enhanced the intelligence and tenacity of the federal law enforcement agency (in this case, the Treasury Department) hunting Cody Jarrett's gang, and because the lead gangster and his cohorts get killed off in various ways, thereby justifying the violence. However, one wonders just why the Breen Office, after viewing the final cut of *Colt .45*, decided to cavalierly release it as-is since the film was, in its own 19th century old west way, just as violent, if not moreso, than the Cagney film.

The film's great advantage was its star, Randolph Scott, the genre actor by which most western films are measured. From being the dialogue coach in the Gary Cooper version of *The Virginian*, to Paramount contract player and star of Henry Hathaway's B-grade Zane Grey series, to up-and-coming A picture leading man, and finally *the* major star of postwar westerns, Scott enhanced the genre not only by expanding on the "strong, silent cowboy" character, but by darkening the image in classics such as *Coroner Creek* (based on Luke Short's novel) and Budd Boetticher's westerns of the 1950s (co-produced by Scott and Harry Joe Brown). His cowboys were tough, stubborn, brutally honest, adhered to their own strong code of honor, never complained, were capable of engaging in rugged fight scenes, yet conveyed a southern charm and occasionally a black sense of humor which lightened tense situations. As he got older, his leading ladies remained on the young side; however, unlike James Stewart, and especially William S. Hart, Scott's restraint in the romance department made his couplings with starlets like Joan Weldon easier to take. Scott knew that his fans weren't looking for romantic moments in his films and he honestly admitted that love scenes made him uncomfortable. (When the studios wanted him to come out of retirement and make talkies, William S. Hart insisted to producers that he make the films *his* way, which included romancing young girls of 20 even as he turned 60.) Scott was also smart enough to bring to the screen the novels of western greats Ernest Haycox and Luke Short, and he used veteran western screenwriters Kenneth Gamet, Tom Blackburn and Burt Kennedy. Belittling his own acting abilities, he modestly gave his supporting players meaty roles, helping to start the careers of future Oscar winners Lee Marvin, Ernest Borgnine and James Coburn, to name but a few. He was smart enough to work for experienced genre producers Harry Joe Brown and Nat Holt, and his late 1940s and 1950s westerns for Columbia are some of the finest in the genre. Delegating production of his films to genre veterans, he also wisely adhered to a certain formula that brought in the public.

In 1951, Scott told Hollywood reporter Bob Thomas that he looked "for a strong, believable story with 75 percent outdoor action and 25 percent indoors. If you get any more of your pictures indoor, you're in trouble."[3]

Which brings us to that great outdoor epic, *Colt .45*. Directed by B maven Edwin L. Marin, doing the sixth of his *eight* films starring Scott, and written by western novelist Tom Blackburn, at the beginning of his Warner screenwriting contract, *Colt .45* became, despite its gross inaccuracies and over-the-top theatrics, one of the biggest hits of the year.

Our story begins in the west of the 1850s. Steve Farrell (Scott) is a former captain in the Mexican War, and a hero who saved others, but today is a gun salesman for the Samuel Colt Company. He is trying to sell his wares to law enforcement officers in the west, including one particular sheriff in the town of Redrock. (This local lawman should really be a town *marshal*. Sheriffs policed the *county*, marshals policed the towns. Even Scott's own 1946 film *Abilene Town*, based on Ernest Haycox's novel *Trail Town* and directed by Edwin L. Marin, pointed out the difference).

Unfortunately, the overworked lawman is pestered constantly by a loud denizen of his jail, the mustachioed Jason Brett (Zachary Scott). After Brett is released, the sheriff says he's a coward except when a gun is in his fist, underlining the film's main theme of "A pistol don't make a man; it's the gent before the gun that counts!" The lawman emphasizes his righteousness by punching the unarmed prisoner in the face. This gives us time to see Brett knocked back to the desk with the sainted .45s. Before you can say "What a stupid lawman," Brett grabs the guns and fires on the sheriff, killing him instantly. Witnessing this murder, Farrell vows to hunt down the killer and get his guns back.

Months go by. In a frenetic montage, Marin shows us Brett's atrocities all over the west. Now armed with the lightning-fast weapons (the actual shooting is preceded by the loud cocking of the hammers—this is many years before the double-action models), Brett and his newly formed gang have robbed stagecoaches, banks, and campsites, the outlaw always murdering helpless men as they stand with their hands raised. As luck would have it, Farrell is within earshot of a tribe of Indians getting shot down in cold blood by Brett.

After the outlaw and his gang depart, Farrell arrives in time to help the wounded chief, Walking Bear (the wonderful Chief Thundercloud). The Cherokee actor is forced to slow his manner of speech down to conform to Hollywood's pigeon-English stereotyping, despite the fact that Blackburn's screenplay takes pains to show the Indians in a positive light. The chief tells us that he and his warriors were attacked by a man whose guns "talk many times," we presume, without letting the other fella get a word in edgewise. It seems that Brett's gang is masquerading as Indians in order to blame Walking Bear's tribe for their upcoming stagecoach robbery. Working fast, Farrell (or rather Scott's stuntman) leaps upon the moving stagecoach and climbs inside where he meets the beautiful Beth Donovan (the beautiful Ruth Roman). The comely brunette has tied a bright cloth to the outside of the coach so Brett's gang will know that she is on the one carrying the strongbox with gold. When the gang shows up, Farrell and his Colt .45s prevent the robbery, despite Beth's attempts to interfere. After arriving in the nearest town, Farrell meets Sheriff Harris (Alan Hale in his second-to-last film; the actor would be dead by the end of the year). Supposedly disgusted with the apathy of the townsmen to track down Brett's gang, Harris deputizes the former gun salesman.

At Brett's headquarters, the outlaw is licking his sizable wounds over the botched holdup, blaming Beth and her weasly husband Paul (Lloyd Bridges). Apparently, Beth despises Brett, but agreed to help with the robbery if he did not kill Paul. Of course, she doesn't realize that her husband, far from being a hostage, is really an enthusiastic partner to Brett's schemes. Paul's ambitions are portrayed as a kind of skewered version of capitalist ambition, as he envisions wealth and power obtained behind Brett's fast-shooting pistols.

Brett, Paul and company are visited by, of all people, Sheriff Harris. Far from wanting to ride out after Brett's gang, the lawman has allowed the gang to operate in "his territory" in exchange for a piece of the action. However, the sheriff (*again*, not marshal) is greedy for more. When Brett knocks Harris away, the lawman grabs the outlaw's two .45s off the table, kinda like when the Redrock sheriff knocked Brett towards the desk where the outlaw grabbed Farrell's .45s in the first reel. The cowardly outlaw is frightened (Scott widens his eyeballs to a ridiculous degree) as he looks into the barrels of his own weapons. Harris is about to kill him when Paul slings a chair at him.

Certainly the bit where Brett, all alone, mutters to the camera that Farrell is in town hiding behind a deputy's badge and then gives a silly drunken smile, might have had a sad truth behind it. It is clear during this scene that Zachary Scott is slurring his words, and there is a heavy suspicion that the actor, depressed over his wasted tenure at Warner Brothers, might have been drunk during the shooting of this film. In fact, after watching Scott's hammy performance in *Colt .45*, Jack Warner ordered his legal department to cancel the rest of the actor's contract.[4]

Back in town, Harris announces that *Farrell*, merely because he also carries two .45s, is the leader of the infamous ".45 gang." However, Walking Bear and his tribe arrive in the nick of time to rescue Farrell. This happens just as Beth rides into town to tell Farrell about her rotten husband; however, just as she's riding down the street, Paul shoots her in the back. On the way out of town, Farrell picks her up off the ground and they and the Indians ride back to their camp. Thanks to the medical efforts of a rather zaftig squaw, it is discovered that, despite being shot in the back, Beth has only received a scratch ("My husband is a terrible shot, Mr. Farrell," she unconvincingly explains). In fact, she is also now attired in a gaudy buckskin jacket that is more Las Vegas than Native American. During this teepee scene, Farrell reaffirms his commitment, not to upholding the law, but only to getting his guns back. "I'm no policeman," he says, and then, a full two years before Gary Cooper did it in *High Noon*, throws his lawman's badge in the dust.

Meanwhile, Brett has effectively used his gang to take over the town, buying up the saloon and other establishments, apparently with the gang's spoils. He and Paul are now in Prince Albert coats and are lording it over "their" town, but the weakling husband is still regretting his shooting of Beth. Drunkenly, he insists on calling Brett his "partner" and putting his arm around him, an act which repels the outlaw boss. Fearing that Paul will talk, Brett takes a little walk with his "partner." Fade out. Later on, Walking Bear and his braves will find the weakling dead from a .45 bullet, with Beth hardly shedding a tear.

After riding out of the Indian camp, Farrell is waylaid by Harris and a couple of posse members. Walking Bear and his braves again arrive in the nick of time and save the gun salesman's bacon; this is accomplished by firing arrows into the chests of Harris and his men. The chief distrusts the white man's justice, and plans to attack the town, but Farrell asks for 24 hours to round up Brett and his gang. (In homage to this scene, Mel Brooks' *Blazing Saddles* has Cleavon Little's sheriff asking the town for 24 hours to get the outlaws, and then boosts his argument when he adds, "You'd do it for *Randolph Scott!*")

In the meantime, Beth is captured by Brett, who is now in total siege mentality, his paranoia and fear knowing no bounds. (Zachary Scott's overacting *also* knows no bounds). The outlaw's paranoia is reinforced by the appearance of the wounded Harris, who lives just long enough to warn Brett that Farrell is in town. Why this crooked lawman, who so recently was ready to kill Brett with his own .45s, would painfully crawl all the way back to town with a mortal wound from an arrow in his chest and warn him of danger, is one of the many mysteries surrounding this film.

When Farrell *does* try to go into town, he is grabbed by Brett's men and, predictably, is saved by the Indians *yet again*. Screenwriter Blackburn was getting awfully tiresome with this routine; doesn't Farrell *ever* do anything by himself? Aided by his Native friends, Farrell single-handedly storms the outlaw's hideout (after Walking Bear's men kill off Brett's gang). However, during the outlaw roundup, Farrell is stabbed in the right side of his chest — another movie wound which bleeds a lot, but apparently is not fatal. Now, the two Scotts face each other. After a brief fight, both men grab a loaded Colt and fire their respective pistols simultaneously. Brett wanders outside, only to then fall dead. Farrell, still bleeding, puts his arms around the loving Beth, again crossing his pistols, though this time it's behind her back. Marins puts the guns in closeup as **The End** comes up on the screen.

There are very few westerns of the time which contained such outrageous over-the-top elements; from the hammy performance of the actor playing the film's main villain to the risible setpieces that are in the screenplay, to its damn-the-logic, full-speed-ahead direction, *Colt .45* is a film where the characters ought to speak with cartoon balloons coming out of their mouths.

Ironically, the most anti-capitalist speeches in the film are uttered by Bridges (who had been a member of the Communist Party). His character is sick of being poor. Paul Donovan hopes to get power and respect via Brett's superior weaponry; in Blackburn's screenplay, it's brute force, not hard work, that buys success in capitalist America. This is reinforced by the cynicism in his screenplay: The law is basically corrupt, it is even part of the problem. The sheriff of Redrock beats a prisoner who is unarmed; the law then locks up an innocent man for the lawman's killing; Sheriff Harris protects Brett from exposure and shares in the loot; his fellow citizens are either cowards or a lynch mob; and, without belaboring it, it is obvious that the town's white population are racists who hate the Indians (who are constantly saving the hero's life). Portraying American authority figures as corrupt, and the use of political terror as a means of attaining riches, Blackburn's screenplay could easily have been written by Party members John Howard Lawson or Lester Cole. Reinforcing this theory is Farrell's ambiguity about being a representative of the law. When he mentions not wanting to be a policeman, was he implying that the United States should not be the world's policeman? Again, I'm not sure just what the screenwriter's intentions were.

STAR PACKER. Western icon Randolph Scott is ready for trouble in Warners' *Colt .45* (1950). The film compared the villain's use of the new Colt revolvers to the Soviets' efforts to build an atomic arsenal.

Certainly, Lloyd Bridges knew better. In a script which shows an unhealthy kinship between outlawry and capitalist success, the actor–Party member delivers his lines with gusto. However, threatened with blacklisting, the actor named names in a session with HUAC.[5] Years later, when the blacklist era was condemned, Bridges apparently rewrote history and acted as if he was always against HUAC. In later years, no one in Hollywood would question just why Bridges was still working during those years while his "friends" in the Party were blacklisted.[6]

Beyond any leftist leanings in the screenplay is an element which crossed all party lines and political systems. Very few, if any, westerns of those days had so blatant a subtext of sexual impotency on the part of the villain as did *Colt .45*. Brett never seems to get up from his chair and go anywhere without taking his guns with him. After Paul knocks out Harris with that chair, Brett reclaims his guns and there is a terribly triumphant look on his face as he lifts them up. Brett's various killings throughout the film imply something else besides just getting rid of witnesses; or as Beth had said, "He's an animal. You should have seen him behind those guns today. I think he kills just to see men die." Or, it is implied, because these guns might be fulfilling some other need.

There also seems to be something implied in Paul's worship of this killer besides just using him to get some fast money. It's plain enough that this weakling doesn't love the woman he married, and it's obvious that he is prepared to give his allegiance, come what may, to Brett. In fact, when Paul cheerfully talks of getting rich, he purposely touches the barrel of Brett's Colt .45, a gesture which causes the outlaw to angrily glare at him, as if the other man had touched something far more personal than just the barrel of a gun.

Even one of the nation's most esteemed critics saw the gun-as-phallic symbol subtext. In his *New York Times* review of *Winchester '73*, dated June 8, 1950, Bosley Crowther wrote:

> They've got a new angle for westerns. It's no longer cowboy loves horse, nor even cowboy loves girl, a motivation which is frowned upon as sissy stuff. This new dramatic angulation might be labeled cowboy loves gun, and it provides quite as much inspiration as any cowboy-horse romance. The Warners used it boldy in their recent *Colt .45*. And now Universal has employed it in *Winchester '73*, a whoop-de-do cowboy picture which came to the Paramount yesterday.[7]

One can easily count of the number of times that the film's characters are punched, slapped, pistol-whipped, conked on the head with both guns and rocks, stabbed, shot and impaled with arrows. Or the many, *many* times Brett tells various characters "Shaddap!" Randolph Scott's noirish westerns for Columbia, like *Coroner Creek* and *The Doolins of Oklahoma*, are full of violent scenes that push the envelope, but the violence in *Colt .45* seems like something out of Punch and Judy or the Three Stooges. Men who are struck with pistols recover quickly without headaches of any kind; a man with an arrow in his chest apparently crawls miles into town with no problem; Beth is shot in the back and recovers within hours; Farrell is stabbed in the chest with a knife, but acts as if nothing was amiss; and, illogically, Zachary Scott's Brett shoots dead more than a dozen people, yet he does not attain the status of a Jesse James or Billy the Kid. (Why are the Pinkertons not after him, why only one solitary ex–gun salesman?)

However, far from being slapstick, the violence certainly bothered Joseph Breen, who insisted that many of "these killings be eliminated." These include "the five men shot down in cold blood in a series of montage shots," "Brett shoots down four Indians in cold blood, three of whom are killed," "one of the chief heavies is killed in cold blood," etc. The censor also complained about the Redrock sheriff being shot to death and crumpling to the ground (on page 6 of the script) and wanted him killed off-stage; ditto for Donovan's "cold-blooded murder."[8] In fact, looking at the finished film, it's quite amazing that Marin and Blackburn totally ignored the censor's suggestions and kept all the killings (with the possible exception of Donovan's off-screen murder). However, Marin doesn't linger on Brett's various victims; as the outlaw pulls the triggers of his guns, the helmsman focuses his camera on the Colts firing, not the bodies of men falling.

Despite its over-the-top histrionics and dearth of logic, *Colt .45* was a box office smash. And even Bosley Crowther admitted, "It is such a hackneyed picture, that it is actually a lot of fun."[9]

In Jack Warner's files, the mogul kept a letter from the ironically named Amos P. Cannon of Baltimore, a collector of Colts. In his letter of May 29, Mr. Cannon called the film "revolting to a Colt Collector." Then the self-proclaimed gun maven added:

> The guns used by Randolph Scott and Zachary Scott were Colt 1848 Dragoons-Caliber .44, as were the cased Colts in the film.

The Colt .45s did not come out until 1870 and the era of the film was immediately following the Mexican War, 1846–1848.

Such a flagrant disregard of facts should not have escaped your technical advisors.

The film should rightfully have been called *Colt Six-Shooter*, but not *Colt .45*, since the repeating firearm was no novelty when the Colt .45 was introduced in 1870.[10]

The studio's next big western would return to the theme of the innocent falsely accused of murder. Unlike *Colt .45*, it was totally devoid of camp. Directed by a specialist in action films, it also starred an actor later known for his portrayals of Vincent Van Gogh and Spartacus....

"A man with no heart makes a bad enemy." —*cattleman Sam Weaver*

By 1950, Kirk Douglas was one of the most popular stars in Hollywood; an actor whose energy on camera seemed almost limitless. He was signed to a contract with Hal B. Wallis and Paramount, but in 1949, he also signed a non-exclusive contract with Warner Brothers, promising to star in one film a year for them. He scored one of his greatest triumphs in *Young Man with a Horn*, directed by Michael Curtiz, but the studio was stumped on how to follow up with a vehicle that would further enhance their new contract star. Their answer, which the studio started shooting in Death Valley in October 1950, was a script originally called *The Travelers*. On January 27, 1951, five months before its release, Jack Warner would change the title to *Along the Great Divide*. It was Douglas' first western.

However, Douglas was already starting to sour on his Warner contract. At Paramount he starred in Billy Wilder's ahead-of-its-time exposé on the American media, *Ace in the Hole*, and then do William Wyler's film version of Sidney Kingley's Broadway hit *Detective Story*. Making what he felt was a B sagebrush saga for Warners was *not* an appealing prospect for the rising star, and he would emphasize that fact in his bestselling 1988 autobiography, *The Ragman's Son*: "I hated the next Warner Brothers picture I worked on, *Along the Great Divide*. I did it just to get my one-picture a year obligation out of the way so I wouldn't be tied up."[11]

Though Douglas was stuck in Warner's B corral, the actor never realized that he was not the studio's first choice for the role of U.S. Marshal Len Merrick. In an amusing letter to studio executive Steve Trilling, dated May 9, 1949, producer and scenarist Anthony Veiller wrote:

> I saw Coop at lunch the other day and asked him if he had yet read *The Travelers*. There was a twenty-minute silence and then he said, "Yes."
>
> Well, I stepped right on his line with a "what do you think?" and he went right back to Shangri-La. When he returned, two slow dissolves later, he said, "Well, it isn't one I could say yes or no to."
>
> I wrapped myself in my confusion and waited for him to make the next move. He made it. He's going to think a couple of more days and then come in and sit down with me on it.
>
> I'll keep you posted.[12]

At one point, John Wayne was also considered for the role.

Our story begins in the southwest. Powerful cattleman Ed Roden (the science fiction genre's favorite military man, Morris Ankrum) is about to hang old cattle rustler Timothy "Pop" Keith (three-time Oscar winner Walter Brennan) for the murder of his (Roden's) son. Also presiding over the lynching is Roden's embittered son Dan (underrated western badman James Anderson) and reluctant rancher Frank Newcombe (Hugh Sanders). Just as Dan is about to eagerly whip the horse out from under Pop, he is rudely interrupted by the arrival of U.S. Marshal Len Merrick (Douglas) and his deputies Billy Shear (John Agar) and Lou Gray (the redoubtable Ray Teal), who takes custody of Keith. Merrick is new to the territory, but then, so is the law itself. The cattlemen have lorded it over the range and hanged men at will; now, with the arrival of Merrick and his men, due process will replace the lynch-law justice of the cattlemen. When Roden argues that the murderer of his son is being allowed to ride away alive, Newcombe convincingly argues that the murder of a federal officer will *really* bring the government's wrath down on their necks. Again, it is established that civilization's move westward will bring with it federal law that will do away with the need for vigilantism.

Left alone, Roden tells Dan that he and he alone will bury his dead son, a decision which enrages the bitter young man, already resentful that the cattle baron has always favored the now dead brother. In fact, as the film progresses, we shall see an entire universe of sinful fathers whose own mistakes have deeply affected their disturbed offspring. Merrick meets with Roden just before he buries his son; and then, after the rancher rides off, suddenly notices a watch left on the ground, supposedly belonging to the dead man. Not thinking much about it, Merrick idly puts the watch into his shirt pocket.

Supposedly grateful for being rescued from a necktie party, Pop steers his protectors to his house, where they meet Pop's feisty, tomboyish daughter Anne (the wonderful Virginia Mayo). However, the group's stay is short; Merrick is warned by rancher Sam Weaver that Roden plans to ambush the group and forcibly seize Pop from them, then continue where they left off at the previous necktie party. Merrick quickly orders the group to saddle up, hoping to escape through the desert (the long way). Anne insists on joining them. During the cinching-up of the saddles, Pop starts singing "Hear the Wind Blow," a song Merrick's father used to sing. Douglas is especially good here, his face a macabre mask as the old man continues to sing the little ditty. Part of Douglas' appeal as a film actor was of his shrewd acting choices. Discussing his performance in his debut film *The Strange Love of Martha Ivers*, he wrote: "I played a weakling, and I always worked on the theory that, when you played a weak character, find a moment when he's strong, and if you're playing a strong character, find a moment when he's weak."[13] It was something the actor put to good use in *Along the Great Divide*; like many of his characters, Merrick is wound up tight, but his tough exterior is used to cover up an obviously tormented man.

Suddenly, the party of five is ambushed in the mountains by Roden and his men. During the shootout, a Roden ranch hand shoots Billy in the back. Furious, Anne seizes the young man's rifle and kills the sniper. Meanwhile, Dan Roden is planning to sneak up on them, but he is captured by Merrick, who threatens to kill the young man unless Roden and his group pull out. Now the party of five has become *six*; this doesn't help their odds since Dan shot a hole in their water canteens, making a desert jaunt a little more dicey than usual.

After Merrick buries Billy, he tells Anne that his father was a lawman who wanted him to help protect a couple of accused killers from a mob. However, the young man refused, claiming that protecting a killer was none of his business. The old man was eventually lynched along with the murderers, to the everlasting torment of the son, who now compensates by being a real stickler for the law. Moved by the story, Anne puts her arms around Merrick and they kiss. However, during the clinch, Anne swipes the lawman's gun. When her attempt to release her father fails, Merrick angrily slaps her, causing Pop to threaten to kill him if he touches his daughter again.

During the journey, Gray changes; he is now starting to openly rebel against Merrick's authority. Of course, looking at it in retrospect, one does wonder what deranged town official would actually appoint *Ray Teal* as a deputy marshal. Taking note of Teal's usual screen persona, a blind man could see that he was definitely not to be trusted behind a badge. Teal also plays a crooked sheriff opposite Kirk Douglas in *Ace in the Hole*, an incompetent doctor in *The Command*, a corrupt town official in *Rage at Dawn*, a ruthless cattle baron in both *Cowtown* and *The Burning Hills*, the leader of a lynch mob in *Hangman's Knot*, a blackmailing private detective (opposite Sir Laurence Olivier) in *Carrie*, and a crooked horse trader in *Gunman's Walk*. I rest my case.

When Merrick and Anne's horse collapses under them, Gray sees the opportunity to kill the unconscious lawman, but Pop grabs a gun and kills the deputy. Unfortunately, the shots drive off the horses, so now the thirsty group is on foot. Pop decently returns the gun to Merrick, but finds that the lawman is ungrateful; and he and Dan Roden, enemies before, are now making bets who will jump Merrick when he falls asleep. Needless to say, despite the fact that she is falling in love with him, Anne is also furious with the tenacious lawman.

Merrick surprises them all and stays awake long enough to guide them to a lake for much-needed water, and then they walk a little more to the next town, where Pop and young Roden are jailed. At the trial, Merrick tells the jury that he believes Pop innocent of the murder, saying that the old man could have murdered him with his own gun had he wanted to, and made his escape. However, when the prosecuting attorney gets Merrick to admit that he is in love with Anne, the revelation helps the jury form a verdict of guilty.

Disgusted with his job, Merrick tears off his badge, and as he does so the pocket watch falls from his shirt pocket. Realizing that it belongs to *Dan Roden*, and that he lost it when he murdered his own brother out on the range, Merrick confronts Roden and the hanging party with the news. Panicking rather quickly, Dan grabs Anne and points a gun at her; as he does so, he angrily indicts his father for favoring the dead man and ignoring him. When the angry Roden approaches his crazed son, he is shot dead. After saving Anne, Merrick chases Dan into a stable where the gunfire upsets the horses. Kirk Douglas would claim in his autobiography that Raoul Walsh purposely endangered both stunt men and horses on the shoot; one unfortunate stunt man gets *uncomfortably* close to the panicking animals as they frantically reared on their hind legs.

After Dan seizes a horse and rides away, Merrick shoots the young man dead; ironically, in the back, just as Roden had shot his own brother.

Gratefully, Anne embraces Merrick as the newly freed Pop looks on in horror. In an ironic comment on the twists and turns the law has taken throughout the film, the old man whines, "You know it's frightening what can happen to a man. A law officer in the family! It's downright terrifyin'!"

The making of the film was not without mishaps, as well as Production Code interference by the Breen office. In a letter to Jack Warner, dated February 1, 1950, Joseph Breen expressed his concern that the end of one scene (on page 59 of the latest script) not end with the implication that "a sex affair takes place" between Anne and Merrick. In another letter to Warner, dated September 22, Breen took issue with a line on page 65, "She's out there with him a long time. By now, *they're probably....*"

In *The Ragman's Son*, Kirk Douglas expressed his disgust with what he called the director's cruelty, citing the helmsman's penchant for doping up the horses on the Death Valley shoot, something that would allow them to fall to the ground more easily.[14] And indeed, horses do collapse and fall in this film, especially the scene where Merrick and Anne's horse

HOLD THE MAYO. Virginia Mayo shares a tense moment with Kirk Douglas in *Along the Great Divide* (1951). Douglas insisted that the script focus more on the need for due process of the law.

falls from under them to the ground just before Pop shoots Deputy Gray. The abuse of the animals was a cause of concern for Joseph Breen, who pointed out a scene on page 68:

> In accordance with Code requirements, please consult with Mr. Mel Morse of the American Humane Association, as to all scenes in which animals were used. We specifically refer to the later portion of the script, in which the horses are described as lame, and in some cases, actually falling to the ground.[15]

There were other accidents on the shoot. In his autobiography, Douglas mentions a scene in which Pop grabs a gun filled with blanks from Merrick as he's on the ground (again, during the final scene in the desert just before Gray is killed). Douglas complained that Brennan's gun could go off near his head, causing the Oscar winner to sarcastically ask (as Pop Keith would), "What are you, afraid?" Douglas let it go, and Brennan almost blew his brains out when he accidentally squeezed the trigger. Apparently, Douglas did not invent this near-tragedy; it was duly reported by columnist Harrison Carroll in the December 2, 1950 issue of the *Los Angeles Herald Express*.[16]

The movie was based on a treatment by B writer-director Walter Doniger, who also did the screenplay; the script was rewritten at the behest of Douglas by scenarist Lewis Meltzer, who received co-screenwriting credit. In an eight-page letter to Anthony Veiller, dated September 12, 1950, Kirk Douglas lists, in painstaking detail, several improvements to be made by Meltzer in Doniger's original script. Of particular concern to the actor was the depiction of Merrick as a standard bearer for the law:

Proceeding from the story's theme, which, as we all agreed, is that the law and justice must be inseparable, that separation of the two leads to disaster, and union to peace and happiness, we also agreed that the central character — Merrick — represents that theme, and, in consequence, his point of view and behavior must reflect it.... To dramatize Merrick's inner conflict, to achieve the point of this story, Merrick *must* go to the other extreme before he is straightened out. His determination to deliver his prisoner must be *more* than that of a good law officer. It must be an *obsession*— an obsession with the *law*, manifested by absolute *refusal* on his part to concern in any way prior to the start of his transformation, with guilt *or* innocence, in other words, *justice*"[17]

Douglas' influence on the script also made for better drama. For instance, in the scene where Merrick grabs his gun away from Anne, Joseph Breen suggested that, instead of slapping her, the lawman should shake her instead. In his letter to Veiller, Douglas insisted on returning the slap to the script, as well as Pop's threat to kill Merrick if he ever touched Anne again. Calling Doniger's watered-down rewrite "almost a reconciliation," Douglas compared the two versions and concluded, "It is obvious which scene has more force and suspense." The actor also insisted on punching up the attraction between Merrick and Anne. Ironically, though Virginia Mayo claimed in her as-told-to autobiography *The Best Years of My Life* that working with Douglas was "awfully hard," she would end up having more lines and the opportunity for more emoting, thanks to the actor's influence on the script. Indeed, on page 6 of his letter, Douglas called for "added tension, suspense, and *humor* inherent in the situation of mutual attraction pulling against mutual antagonism."[18]

In fact, Douglas insisted on keeping up the characters' antagonism to each other all through the film, with allegiances swinging back and forth depending on who gets the upper hand and how desperate their situation; this is underlined by the characters' continually attacking each other for one reason or another, including Anne, who gets slapped or thrown to the ground several times. Actually, with its main plot of a handful of dysfunctional people escorting an accused killer through the wilderness, the film is almost a harbinger of Anthony Mann's *The Naked Spur*, from the hero's obsessions and inner torment right down to the blonde heroine's unusually short hairdo.

Within the film, however, the insistence on adhering to due process is skillfully mingled with a theme of overbearing fathers and their predictably bad influence on their children. Anne is the daughter of a cattle thief and her isolation from other women has obviously caused her to be a hellraising tomboy (though with Mayo, still a very cute one); Merrick's torment is caused when he refuses to join his father on what turns out to be a suicide mission; Dan Roden is insanely jealous of his arrogant father's preference for his brother and, when given the opportunity, kills him. The parental angle, as well as Douglas' tinkering with the script, helped make *Along the Great Divide* a powerful western that reinforced the need for due process and a repudiation of mob rule.

A year and a half after the film's release, another wayward group would be wandering the American landscape while transferring a killer to justice. But only a genius like Anthony Mann could put his own particular stamp on the premise....

"Do business with the Devil and you get it every time."— *Jesse Tate*

There are very few filmmakers (outside of John Ford, that is) who had such a lasting impact on the postwar western as Anthony Mann. Ford's westerns could be poetic and lyrical, rambunctious and irreverent, humorous and self-indulgent, positive and feel-good. Mann's were dark and violent, obsessively commenting on contemporary urban neuroses while Ford's had bucolic settings with a little history thrown in for added color. Instead of

Ford's slapstick drunken brawls, Mann's fight scenes were deadly serious, showing human beings as bestial, clawing animals; whereas Ford showed us the beauty and grandeur of Monument Valley, Mann's use of mountains, valleys and rivers emphasized the dangers behind the beauty; the western landscape portrayed not as a picturesque tourist attraction, but as a foreboding battleground in which men fought against and murdered other men.

As a helmsman, Mann expertly segued from claustrophobic film noir in the 1940s to panoramic A westerns in the 1950s. At Universal-International in 1950, he single-handedly ensured another comeback of the western with his stark and violent *Winchester '73*, starring James Stewart and Millard Mitchell (the film returned Stewart to the genre 11 years after *Destry Rides Again*). It was Mann (*not* Alfred Hitchcock) who was the first to successfully explore the dark side of Stewart's "good guy" persona, allowing the actor to stretch his talent in ways he hadn't before. (Atrociously directed by Hitchcock in 1947, *Rope* miscast Stewart as a sophisticated college headmaster who cherished being "superior." At times, the actor's performance descended into ham and, predictably, the film failed at the box office.)

Winchester '73 showed us a Jimmy Stewart who could be tough, driven; the edge in his screen character that always seemed to be hidden behind a veneer of stuttering awkwardness came to the fore. The quaint anecdotes of a Tom Destry were long gone; *this* Jimmy Stewart had seen war up close. Thanks to Mann, Stewart's comical shyness would be replaced by rage and hysteria, amiability with a dangerous intensity. In Mann's westerns, the Stewart character (like that of Gary Cooper in the later *Man of the West*) had to destroy the evil but charismatic villain: his other half, the worst part of himself. In the follow-up to their first collaboration, *Bend of the River*, a title emphasizing the courses a man must take in his life, Stewart's ex–border raider must literally drown his murderous pal in that symbolic river to be truly free. In 1953, when Mann made *The Naked Spur*, the ugliness in Stewart's character must be revealed in order for him to find his true self; in a year when HUAC and the world's Stalinists would capture our attention, Stewart's Howie Kemp is part of an atmosphere of paranoia and suspicion, not knowing whom to trust or who to believe. As blacklisting, Soviet espionage and the specter of nuclear annihilation dominated the news, Mann gave us a western in which five people out in the wilderness compulsively celebrate acts of betrayal.

Not thirty seconds after the credits disappear, Howie Kemp (Stewart) rides into the frame and hardly bats an eye before he pulls a gun on innocent prospector Jesse Tate (his *Winchester '73* co-star, Millard Mitchell). Enlisting Tate as a guide (for $20), Kemp claims he's just a sheriff tracking a fugitive.

Within that ten-minute time frame, Stewart *again* draws his gun, this time on newly arrived ex-soldier Roy Anderson (the definitive Mike Hammer, Ralph Meeker). It seems that the former bluecoat's "dalliance" with an Indian girl (the chief's daughter, with the implication that she was raped), as well as his all-around malingering, has made him a deserter from the cavalry. After capturing killer Ben Vandergroat (Robert Ryan at his slimiest), the group also meets his friend Lina (a very miscast Janet Leigh). It is then that the sly outlaw reveals that Howie isn't a lawman at all, as well as the fact that the drawling cowboy has neglected to inform his so-called friends that Vandergroat has a price on his head: $5,000. As Ben smiles from ear to ear, Howie now finds himself with two "partners" who greedily include themselves in on his scheme to take the outlaw back and collect the reward money. (*Again* Stewart draws his gun emphatically; in fact, he actually draws *two* pistols.)

All through the arduous trek, Vandergroat plays on everyone's hang-ups and fears, sowing the seeds of dissention. As in all of Mann's best work, character motivation is revealed *gradually*, with the information being processed as we get to know these people. Vandergroat is a charming, yet Mephisthophelean, outlaw; a smiling, enthusiastic manipulator with the guile of an imp and the brains of a seasoned chess player, working the hearts and minds of those around him, including his erstwhile gal-pal Lina. After Ben implies the real reasons behind Howie's quest, the bounty hunter shouts at him to shut up with a fierceness that reveals that the man is deeply disturbed. In fact, he's never been the same since his gal, Mary, ran off with someone else; therefore, he hopes to use the reward money to purchase land and entice the runaway trash back to hearth and home.

When Indians (the Blackfeet, whom Kemp says are peaceful) are discovered in the area, the group rides through quietly and without fuss, until Anderson opens up on the tribe without warning. During the subsequent shootout, Howie is wounded in the leg, but not before he frantically pistol-whips a brave to death. That night, a wounded Howie (obviously wounded in the soul as well as the leg) deliriously screams about "Mary." A concerned Lina quickly pretends that she is Mary to quiet the bounty hunter. (The bonding between outlaw moll and driven tracker had already started. During the shootout with the Blackfeet, Howie had dove off his horse and shoved Lina out of the way as well; after Kemp is wounded, Lina pulls him out of harm's way.)

Howie and Lina continue to bond, with the bounty hunter offering the outlaw moll a chance to join him on the land he's sure the reward money will buy. As strains of "Beautiful Dreamer" play on the soundtrack, he and Lina seal their deal with a passionate kiss. However, their beautiful (if not age-appropriate) romance is rudely interrupted by an attempt by Ben to grab a horse and escape, but he is stopped by Jesse and Roy. Angry at Lina for the betrayal, Howie draws his Colt yet *again*. Then he orders Ben's ropes cut off and the outlaw given is a gun so that the two can shoot it out legally. Vandergroat, needless to say, is a coward when the odds are even; yet the Satanic outlaw defiantly continues to bait Howie, refusing to draw and, as he puts it, give Howie an excuse to murder him. At this point, an excited Jesse declares that he doesn't know who to point his rifle at any more, emphasizing the paranoia which permeates the entire film.

As the group rides to the banks of a river, the thought is ventured that, since the outlaw could be brought in *dead* or alive, perhaps they should ice the felon right then and there. When Roy brings out a rope to use on Ben, the enraged Howie grabs it from the deserter and whips him with it. Here is another one of Mann's set-piece fight scenes, not between hero and villain, but between two angry men who happen to be pretty twisted individuals. As the two roll under a horse, Roy tries to shoot his opponent. Mann cuts to the others for their reactions; we hardly expect Ben to intervene, but why doesn't Lina or Jesse do something? In fact, Mann shows us Lina's worried look as Roy is about to shoot Howie, but she *doesn't* stop him. She had no problem attacking Roy when he was trying to subdue Ben, but now, with the man she is apparently falling in love with in danger, she stands there like a statue. Here, Mann's comment on the characters is hardly one that shows them mercy or even a little understanding; this is not a fight scene from a B western where the hero has to beat the villain in his own manly way in order to prove himself; this is a good guy, albeit a tormented one, about to get his head blown off and the alleged heroine is just letting the carnage go on uninterrupted.

After Howie wins the fight, the dysfunctional crew decides to break camp for the night. Vandergroat, loving every minute of it, talks Jesse into riding with him and Lina the following morning to find some mythical gold strike; of course, without telling Howie or Roy.

After Ben disarms Jesse, he eventually shoots him dead. Though Lina insists that the two ride on, Ben wants to stay so he can assassinate Howie and Roy. When Howie rides into view, Lina prevents the murder, but is knocked unconscious by Ben. After Howie throws his own spur (naked or not) into Vandergroat's face, the outlaw is riddled with bullets by Roy and then falls into the river. Even dead, however, the outlaw has to have the last laugh. When the deserter goes down in the river to retrieve his body, he is killed by a log crashing into him. Ignoring Roy's body, Howie frantically ropes in the outlaw's corpse as Lina stares at him.

AH, WILDERNESS. A short-haired Janet Leigh grabs James Stewart in an anxious moment from Anthony Mann's *The Naked Spur* (1953). With a backdrop of mountains and rivers, the director used his five dysfunctional characters as a euphemism for Cold War tensions.

As he tries to get the felon's body on his horse, Kemp's hysteria mounts as he explains that Ben (referred to previously as a "bag of money") will buy his way back to happiness. However, after a now-penitent Lina tells Howie that she will marry him, the bounty hunter finally relents. *Now*, after 90 minutes of pure hell, Howie realizes that his obsessive quest has almost destroyed him. Tiredly, he pulls Ben's body off his burro for a quickie burial and decides to go with his sweetie to California.

All the actors would praise Mann's direction, especially Stewart. Despite the fact that Ryan neither looks nor sounds like the Dutch-named Vandergroat, the actor neatly steals the film, with the rest of the male cast coming in right behind him for good performances. In Mann's films, Stewart loses the cold calculation of his Destry character and brings us a man bordering on madness. Making his decisions purely for emotional rather than logical reasons (sending Roy on ahead to ride into a Blackfeet ambush seems like a decision made out of spite rather than pragmatism), his Howie Kemp is revealed as a tremendously flawed hero. While he slides down a hill with rope burns on his hands and fails to make the climb successfully, it is *Roy* who succeeds in getting to the top and catching Vandergroat. A man *not* in control, Howie is too weak to fight Ben's taunts; he lets the outlaw get to him in a way the usual cowboy hero *never* would. The wry humor that was part of Destry and any other Stewart characters (that is, in a non–Mann film) is gone; his lack of perspective is equal to his penchant for violence and arrogance; Stewart draws his Colt more times on his erstwhile partners than he does on the Blackfeet warriors who were trying to kill him (the Blackfeet are the only other cast members besides the five leads). Like many a posse leader, to the selfish and deceptive Howie Kemp, it was his way or the highway; even the sadistic Major Tetley in *The Ox-Bow Incident* is more pleasant company than this neurotic, trigger-happy drifter.

Still, a moralist like Anthony Mann could not show a flawed hero without at least *some* redeeming qualities. To Howie's credit, he keeps the journey within the letter of the law; pretending to be a sheriff (that is, until Ben's *faux pas* revelation), he admirably restrains himself from pulling the trigger on the outlaw when he has the chance; knowing that he'll get the reward money whether the outlaw is brought in dead or alive, he stops Roy from lynching Vandergroat and literally fights the deserter to protect Ben's life; with the conniving Ben demonstrating time and again that he will do *anything* to escape, including murder, the bounty hunter does not take any kind of retaliatory action. In fact, outside of binding the outlaw, he never lays a hand on him *once*. Despite his many faults, Howie Kemp still finds some strength to ignore his own homicidal feelings and continues to fight the good fight for due process and the rule of law — even out in the wilderness.

It was a role Stewart loved. In an interview in 1979, the actor said:

IT LOOKS LIKE MORE THAN THE SPUR IS NAKED. James Stewart and a bare-shouldered Janet Leigh in a publicity shot for *The Naked Spur* (1953).

> I think the film stands out today because it was ahead of its time. It's kinda like the films of Clint Eastwood. None of the characters was all good or bad. Not even Janet Leigh's character. Even Robert Ryan had his moments when the audiences kinda liked him. But he had to be the meanest of them all so that his fate could be justified. But most of all, I liked me. I was this man who was ... it was like he was *possessed*. He had a demon that *drove* him. He had a violence that was driving him *mad*. I don't know if it's true, but I heard that Clint Eastwood was influenced by that film ... and my performance in it. Yeah, I liked me in that one.[19]

As for Eastwood being influenced by *The Naked Spur*: An obvious western buff, Eastwood fails to mention this film in any interview when asked about his cinematic influences; in fact, with the possible exception of his bitter lawman in *Hang 'Em High*, his first starring American western which bridged The Man With No Name with a more conventional western hero, the actor's subsequent films demonstrated that the Eastwood persona wouldn't have stood for *half* the nonsense that Vandergroat makes Howie suffer through.

In *The Naked Spur*, Stewart romances Janet Leigh. Opposite the 44-year-old star, and with an unbecoming butch haircut, she looks out of place. When the two suddenly embrace and kiss while "Beautiful Dreamer" blares on the soundtrack, it's the most laughable moment in the entire film, as well as the most unconvincing.

Shot on location in the Rockies, as well as Lone Pine, California, *The Naked Spur* continued the string of successful Mann-Stewart collaborations until a schism developed between the two men on the set of U-I's *Night Passage* four years later.

In the meantime, in that western-heavy year of 1953, depictions of old west justice were about to be given a savage new twist. Taking a belated cue from *Destry Rides Again* (the Stewart version), women were once again going to take charge of the action; and, as one feisty heroine would prove, she didn't need "a big, strong man" to defend her....

"Ain't nobody wants to tangle with a wildcat, ma'am..." — *a citizen of Border City*

In 1953, the Civil War, like the Indian Wars, continued to be good material for the western. The tragedy of "brother against brother" played well in an America haunted by the specter of Communism and the A-bomb. One such film which depicted the War Between the States would be made by a company always known as "the little cowboy studio."

That year, Republic released *The Woman They Almost Lynched*. Based on a *Saturday Evening Post* story by Michael Fessier and with a screenplay by western and thriller author Steve Fisher, the film is set in the mythical, and appropriately named, Border City, lying somewhere between Missouri and Arkansas. We are told, several times, that Border City is a "neutral zone" between the Union and the Confederacy. Here, both Quantrill's men and presumably Jayhawkers can congregate without any animosity between them. That is because the town is run by a female mayor (since "no man is brave enough to take the job") who has banned anyone coming through town in the uniform of either army. It is a locale that could only exist in Fantasy-Land, but veteran helmsman Allan Dwan obviously saw the premise for the nonsense it was and set about giving this work a slightly subversive, and definitely feminist twist; which, despite the oddball plot, made it a cinematic rarity — a camp film which had something meaningful to say (kind of like *Johnny Guitar*, but with prettier female leads).

It is the spring of 1865. As Civil War battle footage from previous Republic westerns is played in the background, veteran narrator Marvin Miller tells us of the rise of Confederate guerrilla leader Quantrill and his band of bushwackers as they ride with a flag that clearly says "Quantrill" on it, as if the guerrillas were some kind of sports franchise.

Then Miller tells us about Border City. In fact, we are just in time to see a lynching. Here, a Mrs. Stuart (Minerva Urecal) tells the rather zaftig Mayor Courtney (Nina Varela) that lynching is murder, but the hanging has the mayor's backing because the accused was guilty of making "inflammatory speeches" which would have caused riots. Therefore lynching is tolerated because there is no "law machinery" in Border City. Her speech is mockingly applauded by ranch foreman Lance Horton (the top-billed and versatile John Lund).

The catalyst that will change all this madness happens to be on her way to town on the noon stage.

When a Union patrol halts said stage, the young lieutenant in charge is stunned (and charmed) to see that the only passenger is Sally Maris, played by the gorgeous Joan Leslie.

A star at Warner Brothers during the war years who appeared in some of their biggest films, Joan complained about her billing in one film (*Two Guys from Milwaukee* with Dennis Morgan and Jack Carson) and soon not only found herself kicked out of Warners, but that Jack Warner personally had her blacklisted at every other major studio in town. In the next few years, her bread and butter would be the Bs (though Eagle-Lion's *Repeat Performance* is outstanding). Segueing into westerns (like *Northwest Stampede* with James Craig), Joan's work was soon noticed by Herbert Yates. Not giving a damn about Warner's blacklist, he signed her to a Republic contract in 1950. Far from her teen years at Warners, Joan was still a knockout at 28, as every male cast member in the film is convincingly attracted to her, except, that is, Quantrill.

As the stage continues on its journey, Quantrill's band appears and slaughters the cavalry escort, including the lieutenant. The stage is overturned, and two Rebs remove Sally from the wreckage. Feisty to a fault, the young lady verbally indicts both Quantrill (for some reason, he is called *Charles* Quantrill, and played by Brian Donlevy) and his black-garbed wife, Kate (Audrey Totter).

Usually, whenever there was a Civil War western made during those years, the studios would *always* cast a mature character actor to play Quantrill. And so, 51-year-old Donlevy portrays the guerrilla chieftain merely on the merits of his performance as Quantrill in U-I's 1950 Civil War picture *Kansas Raiders,* which starred Audie Murphy as Jesse James. In that film, the writers and director (genre veteran Ray Enright) portray the guerrilla leader as a pseudo–Hitler figure, spellbinding in his grand plans to destroy the Yankees and institute a New Order for the Confederacy; even his bushwackers act like sagebrush Gestapo when they enter a northern town. In fact, this film is the closest example in the postwar years of using Quantrill's raiders as a euphemism for Nazi terror.

However, the *real* Quantrill was 27 when Union troops surrounded his Kentucky cabin and mortally wounded him. He died in a Union hospital several months later.

There is some debate, however, as to whether the guerrilla chief actually married Kate McCoy (and one wonders if even *that* was her real name). Apparently, like some disturbed young women who write letters to serial murderers, the real Kate became a Quantrill groupie and, though there is no surviving wedding certificate to back her up, always claimed that the two were man and wife. Even up to the 1920s. several old women would claim to actually *be* Kate; however, nothing could be proven.

The guerrillas decide to escort the now up-righted stage back to town and Quantrill and Cole Younger (the underrated Jim Davis) order a wounded young man (the *always* youthful-looking Ben Cooper) to ride in the coach with Sally. Here, the eastern babe will try to talk this young man out of his life of war crimes. Responding to her beauty, if not her words, the innocent-looking youth tells Sally of his dreams to settle on a farm and marry a (his eyes go up to Sally's red hair) red-haired lady of class and refinement. If nothing else, this is certainly one of the few films that would dare show us a gunfighter with a case of puppy love.

Once they arrive in town, Sally is shocked to find that this innocent-looking youth is actually Jesse James. Dwan and Fisher must be given credit for showing us James as a teenager, which is what he actually was during his time with Quantrill. In the film, the proud Jesse tells Sally he is 27, though the script says he's 16. When the film was made, Ben Cooper was 19, but his eternal youthfulness would make him look younger. In the spring of 1865, James was actually 17.

It seems that Sally is in Border City to see her brother Bill (or "Bitterroot Bill" to the rowdies in town). And it also seems that Bill (Reed Hadley) is a saloon owner who has not seen Sally since she was little. Still, the next scene is somewhat shocking for 1953. Believing Sally to be another candidate for dance hall girl, he "inspects" his sister, turning her around and looking her up and down. As if this weren't bad enough, he flirtatiously tucks her under the chin and tells her to be "*real* polite to the boss; that's me!" Bill is duly horrified when he learns her true identity. He convinces Sally to stay in his room at the saloon (he moves across the hall). Sally is shocked that Bill, who has had so much promise, has turned to "drinking and gambling."

When Kate shows up at the saloon with her hubby Quantrill, it is revealed that she and Bill were to marry until she was kidnapped by the bushwacker. ("I like *masterful* men," she says while swooning against the guerrilla leader's chest.) Then she orders the piano player to play the popular standard (*not* written in 1865), "All My Life." This is done to make Bill wallow in his pain even more. Totter's performance (she is obviously dubbed by a real singer), full of operatic gestures and sexual gyrations unheard of in 1865, purposely done in order to taunt both Bill *and* Quantrill, is a camp delight. Republic's films, particularly their westerns, never went *this* over-the-top.

However, the performance goes too far and a drunken Bill, pushed to the brink, pulls a gun on Kate. This forces Lance to gun him down. When Sally finds out, she calls for Horton's arrest until she is told that there is no law in town.

Ordering everyone to leave the saloon (the refined easterner is now the new owner), Sally stubbornly declares that she will stay in Border City. However, when Lance defies her threat to shoot him ("What with, a powder puff?"), Sally expertly uses Horton's own gun to shoot his whiskey glass off the bar. Then she issues the boldly feminist line, "Still think I need a *big, strong man* like you to look after me?" This was not the kind of line one hears from a western made in 1953, especially at Republic.

Now forced to reopen the saloon, she rehires the three dance hall gals she had just fired (one of whom is Virginia Christine), abandons her prim outfit and dresses as a saloon queen.

Meanwhile, Quantrill threatens to reveal that Lance is actually a Confederate officer (without a southern accent). In a scene in Quantrill's hideout, Lance denounces the bushwackers and claims that Robert E. Lee and the Confederacy washed their collective hands of the guerrillas long ago. According to the film, Quantrill and his men have *very recently* been on the run because of their raid on Lawrence, Kansas, Steve Fisher neglecting to inform us that the Lawrence Massacre was in August 1863 and nowhere near the spring of 1865. It was true that even the South was shocked by the barbarity of what happened in Lawrence; however, the Rebs, far from disowning him, continued to work with Quantrill to the very end of the conflict. It was his own gang gradually leaving him that resulted in the guerrilla chief's downfall.

Back at Sally's place, the former prim eastern babe now has a smile and a beautiful pair of shoulders to display before the male inhabitants of her swanky saloon. When news of a nearby southern garrison prompts Kate to start singing "Dixie" (which would trigger a gun battle between opposing sides in the saloon), Sally jumps her and the fight is on. Not since *Destry Rides Again* had there been a more lively saloon catfight. Leslie later claimed in an interview with TCM that she had never hit anyone in her life, though from what we see of the fight, she definitely has a mean right hook.

In an interview with the online magazine *Western Clippings* she said,

> Audrey Totter was so very good — we got a tremendous kick out of the fight.... I was supposed to hit Audrey and I just couldn't. Not hit her on the face! Allan Dwan tried to explain and

Audrey told me to go on and do it. Somehow it did get done, but it was a very difficult thing to do.[20]

After having her hair pulled all over the place, Sally triumphs and physically drags the unconscious Kate out the door, buying her a new respect from the saloon patrons as well as the girls she employs. However, after everyone leaves, she bursts into tears with, "Brawling! Like a common hussy!"

Joseph Breen didn't find anything amusing about the catfight. In an October 6, 1952, letter to Republic executive J.E. Baker, the censor insisted, "This fight between the two women will have to be handled with the utmost care to avoid any excessive brutality."[21]

When Lance visits her at the saloon, Sally tells him she knows the truth about the gunfight that killed her brother, and Lance admits to being a Reb officer. This mutual display of trust ends with a kiss. Afterward, they playfully call each other "Yankee" and "Reb," Dwan purposely framing the shot with an American flag in the background.

Meanwhile, an angry Kate is gunning for Sally. To Jesse's surprise, the eastern gal refuses to run away, so he gives her his own extra gun and holster. Instead of waiting for Kate to arrive, Sally plans on meeting her in the street, saying, "Back in Michigan, we didn't wait for wild beasts to close in on us." (Joan Leslie was born in Detroit). Finally, the big shootout occurs, with Sally, doing a cross-draw, easily shooting the gun from Kate's hand. (In Fisher's October 28 synopsis, he writes, "Kate's gun-hand is reduced to a bloody pulp by the bullet."[22]) Afterwards, Sally calls Kate a disgrace to women.

Suddenly, things start falling apart. Quantrill is leaving town with Lance as a hostage but Jesse purposely lets the Reb officer grab his gun, thus ensuring his escape. Storming the saloon, Lance is able to prevent Cole from kidnapping Sally, but is wounded in the process. (Shot *several* times, he should have been killed, but since he's the hero...) Just then, the Union garrison arrives and attacks Quantrill's men. Falling off her horse in front of the saloon, Kate is helped inside by the compassionate Sally.

When the Union captain and his men arrive in the saloon looking for Kate, they are stunned to see a new saloon gal do a number (with dubbed voice and operatic gestures). Logic would dictate that the hunted Kate would want to rush the blue-bellies out the door, but *no*! Kate singles herself out by singing this song, *then* she outrageously flirts with the stiff-necked captain. ("Forget her, will *I* do?" she asks, not missing the irony of the moment.)

To prevent Lance from falling into Union hands, Sally allows herself to be captured, claiming in a handwritten note conveniently dropped in front of the troops that *she* is the Reb spy, not Lance. The outraged mayor orders her hanging, ridiculously using her local authority to supersede the Federals— and the captain buys it. But before the mayor can hang Sally, Kate rides up and reveals her true identity, telling them all that the eastern gal has merely bought time so that Lance can get to the southern garrison outside town. Soon, the war is over, and Lance returns to Border City to reunite with Sally.

If one must admire any of the performers of this film, it is Joan Leslie, one-upping Jack Warner and proving beyond a shadow of a doubt that she can carry a film for another studio. Leslie is ridiculously billed *fourth* under Lund, Donlevy and Totter despite the fact that her spunky Sally Maris is the focal point of the film (she's even in the title). Showing defiance against Kate, resistance to Cole Younger and other randy men, and determination to succeed despite opposition from the mayor and the town's so-called respectable women, Joan takes center stage and captures our hearts as few western heroines of the day have. Even Quantrill remarks to Kate, "Why don't you quit? She fights better than you, shoots better than you and even talks better than you!" Throughout her career, she had always played the "good girl," but no one played the part better than Joan Leslie.

Woman They Almost Lynched is full of barbed comments on sexism. Kate admits to taking her rage out on the world because of her rejection of a good man, Bill, for an evil one, Quantrill; acting like him and the rest of the guerrillas, she has lost her humanity, or, in this case, her femininity (or what passed for it, according to the 1950s). When Kate announces that she's going to kill Sally, Bob Younger says, "Listen to her, she thinks she's a man!" Pointing her gun at the Youngers, she makes them admit that she can shoot and ride as good as any man. To these sagebrush thugs, violence is the only qualification for equality of the sexes. This characterization had already been established in Steve Fisher's October 28 synopsis, where the writer describes Kate as being "a legend by the time this story picks up. She rides like a man, dresses like a man, kills like a man. She is immune to all the softer emotions ... except love."[23]

Still, Kate has enough sand to openly flirt with the stiff-necked captain, who, despite his reserve, is bending to her charms. After he and his men allow Kate to escape across the prairie, the captain orders his men to turn around, yet Dwan has the officer linger a little longer as he looks in the direction his attractive enemy has gone; a nice touch.

However, it's obvious that the captain is ill at ease when dealing with females. Despite the officer being ultra-serious about his job, Kate obviously pierces his hard shell; when the mayor bulldozes her local authority over that of the Federals, he is helpless yet again; finally, Sally, in her phony note, refers to him and his men as "pig-headed beasts," a comment that infuriates him. Earlier, before Quantrill massacres his men, the doomed lieutenant is easily charmed by Sally after barely knowing her. Throughout the film, it seems that men in uniform are putty in the hands of these women.

Though delivering sexist comments to Sally in the beginning, Lance comes to respect her *first*, then falls in love with her. Their love, symbolizing the reunion of the north and the south, does show the lengths they will go to protect each other.

However, romance was not on the censor's mind when he read early drafts of the script. In a letter to J.E. Baker, dated October 6, 1952, Breen said the story was acceptable to the Code, with one glaring exception:

> The element to which we refer is the casual treatment of lynching found in the opening and closing scenes. These scenes add up to a justification of lynching, which is in direct violation of the Code. We venture to suggest that a possible method of correcting this difficulty could be found by simply having the majority of the people in these scenes refer to the hanging, and attempted hanging, as executions rather than lynchings.[24]

Reminiscing about the film more than 50 years later, Joan Leslie admitted that

> the story is a little odd, although I like that I later hide Audrey upstairs in my bedroom. The movie is dramatic but silly. Actually, it's a pretty fast-moving little movie. It's odd the way Republic brings music into the story—it's a scream! It seems out of place! Not legitimate. Audrey later told me she played the whole thing for farce, while I was doing it straight.[25]

This was hardly Joan's fault since director Dwan didn't tell anyone to play it for laughs. When Peter Bogdanovitch asked Dwan in 1971 why he didn't tell the actors he was aiming for parody, the helmsman responded:

> No—then they'd try to be funny. You tell some of those characters "This is a very funny scene," they'd horse it up, put things in. But imagine—we had a gunfight between two gals—going down the street like the cowpunchers. If they'd had anything but skirts on, I'd have shot between their legs. I couldn't do that with girls. [Dwan apparently forgot that Audrey Totter was wearing pants.] Of course, today they would strip for it![26]

THIS TOWN AIN'T BIG ENOUGH. Joan Leslie hides from a gun-toting Audrey Totter in a posed publicity shot for *Woman They Almost Lynched* (1953). In the film, not only does Leslie's character stand up to Totter, but she also has a saloon brawl with her.

When Bogdanovitch asked him if writer Steve Fisher was in on what he did, Dwan replied acidly: "I don't think he'd know *now* that it wasn't serious. If the actors said the words, it was all right with him."[27] However, to "Brog" of *Variety*, it was *Dwan* who didn't know what he was doing. In their March 30 review, besides calling the film "pretentious to extremes" (apparently they missed Dwan's attempts at parody), the paper further criticized the helmsman: "[The film] has been unevenly directed by Allan Dwan, who was unable to master the welter of story tangents, characters and gabby dialogue...."[28]

To quote Joan Leslie, *The Woman They Almost Lynched* was indeed "odd and silly." However, its feminist slant, its insistence on breaking through barriers between male and female as well as north and south, and its condemnation of mob rule, even when that mob is sanctioned by a misguided mayor, make this film stand out as one of the more enjoyable and provocative westerns of the 1950s.

Indeed, Republic proved that a quality western that depicted miscarriages of justice didn't always have to come from a major studio. Its rival, Allied Artists, could also produce a little gem or two. Later that year, the studio released a film about one of the most terrifying gunmen of the west. What made this man truly frightening was that he was not an outlaw at all, but a respected member of the community; and worse, he was charged with the task of ridding the country of outlaws....

> "I'll live long enough to wear your ears on my watch chain!"—*a bullet-riddled Jack Slade*

The old west was a place populated with more colorful characters in one location at one time than probably any other in world history, neat, separate categories: Billy the Kid, outlaw; Pat Garrett, lawman; Belle Starr, bandit queen; Wyatt Earp, lawman; Jesse James, outlaw; and so forth. The name of Jack Slade was not as famous as these iconic figures of the west. This is because Slade was neither lawman nor outlaw; he didn't rob any banks, nor did he wear a badge, nor, like the James boys, did he exploit the injustices of the times to excuse his sins. And he didn't die in the prescribed manner, full of tragic and ironic dimensions, such as being shot from ambush by his best friend or being shot from behind by a distant relative who wanted the reward money, or shot to pieces by well-armed townsmen during a bank holdup. All of the above elements, considered "requirements" for western immortality, are missing from Slade's life. Instead, Slade was an accepted member of society; indeed, today he is considered (if he is considered at all) as one of those tenacious hard-working individuals who helped to open up the west to communications with the east. But Slade was something else as well. Possessed of an explosive temper when drunk, he became a bully and a killer; once sober, he apologized profusely for the trouble he caused and gladly paid for any damages he incurred. Dedicated to his job, loyal to his wife, hard-working, industrious and sociable, Slade was a respected figure whose deeds ultimately helped in the building of our country; drunk, he was society's scourge; he hurt people, damaged property, and ultimately murdered those he considered his enemies. And it was this dual personality, his tenaciousness in getting the job done, as well as his weakness for alcohol and inability to handle his rage, that make him the most frightening character in all the west.

For in a much later day, had he been surrounded by the pressures of a modern industrialized America, Jack Slade could have been one of us....

Joseph Alfred Slade was born in Carlisle, Illinois, on January 22, 1831. His growing-up was basically normal except for one incident which was a harbinger of things to come. Already developing an explosive temper, teenager Slade killed a man who had been bothering him and his friends (Slade struck him in the head with a rock). At the age of 17, Slade enlisted in the army and fought in the Mexican War, though "fought" might be stretching it a bit; by the time he served in the military, he and his men were going to garrison newly captured towns that bordered Mexico. Though not firing shots on the battlefield, the men had to fight the hostility of former Mexican citizens who had no love for "gringos." It's not known whether Slade released some of his burgeoning hostility on the people he and his buddies routinely called "greasers."

While in Texas, the former army veteran met and married Maria Virginia Dale (or, as some called her, Virginia Maria Dale). Slade was 5'8" and 180 pounds, while Virginia was actually quite tall (without high heels). A striking woman, Virginia was a crack shot, an expert horsewoman, and a fiery individual who could drink and curse a blue streak better than any man. Unlike the extroverted Virginia, Slade basically kept his demons on the inside, until, that is, something triggered their release. After the couple moved to Colorado, Slade put his energies to good use by becoming a freight wagon driver through most of the 1850s. As he went about his job, he developed the traits which make him an outstanding worker: endurance, professionalism and a can-do attitude. The life of a freighter was not an easy lot. He had to haul his cargo through rough weather; and if transporting supplies to far-reaching outposts wasn't hard enough, he had to do it on a tight schedule. (Freighting companies fought like tigers for precious government mail contracts; speed was essential if these companies were to stay in business.) The freighter could be rowdy and drunk, but he had to be alert and sometimes endure the unendurable. Thus, escaping the larger-than-life presence of his stunning wife, Slade enjoyed the all-male world of the freighter, eventually becoming a wagon captain over dozens of tough, undisciplined men.

In 1857 or 1858, Slade joined John M. Hockaday & Co. and was appointed the division supervisor of the Green River section, more than 300 miles west of his usual headquarters at Horseshoe Creek. However, despite his dedictation to his job, Slade's demons were never far away. On May 20, 1859, while Slade was in charge of a supply train headed towards Salt Lake City, the inevitable happened. According to the account of William Ashton, former agent of the Green River division:

> On the 20th, a difficulty occurred between Mr. Slade [the agent of J.M. Hockaday & Co.] and some of the men in the trains belonging to that company. In the fray, one Andrew Ferrin was killed. From the best information I can get, Mr. Slade was justified in shooting him.... On the day of the fatal accident, Mr. Slade, meeting the train, found that some of the men had broken into boxes containing liquors [sic], and having helped themselves abundantly, were prepared to resist anything.[29]

However, according to the memoirs of frontier trader Granville Stuart "The wagon boss had gotten drunk, about fifteen miles back, was cussing the driver about some trifle, the driver had talked back, and the 'boss,' who was J.A. Slade, drew his revolver and shot the man dead."[30]

According to Stuart, the dead man was wrapped in his blanket, quickly buried and the incident was forgotten. As a freighter, Slade had taken full command of dozens of rough, sometimes drunken men, and whipped them into a dedicated unit of professionals transporting the mails along what they called the Cumberland Line. He was too good a man for the company to throw to the wolves. However, one man who made sure the Ferrin killing would be remembered was a writer named Samuel Clemens. According to the writer who was known as Mark Twain, Slade and Ferrin agreed to settle their differences with their fists and Ferrin threw down his gun first; in response, Slade laughed and shot the man dead for trusting him. Complementing this account, western artist Charles M. Russell worked on a painting he called *Laughed at for His Foolishness and Shot Dead by Slade*. Art now reflected life, and as far as Jack Slade was concerned, his life would be influenced by art, as well as media accounts of his alleged bloodthirsty acts.

Twain did not alter his opinion even after meeting Slade. Traveling with his brother Orion, Twain stopped at one of the Overland's many stage stations, where he ultimately met the object of his endless fascination. As the future author of *Huckleberry Finn* put it:

> The most gentlemanly-appearing, quiet and affable officer we had yet found along the road in the Overland Company's service was the person who sat at the end of the table, at my elbow. Never youth stared and shivered as I did when I heard them [freighters] call him Slade![31]

Despite the fact that Slade did nothing more hostile than offer the budding author another cup of coffee, Twain let his imagination get a little carried away: "It was hardly possible to realize that this pleasant person was the pitiless scourge of the outlaws, the rawhead-and-bloody-bones the nursing mothers of the mountains terrifed their children with. And to this day I can remember nothing remarkable about Slade...."

At this time, John Hockaday sold out his company to Russell, Majors & Waddell; their Leavenworth & Pike's Peak Express Co. stages went from St. Joseph, Missouri, through the territories of Kansas, Nebraska and Colorado, and ultimately ended in Salt Lake City, Utah (as compared to the Butterfield Line which traveled through the warmer southwest and ended its run in California). Slade was the line boss, the district supervisor in charge of the stagecoaches carrying mail and passengers headed through those mountains buried in snow and passes flooded from persistent rains; at times Slade even took the reins himself and suffered every bit as much as the men under him. When Shoshones attacked his stagecoach, he reportedly stood out in the open without regard for his safety and, just using his revolver, killed several warriors. Suspecting that the white man shooting at them was mad, the frightened Indians quickly rode away. After they left, Slade took out his knife and cut off the ears of a warrior to put on his watch-chain. The warrior may not have been dead when he did it.

As the Overland's line boss, Slade also had little tolerance for outlaws who preyed on his stagecoaches. If outlaws robbed or molested any of his men in any way, Slade didn't think twice: He hanged them. Literally dozens of killers and horse thieves would end up dangling from the end of a noose by order of Jack Slade. However, the company couldn't argue with the results. Slade's liberal use of the hangman's rope did the trick: Outlaw depradations stopped. A further result of his take-no-prisoners style was a new title; from then onward, he would be referred to as "the Law West of (Fort) Kearney."

In 1860, Slade supervised the building of 200 relay stations for Russell, Majors & Waddell's newest venture, the Pony Express. Much romanticized by Hollywood, the operation barely lasted 18 months, though Slade did reportedly hire a scrawny 15-year old named Bill Cody, who later added "Buffalo" before his name. As the future showman and Indian-fighter wrote in his autobiography many years later, "Slade, although rough at times and always a dangerous character — having killed many a man — was always kind to me. During the two years that I worked for him as pony-express-rider and stage-driver, he never spoke an angry word to me."[32]

In 1860, with the nation rapidly sliding toward civil war, another war of sorts would break out between Slade and a man who was everything the tenacious line boss hated. At a small stage station in a tiny village in Colorado called Julesberg, named after its owner, Slade met one of the most important individuals in his life; one who might have indirectly set him on the self-destructive course he would take for the rest of his life. Jules Beni, a French-Canadian saloonkeeper and trader, was *not* considered the territory's most honest man. Indeed, when Beni ran the station, Russell, Majors & Waddell's horse-flesh would mysteriously disappear. The company took this thievery for a while, until its district supervisor finally did something about it. Accosting Beni in his saloon one day, Slade fired him, an act which caused the French-Canadian roustabout to take a quick dislike to the company's line boss; the dislike soon grew into homicidal rage. In March 1860, Beni took matters into his own hands.

One day, while Slade headed to the station's restaurant, Beni appeared at the door with a loaded revolver, which he promptly emptied into Slade. As the wounded line boss staggered around the side of the building (for some reason, Slade did not fall), Beni retreated inside and then appeared with a double-barrelled shotgun. This too he emptied into Slade. Then, after Beni told Slade's men to "put him in a blanket and bury him," the mortally wounded Slade reportedly gazed up at his enemy and threatened to live long enough to cut off his ears and put them on his watch-chain. Amazingly, after being transported hundreds of bumpy miles back to St. Joseph, Missouri, by wagon and then undergoing a difficult operation to remove several dozen shotgun pellets and six .44 caliber bullets imbedded in his body, Jack Slade lived.

Many months later, after a full recovery, Slade returned to Julesberg, but first he had a couple of his men capture Beni and hold him until his stage arrived in the village. According to the most famous account, Slade had his enemy tied to a post and then methodically shot him to pieces, firing into his appendages first before delivering more serious wounds so as to increase his victim's pain. Then Slade pulled out his knife, sliced off Beni's ears and put them on his watch-chain. Again, it's not known whether Slade waited for Beni to die before he did the cutting.

The less colorful account has Beni attempting to escape, causing Slade's men to shoot him dead. Though frightened of what Slade would do (he issued instructions for them to keep Beni *alive*), they were surprised to find that their boss just shrugged off the killing, apparently satisfied that his enemy was dead. *Then* he cut off Beni's ears and put them on his watch-chain.

There are those who theorize that Beni's murderous attack on Slade and his being at death's door had totally warped the already troubled line boss. In fact, one would be hard put *not* to have his or her mind permanently altered by Beni's attack — or the grisly retaliation which followed.

This traumatic change in Slade's personality caused by his shooting is even acknowledged by medical experts today. In a letter to Dan Rottenberg, author of *Death of a Gunfighter, the Quest for Jack Slade, the West's Most Elusive Legend,* Dr. John DeShazo commented on the attack on Slade and his mental condition afterwards. A former captain in the U.S. Air Force in Vietnam from 1968 to 1970, and assigned to the 659th Tactical Hospital, Dr. DeShazo had dealt with men wounded in battle. In this letter, dated October 7, 2009, the doctor made a trenchant comparison between Slade the gunfighter and men in front-line combat:

> Anyone who has known people who were shot will say that virtually all of them are mentally changed by the experience, even if they recover. Physically and mentally, getting shot is not a minor experience. Those of us in the military who knew soldiers personally who have been shot will tell you a wounded soldier is a changed soldier.
>
> It takes longer to recover mentally than it does to heal physically. Slade undoubtedly suffered from this effect. An explanation for his erratic behavior may be that he recovered physically but bore mental scars that were not properly treated.
>
> In military medicine, we have learned how to help wounded soldiers recover physically as well as mentally, but in Slade's day, only a little was understood about the physical effects of a bullet wound, and nothing about the mental. He was left to his own devices — perhaps only his whiskey — to deal with it. There were no wounded soldiers to tell him, "I know what it's like to be shot and you are acting like someone who needs time to come back. So stay with me here, buddy, and let's help each other get well." On the other hand, pouring salt into his wounded mental state, Ben Halladay was pushing Slade to get into another gunfight, which is probably the last thing anyone wants to do who has been shot.
>
> Based on the behavior you described, I am pretty sure Slade suffered from post-traumatic stress.[33]

If this was indeed Slade's state of mind after his March 1860 shooting, it comes as no surprise that from then on, his consumption of alcohol increased.

As time went on, Slade actually started shooting up the company's stage stations. Afterwards, he would always apologize profusely and pay for the damages; and for a while he would try to be a model of decorum and respect other people's property — that is, until he did it all over again. Surrounded by wild freighters of equal rowdiness (though without Slade's complex personality), the company's line boss was frightening passengers and employees with his rude and ultimately psychotic behavior. Shooting up company property and then apologizing for it afterwards soon became a running joke. In time, an unamused Russell, Majors & Waddell got fed up with this routine. In 1862, after he shot up the civilian-run sutler's store at Fort Halleck, they fired him.

Taking the firing philosophically (meaning, he *didn't* go gunning for his bosses), Slade decided to pack up and leave Colorado with Virginia. Inevitably, Slade would be one of the men in charge of dozens of miners and their families when they formed a caravan headed towards the gold fields of the northwest, particularly Idaho Territory, which encompassed the future state of Montana. Prospector Bill Fairweather (Slade's future drinking companion) had discovered gold in Alder Gulch, Montana, and hundreds were flocking to the site (a novel about the campsite, titled *Alder Gulch*, would be written by western giant and Oregon native Ernest Haycox). During the caravan's trek, Slade got drunk, and his rowdiness cost him the chance to be voted wagon captain over his rival, one James Williams. It is even said that Williams, slightly taller than Slade, as well as heavier, bested him in a fistfight.

Eventually, Slade and Virginia made their home on a rambling little spread which Slade dubbed "Virginia Dale." But Slade was not a man who could live a quiet life any more than he could stay away from the sauce. And so (perhaps to stay away from his overbearing wife?), Slade spent long days and even longer nights in nearby Virginia City with his equally rowdy pals, drinking, going wild, and causing a lot of damage, mostly with his gun. At the same time, Virginia City, despite having its own marshal and courts, had another faction involved in enforcing the law, if unofficially. Calling itself the Committee of 100, a group of men consisting of miners, merchants and professionals had decided long ago to do away with trial by jury and enforce the law their own way. Plagued with a persistent outlaw problem, Virginia City had backed the vigilantes to the hilt and, since they ruthlessly dispensed justice by noose, the group was responsible for the deaths of many outlaws, much as Slade and his men had been back in the day. As an added irony, the group was led by James Williams, Slade's antagonist on the Alder Gulch wagon train. After many weeks of Slade and his bully boys blasting away at polished mirrors and other breakables behind the bars of many a saloon, things finally came to a head on March 10, 1864.

Staying in town a little too long, a drunken Slade and his buddies shot up another saloon when the miners, led by Williams, got together and decided to put an end to the madness. Though his friends more or less got tired of the destruction and drunkenly wandered away, Slade wouldn't stop. Promising to leave town, he defiantly remained; apologizing for the mayhem, he continued disturbing the peace. It is said that one of the reasons for the vigilantes' wrath is that Slade had drunkenly sung a dirty song about the town marshal, a main vigilante supporter, and that the ditty contained some unflattering lyrics about a certain part of the lawman's anatomy.

Despite the pleas from decent citizens who liked Slade personally, including Judge Alexander Davis who begged Slade to leave town, the drunken man remained. But by then it was too late. Slade was captured, tied up and led to the edge of town where, surrounded by dozens of miners and citizens, he was put on a platform between two barrels and had a noose placed around his neck. The situation sobered him up immediately. With tears in his eyes, the former executioner of many an outlaw begged for his life. But Williams and his men had no mercy. Indeed, Slade's sudden tears and begging for his life turned off the many miners who might have entertained any show of mercy for the former "Law West of Kearney." As Slade's friend Henry Gilbert reflected years later, "The miners believed that any man who had not hesitated to inflict death upon so many of his fellows ought to at least meet his fate with manliness."[34]

Manliness, however, or the old west's version of it, did not make the noose seem any less tight to the man who was about to swing from it; and so, Jack Slade died, in tears, begging for his life, and without dignity, and all because he went on one bender too many.

> The Only Law the outlaws taught him was to kill ... kill ... kill! The only way the law could get him was through the choking smoke of his blazing guns!

The above quote was the usual Hollywood over-the-top tagline; this time it was for Allied Artists' newest western *Jack Slade*, the only film based on the gunslinger's life where he is the central character.

In a small town in Illinois (they don't say Carlisle), 13-year-old Jack sees a man beating a boy and kills the assailant with a well-thrown rock. Now that things are a little too hot for them, Jack and his father leave town (there is no mention of Jack's many brothers and sisters or what happened to Mom). When outlaws stick up the stagecoach they're riding, Jack's father is killed and stage driver Tom Carter (Harry Shannon) unofficially adopts the boy. The killing on the stage has already instilled in Jack a hatred for outlaws and, after a spell in the army during the Mexican War, the young man admits to Tom that he attracts trouble. Of course, saying that Jack Slade attracted trouble is like saying a torrential downpour might contain a little water. As Slade (former Fox star Mark Stevens) grows into manhood, his shooting skill increases. After he takes a job as a freight wagon driver and is confronted by outlaws, he not only subdues them, but has them hanged as well. Though the local marshal pressures the company into firing Slade, the young man has no trouble being hired by Dan Traver (frequent B western and sci-fi veteran Paul Langton), an official for another freight outfit. Traver hires Slade as the line boss; the new hireling replaces the alcoholic Jules Reni (not *Beni*; and played by Barton MacLane). It is said that Reni is in league with other Julesberg outlaws, like the Dantons, in stealing horses from the freight line. Traver also introduces Slade to the tempestuous Virginia Dale (on her way to an Oscar, Dorothy Malone). It soon becomes apparent that Virginia can ride fast and shoot faster. Smitten, Jack marries her.

But there are enemies about. Challenging Slade to a gundown, Reni drunkenly shoots the line boss when his back is turned. Needless to say, the back-shooting in the film is not the full-blooded riddling of shot and pellet that the real Slade endured.

Appointing himself the unofficial lawman of Julesberg, Slade rides over to the Denton ranch where he decides to serve warrant on the outlaws. When one of the surviving Dentons guns down a boy they had kept as a hostage, Slade kills the man instantly. The shaken, scared boy reminded the hardened Slade of himself and the child's killing causes the line boss to turn to drink. Later on, storming the hideout of the infamous Prentice brothers, Slade is horrified to find that Tom, his adoptive father, has been cruelly sent outside to take the posse's bullets. Furious, Slade guns down all the Prenctices except for Ned Prentice (Ron Hargrave), who has surrendered. This means little to the vindictive Slade, who promptly hangs the prisoner without trial.

After going on a drunken binge in which he terrifies saloon patrons, Slade rides out of town and accidently runs over a little girl, crippling her. The citizens' committee calls for Slade's removal and its leader, Farnsworth (former B western star Jim Bannon), wants him hanged.

When Slade arrives in the local saloon to bitterly announce that he's leaving town, Jules Reni and two of his men take him prisoner. Virginia arrives and guns down one of the outlaws. After Slade kills the other man, he wounds Reni and then threatens to shoot him apart "piece by piece!" Virginia tries to stop him, but he shoves her out of the way and slowly empties his pistol into the now-tearful, begging murderer. After Reni dies, Slade is pursued out of town by Traver. Given a chance to surrender, Slade refuses, forcing Traver to gun him down. As he dies, Slade warns his friend that *he* will now be known as a gunfighter, the man who killed the infamous Jack Slade.

Since the film as written by Allied Artists screenwriter Warren Douglas and B veteran Harold Schuster, Slade's complicated life is simplified to the point of idiocy. Still, both men instill in this respectable low-budget effort a sense of tragedy and misfortune that few westerns of the time had. Its hero is cursed by the Fates; outside of his good fortune in marrying the loyal and vibrant Virginia, Slade is headed for a tragic end the moment we see him kill the man at the beginning of the film with that rock. Nothing is told of Slade's family background (his family was well-off; his grandfather had started the town of Carlisle, where Jack was born). Less is shown of the behind-the-scenes machinations of Russell, Majors and Waddell, or those who operate the freight line business. Slade's rages, fueled as they are by liquor, are always provoked by others. There is nothing here about the Ferrin killing, his purposeful hangings of outlaws who had nothing to do with the deaths of close friends (or, as in Tom's case, a father figure). And his great service to the country for helping to link east and west is not mentioned at all.

What the filmmakers *have* done, however, is give us a portrayal of a flawed hero who *could* have done great things had he been allowed to. But Slade's multi-faceted personality is still simplified along B western lines and dime-store psychology. In this film, Slade drinks because of the many deaths of innocent people he has witnessed, particularly the deaths of the little boy at the Prentice ranch and the accidental shooting of his father figure, *not* because he was a man under pressure while doing a Herculean job or working insane hours for the stage line. (In the pro-capitalist, anti–Communist 1950s, no one was about to say that companies, even in a B western, put their workers under intense pressure.)

Though Mark Stevens is short and slight of build, just like the real Slade, he fails badly at showing us what makes Slade tick. A good actor who was gifted in showing us the inner torments of his characters would have done justice to the role; someone like Robert Ryan perhaps. Whether playing psychotic bad guy or tormented hero, Ryan always made you sympathize with him, especially after he articulated his thoughts and feelings. Stevens has none of this talent. After doing more B westerns, his career, long past his starring roles for Fox, continued to go downhill.

On the other hand, Dorothy Malone was going in another direction; like winning an Oscar for her extremely mannered performance in Douglas Sirk's overwrought *Written on the Wind*. In the late 1940s and early 1950s, however, after her Warner contract ended, Malone was a much-utilized ingénue in B westerns, almost always playing the rancher's daughter. Virginia Slade was quite different from characters she had done before, but her gun-toting hellcat is still far more quiet and introspective than the real Virginia, a woman who didn't think twice about anything and who was quick to anger. (She originally wanted to kill all the men who were responsible for her husband's lynching). Malone does not convey this at all; she is a 1950s idea of a gun-toting hellcat, as she demonstrates when she tries to stop her husband from shooting Reni to pieces. The *real* Virginia would have joined him.

In another Allied Artists B western released in 1953, the studio took a small part of Slade's life that they didn't use for their film, his lynching, and expanded the premise to revolve around a town held in the grip of vigilante law. Though it was made on a low budget, it starred a B western icon who had been prominent in the genre since the late 1930s. Wearing his guns the same way as Wild Bill Hickok, for almost 20 years this cowboy hero fought like a demon to bring law and order to the west. While at the same time claiming that he was just a "peaceable man"....

> "Well, folks seem to have forgot about it, but there used to be a thing called law and order." — *"Strummer" Jones*

There are very few cowboy heroes of the movies whose fame was partially based on his on-screen name, especially if part of that name had already belonged to a famous lawman. However, the man who was known by the moniker Wild Bill Elliott proved that there was a lot more to him than a just a gaudy name. Born in Pattonsburg, Missouri, on October 16, 1904, Gordon Nance was raised on his parents' ranch. After his family moved to Kansas City while he was still young, his father Roy became a stockman at the Kansas City stockyards. It was here that the youngster grew to appreciate horses and attended many a local rodeo or horse breeders' contest where he watched the local cowboys go through their paces. At the tender age of 16, Gordon won first place in the American Royal Horse & Livestock Show, and through his father, he met experienced cowboys who took the eager young man in hand. In time, Gordon learned how to control his horse with his knees instead of yanking on the reins, the sure sign of a master horseman. Added to this experience with actual cowboys (many of whom were born in the waning days of the actual "wild west"), the young man was enthralled by the silent westerns of William S. Hart and Tom Mix. Much of this love for all things western grew until he decided to drop out of high school (which he finally did on February 22, 1921) and go to Hollywood where he hoped to get steady work as a cowboy extra. Around this time, his mother Maude allegedly predicted that he would become a western movie star.

He enrolled at the famed Pasadena Playhouse, where he appeared in plays with future star Robert Young and a future co-star in Warner Brothers films, Addison Richards. Soon, Gordon was spotted by a talent scout, who promptly changed his last name to Elliott. In 1926, Elliott made his film debut in *The Plastic Age* opposite Clara Bow. The next year, he actually got fourth billing under his idol Tom Mix in *Arizona Wildcat*. As the 1920s progressed, Elliott's carrer continued to grow until the talkies came in. For some reason, the size of his roles was suddenly reduced. He was either an extra or bit player in low-budget talkies until he signed a contract with Warner Brothers in 1933.

Steadily employed at the Burbank studio, Elliott was still playing bit parts, but at least they were interspersed with featured roles. He was a gigolo trying to pick up Louise Fazenda (Mrs. Hal B. Wallis off screen) in *Wonder Bar* with Al Jolson and Kay Francis; he was a red herring in one of the studio's Perry Mason mysteries, and revealed to be the murderer in another; he was the romantic rival of (of all people) Joe E. Brown in *Alibi Ike*; a bootlegger in *"G" Men*; a radio announcer in *The Walking Dead* (a scene which took advantage of Elliott's clear and distinctive speaking voice), and played the role of Rutherford, a horseback rider, in *Dr. Monica*. He supported the biggest names at the studio: Paul Muni, James Cagney, Kay Francis, Al Jolson, Warren William, Edward G. Robinson, Humphrey Bogart and Bette Davis. When he played the sympathetic government agent in Dick Foran's *Moonlight on the Prairie* (where Elliott's character is murdered by the villains) he attracted the attention of Columbia Pictures. As he continued to support Foran in his westerns (sometimes playing villains), the studio of Harry Cohn was looking for someone to star in a western serial and eventually a series of Bs to add to their profitable Charles Starrett series. Cast in the title role in *The Great Adventures of Wild Bill Hickok*, Gordon Nance finally lived his dream of becoming a western star. The picture's success with serial and western fans spawned a series of Bs in which Elliott mostly portrayed a character named Wild Bill Saunders.

Though not *exactly* Wild Bill Hickock, Elliott's character wore his guns with their butts forward, like the real Wild Bill. And though he never sported the longish hair and bristling mustache of the real lawman and gunslinger, Elliott instead used the "Wild Bill" moniker itself to make a sardonic comment on his character's allegedly violent reputation. After introducing himself to someone, that person, whether it was the heroine, a supporting character, or even a little boy, would almost invariably say, "You don't mean *Wild Bill!*" To which Elliott would predictably reply, "I don't know why folks call me that. I'm a *peaceable man.*"

No cowboy star in the history of motion pictures would became so identified with a catchphrase as did Elliott and his constant protestation that he was, and forever onward would always be, a peaceable man. This was, of course, said after some well-staged fight scene or display of his shooting skill. Off-screen, Elliott was a man from the Midwest, not the west. Unlike his future co-star Tex Ritter, he didn't *sound* like he could have been a real cowboy. However, to his advantage, like his fellow Columbia co-star Charles Starrett (from New England), he was an articulate, well-spoken individual with a direct, no-nonsense manner; both skills served him well when confronting the villains or asking the the rancher's daughter (usually Iris Meredith) "What seems to be the trouble?" Elliott's cowboy hero not only used his fists (with a very distinctive kind of fighting style) and his guns, but also used his mind to come up with clever ways to psyche out the villains and cause them to trip themselves up. Starrett, whether playing the Durango Kid or not, would also employ ways to trick the bad guys (usually Dick Curtis) into ruining their own plans. Accompanied by talented comic relief (and a good straight actor as well), Dub Taylor, the Columbia Wild Bill series is still enjoyable to this day.

After a long stay at Republic, Elliott signed with Allied Artists in 1951. Republic had tried to put Elliott into "A" westerns, and billed him as William Elliott. There was even talk that he would star in a screen bio of his boyhood hero William S. Hart. However, Elliott was a man who appreciated his young audience; he was their hero as he portrayed a man who was both clean in word and deed. Moving over to more "adult" films, with their propensity for violence and mature plotlines, was *not* a prospect the self-proclaimed peaceable man relished.

Elliott's career came full circle as he returned to Bs. Low-budget, austere and sometimes gritty, these Allied Artists westerns put Elliott into more realistic situations than did his cult-of-personality Columbia and Republic westerns. Efficiently directed by studio helmsmen Thomas Carr and Lewis Collins, these films put the Elliott hero into situations that reflected some period in history, like the Gold Rush or the westward expansion of the railroad.

In the spring of 1953, Allied Artists was preparing a shooting script that showed a town under the thumb of vigilante law. Elliott had appeared in Bs for both Columbia and Republic where his heroes stopped many a lynching as they loudly proclaimed that if the mob had a legitimate grievance, they should take it to the law. Now, still a western star at 48, but without the larger budgets or infallible image he had projected earlier, an older and wearier Elliott would take on men who mocked due process and instigated lynchings for their own personal gain.

As his screen career came to a close, the former peaceable man proved that he could still fight the good fight....

Over the credits of *Vigilante Terror* is a drawing of a hangman's noose, and a foreword scrolls up on the screen apprising the audience of the discoverery of gold in California and how thieves and cutthroats held sway, forcing the formation of a "Vigilante Committee" in the town of Pinetop. "But in fighting violence with violence, they ignored justice," the titles proclaimed. Outlaw gang leader Brewer (B western and serial veteran George Wallace) distributes several sheets of calico to his gang to wear as masks during the upcoming stage holdup of the mining payroll. During the robbery, Sperry (Denver Pyle) drops his mask before the gang makes their getaway. Meanwhile, riding into Pinetop is lone cowboy Tack Hamlin (Elliott) to post a letter at the local general store-post office run by Matt Taylor (Stanford Jolley) and his daughter Lucy (another Republic veteran, Mary Ellen Kay).

In a report to the Vigilante Committee, Gene Smith (Robert Bray) declares that the organization can't go after Matt Taylor merely because he had sold calico to one of the stage robbers. However, looking to hang innocent people is the vindictive Brett (the underrated Myron Healey). That night, the committee members, wearing neckerchiefs over their faces, force their way into Matt's store and find the pre-planted evidence to frame the merchant.

At the same time, Tack meets his outlaw brother Jed out in the woods. The young man wants to leave Brewer's gang, but they won't let him. During the rendezvous, Brett's gang rides into the clearing and is preparing to lynch Matt Taylor until Hamlin intervenes. As he had done many, *many* times before, Wild Bill Elliott stops another lynching. Unfortunately, after making sure Taylor is able to ride away, Tack is shot from behind; this causes Jed to call out to his brother and make his presence known. Cut to the next morning, when Tack wakes up (it's not explained why the bullet didn't do any damage) and finds that the vigilantes have hanged his brother.

Back in town, Tack runs into his old pal "Strummer" Jones (B western sidekick Fuzzy Knight). At the local saloon, Brett is stunned to see that Tack is still alive. (During this scene, we see Wild Bill and Fuzzy drinking beers, a bit that underlines the fact that Elliott might have been aiming his features for adults rather than his traditional child audience.) When a saloon patron kills one of Brett's cheating dealers (who drew first), Tack knocks the man out, but then finds himself protecting the fallen man from Brett and a lynch mob. Mayor Winch (Henry Rowland) quickly offers Tack the job of sheriff; he is reluctant to take it. "Strummer" asks his bitter friend whether he wants to see a hanging. With painful memories of the recent lynching of his brother, Tack changes his mind and accepts the job, making "Strummer" his deputy. As time goes on, the two are soon locking up assorted felons and hellraisers, the aim being to disarm and capture them rather than kill them.

With Tack's success as a lawman, Brett and his Vigilante Committee find themselves up against the wall. Though Gene Smith and the town like Tack's work, Brett insists, "It's Hamlin or us!" Soon it is revealed that Brett is in league with Brewer and his gang to rob the mining shipments, then frame innocent citizens for the crimes and lynch them.

Stirring up a mob, Brett tells them that Tack's brother Jed was in the Brewer gang. Quickly, the mob grabs Tack, "Strummer" and Taylor and are about to lynch them. A rifle-toting Lucy rescues them and they all ride out of town. Brett, Smith and the Vigilantes give chase, but their presence is soon discovered by Brewer. Mistakenly believing that Brett, his partner in crime, has actually led the vigilantes after *him*, Brewer opens fire on the posse. Soon, the gang and the vigilantes kill each other off, with help from Tack, "Strummer" and Taylor. During the shootout, both Brett and Brewer are wounded. However, still angered by Brett's "double-cross," Brewer kills the vigilante leader with his last bullet and confesses to the whole scheme. Smith apologizes to Tack for his role in the vigilantes and promises that, with law and order now reestablished, the group will be disbanded.

Vigilante Terror is a standard Allied Artists B western, low-budget, badly photographed in black and white, with workmanlike direction and B movie acting, but underneath its cheap trappings, there is urgency in its message. As actual and perceived Communists were being kicked out of their jobs, and millions were still being taken away in the middle of the night in Russia never to be heard of again, the American western continued to make a plea for due process and the rule of law. In *Vigilante Terror*, scenarist Sidney Theil *does* stack the cards by making Brett one of the gang hiding behind a cloak of respectablilty. Though the Vigilantes' methods are condemned, Brett is portrayed as filled with bloodlust due to his framing innocents for the gang's robberies, *not* because he is a law-abiding citizen sincerely believing in the death penalty as a deterrent against crime. Still, the dialogue leaves no doubt that vigilante rule is to be condemned as un–American. Fuzzy Knight, a good actor capable of sincerity when the situation called for it (and when he's not playing the stereotypical clown sidekick), tells Tack, "Sometimes I get the feelin' that killin' ain't the way to stop killin', no matter how it's done." Here is a line that doesn't only come out against vigilante justice, but is an impassioned plea against the death penalty. Tack beats up Brett after the vigilante leader has threatened the new sheriff and refused to move his belongings from the lawman's office. A man who believes in the law of the rope, Brett has stored crates and barrels in what was once the sheriff's office, an obvious gesture of contempt for those who enforce the law.

At first, Tack is bitter and wants revenge against his brother's killers, but he uses his anger against the vigilantes to fight the good fight for law and order, arresting lawbreakers instead of killing them. Again, the message is emphasized that the law can be applied without the need for deadly force. When the saloon gambler is about to be lynched, Tack declares, "This man rates a trial." After Tack turns down the sheriff's job, "Strummer" sways him by asking whether he'd like to see a hanging; here, the memory of the horror that befell his brother causes Tack to forget his own personal bitterness and take the job in order to stand in the way of mob rule.

When Tack and Taylor are about to be lynched, it is Lucy who rescues them — a B western showing a rare act of heroism from a woman for a change. Later, as they ride after the Brewers, and with the vigilantes in pursuit, Tack hits Lucy with the time-honored line, "This is no place for a woman." She defiantly replies that she expects that coming from a man, especially one she had just rescued.

Though essentially agreeing with the vigilantes to protect his gold shipments, Gene Smith lacks Brett's bloodlust and sees the hangings as extreme. A good man, he looks upon Brett's vigilantes as a necessary evil; by the end of the film, he sees them as *pure evil* and totally unnecessary. Even the ending promotes community responsibility and heaps contempt on a take-no-prisoners attitude. Storekeeper Matt Taylor, a near-victim of *two* lynchings, is the one who wounds Brett when he is about to gun down Tack.

However, it might not be Thiel's live-and-let-live screenplay which dictated the heroes' reluctance to use deadly force. In a letter to Westwood Productions president Vincent Fennelly, Joseph Breen wrote: "[I]n an effort to overcome what is considered to be a seeming wanton disregard of human life, it is requested that this total [number of killings] be materially reduced, and that some of these killings merely be woundings or incapacitations."[35]

Never has a western had as many woundings-in-the-shoulder as *Vigilante Terror*.

Sperry is wounded during a payroll holdup and both Brett and Brewer are hit at the climax. However, Breen's advice still couldn't sway the filmmakers to drop scenes in a film where *two* men get shot in the back, one riding away who is plugged by Brewer, and the outlaw's right-hand man getting it on the mountain during the climactic shootout. In another example of ignoring Breen's warnings, one of the vigilantes is hit in the face (the actor merely recoils and covers his face before falling to the ground).

After warning Fennelly about showing restraint in how to dress the film's female characters (there was only one woman in the film, Mary Ellen Kay, who didn't come anywhere near getting out of her clothes), Breen turned his attention to the scene on Page 17 of the script that depicts Jed's hanging: "In order to be acceptable in the finished picture, the 'shadow of a dangling man' will have to be eliminated. In this connection, we believe the photographing of the business described in Scene 67 will be sufficient to indicate that Jed has been hanged."[36] The censor also insisted that "the details of the actual robbing of the safe should be masked from the audience."

After the B western series became passé in 1954, Elliott stayed with Allied Artists and did a series of B-grade police procedurals which cast him as a police detective solving crimes alongside his sidekick, B-western veteran Don Haggerty. Elliott would never make another film after 1957. Despite his now-tumultuous personal life (he left his wife of 30 years for a younger woman and then found out that his first wife had cleaned out his savings account), he tried to stay in the business by hosting local TV shows that featured his westerns. A former commercial pitchman for Viceroy, Elliott developed cancer of the throat from his lifelong cigarette habit and lost his fight with the disease on November 26, 1965; he was 61.

Like many B western stars, Elliott conveyed a persona that stood for justice and the rule of law; he showed kids in the audience a way to live and carry oneself in life and to do it with honor and dignity. There are those who say that such characters are unrealistic and were an insult to the harsh realities of the old west; and while some of that is undeniably true, one cannot fault men like Bill Elliott for their sincerity, or the faith they had in their mostly juvenile audience in wanting to see right and the rule of law win out in the end.

Meanwhile, over at Universal-International, the "A" version of the B cowboy hero would be another near-victim of lynch law. And the man playing the accused would be a real-life hero who had seen killings up close....

"I left everything I owned because I believed in him."—*Louella Buckley*

When Universal filmed *Tumbleweed* in the spring of 1953 as a new vehicle for Audie Murphy, it was not as if the studio considered the material new or innovative. Taken from a pulp novel written in 1937, its story was as old as the western hills. It was the plot of the innocent cowpoke accused of murder and on the run from both the bad-guys and the law. The novel by Kenneth Perkins was published under the title *Three Were Renegades*; that is, when it wasn't published under the title *Three Were Thoroughbreds*.

The story starts off with rootless cowpoke Nick Buckley looking for shelter for his pregnant mare, a thoroughbred horse. During his journey, he meets Louella Purdy, one of the west's many female peddlers, traveling with her own wagon. When the horse, having given birth to a foal, is killed by a claim jumper, Buckley kills the thief and is later accused of murdering the man for a map to hidden gold which had been sewed into his vest. Tracked by a hard-drinking sheriff and his crazed posse, as well as a crooked gambler and his gang of outlaws, Buckley eludes his pursuers over a period of several weeks—or perhaps reading this cliché-ridden novel will only seem that long.

The book was first filmed by Columbia in 1948, starring Robert Young (no cowboy he) and the most beautiful female peddler ever seen in the old west, Marguerite Chapman (who later played Kate Clarke [a Kate Quantrill clone] opposite Murphy in *Kansas Raiders*). Shot in color by George Sherman, the Columbia film is faithful to the book, though Sherman's skill and the production mounting make Perkins' cliches tolerable.

However, in the 1953 Universal film, Perkins' story of the hero fighting to prove his innocence gets turned on its head. Shot at the height of the Cold War, *Tumbleweed* turns one man's guilt into the universal guilt of many. For in its own way, the film underlines the theory that if the law is *not* an ass, at times it sure acts like one.

Wagon guide Jim Harvey (Audie Murphy) is riding through the desert on a horse when he finds a wounded brave. He is Tigre (Latino actor Eugene Iglesias, who would work with Audie in several more films), son of Aquila, the Yaqui chief. Despite a half-hearted knife attack and Tigre bitterly calling him "white man" every two seconds, Jim gives the wounded racist his water and removes the bullet in his shoulder. Later on, as Jim guides a small wagon party across the desert, the party is attacked by the Yaquis. Thinking ahead, the young guide takes the women and hides them up in the hills. In a bid to talk to Aquila, Jim is captured by Yaquis while the men at the wagon train are massacred. By coincidence, Jim is held captive by Tigre's mother, who, having heard of the kindness he gave her son, promptly releases him. Jim then leads the women back to town.

MURPHY'S LAW. Audie Murphy in a publicity shot from *Tumbleweed* (1953), the film version of Kenneth Perkins' *Three Were Renegades*. It improved on the book by adding a plot about collaboration in a wagon train massacre.

Upon his arrival, the townsfolk are ready to lynch Jim, believing him to be a collaborator with the Indians who set up the massacre. Arrested by Sheriff Murchoree (the genre's premier ham, Chill Wills), Jim doesn't know that one of the deputies, Marv (future spaghetti western superstar Lee Van Cleef), and others plan to break in and lynch the helpless man. However, Tigre bursts in and knifes a deputy before releasing his friend but is shot dead during the breakout. A wounded Jim flees to the ranch of Nick Buckley. Why screenwriter John Meredyth Lucas would shift the name of Perkins' hero to that of a rancher who believes in Jim's innocence is anyone's guess. We can only assume that the name sounds like that of a shady gambler rather than the guileless character that would fit Murphy's image. Buckley is played by Roy Roberts, virtually repeating his helpful rancher role from Murphy's *The Cimarron Kid*. There is more irony in the characters' names: Screenwriter Lucas then

MURPHY'S LAW, PART II. Falsely accused Audie Murphy is behind bars as his girl Lori Nelson stands by in *Tumbleweed* (1953). Besides its plot elements of lynch mobs and war with the Indians, the film took aim at how people can be fooled by appearances.

gives Buckley's wife the name of the female peddler in Perkins' novel, Louella (the character is excellently played by K.T. Stevens).

Buckley gives Jim his "best horse" to escape on: Tumbleweed (there had to be an excuse for that title). Tumbleweed is no thoroughbred in the accepted sense of the word; instead, he is an odd-looking hybrid of horse and burro. Left alone with the poor creature, Jim laments that the rancher, and society at large, doesn't think much of either of them. All cowboy stars have done the Framed Cowboy plot, but Murphy's youthfulness and sincerity added an extra dimension. Kids in the audience, and those adults with a bit of the child in them, responded immediately. Few western stars would convey these qualities as frequently (or as successfully) as Audie Murphy.

Though Jim sees him as a pathetic freak, Tumbleweed ends up saving the young man's life again and again. Using his natural burro's skills, the maligned creature climbs mountains where ordinary horses cannot follow and helps Jim find water in the desert. Ridiculously called Clodhop in the novel, Tumbleweed eventually wins Jim's grudging respect.

Jim is captured by Sheriff Murchoree and his posse far out in the desert. The group is attacked by the Yaquis, who happened to have brought along their chief, Aquila (Ralph Moody). Also arriving for the climax is Lam Blandon (Russell Johnson) and Laura (the Louella Purdy part, sans peddler's wagon, played by Lori Nelson). Typical of Johnson's screen character during his Universal years, he's the one who leads the lynch mob trying to hang Audie back in town.

For Nelson, it is another ingenue role; she plays Laura with appropriate sincerity as the only one in town who refuses to speak out against Jim. As this film indirectly shows, the refusal to condemn someone in front of a crowd of his persecutors is an admirable trait. In 1953, Laura's reluctance to point an accusing finger had another meaning: As *Tumbleweed* went into release, the McCarthy hearings were in full swing.

As the film progresses, it is soon revealed that a white man put the Indians up to attacking the wagon. After Marv gut-shoots Aquila, the dying chief fingers Lam Blandon as the one who tipped the Yaquis off about the wagon. Apparently, the evil Blandon was hoping to start a war with the Yaquis so he could steal the riches on their land, a typical scheme of western badmen of the fifties, but much better than the hidden-gold-map-in-the-vest plot contrivance in the book.

After blowing away Marv, Blandon makes his escape. But Jim quickly gives chase on Tumbleweed. In many of his films, Audie would turn down the chance to use a stunt double; of course, this was not always the case, but it would seem so here. During the climactic chase and fight with Johnson, it is clear that Audie is doing his own stuntwork, including his falls onto stone surfaces and his slides down the side of a rocky hill. Yet even in this rough-and-tumble sequence, mistakes are made. Such a moment happens during the fight when Johnson's hand is covering Murphy's face and Audie takes a swing at him. The punch clearly misses, yet Johnson still recoils and falls back to the ground.

Honest Foringo and his outlaw gang, a typical cliché of the pulp western, are not in the film. Neither is the ignorant, imbibing sheriff who tracks Buckley. The character is now an honest, upright lawman who stops the mob from lynching Jim; though tenacious in his pursuit of the wagon guide, the sheriff proclaims rather proudly what our Bill of Rights made plain, no man is gonna be hanged in *his* town without a fair trial. Though the righteous lawman is played by veteran character actor and obnoxious scene-stealer Chill Wills, the old ham's performance is kept remarkably in check by Nathan Juran, a director not known for subtlety.

No Indians appear anywhere in Perkins' novel. In the film, however, the innocent hero is accused of collaboration in a massacre. The subtext of guilt over the mass murder of innocent people definitely had more of an impact than the killing of the claim jumper in the novel. Eight years after the end of World War II, mass killing had come to the western, with Native Americans murdering white characters and vice versa. By the postwar years (especially after the weakening of the Production Code in 1952), the western would focus on the issue of race war, showing both Indians and whites as capable of committing atrocities. With fresh memories of recent ethnic cleansing in both Europe and Asia, the western film would now comment, indirectly, on the horrors of war in our own time. Right in the middle of this groundbreaking change in the genre was Universal's biggest western star, a combat veteran who was all too familiar with those very same horrors.

By 1953, Murphy's acting had improved considerably. He was now totally sincere in his roles; the stiff novice of 1948 was a box office draw by 1953. This would not be the case if he had not developed into a good actor. In *Tumbleweed*, Audie is especially convincing in his confusion and fear once the townsfolk attack him. In the years ahead, he would again face angry townsfolk and a hangman's noose in *Drums Across the River*, *Six Black Horses*, *Hell Bent for Leather* and, in an even darker vein, *No Name on the Bullet*. In these films, we have the bizarre spectacle of the most decorated soldier of World War II as the focal point of mob fury. In *Tumbleweed*, the Murphy persona is now a scapegoat for factional hatred; when Jim Harvey arrives in town after the massacre, his friends at first scorn him, then assault him. In Murphy's *No Name on the Bullet*, Asa Canfield's remark that "a man's guilt is his own burden" could have been a comment on the pursuit of Jim in *Tumbleweed*, where the guilt of one man is nothing compared to the guilt of those westerners, both white and red, who accept racism and mass murder as a means to an end. (And even though his innocence is proven in the end, I imagine Jim would think twice about these townsfolk he had once considered "friends.")

The film also reiterates the moral that one cannot tell a book by its cover. Just as Jim is falsely accused of a crime, Louella tells Laura Saunders of her husband's being falsely accused of a crime and how she believed in him, an obvious comparison to Laura's faith in the innocent wagon guide. Though seen as a freak because of his mixed breeding, Tumbleweed is instead a multifaceted animal whose strength and endurance constantly save the day. Like the innocent man riding him, the half-breed horse is far more resourceful than those pursuing him.

Tumbleweed is a significant film in the Murphy canon. Released just two days before Christmas of 1953, it was not exactly a holiday film that depicted Good Will Towards Men. However, by euphemism, *Tumbleweed* concerned itself with topics that were all too relevant to the postwar era: themes of guilt and innocence, race war and mob rule, and how easily the law can be twisted to suit the greed of others.

At the end of the film, after Blandon accidently falls to his death and Jim is proven innocent by Aquila's deathbed confession, the young man finally gets together for a clinch with Laura. They are both shy about kissing until Tumbleweed, like all faithful horses of the past, acts as matchmaker and pushes them together. The bit is as old as the silents and used by everyone from Ken Maynard and Buck Jones to Steve McQueen (in *Tom Horn*). This bit alone would cement Murphy's image as the inheritor to the tradition of the Saturday matinee hero, despite the higher budgets of his films and the better casts. Still, Audie is allowed to angrily scold his faithful horse after the shove, something Ken Maynard and Buck Jones never did.

Meanwhile over at Warner Brothers, *their* number one western star was facing another lynch mob.

"That's what hate does to a man, it makes ya careless...."—*Larry DeLong*

The success of *Colt .45* prompted Warners to find appropriate stories for their new western star, Randolph Scott. In the next few years, the star would shuttle back and forth between Warners and Columbia, with Harry Cohn's studio constantly trumping their neighbors in Burbank in providing much better material for Scott. Warners' *Carson City* and *Fort Worth* would never rise to the level of a *Man in the Saddle*, *The Nevadan* or *Hangman's Knot*. At Columbia, Harry Joe Brown and his unit made sure that a Scott western provided the public with stories and performers which complimented the actor; at the Burbank studio, Jack Warner sometimes threw his contract players into films whether they fit their roles or not. Also working against a film's quality was the miserly Warners "one-take" dictum which forced a director to print takes that were, let's say, less than flawless.

One exception was the work of the European-born and -bred Andre DeToth, who also shuttled back and forth between Warners and Columbia, adding to the quality of Scott's films. Yet even *he* was forced to adhere to the "one-take" standards of Jack Warner. The helmsman's work on Scott's major Warner release of 1954, *Riding Shotgun*, would bear this out.

Our story begins with shotgun guard Larry DeLong (Randolph Scott) and his stagecoach stopping at a stage station on the way back to the town of Deep Water. DeLong has been taking several odd jobs all over the west while going after outlaw-murderer Dan Marady (the underrated James Millican), an outlaw whose unusual trademark is a two-shot Derringer pistol. Fully aware of DeLong's pursuit of him, the outlaw sends one of his men to the stage station to lure DeLong into a trap by pretending to sell his precious Derringer at the station's general store. After riding away and leaving his passengers unprotected, a totally careless act, DeLong is predictably captured and tied up. Prominent in the gang is Pinto (the up-and-coming Charles Bronson), who wants to kill DeLong right away. Now with the great Larry DeLong out of the way, Marady and company ride down, plunder the unprotected stage and kill stage driver Bob Purdy (versatile contract player Paul Picerni); the gang also plans to rob the town's filthy-rich casino, the Bank Club. Unfortunately, they rather stupidly leave their mortal enemy tied up right near the loaded Derringer pistol, which Delong uses to shoot off his ropes.

Unfortunately, the townspeople believe that DeLong, having stupidly rode off with a gang member, is one of the robbers and that he murdered Purdy as well. Arrogant town boss Tom Biggert (Joe Sawyer) leads the way for a movement to stretch our hero's neck and make it DeLong-er than it is.

After arriving in this lovely hamlet, DeLong is attacked by an old woman, hit in the head by a little brat's slingshot and beaten by Biggert (who gets back everything he gave). With the marshal out of town hunting the gang (who ride *into* town unchallenged), the man in charge of the law is the appropriately named Tub Murphy (Wayne Morris), a man who'd rather eat than fight. In the late thirties, Morris was Warners' number one handsome juvenile, and appeared in Michael Curtiz's *Kid Galahad* opposite Robinson and Bogart and other classics. After he enlisted during World War II, Morris became a hero bomber pilot, bravely flying dozens of missions over Germany. Returning to Warners after the war, he found that the momentum of his career was gone, and the former juvenile descended into B westerns for Allied Artists and other low-budget outfits. In fact, to this day, Morris is known among western film fans as the last star of a regular B western series, one which ended in 1954, the same year as his appearance in *Riding Shotgun*. Unfortunately, Tom Blackburn's script (Blackburn gave us the over-the-top *Colt .45*), based on a story by hack writer Kenneth Perkins (the author of the awful *Three Were Renegades*), practically insults the former war hero as it makes light of the actor's persistent weight problems. No sooner is there some important decision for him to make than the deputy flees to the nearest restaurant for about ten slices of pie.

Chased by the townsfolk, including a young hotshot deputy and a former stagecoach guard who desires our hero's job, DeLong hides in a cantina run by, of all people, Fritz Feld. Jack Warner would bitterly complain that DeToth would do nine takes with the stuttering actor and immediately ordered the helmsman, once again, not to do more than *one take*. Also making an appearance is a weasly little man (Vic Perrin) who has no lines throughout the film, but constantly walks around the street dangling a noose. Meanwhile, several of the town's respectable young women, as well as the pretty painted ones, watch DeLong's siege with almost a sexual thrill behind every look. Having an accused murderer in town apparently turns them on; and Blackburn's rather odd script even has one of the town's "loose" women ask the little weasly guy, "What're you doing fiddlin' around with that rope for, honey? Don't ya like *me* any more?" What was *that* supposed to mean? Unfortunately, Blackburn never explained it.

WAYNE'S WORLD. A young Charles Bronson watches lynch-happy Vic Perrin get roughed up by Deputy Marshal Wayne Morris in *Riding Shotgun* (1954). Western novelist Tom Blackburn's screenplay attacks the lynch mob mentality of the Cold War years.

Prominent in all this mishagas is DeLong's half-his-age sweetie, Orissa Flynn (contract player Joan Weldon), the daughter of the man who owns the casino that Marady and his gang hope to rob. During the siege in the cantina, the townspeople spew their hatred and contempt, all of them wanting to lynch DeLong to appease their righteous rage, yet too cowardly to really get near the place and capture him (that's because our Randy is a crack shot). Indeed, studio correspondence made it very clear that they were hoping the film would be another *High Noon* (leftist screenwriter Carl Foreman's dig at American civic responsibility, as well as HUAC). Here, the left-leaning Blackburn rips the townpeople and their civic leaders as arrogant and bloodthirsty hypocrites; very brave when facing one lone cowboy in a cantina, but totally asleep when Marady and his gang of killers ride in to plunder the town.

Unfortunately, except for a few half-hearted attempts to get DeLong (by individuals who are far more dysfunctional than even Marady), the film becomes a bore. One must give credit to DeToth for trying to keep things interesting with candid close-ups of the townspeople, their facial expressions revealing them to be either thrilled with the siege (for very odd reasons) or hoping for blood to be spilled. Through it all, Vic Perrin waves his noose and crawls around the Deep Water streets like some malevolent little mole. Tub Murphy takes a principled stance (DeLong is also his friend) and asks for restraint from everyone, but the moment the deputy has to make a decision, he's back in the restaurant contemplating the square root of Pie.

Finally, with the brave townsmen having had enough (even Blackburn must have known that the scenes were getting nowhere), they decide to storm the cantina. However, DeLong has escaped and made his way to the casino. After cutting the cinches off the outlaws' getaway horses (which hold the saddles on the horses' backs), DeLong breaks into the Bank Club and a shootout and brawl ensue. When the outlaws escape and mount their horses, the saddles slide off and their keisters hit the ground hard; *now* the townsmen capture them.

Meanwhile, inside the casino, Marady tricks DeLong into firing all his bullets, leaving his gun empty. But just as Marady stalks DeLong with a loaded gun, the shotgun guard kills the outlaw with his (Marady's) own Derringer (poetic justice — ya gotta love it). When Pinto tries to assassinate DeLong, the bratty kid slings a rock at the outlaw's head, and our hero kills him with a townsman's gun.

Now that the evil outlaws have been vanquished, DeLong enters the casino-restaurant arm in arm with his buddy, Tub Murphy (with Orissa trailing behind them) for some much-needed food. Never has lynch law been defeated in such a ridiculous manner.

In Kenneth Perkins' original story, written in 1942, the chief outlaw is called "Pops" Marriday, and he is DeLong's friend; Marriday's *gang* are the bad guys. Blackburn's screenplay turned the sympathetic old man into a young killer who is DeLong's bitter enemy. However, the role of the "young killer" would be cast with the 44-year-old James Millican.

The film's director harbored great reservations about Blackburn's script revisions. In a detailed four-page letter to producer-writer Ted Sherdeman (the scenarist of *Them!*), dated December 10, 1952, DeToth pointed out the many problems with the script, then titled *Riding Solo*. After mentioning that "the basic ingredients, which made *High Noon* and pictures of its type a success, are missing from *Riding Solo*," the helmsman wrote: "In America, they always used to hang people out of town. The only killings in town were in bars and on the streets — otherwise our ancestors of the West were quite hygienic and clean people, usually getting rid of their fellow men out of town."[37]

Perhaps we should take the Hungarian director's remark about "our ancestors of the West" with a grain of salt (Budapest, the toughest town in the West?). Still, his comments about lynchings in town made a certain kind of sense; though hangings in the west were public, lynchings, by the very nature of the crime, weren't always. This observation by the film's director already puts a huge hole in Blackburn's script; for if DeToth didn't believe in lynch-happy townspeople, how could he convince *us*?

In fact, throughout his letter, DeToth expresses skepticism toward Blackburn's script. In some instances, he vetoed scenes because of the expense of building sets. In Blackburn's script, a woman and boy on DeLong's stage are wounded by Marady's men; a subsequent scene has the shotgun guard visiting them in the hospital, necessitating the construction of a hospital room set. DeToth continued,

> Why, in *High Noon*, we had a rooting interest since the returning killer was a famous and a ruthless one, fortified with three menacing and matching henchmen. Here, none of these are available at present.
>
> The great value of *High Noon* was the clear cut picture and geography of events. We knew the road Cooper had to travel and we set the heavies in his path. Here, we are not aware of the impending danger and the plan of Marraday [the spelling in the story] to hold up the town's Bank Club until it is almost over, and the quick flurry of action at the end will not remedy retroactively the faults from the middle of the outline and original story as it goes and the creeping shadow of the Hanging Tree will not match the menace of the desperadoes of *High Noon* or other similar pictures.

The simplicity of *High Noon* is missing in *Riding Solo*. Both the outline and the original story get too complicated and in the end, using Marraday as the *deus ex machina* leaves our hero, Larry DeLong, doing nothing.[38]

Then DeToth mentions the anointed classic another bunch of times before declaring that *Riding Solo* has "the potentialities [sic] for one of the greatest western farces" unless the script is severely changed (again, to match the power of the Fred Zinnemann film). This is an interesting comment in light of a 1996 interview DeToth gave to Anthony Slide for the publication of *DeToth on DeToth, Putting the Drama in Front of the Camera*. After Slide admitted to never having heard of Tom Blackburn, DeToth defended the man whom he claimed had written "one of the great western farces": "He was a good writer. If somebody didn't like the film, it shouldn't be held against Blackburn. He wrote several western novels...."[39]

In a letter to Ted Sherdeman from Warner honcho Steve Trilling, the executive wrote: "A lengthy conference this morning with Andre DeToth and Tom Blackburn reveals that Mr. DeToth has considerably more enthusiasm for the story than his memorandum indicated."[40] (One wonders if, during the conference, the director was able to restrain himself from mentioning *High Noon*.) Apparently, despite its truly ridiculous screenplay, *Riding Shotgun* was a box office smash for Warners, earning $1,400,000 in the United States alone.[41]

In the meantime, as HUAC continued its hearings on Communist subversion, another western was filmed depicting a falsely accused hero under siege by a town full of ignorant citizens.

And like the deeds of a certain power-hungry Senator of the times, the project illustrated the dangers of believing the accusations of a self-righteous demagogue....

"A man's life can hang in the balance ... on a piece of paper!"— *Dan Ballard*

On February 9, 1950, an obscure West Virginia Senator named Joseph McCarthy made a speech to a women's club at the McClure Hotel in Wheeling. Holding up a piece of paper, the Senator melodramatically announced that he had in his hand a list of 205 Communists who were "known by the Secretary of State" to be card-carrying Communists working in the State Department. By the time the Senator got to the next stop on his tour, Salt Lake City, the number of "card-carrying Communists" had amazingly dropped down to 57.[42]

Did the other 148 Communists suddenly misplace their cards?

The early 1950s were McCarthy's peak years. He rode the crest of popularity on a hunt for Communists in the United States government. The fact that there really *were* some Communists in the government who were secretly spying for the Kremlin was beside the point. The accusations by McCarthy and his aides Roy Cohn and G. David Schiene were wild and all-encompassing; instead of pointing the finger at actual Reds, their net fell over many innocent liberals who were loyal to the nation. Backed by J. Edgar Hoover's FBI, the Senator slandered so many people that his efforts at uncovering alleged Communists actually damaged the genuine attempts of sincere FBI men to entrap *real* Communist spies. As Special Agent in Charge Robert Lampiere said, "McCarthyism did all kinds of harm because he was pushing something that wasn't so...."[43] Lampiere also maintained that the Red-baiting atmosphere perpetuated by the Senator "harmed the counter-intelligence effort against the Soviet threat because of the revulsion it caused."

In 1953, McCarthy and his committee launched an investigation into alleged Communist infiltration into the United States Army, his probe focusing on the Army Signal

Corps laboratory at Fort Monmouth, New Jersey. Though the committee's investigations went nowhere, the Army fought back by bringing to light the fact that Senator McCarthy had sought preferential treatment for his aide Schiene, who had been drafted into the army as a private that same year. Behind the investigation (and never very far from the surface) were the heavy implications of another taboo of the times: homosexuality. It would be revealed years later that Cohn and Schiene were gay, along with the rumor that the Red-baiting Senator was probably involved with both men as well. Convened on April 22, 1954, the Army-McCarthy Hearings were the most-watched TV event up to that time. By the conclusion of the hearings on June 17, the U.S. Army triumphed. Watched by an estimated 80 million people, the hearings did more than just provide a stirring parable to the triumph of due process in a constitutional democracy, it triggered the downfall of the most notorious Senator of modern times. In a Gallup Poll conducted in January 1954, 50 percent of Americans had a positive view of Senator McCarthy; by June of that year, at the conclusion of the hearings, the Senator's popularity fell to 34 percent, with those having a negative opinion of him rising from 29 percent to 45 percent. On December 2, 1954, the United States Senate voted to censure McCarthy by a vote of 67 to 22, keeping him in the Senate, but destroying his influence forever.[44]

Then, on July 23, a little over a month after the hearings, RKO released a western produced by liberal producer Benedict Bogeaus that made a powerful comment on how a false rumor could ruin a man for all time.

In the little southwest town of Silver Lode, four mean-looking hombres ride down the main street just before the Fourth of July celebrations. Children playing in the street sense something bad about these men and fearfully clear out of their path. It is an audacious beginning to an audacious film.

Silver Lode was written by veteran scenarist Karen DeWolf (wife of B producer Frank Strieber) and directed by Allan Dwan, helmsman of *Woman They Almost Lynched*; it's a far more serious film than the Joan Leslie vehicle. In fact, everyone involved showed how much drama and entertainment they could pack into a tight little 77 minutes.

The leader of the forbidding horsemen is U.S. Marshal Ned McCarty (the memorable Dan Duryea), who is accompanied by his "deputies," Kirk (Alan Hale Jr.), Wicker (Stuart Whitman), and Johnson (the ubiquitous Harry Carey Jr.). The four arrive just in time to interrupt the wedding of Dan Ballard (John Payne) to rich gal Rose Evans (Lizabeth Scott); also attending the ceremony are Rose's brother Mitch (John Hudson) and two veterans from *Along the Great Divide*, Morris Ankrum (as Rose's father, Zachery) and Hugh Sanders (as Reverend Field), as well as the town's tough lawman, Sheriff Woodley (the wonderful Emile Meyer). McCarty has a very official-looking warrant for Dan's arrest for robbery and murder, as well as official-looking credentials identifying him as a marshal.

When the marshal and deputies try to seize Dan, his many friends are willing to fight them, but the accused man counsels restraint. According to McCarty, Dan murdered McCarty's brother and robbed him of $22,000 two years ago, about the time the rancher showed up in Silver Lode and started a life for himself. The town is mostly on Dan's side, including (it is implied) an unnamed gunman played by veteran B western player Myron Healey. At first, Dan's friends want to accompany him and the "lawmen" back to Discovery, California (an obvious comment on the film's theme of false accusations), but McCarty agrees to Dan's request for two hours to so that Judge Cranston, the premier legal authority in Silver Lode, can decide on the merit of McCarty's warrant.

In the meantime, Dan has been trying to enlist the aid of randy saloon gal (and apparently ex-flame) Dolly (Dolores Moran), but the bitter fallen woman refuses to help. Dan also tries to have the town's telegrapher, Paul Herbert (comic actor Frank Sully, who turns up frequently in the FBI's COMPIC files), to wire the federal office in Sacramento and also wire Discovery to verify if McCarty actually is a marshal. Before he can send the messages, however, Herbert discovers that the telegraph wires have been cut, so he rides out to repair them. In the saloon, Deputy Wicker claims that Dan shot McCarty's brother in the back over a poker game and stole his winnings, $22,000. In reality, Dan had legitimately won the money; this caused McCarty's angry brother to draw first and Dan was forced to kill him. During this time, Dan learns that Johnson is a weak link in the deputies, and will sell out McCarty in two seconds for money. Alone with the "lawman" in the local stable, Dan finds out that McCarty had an expert forger named Williams forge his warrant and his identification to make them look legitimate — and then murdered him so that he couldn't talk.

Tracking Dan to the stable, McCarty kills Johnson, then shouts to the whole town waiting outside that Dan killed him. However, Woodley has climbed in through the loft and heard the "marshal's" attempt to blackmail the accused man. Thinking quickly, McCarty turns and kills the sheriff, but Dan knocks him out and takes both of the dead men's guns. Finally, when the townspeople burst in, they see their beloved sheriff dead and Dan menacingly holding two loaded guns. When the sheriff's widow accuses him of murdering her husband, the cry is taken up by the others and Dan is forced to threaten them at gunpoint as he leaves the stable. Rumor has now been backed up by "fact."

During his escape, Dan expertly guns down the two remaining deputies, and is even chased up to Dolly's room, where he finally convinces the painted tart to help him. Fleeing to the church, Dan is given sanctuary by the compassionate Reverend Field. Soon, the bloodthirsty crowd, consisting of his former friends and future in-laws, show up outside the church. McCarty forces his way past the reverend and confronts Dan up in the belltower.

Meanwhile, Rose has teamed with her former rival Dolly to coerce Paul Herbert into writing a false telegram claiming that Dan is innocent and that McCarty is a murderer and thief. If he doesn't, Dolly will tell Paul's wife he said more than "hello" to her while they were alone.

Back at the belltower, our bleeding hero is actually willing to give McCarty *anything* to escape the vengeance of the crowd. However, when Rose arrives with the phony message and announces that McCarty is the guilty one, the crowd is all-too-willing to agree with the false piece of paper and prepares to storm the belltower. Panicking rather quickly, McCarty fires at Dan, but the accused man swings the heavy bell at him, one bullet finally ricocheting off its surface and striking McCarty in the heart, killing him. When the townspeople realize that Dan had no gun and that the ricochet off the bell killed McCarty, the reverend proclaims it "an act of God," though one wonders why God would put Dan through all this to begin with.

Dan angrily indicts his former friends. As he takes the loyal Rose by the arm and leaves the church, it is heavily implied that the two will leave Silver Lode forever. Meanwhile, Paul and Dolly receive the *real* wire from Discovery referring to McCarty as a phony and that a *real* U.S. marshal is on his way to Silver Lode to straighten out the mess.

Dan is obviously a man with a dark past; he is, from what we can guess by his frighteningly expert aim, a gunslinger who has now reformed and is using his poker winnings to start a new life. At first he counsels against violence; only when he finds that there is no

UNAMERICAN ACTIVITIES. Surrounded by unidentified extras, John Hudson (left) faces a gun-toting Dan Duryea in *Silver Lode* (1954). The film used the western to attack Senator Joseph McCarthy and HUAC by casting Duryea as a phony U.S. marshal named McCarty.

escape does he use a gun; and even then, he only kills to defend himself, shooting dead the two phony deputies, but wounding the misguided Mitch in the hand. There is no mistaking what screenwriter Karen DeWolf thinks of McCarty/McCarthy. More than once, Dolly calls the phony marshal a rat to his face. When the bogus lawmen ride into town, ironically before a banner celebrating the Fourth of July, a symbol of our democracy, kids flee in terror, even though McCarty and his men had done nothing to merit this display of fear. Shouldering their horses through crowds as if they were fascists on horseback, these "lawmen" only show their ruthlessness to the town's adults, some of whom are wary of them before they even state their purpose.

When Dan hides behind the Fourth of July tables adorned with American flags, we see that only the forces of reason and democracy can protect him; up in the church's belltower, it is the huge bell, its appearance here reminding us of the Liberty Bell, that finally saves Dan and instead signals a death toll for McCarty, the enemy of freedom. In reality, the film's prediction of death for the man who inspired the character of Ned McCarty would come true; Joseph McCarthy would be dead of hepatitis in 1957, three years after the film's release.

In the *N.Y. Times*' July 24 review of the film, Oscar Godbout totally missed the film's anti-blacklist point of view:

> It's a meaningless sort of charade Allan Dwan, the director, has concocted in what appears to be a rented western town. But perhaps he couldn't help it, since the script ... was a complete misfire.

Silver Lode will probably inspire the kiddies to buy more caps for their six-shooters for a while and then expire, its epitaph a line of small type in an industry reference book. Justice will be served.[45]

The review in the May 12 issue of *The Hollywood Reporter* wasn't exactly a rave:

Silver Lode is a feeble western that will manage to get by as a programmer only on the strength of such names as John Payne, Lizabeth Scott and Dan Duryea. The Karen DeWolf screenplay is burdened with implausible situations and unconsciously funny dialogue that drew continuous laughs from a Pantages preview audience, all of them coming in the wrong places.[46]

The May 12 review in *Motion Picture Daily* praised the film's "[R]ealistic mob sequences, sufficient action and suspense, plus enhancing Technicolor photography, overcome a complicated plot to rate *Silver Lode* a better than average item for houses specializing in period westerns."[47] Still, the above review praised the film for its entertainment value, *not* as powerful social commentary.

The Production Code office had other concerns besides the project's political subtext. In a December 10, 1953, letter sent to Benedict Bogeaus, Joseph I. Breen made his complaints known on the production then known as *Desperate Men*. Patiently, he listed some of the problems he had with the script:

Page 14: The gun-whipping seems excessively cruel.
Page 85: The cries of the mob calling for lynching should be kept down as much as possible.
Page 93: Dolly should be attired in a bathrobe or at least something similar.[48]

The fanatically religious Breen had special instructions for the film's climax:

Page 118: The section of this picture that will need to be handled with extreme care and good taste is this concluding action within the church proper. The men should be respectful as they enter the church and once inside should conduct themselves as though they remember that this is a house of God.... Such things as the flourishing of guns should be deemphasized as much as is consistent with story telling purposes.[49]

The stiff-necked censor also surprisingly suggested a far grislier death for the film's main villain:

Page 123: In the same vein, we feel that it would be in much better taste if McCarty's body were to fall out of the steeple and land on the ground outside the church, rather than plummeting down the stairwell. This change of action would avoid subjecting you to the charge that you are profaning the church with murder, brutality and gruesomeness.[50]

Breen's suggestion was ignored; in the film, McCarty plummets down the stairwell. However, Reverend Field pronounces the violence as okay since it was "an act of God," thus soothing the usually stuck-up censor. However, Dwan and DeWolf defiantly refused to let Dolly appear in a bathrobe.

One must praise the two best actors in the film, John Payne and Dan Duryea, for giving wonderful performances. Abandoning his Broadway and Fox musical past, Payne was the perfect embittered hero of the 1950s action film; he would give an even better performance playing another falsely accused victim in Phil Karlson's excellent noir *Kansas City Confidential*. The character of McCarty lacks the sense of humor that Duryea's best characters possess: There is no charm or laughter in his phony marshal.

Released around the same time as Nicholas Ray's anti-blacklist western *Johnny Guitar*, the lower-budgeted *Silver Lode* is, in some ways, a more direct attack on the outrages of McCarthyism, as it uses the old west canard of false accusations and vindictive lynch mobs to comment on the blacklist period.

Salus populi suprema est lex! ("The safety of the people is the supreme law!")
—the leader of the Jackson County Vigilance Committee

On the night of October 6, 1866, three men boarded the eastbound express of the Ohio and Mississippi Valley Railroad at Seymour, Indiana, took their seats and then patiently waited for the train to travel far out into the countryside. Once they felt it was safe, they donned masks and quickly made their way to the express car where they promptly pulled guns and held up the Adams Express Company messenger. They grabbed two safes, pulled the emergency cord that prompted the engineer to slow the train down and then leapt out of the car with their booty. One safe contained $30,000 and the other $15,000. However, because the safe with the $30,000 was built much sturdier than the other one, the gang was forced to abandon it, but were able to plunder the other safe and still escape into the darkness with the $15,000.

The robbery triggered one of the most intense manhunts in the west, finally ending in what one Chicago newspaper called "one of the most violent nights in the history of our country." The three men were petty thief Frank Sparks, John Reno and Simeon Reno, the latter two brothers who, with their siblings Frank and William, were the core members of a group of outlaws to be known for all time as the Reno Gang. Little did the three men realize, on that hectic night, that they had just made a dubious kind of history: They had just committed the first train robbery in the United States.

If the James-Younger Gang, two sets of outlaw brothers who united to rob banks and railroads, were merely getting back at northern establishments whom they saw as exploiting a defeated South, then the Reno Brothers couldn't even conjure up *that* excuse. Their home state was Indiana, a Midwest bastion of the victorious North. In, fact, though the James-Younger outfit was made up of seasoned robbers and murderers, even they didn't go about their various crimes with the purposeful ruthlessness and savagery that was the trademark of the Reno Brothers. How they grew into their antisocial roles is a horror story in itself.

Their parents, J. Wilkison and Julia Ann Reno, owned a 1,200-acre farm in Rockford, Indiana (two miles north of Seymour, and not far from that historic first train robbery). Frank was the first son born in 1837; John in 1838; Simeon (or Sim) in 1843; Clinton (or Clint) in 1847; and William in 1848. A girl, Laura, arrived in 1851.

Childhood was not all that rosy on the Reno farm. Besides resenting long hours of farm work, the siblings were pressured (physical force might have been used) by their fanatically religious parents to study the Bible on Sundays, as well as attend school and church. Resenting the Bible-or-a-Busted-Nose school of religious teaching, the siblings turned — and, boy did they turn! That is, all except Clint, who became the parents' favorite because he actually studied the Bible; this caused the other siblings to sneeringly dub him "Honest Clint."

Soon they were coercing travelers who passed along their farm road into crooked card games. They graduated to stealing horses, robbing businesses in and around Rockford, and setting fire to establishments which didn't pay them a "tribute." But the next crimes topped even these outrages.

When the Civil War started, the Renos were not what one would exactly call "patriotic." At the time, federal authorities paid a bounty to cash-strapped young men who signed up for the army. Frank and John, feigning patriotic motives, joined up, pocketed the cash and promptly deserted. This scheme, known as "bounty jumping," would be refined by the

Reno boys in the coming years. After running off with the money, they would go to another area which had never heard of them and they would go through the process all over again.

With the war starting to swing towards a Union victory by 1864, the Renos returned to Rockford. Having already met several more "bounty jumpers" in their travels, they decided to form a gang and do some *serious* pillaging. In late 1864, the gang, which included Frank Reno and a young man named Grant Wilson, robbed the federal post office in nearby Jonesville. Afterwards, the post office robbers were captured by U.S. marshals, but they were able to post bond with a promise to reappear for their trial date. Not only were the Renos noticeably absent on the date of their trial, but two more post offices mysteriously lost their currency in nearby Seymour and Dudleytown. Wilson decided to turn State's evidence against Frank Reno; however, on the eve of his testimony, the former robber fell victim to lead poisoning. And so, the oldest Reno brother was exonerated.

Making their headquarters at a hotel in Seymour called the Radar House, the gang apparently had no moral qualms about robbing their own guests. One guest said that he was going to report his hosts to the sheriff; the unfortunate man's head was found floating in the nearby White River the next morning. In the meantime, the gang terrorized the Midwest, robbing retail establishments, post offices, trains and even engaging in a little "mugging," initiating new heights of brutality in the treatment of their victims. Predictably, they were arrested many times, but were mysteriously released soon afterwards. The reason for this might be explained in their arrogant boasts that they either bribed or terrorized state officials.

On September 28, 1867, when two men robbed another train leaving Seymour, the Renos were instantly blamed. However, the two men, Michael Colleran and Walker Hammond, were actually part of the gang, and decided to "freelance" on their own (the robbery netted them $8,000). The Renos decided to take action. The result was a midnight visit from John Reno and other unhappy members of the gang who beat up both men and turned them over to the Jackson County sheriff; the only thing they *didn't* turn in was the $8,000.

Soon, however, things were going to change for the outlaw Renos; the downfall began when the Pinkertons entered the case. On November 17, 1867, John Reno and gang member Val Elliot robbed the County Courthouse in Gallatin, Missouri, making off with $23,000. On December 4, John was captured by Pinkerton agents in Seymour. Returned to Missouri by the agents (all while they and their hands-on boss, Allen Pinkerton, were getting death threats from the gang), John Reno was found guilty on January 7, 1868, and sentenced to 25 years at hard labor at the State Penitentiary in Jefferson City.

The Pinkertons caught Frank Reno and gang members Miles Ogle and Frank Perkins and locked them up in the jail at Council Bluffs, Iowa, but the three men escaped on April 1 by somehow digging a huge hole in the cell wall. Feeling uncharacteristically puckish, they left a note which said "APRIL FOOLS!"

On July 9, three non–Reno members of the gang held up another Ohio and Mississippi Valley train near the watering station at Brownstown. However, when the robbers attempted to enter the express car they were met with a hail of Pinkerton gunfire. After the shootout, the agents scoured the woods and captured the three men. On the night of July 20, local law enforcement officials were transferring the three outlaws by train. At a point three miles west of Seymour, a large group of hooded men halted the locomotive and, at gunpoint, took the robbers from the wide-eyed lawmen. The hooded men then wasted little time in pulling out nooses and hanging the three outlaws from the nearest tree. The lynchers belonged to the recently formed Jackson County Vigilance Committee.

Meanwhile, Frank Reno and gang member Charlie Anderson were sitting pretty in Ontario, Canada. The Pinkertons tried to have them extradited, but hit a brick wall with Canadian authorities who feared that the two would be lynched as soon as they were returned to Indiana (the vigilantes had loudly announced their intentions to anyone who would listen). Finally, after much international wrangling, Lord Monck, the governor-general of Canada, granted extradition. Frank would soon be joining his brothers in the Scott County Jail in Lexington (William and Simeon were finally captured by Pinkerton agents in Indianapolis). Fearing that a lynch mob would storm the flimsily constructed jail, their loyal and quite ignorant sister Laura paid county officials to move her brothers to the more secure jail in New Albany. There they were guarded around the clock by Sheriff Fullenlove and his hand-picked guards. In fact, the proud lawman actually boasted to reporters that no one could penetrate his jail — except perhaps the 50 armed men wearing hoods who broke into the place before sunrise on December 12, 1868.

Bravely, the sheriff refused to turn over the keys; after he was beaten up and even shot in the arm several times, his wife handed the hooded men the keys. Breaking into the outlaws' cells, the vigilantes dragged them out, put nooses around their necks, threw the ends over the ceiling beams and pulled them up off the ground. Charlie Anderson slowly strangled to death (his noose broke and the hooded men were forced to string him up yet *again*). With the toes of their boots barely off the ground, the three Reno brothers strangled slowly. Afterwards, the vigilantes returned to their homes feeling good about themselves. Federal and state officials, relieved that the cancer in their midst was finally gone, hardly lifted a finger to find those responsible.

After viewing the bodies of her outlaw brothers, with their faces turned blue and their eyes bugging out of their sockets, Laura angrily indicted the people of New Albany for allowing her brothers to be lynched. However, there were those who would indict *Laura*, a rather dense young woman who enabled her older siblings' murderous behavior for years. Surprisingly, Laura would eventually marry and become a responsible citizen. Meanwhile, John, every bit as despicable as his brothers, was ensconced in the state prison in Jefferson City. After his release in 1878, he returned to Seymour. In 1885, he was arrested for passing counterfeit currency and served three years in Indiana State Prison. After serving that stretch he again returned to Seymour, keeping his nose clean and even writing his memoirs. Needless to say, the alleged "non-fiction" portrayed him and his brothers as saints and indicted his pursuers. He died on January 31, 1895; few showed up at his funeral.

Clint Reno, who never partook of his brothers' illegal activities and supposedly followed his parents' strict religious teachings, was arrested for assault and battery in 1874; accused of selling liquor to a minor in 1878; and arrested twice for keeping a gambling house in 1885 and 1890, respectively. Ultimately, he moved west and died in an insane asylum in Topeka, Kansas, in 1921; reportedly, he was suffering from "religious delusions."

As far as history was concerned, the Reno family even lost out in popular culture as well. The James-Younger Gang would be (and to this day would remain) the ultimate yardstick by which all 19th century outlaw gangs were measured. It would forever be Jesse James, not Frank Reno, who would galvanize the public's imagination. Hell, the Renos weren't even killed in any exciting shootouts with representatives of the law; they were ignobly lynched by bitter middle-aged men wearing pillowcases. There would be scores of films depicting the Jameses and their exploits, but there would be none featuring the Reno Brothers until 1955.

By the middle of the 1950s, RKO was in serious trouble. Bought by flighty (in more ways than one) and filthy rich Howard Hughes, RKO was soon run into the ground by the batty billionaire. Using the studio as his own personal toy, rather than as an entertainment conglomerate, Hughes ruined the company that gave us *Citizen Kane*, Val Lewton and Astaire & Rogers. Around this time, producer Nat Holt, who had worked on Paramount westerns in the early 1950s, hired one of his former screenwriters, pulp novelist Frank Gruber, to concoct a treatment for a new Randolph Scott western, *Rage at Dawn*.

Realizing that the Pinkertons had not only sought to catch the Renos, but did indeed spy on them as well, Gruber simply used the oldest old-hat plot in his non-imaginative repertoire of ideas to flesh out his treatment. Scott would play a Pinkerton (here called "Peterson") agent who would pretend to be an outlaw and infiltrate the gang, getting the goods on them and helping to capture them in the process. In literally countless western novels and pulp mysteries he had written, Gruber fell back on this cliché, an ancient and lazy plot device even before the advent of the talkies. Another Gruber-ian cliché would be the tendency of his characters to get hysterical, usually over small matters, ending many of their sentences with two or three exclamation points. Still another trait of Gruber's was his addiction to having several characters enter a scene at once, figuring that if a conversation between two characters was getting nowhere, introduce even *more* characters and hope against hope that *some kind of conflict* gets going. Gruber's *Peace Marshal* and *Town Tamer* are two of his pulps where many of these time-wasting gimmicks are employed.

However, the prolific hack, busy with blessing the new medium of TV with his clichés, couldn't do the script for the Scott picture; *that* was written by Horace McCoy, a much more talented author who had written western novels, noir-like thrillers (*Kiss Tomorrow Good-bye*) and noir-like melodramas (*They Shoot Horses, Don't They?*). Unfortunately, even *he* couldn't bring a sense of brutal reality to Gruber's clichés. McCoy would be dead at the age of 58 on December 16, 1955.

The film's director was Tim Whelan, who was born in Indiana just twenty-five years after the Renos were hanged. Signed to an RKO contract in the 1940s, after *The Thief of Baghdad*, he received progressively worse assignments, reducing him to B film status. (He would direct the entertaining Randolph Scott vehicle *Badman's Territory*.).

Our story begins in 1866 in Southern Indiana. As the narrator tells us, this is the true story of the Reno Brothers, which, of course, it *wasn't*. For example, the film will concentrate on the brothers alone and totally ignore the non-family members of their gang (dozens of outlaws over the years). Generously helped by subtitles, we see who the brothers are: Frank (Forrest Tucker), Simeon (the usually scene-stealing J. Carrol Naish), John (genre veteran Myron Healey), and Bill (Richard Garland). Their plan is to go into the peaceful hamlet of Seymour and rob the bank.

Meanwhile, the Seymourians are armed to the teeth. The sheriff (the outlaw leader in *Vigilante Terror*, George Wallace) announces to the assembled townsfolk *not* to fire on the Renos until after they leave the bank with their swag. Predictably, the Renos arrive in town, leap out of the buckboard with their guns drawn, and before you can say "Open fire!" someone opens fire. The townsfolk end up killing Bill; in real life William Reno outlived the other brothers by thirty years. Also jarring in this scene is the blatant appearance of telephone poles in the background.

The remaining brothers regroup at the home of their younger sister Laura (the very cute Mala Powers). Ms. Powers would become a well-known acting teacher many years after her filmmaking days were over; however, her performance in this film is dangerously close to ham. Her anguish-filled lines and the soap-opera situations she's forced to deal with don't help. In the scene where Laura loudly argues with her brothers, Tucker's underplaying constantly trumps Powers' wide-eyed hysteria. The scene is unintentionally funny anyway; as the three surviving Reno men attempt to eat their dinners, the pall of the raid's failure and Bill's death almost make the scene a parody of Ingmar Bergman.

Typically (with Gruber material anyway), since the scene is getting nowhere, Laura enters, shouts and wrings her hands; and when she's through, and to keep the scene moving, "good" brother Clint (Denver Pyle, another genre veteran and frequent Scott co-star) enters and then *another* argument ensues. The brothers surmise that *someone* is leaking information about their plans to the Petersons. Working on a hunch, Sim goes to the local saloon and boasts about their next robbery to bartender Murphy (talented character man Arthur Space). When the gang catches Murphy about to saddle his horse for a 1 A.M. ride, they realize that he is a Peterson agent. He is slugged and tied up and the barn is set on fire, with the agent perishing in the flames. This situation might have been based on the fact that Allen Pinkerton had his men constantly watching the Renos by pretending to be various residents in the town. One ace operative, Dick Winscott, pretending to be a shady character from the east, opened a saloon in Seymour and kept his ears open as the gang got drunk and boasted of their plans. Unlike the film, however, Winscott was not caught; he would be very much alive to join lawmen in hunting the gang.

At the office of Amos Peterson (William Forrest) and his youthful son Amos Jr. (the *always* youthful-looking William Phipps), agent Monk Claxton (Kenneth Tobey) is told that the agents have hired former Confederate operative (read that as *spy*) James Barlow (Randolph Scott) to help run down the Renos. We are told that Barlow is as good as the whole Confederate army, the screenwriters neglecting to mention that they *lost*. The Petersons decide that Barlow will pretend to be a painter, and then, as if this pretense isn't enough, pretend to be an outlaw pretending to be a painter.

After arriving in town, Barlow and Claxton meet storekeeper Fisher (Trevor Bardette) and his clerk Detrick (Henry Aldrich himself, James Lydon). Barlow is instantly attracted to customer Laura, follows her out and insists on seeing her again. When two members of the gang (not family members) try to interfere, Barlow rather unfairly assaults them first, easily knocking them out. Clearly, Frank does not like the attention this "painter" is paying to his sister. Ultimately charmed by his stalking her, Laura soon warms to her persistent Virginia-accented suitor.

Barlow pays for his groceries with marked bills from a recent train robbery (staged by Barlow and the Petersons and promptly reported in the press). This news reaches Seymour's crooked judge (another frequent Scott co-star, Edgar Buchanan), corrupt D.A. Latimore (Howard Petrie), and his no-good sheriff (Ray Teal), all in the employ of the Reno Gang. After being arrested, Barlow promises to make them rich with his ideas for even bigger train robberies. And so, to Frank's dismay, Barlow becomes one of the gang. The film now reenacts the raid on the Council Bluffs Courthouse. Meanwhile, Laura is falling for her twice-her-age suitor and is horrified when she overhears him plotting a train robbery with her brothers; this give Powers gets another chance to overact.

During, the train robbery, Amos Peterson himself pulls open the door of the express car and opens fire with his men. Claxton and several gang members are killed, and Frank and Sim are wounded. During the gunfire, John Reno is shown to be a coward. Healey, who was always best playing either charming criminals or stalwart good guys, uncharacteristically overacts the hysterical bit to show he's *yellah*.

After being locked up in the Seymour jail, the three Renos are taken from their cells

ROPE JUSTICE. An unidentified extra doing the "stringing up," James Lydon (with neckerchief and glasses), Trevor Bardette (with light-colored neckerchief and white hat) and a gun-toting unidentified extra do their grisly work as a horrified Randolph Scott is forced to watch in *Rage at Dawn* (1955). The film was a clumsy attempt to portray the lives of the little-known Reno Brothers.

by hooded men led by Fisher and Detrick. Hearing about the plot, Barlow rushes to the jail to stop them, but ultimately he becomes an eyewitness to their lynching. Scott is excellent in this scene; the camera focuses on him as he gives a painfully realistic reaction to the hangings. The many things historically wrong with this scene start with the fact that Charlie Anderson is absent, and John, who was safely locked up in state prison in Indiana, was *not* lynched.

Laura shows up after the lynchings in a buckboard driven by Clint. When Barlow arrives to console her, Clint symbolically hands the reins over to Barlow.

Early drafts of the script did not please the Breen Office. Some of the actions the censor wanted removed were: One man attacking another with the butt of his carbine, outlaws kicking opponents while they're down, several pistol-whippings, and phrases like "God knows," "Mother of God" and "ball of pus" ("unduly vulgar" snapped the censor). As for the romance between the two leads: "We could not approve an overly suggestive termination of the scene between Barlow and the girl."

Predictably, the film's final scene drew a sharp rebuke from the censor even as the script was being prepared. In a letter to RKO executive William Feeder, dated October 5, 1954, Breen pointed out his biggest complaint on page 129 of the latest script draft: "The most important Code violation in this script is found in the lynching of the three criminals. We cannot approve this casual treatment of such a serious wrongdoing. Furthermore, this lynching is clearly justified at the meeting of the townspeople. We must ask that the fate of the criminals be resolved in some other manner."[51]

Ultimately, Feeder and McCoy corrected the scene along the lines of Breen's suggestions. Unlike real life, where the authorities did nothing to find the Renos' murderers, in the film, the sheriff locks up Fisher and Detrick, proclaiming that he finds them no better than the outlaws they lynched. It is implied that a lengthy jail sentence will loosen the tongues of the storekeepers and they'll spill the beans on the men who joined them.

Filmed in color, with a screenplay and direction by two dying men (McCoy would be dead by the end of the year; Tim Whelan would be dead less than two years after the film's release), *Rage at Dawn* is a pretty awful picture. Though the screenplay does depict several important events in the history of the outlaw gang, these various bits of information, as well as the time frame in which the events occurred, are altered enough to show that the "true story" of the Reno brothers was nothing more than a cliché-ridden Frank Gruber plot. Just three years after the film's release, RKO studios would close (its facilities were eventually bought by Desilu Productions), and *Rage at Dawn* would go into the public domain where it can still be had either on video or DVD for literally pennies.

The horrors of mob rule and lynch law would continue to preoccupy the turbulent 1950s. However, with both Senator McCarthy and Joseph Stalin now dead, some in Hollywood wanted America to get back to basics and remember that, through all the threats of Communism and native despotism, our Constitution and democratic values still triumphed in the end. These filmmakers decided to take a look back at the old west, and what they found were uncomfortable parallels between those in the twentieth century who destroyed lives and livelihoods and those in the nineteenth who lynched innocent men.

And so, as spanking new hot rods raced across the landscape and young people danced to rock 'n' roll, the western reaffirmed its dominance at the box office by providing stories that celebrated duly-appointed lawmen who fought the Cold War–like passions of the mob....

4

Badge-Toters: 1956–1959
Reaffirming the Rule of Law in the Old West

"I don't go around just shootin' people down. I work quiet, like you."
— Ben Wade

The works of Elmore Leonard have endured for more than 60 years, with the author still going strong at age 90. His thrillers and crime books have sold in the hundreds of millions, and many of them have been made into successful films. However, the bestselling author of heist and caper books actually started his career 50 years ago writing westerns.

Decades before audiences cracked open *Be Cool* and *Tishomingo Blues*, Leonard's western short stories ran in *Zane Grey's Western Magazine* and *Argosy*. The stories emphasized the standard elements of the time, like romance and adventure; however, the author also instilled in them some interesting and unconventional characterizations. Leonard's westerners were never just the standard "hero," "heroine" and "villain." Their survival in a brutal and hostile frontier was always based on realistic choices, not pie-in-the-sky morality. Leonard's persistent refusal to judge his characters as either "right" or "wrong," as well as his rejection of racial stereotypes, characterizes much of his early work. This stand against bigotry grew with the coming years as the theme of racial awareness became acceptable in the western genre. Another trait in his work was in preferring the hero's thorough experience in his chosen occupation to that of the bureaucrats and armchair deciders who *really* affected the outcome of events; for instance, the plain truth coming from the seasoned Indian scout rather than the stiff-necked cavalry officers who had no idea of the real situation *vis-à-vis* the Apaches. This last was a new and earthy twist to the pulp western that more established authors like Ernest Haycox and Luke Short, men who had written since the 1920s and 1930s, would totally miss (Haycox died in 1950 and Short's work would more or less remain unchanged till his death in the 1970s).

He rejected the stereotype of the savage Indian; though many of his early stories *did* feature murderous Apaches, they were also viewed as intelligent — or, more likely "crafty." Leonard featured the Natives as a force to be reckoned with, while portraying white military officers as blustery, homicidal and basically dumber than a sack of hair. Certainly, opposite the savvy, street-wise scout or cowboy (whose basic requirement as a know-it-all was his mandatory childhood being raised by the Apaches, presumably without having to deal with *their* racism), the fort commanders in Leonard's works all had sizable broomsticks up their blue britches. Though Leonard sometimes came perilously close to echoing the anti-white racism of rabid Native American–ophile Will Henry, he lacked the latter's bitterness or oddball need to portray himself personally as some kind of Native warrior.[1]

However, Leonard was an author who was well aware of the injustice of Jim Crow and racial oppression to America's people of color. After his first novels *Gunsights* (originally written as a screenplay) and *The Bounty Hunters*, Leonard wrote *The Law at Randado*, a novel that depicts the coming of age of a street-smart young man who has been appointed marshal of the growing town of Randado. The villain of the piece would return, in one form or another, in the coming years: a rich, privileged young white man who wants to be Boss of the Valley. In this case, the dude is Phil Sundein, a character name that the author would use again. And though the focus of the novel is the young lawman hero, the galavanizing event that confirms Sundein's evil occurs when the hero is not around. Midway through the novel, the rich-boy villain railroads two innocent Mexicans of murder and incites a racist town mob into lynching the pair. Here, Leonard parts radically from his previous pulp western stories and provides a powerful euphemism on southern lynching and racist hysteria that was all too prevalent when he wrote the novel in the early 1950s.

In 1961, Leonard wrote the groundbreaking *Hombre*; as far as I'm aware, it's the first western novel featuring a white hero raised by the Apaches who is actually more Indian than white in his thinking, his actions and even his way of speaking. Dozens of novels had Indian-raised white heroes, but *Hombre* dared give us a white hero whose Native way of thinking is seen as positive, and ultimately ends up saving lives. In *Last Stand at Saber River,* set after the Civil War, we have men who are antagonists from the North and the South, yet the real villains exploit these divisions, and the ending, where the two realize that they are not the enemy, symbolizes a reconciliation.

However, in the early 1970s, as films like *Shaft* and *Come Back, Charleston Blue* played the theaters, Leonard provided stinging racial commentary in *Forty Lashes Less One* and *Valdez Is Coming*. In the former, two convicts of Yuma Prison, one Indian and the other black, are trained by a white-dominated system to hate each other; and it is not until they start to respect their own ethnicity that the two men unite to fight back against the racist white prisoners as well as the oppressive and bureaucratic prison overlords (with Leonard portraying the goody-goody religious warden as sexually frustrated). In *Valdez Is Coming*, one of his short stories expanded into a novel, Leonard tells the story of a powerful white businessman whose posse had murdered a falsely accused black man. When the territory's Anglicized Latino lawman insists on some kind of financial compensation for the victim's Native American widow, the businessman (whose treatment of "Bob" Valdez bordered on racist condensation) refuses and punishes the lawman by sending his men after him. As time goes on, pursued by the businessman's mob, the lawman goes back to his Latino roots, becoming "Roberto" Valdez, a man whose pride in himself and his heritage cause him to take vengeance on his racist pursuers. In the film version of the novel, Burt Lancaster, who sincerely believed in the story's anti-racist message, cast himself as an unusually blue-eyed, New York–accented Latino avenger (with the liberal actor ironically perpetuating a racist casting choice by giving himself the starring role). Early in the novel, the businessman figures to teach the upstart Latino a lesson by having him tied to a huge crossbeam with his arms outstretched against the wood, a scene that was also in the film version. In a later interview, Leonard vehemently denied that he was portraying Valdez as a victimized Christ figure.[2] (Ironically, in the ending of Leonard's original short story, Valdez eventually turns outlaw and is shot dead during an attempted bank holdup.)

However, back in March 1953, eight months after the release of *High Noon* (July 30, 1952) and around the same time Gary Cooper won the Oscar for his performance in it, Leonard wrote the short story *3:10 to Yuma*, which came out in *Dime Western Magazine*. It told the story of a Bisbee, Oklahoma, deputy marshal named Paul Scallen, a twenty something lawman who transports a young and ornery outlaw leader named Jim Kidd to the train to Yuma.

In the meantime, he must avoid Kidd's loyal gang members who want to spring him, especially the hellion's loyal-beyond-loyal second-in-command Charlie Prince. In John Cunningham's original story "The Tin Star," and Fred Zinnemann's film *High Noon*, the lawman remains in town and fights the four vengeance-crazed outlaws coming in on the noon train. In Leonard's *3:10 to Yuma*, the outlaw is already in town and the arrival of the train, seen as a vehicle bringing evil to town in *High Noon*, is a welcome sight to the lawman character: He can use it to remove the outlaw from society and put him in prison (while avoiding the outlaw's friends, that is). Quickly seeing the parallels between the Zinnemann film and Leonard's story (with the author merely reversing the original's formula), Columbia Pictures bought the rights to the story in the mid–1950s.

Shot by one of the most underrated directors of the genre, Delmer Daves, between November 28, 1956, and January 17, 1957, *3:10 to Yuma* radically expanded Leonard's original story and altered its lead characters, both to the story's ultimate benefit. With a screenplay by Halstead Welles, the film changed the playing field slightly by casting two middle-aged actors as the two central figures in the story, again to the story's benefit.

In Oklahoma, farmer Dan Evans (Van Heflin) is herding cattle with his two young sons when, from a safe vantage point, they see outlaw Ben Wade (a charismatic Glenn Ford) and his gang hold up the Butterfield stage. Inside the coach is the line's owner, Mr. Butterfield (Robert Emhardt), who warns Wade against robbing the line. When stage driver Bill Moons grabs one of the outlaws and holds a gun to his head to make the gang surrender, Wade quickly guns down both Moons *and* his hostage. Seeing these murders from afar, Dan's sons try to get their pa to ride down and stop the gang, but the frightened father keeps bringing up excuses to stay where he is.

Later, Dan's wife Alice (Leora Dana) questions why her husband merely sat his horse and just watched the robbery rather than taking action. Meanwhile, Wade and his gang have spent their time drinking in the nearby saloon run by the lovely Emmy (Felicia Farr). After the gang leaves for Nogales, Mexico, Ben lingers behind. With the outlaw leader and the lonely saloon owner plainly attracted to each other, the two head to the back room. Ben's tryst with the gorgeous tavern girl gives Dan and the marshal's posse time to apprehend him. Not interested in escorting the badman on the 3:10 train to Yuma, the debt-ridden farmer quickly changes his mind when Butterfield offers a reward of $200 (at a time when the average cowboy earned a dollar a day for his labors). In Leonard's original story, the young lawman earned $150 for the job.

One of the men detailed to help Dan is the drunken and dysfunctional Alex Potter (the wonderful Henry Jones). On the way to Contention City, the trio stop at Dan's house where Ben tries to charm the wife, and the boys boast of their old man's courage. After arriving in Contention City, Dan and Wade hold up in the local hotel while waiting for the 3:10. Potter and Butterfield are also there to back Dan up. Unfortunately, also aware of their stay is Charlie Prince (the always formidable Richard Jaeckel), the psychotic little second-in-command whose loyalty to Wade is beyond question. The gang members quickly converge on the town.

During their hotel stay, Ben baits the poor farmer with promises of money if he'll just take the handcuffs off him and look the other way as he makes his escape. Wade cleverly uses the farmer's financial plight to weaken his resolve. Suddenly Bob Moons (an awful performance by the unknown and New York–accented Sheridan Comerate), the brother of the stage driver killed by Wade, bursts into the room and plans to kill the outlaw, but Dan bravely ignores his gun and punches him out.

Out in the street, Prince puts a gun in Potter's back. A gang member is about to shoot Dan from the rooftop across the way until Potter shouts a warning. Viciously, Prince shoots Potter in the back and then hangs the screaming man in the hotel's lobby. By this time, Wade predicted that those helping Dan would abandon him one by one. Men from Bisbee, frightened of tackling Wade's gang, leave the scene; and even the staunchly loyal Butterfield ultimately begs Dan to release Ben, saying he'll pay him the $200 anyway.

Worried about Dan, Alice shows up at the hotel (seeing the hanged man's body dangling over the lobby, she seems remarkably unfazed). As Butterfield holds a gun on Wade, Alice also implores Dan to release the outlaw, delivering the unintentionally funny line, "Oh, Dan, I don't want a hero, I want *you*!" However, a change has come over Evans. He had been scared and at one point actually considered Wade's offer of money to release him, but the farmer's backbone has now stiffened. He tells Alice that even Potter, the town drunk, gave his life so that folks can live decently and in peace. "Do you think I can do less?" he asks.

After she leaves, the time comes for the train to arrive at the station, and Dan, holding his shotgun close to Ben's head, is able to maneuver their way through the streets, even though Wade's gang is all over the place. However, just as the train pulls out, the two men are confronted by Prince and the gang. Ignoring Prince's pleas to drop to the ground so he can kill Dan, Wade jumps into an open car with Evans right behind him. As Prince runs after the train, he fires at Dan, but the farmer is able to gun down Potter's killer as the train pulls out. After Dan asks the outlaw why he decided to help him, Wade responds that it was because the farmer saved his life at the hotel, and he didn't like owing people favors. Besides, he boasts, "I've escaped from Yuma before...."

As the train passes Alice's buckboard, they are all witness to a sudden thunderstorm, providing much-needed rain to the valley that will save their parched farm.

Delmer Daves was a first-class western director, and *3:10 to Yuma* is only the second of his outstanding genre trilogy with Glenn Ford at Columbia. *Jubal*, made the year before *3:10*, was based on the Paul I. Wellman novel *Jubal Troup*, with Ford playing the title character opposite Ernest Borgnine, Rod Steiger, Charles Bronson and Felicia Farr. *Cowboy* came in 1958 with Ford cast as the veteran cowboy who has to deal with tenderfoot Jack Lemmon. Yet *3:10* attained classic status, and is the first Ford western since *The Man from Colorado* which made a powerful statement about the need for due process.

Heflin, a versatile actor, brought heroic dignity to his reluctant lawman role. A peaceful farmer who can, nevertheless, "hit anything he shoots at," Dan Evans takes the role of a deputy guarding an outlaw leader for the promise of money; by the end, with the money promised by Butterfield anyway, he now stubbornly stays on the job because of a newborn commitment to law and order. Heflin is excellent as he shows the change in his character, conveying genuine fear and even weakness when it looks like the gang will retake Wade and murder Dan. After the horror of Potter's lynching, Evans relaxes and soon grows comfortable in his lawman role, skillfully using smarts he didn't know he had to maneuver his way through the streets even as Wade's gang has their guns trained on him.

Yet it is Ford who surprises in a bad-guy role. It was not his first villain role (*Lust for Gold* and *The Man from Colorado* were examples of bad guys he played in the 1940s). However, in an interview with C. Courtney Joyner (Ford's last), the actor expressed regret that he had played Judge Devereaux in *The Man from Colorado*, saying that the studio received bundles of mail in protest. Elmore Leonard has claimed that the actor initially turned down the role of Ben Wade (he thought he was going to play the good-guy). Yet Peter Ford, in his biography of his father, wrote: "What made *3:10 to Yuma* an unusual project for Glenn Ford was that in this one he would not be playing the stoic hero. That role, Dan Evans, would go to Van Heflin. Glenn chose instead to play against type as the villain — the leader of the stagecoach-robbing gang of desperadoes, Ben Wade."[3]

Certainly, if Glenn was dissatisfied with playing the villain, one would never know this from his performance. With a quiet voice and the confident strides of a two-legged alley cat, Ben Wade is one of his best characters. Lying on a moldy bed in the "bridal suite" of a two-bit hotel, his Stetson low over his eyes, he quietly manipulates the mind of the farmer-turned-lawman guarding him. Oozing a seedy charm, Wade tempts the dirt-poor farmer with promises of money and even expresses admiration for Dan's wife that is just short of sleazy innuendo (though it still makes Dan mad enough to threaten to unload "both barrels" at the outlaw). As he plays on the farmer's vulnerable state of mind, Ford turns Wade into a Stetson-wearing snake tempting Dan with promises of stolen loot that will settle all his financial burdens. Yet the actor also makes us see the outlaw who, if not exactly regretting his choices in life, still harbors some admiration for the farmer who married a good woman and raised two fine boys. When Alice visits Dan at the hotel, while Butterfield holds the shotgun on the outlaw, director Daves wisely cuts to a shot of Wade as he earnestly watches the two meet out on the landing, with Ford causing us to wonder whether the outlaw was regretting that *he* didn't end up with a loyal woman like this.

Ford's admiration for his co-star and director was certainly genuine. He would call Van Heflin "one of the finest actors he ever worked with in Hollywood" and "brilliant."[4] Elmore Leonard later claimed that the actor's final line about breaking out of Yuma was put in because "he's [Ford] the star, they gave him that. Kind of a fun ending."[5] However, according to the actor:

> Nothing happened in a Delmer Daves film that wasn't intentional from the camera setups to the wardrobe. He was like Fritz Lang in that way. For some reason, and it has nothing to do with me, *Jubal*, *3:10 to Yuma* and *Cowboy* are three of the best westerns I made. It could be the good stories, but you've got to give Del a lot of credit.[6]

The final line, though not approved by the story's author, perfectly fit the character of Ben Wade. Obviously glad that Dan is still alive, Ben has to tell the farmer, and probably himself, that he didn't like "owing anyone favors" and idly brags that he's escaped from Yuma before. It makes the audience wonder, was it an idle boast? Or was he merely saving face by not admitting that his admiration for Dan Evans caused him to throw his freedom away?

Certainly, Ford's charming heavy is much better than the rough-and-tumble psychopath played by Russell Crowe in the mean-spirited remake. Though Crowe himself is an excellent actor, and good in westerns, the remake was far more cynical and depressing, with a cartoonish, ridiculous ending as compared with the optimistic one in the original.

An added plus to the 1957 version is Henry Jones' pathetic drunk. Jones was a plain-looking character actor with droopy eyes and a sallow face who, with impeccable timing, could put comedy into his dramatic roles and drama into his comedic roles. He is outstanding as the sardonically unctuous judge in Hitchcock's *Vertigo*, proclaiming Stewart's hero innocent even as he tears him apart. At times, his characters may be sleazy, but the actor playing them also makes them hilariously funny. As the comical Alex Potter, Jones projects both comedy and, later on, sympathy, as the catalyst who causes Dan Evans to fight the Good Fight.

However, the script depicting Good Fight had to go through the Production Code office. Its strictures severely loosened in 1953, thanks to Otto Preminger's *The Moon Is Blue*, the PCA still had the power to censor American films. With the banishment of the fanatical Joseph I. Breen (or as Breen liked to put it, his *retirement*) in 1953, the agency was taken over by the kinder and gentler Geoffrey Shurlock. In a letter to Columbia president Harry Cohn, dated October 5, 1956, while the script was being prepared, Shurlock had a problem with one particular scene:

> Page 38: The dissolve on Page 31, together with the opening of Scene 66, seems unavoidably to infer an illicit sex relationship between Emmy and Wade. Which would not be acceptable in your finished picture. By way of avoiding this objectionable flavor, Emmy and Wade, in Sc. 66, should not be coming out of the back room. It should be made clear that, during the intervening time following the dissolve on Page 31, they have remained in the saloon, possibly sitting at a table talking. Further, the dialogue on Page 38, "I got something to remember," and "Me too," should be changed, because of its present connotation.[7]

Delmer Daves and scenarist Halstead Welles, showing the stubbornness of Dan Evans, had their own way of dealing with the censor's objections. In a follow-up letter to Cohn, dated November 27, a clearly annoyed Shurlock complained:

> Comparing this script with the script dated September 27, 1956, the only change we note, in this connection [Wade and Emmy having sex] is a change in wording in your stage directions from "back room" to "sitting room."[8]

In fact, as we can see by the finished film, when Ben and Emmy leave the back roo—I mean the sitting room, she's patting the hair on the back of her neck and he's adjusting the lapel of his jacket. Not only do the two look at each other lovingly as Ben leans over the bar, but the forbidden lines (Emmy, "I've got something to remember" and his quiet reply, "Me too") are very much present.

The censor was still able to successfully get other parts of the script either toned down or removed altogether: Dan's kneeing Ben in the face when the outlaw makes a grab for his shotgun; toning down Wade's lines to Alice about the sea captain's daughter ("An' she'd never take any money," he would have said); removing Wade's salacious dialogue to Dan when talking about Alice ("A woman like that every night close...."); cutting down shots of Potter's hanging body to the "barest amount of footage"; and avoiding "objectionable gruesomeness" in the scene in which Prince is killed.

In his *New York Times* review of August 29, 1957, after favorably comparing it to *High Noon*, Bosley Crowther called *3:10 to Yuma* "a good western film, loaded with suspenseful situations and dusty atmosphere."[9] In a *Village Voice* review of the remake nearly fifty years after Crowther's, J. Hoberman made some pertinent comments on the original:

> *3:10 to Yuma* had an obvious kinship to *High Noon*, which appeared five years earlier. In both, a lone citizen is pitted against an insouciant criminal (and his gang), as well as confounded by a social order too craven to defend itself. The various moral issues are subsumed in the 11th Commandment that a man's gotta do what a man's gotta do. If *3:10 to Yuma* lacked *High Noon*'s

stripped-down drama, it strove for additional psychological complexity in contrasting two American types: the stolid working-stiff everyman and the charming hipster sociopath. In one of his most resonant bits, *Yuma* juxtaposes Heflin's dutiful marriage with Ford's passionate seduction of a lonely barmaid.[10]

Released on September 1, 1957, at the height of the JD craze (which mostly began with the box office success of *Blackboard Jungle* starring Glenn Ford) *3:10 to Yuma* starred two middle-aged actors in a story that made a powerful plea for due process and upholding the law. As America's youth grooved to rock 'n' roll, and packed the theaters that played schlocky AIP JD flicks, Ford, Heflin, Daves and Welles gave us a classic film which used the setting of the old west to set a moral compass for us in the mid-twentieth century and beyond.

Almost two months later, Paramount released a western that made another plea for due process and trial by jury against the hysteria of mob rule. However, unlike *3:10 to Yuma*, where an ordinary guy learns the value of law and order, this film showed the relationship between a young sheriff and the veteran ex-lawman who teaches him when and how to enforce the law.

And it starred a genre veteran who had his own enduring contempt for mob rule off screen as well....

> "A gun's only a tool. You can master a gun if you've got the knack.
> It's harder to learn men."—*Morg Hickman*

After seven years on Broadway, Henry Fonda, the actor who brought to life such classic characters as Tom Joad and Wyatt Earp, returned to Hollywood to star in the screen version of his stage hit *Mister Roberts*. From all reports, the actor didn't miss the film capital; and in the intervening years in the Big Apple, he had avoided the paranoid, contentious atmosphere in Hollywood during the Blacklist Years. Fonda was no Communist, but his hatred for HUAC and contempt for their aims caused a famous split with his conservative pal, James Stewart. During those years, Stewart returned to the western genre (and ushered in "percentage of the profits" deals) in the groundbreaking works of Anthony Mann. With the exception of his 1940s movies with John Ford, Fonda would not have a helmsman with such a consistently strong background in the western genre; and even then, his relationship with Ford would end, this time over conflicts dealing with the film version of *Mister Roberts*. Still, the Navy comedy was a hit (thanks to Mervyn LeRoy taking over the direction after Ford became ill—meaning he fell off the wagon again). With the success of *Mister Roberts* coming on the heels of the disgrace of Joseph McCarthy in the 1954 Army-McCarthy Hearings, Fonda returned to films with a vengeance.

Whether by design or not, though perhaps with the recent abuses of McCarthyism in mind, Fonda's choices of film material became more concerned with social responsibility and the rule of law. Some of his films of the past had already addressed this theme, like his *Young Abe Lincoln* and *The Ox-Bow Incident*. However, with the recent rush-to-judgment atmosphere in the Red-baiting Hollywood of the early 1950s, Fonda felt an urgent need to tailor his material more along pro-democracy lines, sometimes using his characters as symbols of freedom pitted against the forces of demagoguery. After he was miscast in the atrocious *War and Peace*, the actor appeared for the only time for Alfred Hitchcock in *The Wrong Man*, in which he played a husband falsely accused of a robbery; then came *Twelve Angry Men*, in which his calm but persuasive juror helps defeat bigotry and indifference and re-establishes the need for due process while he and his fellow jurors decide the fate of the accused.

Fonda's reasons for choosing to do certain film projects were far more personal than audiences realized at the time: As a youngster back in his native Nebraska, he had witnessed a lynching. With this horror engraved in his memory, the actor dedicated himself to doing material that emphasized the need for due process and condemned mob rule.

In 1957, Fonda signed up to do *The Tin Star*, his return to the western genre for the first time since Ford's *Fort Apache* of 1948. Produced by William Perlberg and director-scenarist George Seaton for Paramount release, *The Tin Star* focused on the relationship between a novice sheriff and a seasoned ex-lawman, and how those representing law and order must gain the respect of the people they're sworn to protect.

The film was directed by an old hand at the western, the helmsman who had so recently reestablished Fonda's friend Jimmy Stewart in the genre, Anthony Mann. Ironically, at the time when Stewart renewed his friendship with Fonda, he split with Mann. The bone of contention was the director's abrupt exit from Universal-International's *Night Passage*. After a brief stay at Warners where he made the film version of James Cain's *Serenade* with Mario Lanza, Mann returned to the western genre with a script (by Dudley Nichols, scenarist for *Stagecoach*) that he apparently had more respect for than the one for *Night Passage*.

Morg Hickman (Henry Fonda) rides into town with something under the white blanket on the back of his pack horse. As the entire town stares at him, they can clearly see a man's hand hanging down from under the sheet. Mann's camera focuses on the corpse's arm in a way the Breen Office never would allow him to do just a few years before. Hickman is a bounty hunter, that breed of man who goes out on the trail of wanted men and brings them in dead or alive for the reward money. Appalled by his presence (as well as the corpse's), the townspeople want nothing better than for Hickman to leave. When Morg enters the sheriff's office to look for the lawman, he finds that Ben Owens (Anthony Perkins), a wet-behind-the-ears young man who drops his pistol while practicing his "fast draw," is actually the sheriff. Forced to wait until the express mail company which posted the reward can verify his bounty claim, Hickman finds no friends in town, barred from staying at the local hotels and unable to leave his horses at the local stables. Following Kip Maynard (Michel Ray), the horse-crazy little boy who hangs around the stable, Hickman is offered a place to stay by the boy's gorgeous widowed mom, Nona Mayfield (Betsy Palmer).

Quickly noticing the boy's dark coloring opposite his blonde mother, Hickman wonders who his father was, and is shocked when Nona replies that his father was an Indian. Here, Hickman is forced to fight his own racism and deal with the likable youngster and his mom's compassion for Native Americans on their own terms. A principled man, Kip's father was murdered by bigoted whites; aware of who the boy's father was, the townspeople avoid Nona and Kip like the plague.

When Hickman returns to town to see if his reward money is forthcoming, he finds that Ben's girl Millie (Mary Webster) wants Ben to give up the badge, but the stubborn young man refuses. When town bully Bogardus (perennial western bad guy Neville Brand) shoots a saloon patron, the innocent Ben hesitates when he tries to arrest him; in fact, the bully almost guns Ben down, but Morg shoots the gun out of his hand. After this near-tragedy, Hickman reluctantly agrees to teach the young sheriff how to be a lawman. Morg admits to the young man that he was once a lawman forced to turn to bounty hunting to make enough money to transport his dying wife and son to a warmer climate; but his quest for one outlaw took too long and they died before he could return. Hickman's contempt for the office of sheriff and the business interests who refused to help his family caused him

HIDDEN DRAW. Bad guy Neville Brand (back to camera) tries to pull off a sneaky draw on naive sheriff Anthony Perkins in director Anthony Mann's *The Tin Star* (1957), as Henry Fonda (in the center) tries to stop it. This shot is typical of the brilliant helmsman's use of the frame.

to become a bounty hunter full-time. However, the cynical ex-lawman's heart is gradually melting thanks to the love he receives from Nona and Kip. Already fond of the boy, Morg uses part of his reward money to buy him a horse.

Harsh realities enter this idyll. The area is plagued by stagecoach robberies later revealed to be committed by the half-breed McGaffey brothers, Ed (Lee Van Cleef) and Zeke (Peter Baldwin), and Bogardus sees himself as the new sheriff who will stop them. Knowing that Bogardus will turn the lawman's post into a lynch mob nightmare, Ben stubbornly stays at his job. After Ed murders the town's beloved physician Dr. McCord (Mann veteran John McIntire), Bogardus leads a rowdy posse to find them. Realizing that the fugitives can only be caught by one man instead of a noisy mob, Hickman insists that Ben go after them alone.

Riding his new mount far from home (and following the McGaffeys' pet dog), Kip unintentionally succeeds in finding the outlaws where Bogardus' posse fails. After Ben foolishly stands up and requests the McGaffeys' surrender, Ed's rifle bullet creases the young man's skull. This forces Hickman to use burning brush to smoke them out of their cave and then knock Ed unconscious with the butt of his rifle when he appears.

With the McGaffeys locked in jail, Ben must deal with Bogardus and his lynch mob. After they attack the jail, Ben meets the mob with a shotgun (Morg's suggestion). Throughout his stay, Morg has rejected Ben's offer of wearing the tin star, but after seeing the young man stand up to Bogardus, he now appears before the mob wearing the badge. "Will you hold this, sheriff?" asks Ben, handing over the shotgun with a smile. When Bogardus tries to draw on him, the young lawman shoots the bully with both of his guns. Mann films the scene with Neville Brand's body practically crashing into the camera after the bullets make impact.

With the mob's leader dispatched, the formerly vindictive crowd backs down; the McGaffeys, though contemptible murderers, will get a fair trial. At the fadeout, Millie comes to accept Ben's position as sheriff and Morg and his new family will leave for another town where it's implied he'll return to his previous profession. As the buckboard with Morg, Nona and Kip leave town, Mann's camera purposely pulls back to the original position it was in when Morg entered town with a corpse on the back of his horse. Symbolically, when Morg entered town, he brought death with him; now, as he leaves it with those he loves, he's on his way to a new life.

The Tin Star lacked the usual frantic ingredients of the typical Mann western, and it's obviously this serious treatment of an important topic (the law vs. mob rule; tolerance triumphing over bigotry) which attracted Fonda to the film in the first place. A master at underplaying, the actor never allowed himself to go over the top as his pal Jimmy Stewart sometimes did, *especially* in Anthony Mann westerns. Unlike the usual Mann films, *The Tin Star* is not only a coming-of-age film, showing us the growth of a young man who happens to be a sheriff, but also shows us how a jaded, cynical ex-lawman once again comes to respect the need for law and order. It lacks the sadistic fight scenes and panoramic vistas of previous Mann films (*The Tin Star* is in black and white). The director reinforces the film's twin themes of the need for due process and the rejection of demagoguery in an era dominated by HUAC and the Soviets. Fonda would actually point out *The Tin Star*'s lack of grandeur and Mann-like scenes of violence:

> [T]his is my first western since 1947 when I did *Fort Apache*. I felt, at the time, that I had played enough strong, outdoor roles to last a while, and frankly didn't care whether or not I ever saw a horse or six-gun again.... Actually I guess the reason I returned to westerns was because I happened to like this particular story, which doesn't sell cowboy scenery or gunshots. It's the new approach which Perlberg-Seaton, in making their first western, call "people rather than horse opera" theme.[11]

Though the actor *did* like the story, it was not as if the script's important themes were the *only* attraction for his working on the project. For his role as Morg Hickman, Fonda was paid $175,000; in contrast, Paramount contract player Perkins was paid $45,000 ($4,500 for ten weeks' work).[12]

Being a western, especially an Anthony Mann western, injuries were to be expected. A studio progress report on the film stated: "Henry Fonda suffered an eye injury yesterday on the Janss Ranch location set of Perlberg-Seaton's *The Tin Star*. Mounting his horse, the animal reared and Fonda's head was thrown hard against the saddle horn. The lid of his right eye was cut and his forehead was bruised."[13] And Fonda's wasn't the only injury. On October 23, 1956, during the scene where Fonda, Perkins and Michel Ray were tracking the McGaffeys, Perkins' horse "stumbled over a rock coming down a steep incline on location" and Perkins was "thrown over the head of the horse and landed on his shoulder."[14] The studio report, ultimately released to the press, rather ridiculously called Perkins "an expert rider" who immediately "hopped back into the saddle." Of course, if the future Norman Bates was an expert rider, why did studio coach Bill Hurley have to teach him how to ride? Showing the boys a thing or two, equestrienne Betsy Palmer wanted Nichols to write in a riding scene for her. As we can tell by the finished film, the closest she gets to a horse is having it pull her buckboard.

And it wasn't only the good guys who got hurt. According to a Personal Injury Report filed November 6, Lee Van Cleef was also trounced. This mishap occurred the day before, during the scene where Ed McGaffey leaves the cave through the burning sagebrush to confront Hickman: "Actor in jumping over brush fire, 4" in height, heavily smoked-in leaping struck left knee on rock on ground. Actor didn't realize injury occurred until morning of 11/6/56."[15]

Paramount would release more dispatches about filming, this time emphasizing harmony on the set, which apparently there was (the normally reserved Fonda even ended up telling Perkins his life story while the two were being driven to the film's location). Ruminating on a possible blowup between the veteran Fonda and newcomer Perkins, one PR release announced:

> The bomb never went off. The veteran and the newcomer left the final day of shooting with respect for each other. Director Anthony Mann watched them go and said, "Now if they had been *women....*"

The studio PR machine released more blather to the press, gleefully reporting that the married Betsy Palmer is planning for a family of "oh, four or five," and that she "was equipped for the nursery routine since her husband is Dr. Merendino, a *pediatrician.*" However, the missive ended on a sad note with "so far, no little Merendinos."

Anthony Perkins also came in for his share of phony gossip. At the time, the closeted bisexual actor was seeing Warner's favorite leading man, Tab Hunter, but you wouldn't know that from the studio pressbook:

> Anthony Perkins is coming out of his no-romance shell and is playing the field, with Norma Moore, Elaine Aiken and Maria Cooper (Gary's daughter) all on the whirl. He'll see Norma at Christmas time in New York after he finishes *The Tin Star* at Paramount.[16]

In fact, Tony's bisexuality almost cost him the role. He would later claim that there was a rumor that producers Perlberg and Seaton "wouldn't have me in their picture for a million dollars."

According to Perkins' biography, *Split Image*, author Charles Winecoff wrote:

> Because of the rumors that were starting to circulate about him, Tony had to make twice the effort to keep up his guileless image for the Paramount big boys. He could no longer afford to be seen around town with the wrong people, and now he knew it.[17]

Though Paramount's pressbook claimed that Fonda would not do another western after *The Tin Star*, it was reported that the success of the Mann film "prompted Paramount to air mail another old west script to Hank. It's an off-beat yarn by Missouri writer Hugh Telford and said to be perfect for Fonda." A quick scan of the Internet Movie Database did not reveal anyone named Hugh Telford who had ever done any work in film or TV. However, Paramount *was* preparing another western at the time which cast Anthony Perkins as the disillusioned son of an ex-outlaw. Ultimately called *The Lonely Man*, the western instead cast Jack Palance in the role purportedly slated for Fonda.

In an October 15, 1957, review, *The Hollywood Reporter* accurately pointed out *The Tin Star*'s many assets:

> There is very little actual gunplay here, although there is enough to make the threat more potent. What [Dudley] Nichols has done is to make the character development of his young man an exciting experience. Anthony Mann, the director, has fully realized every possibility inherent in the story and in his fine cast. Fonda is never consciously heroic: in fact, his lines and gestures seem the opposite of a man who believes in stability of the law.... Mann uses each scene for all it is worth in itself and also a part of the whole, pacing and emphasizing his developing story.[18]

GUNFIGHTING 101. Novice lawman Anthony Perkins is taught the dos and don'ts of the fast draw by veteran ex-lawman Henry Fonda in *The Tin Star* (1957). Anthony Mann's film took aim at lynch mobs and Old West racism.

Bosley Crowther, in his *New York Times* review of October 24, called *The Tin Star* "a fairly routine story," adding that it was "played in that lean, laconic fashion fancied in Western films, and it has plenty of dusty action in it, but you can always see what's going on." Though impressed by Fonda's performance, the critic referred to Perkins as "a bit too much of a hayseed...."[19]

A year after the release of *The Tin Star*, Mann returned to the violent western which featured a hero fighting bad guys who were a projection of his own inner demons. As for Fonda, his next western, *Warlock*, would continue the theme of the need for law and order in the old west.

And Anthony Perkins, despite his insistence on being cast in a western, would only appear in just two more: *The Lonely Man* (directed by Henry Levin, the helmsman of *The Man from Colorado*), and a small role in John Huston's *The Life and Times of Judge Roy Bean* in 1972.

Meanwhile, over at Warner Brothers, another handsome young actor not known for being a western player was having his own problems playing an outlaw. However, the role he would be playing was no ordinary badman, but a young icon who made his mark in history. The story of Billy the Kid was a primer for a tale of by-the-book law and order against that of personal vengeance.

Now, the up-and-coming Paul Newman was about to find out that even when a young actor played a surefire character like Billy Bonney, he could still come up with one of the most laughable performances of the decade....

"I *am* the Law!"— *William Bonney* (aka Billy the Kid)

Billy had been the subject of a number of films since *Billy the Kid* (1930) with Johnny Mack Brown. In 1941, MGM made *Billy the Kid* with the overaged and dark-haired Robert Taylor as the "Kid," and in 1954, Columbia and future horror director William Castle gave us the overaged and dark-haired Scott Brady as Billy in *The Law vs. Billy the Kid*. Outside of Castle's usually good direction and a wonderful performance by the underrated James Griffith as Pat Garrett, the film was awful. Audie Murphy was the closest in age to the Kid when Universal starred him in *The Kid from Texas* in 1950. Billy even made an appearance as a hair-triggered young time bomb in Warners' *The Boy from Oklahoma*, directed by Michael Curtiz and starring Will Rogers Jr. as a non-violent sheriff. We'll skip PRC's Billy the Kid series of the 1940s; starring a good actor, Larry "Buster" Crabbe, the films themselves were dreadful, as they portrayed Billy as the *good guy*, much in the same way Republic would cast Clayton Moore as a heroic Jesse James in two of its serials. The depiction of Billy as a hero caused controversy, as parents complained bitterly to PRC that a desperate outlaw and killer was now supposed to be cheered on by little boys in the audience. The studio quickly solved this problem by naming Crabbe's character Billy *Carson*.

In 1957, Warner Brothers had discussions with Gore Vidal (writer of the recent teleplay *The Death of Billy the Kid*) and their young contract player, Paul Newman, and decided that the time was right to bring Billy the Kid back into the world of the "A" western.

In later years, Vidal expressed bitterness over the fact that Fred Coe (producer of the TV version), scenarist Leslie Stevens and the studio supposedly hijacked his (to him anyway) wonderful script and turned it into "an auteur film; I say no more." This last snipe was due to the fact that Coe hired one of his friends to shoot the film version, a young TV director named Arthur Penn, who was making his feature debut as a director. Since all this rewriting took place behind Vidal's back, the playwright-novelist had feelings of resentment towards Paul Newman, the man who was supposed to fight for his script. Referring to the young actor as a "lunkhead," Vidal said, "Paul, no tower of strength in these matters, allowed the hijacking to take place."[20]

However, topping the author's diss list was the man who turned his movie project *The Legend of Billy the Kid* into the new and supposedly improved *The Left Handed Gun*: "[Fred Coe] sees what he thinks is a studio movie star in Paul Newman and a scatterbrained playwright who's all over the place in me, and he has an opening to get in and take over and [he] did."[21]

Perhaps with Vidal's "auteur" crack still sitting in his craw, Penn himself had his own take on the playwright's work many years later: "The Gore Vidal script didn't particularly sit well with me. It seemed too specialized and narrow."[22]

Touted as a young leading man in the days before the studio signed Tab Hunter, Newman had tried out for the role of James Dean's brother in Elia Kazan's *East of Eden*. After

Dean's tragic death on September 30, 1955, it was Newman, not Dean, who was loaned to MGM for his star-making role in *Somebody Up There Likes Me*. Other roles that seemed perfect for Dean fell, one after the other, into Newman's eager hands, including playing the ultimate bad boy of the west, Billy the Kid. Newman was a terrible actor in the 1950s, alternating between performances of sheer dullness or bad impressions of Marlon Brando. In *Somebody Up There Likes Me*, it seems that director Robert Wise is constantly shooting profiles of Newman, so as to accentuate his prominent Brando-like nose, as the actor does a horrible impression of Stanley Kowalski as a prizefighter. Not until the 1960s would Newman lose the Brando mannerisms and finally come into his own as an actor. In the meantime, however, the young hellion who participated in the Lincoln County War was going to be played by a man who would substitute Billy's natural cunning with angst, and turn his penchant for outlawry into Freudian neurosis. In other words, there would be a Method (acting) to Billy's madness.

A young man named William Bonney (Paul Newman) is *schlepping* his saddle across cattle range belonging to Englishman John Tunstall (English actor Colin Keith-Johnston). When the cattleman and his men surround Billy, they naturally ask him why he's on their range. As soon as Newman takes a *long* pause before he even opens his mouth, we already know how he's going to play the role. Apparently, with Penn's encouragement, Newman is waiting to be "into the moment" before reacting. (A delay like that would be considered highly dangerous when someone asked you a question in the old west.)

Tunstall's ranchhands have heard that Billy is from El Paso, not Kansas City, as he claimed, and that at age 11 he murdered a drunk who insulted his mother. Here, Vidal and Stevens continue to perpetuate the lie that Billy had his first kill as a kid while protecting his mom. And Billy was not from Kansas City, but New York's Hell's Kitchen. Even Warners' own tagline for the movie made that plain, referring to him as a "juvenile tough from the back alleys of New York." However, his birthplace in the Big Apple is not mentioned once in the entire film.

Tunstall takes a liking to the quiet young man and teaches him passages from the Bible. Unfortunately, Tunstall and his cattle are a thorn in the sides of the "Brady-Morton" faction, Vidal and Stevens' emphatically non-Irish version of the Murphy-Dolan combine. And with this change from historical reality, the underlying British-Irish antagonism that was always lurking somewhere beneath the simmering conflict disappears from the film, never to return. Therefore, when Tunstall, a man who foolishly never wears a gun in the old west, goes riding up a lonely hillside on his range and is gunned down by both Morton and Sheriff Brady, as well as their lackies, not one brogue is heard on the soundtrack.

Despite the fact that the usually taciturn and easily confused Billy hadn't shown one bit of affection for his English employer, he now agonizes over his death. After discovering the body, Newman is not only channeling *any* scene where Marlon Brando conveys torment, but throws in a little Dean (who uselessly hits the side of a metal desk in the police station scene from *Rebel Without a Cause*). Having made friends with two other young ranchhands, Tom Folliard (Kentucky-born western veteran James Best) and Charlie Boudrie (actually Bowdre; and played by James Congdon), Billy contrives to avenge the death of the man whom he just barely met (a fact pointed out by Folliard) and enlists their help.

Confronting both Morton and Brady as they're riding into town, Billy calls them out and then, with little hesitation ("You've been called!"), guns down both of them. Now chased into the home of Tunstall's right-hand man McSween (John Dierkes), Billy admits

METHOD OUTLAW. Paul Newman (left) as an overacting Billy the Kid in *The Left Handed Gun*. Standing behind him are (from left to right) John Dierkes, unidentified actor and Colin Keith-Johnston. Director Arthur Penn's film version of Gore Vidal's TV play is still funny to this day.

that the town is after him merely because he killed Morton and Sheriff Brady. Enraged, McSween attacks Billy; however, since the men of Lincoln are applying torches to his house, he forgets about Billy and tries to put out the fire. Here, Penn's (and apparently screenwriter Stevens') eccentricities are on full display: As his house burns down around him, McSween is upset that an errant bullet has hit his prized piano. McSween dies in the flames while an injured Billy crashes through the back window and escapes.

Making his way to a Mexican village, he is treated by Celsa (played by a nice Jewish girl from Brooklyn, Lita Milan) and her father Saval, played by Martin Garralaga. Ironic casting here: In 1950, the Latino actor was a member of Billy's gang when Audie Murphy played the outlaw in Universal's *The Kid from Texas*. Running into his friend Pat Garrett (one of the best actors *ever* to play the role, the wonderful John Dehner), Billy joins in the festivities before Pat marries his Latina sweetheart (played by the dark-haired non-Latina Jo Summers). The film doesn't specify whether she's supposed to be Garrett's first wife, Juanita Martinez, or his second wife, the petite Apolinaria Gutierrez. (Since Juanita died shortly after the wedding, of unknown causes, we can assume that this is Apolinaria.)

While loitering at Pat's cantina, Billy locks horns (and pistols) with the arrogant Joe Grant (Ainslie Pryor). Though Grant takes a dislike to the swaggering young outlaw, it's equally obvious that Billy is purposely prodding the hot-tempered giant to draw on him. There are several different versions of Billy's real-life encounter with Joe Grant; either way, one thing was for sure: Grant was *not* a nice young man. In one version, Grant and Billy were in a saloon at Fort Sumner when, after too many drunken boasts and name-calling, the bigger man pushed Billy and wrestled him to the ground. After somehow getting loose, Billy grabbed his gun and shot Grant in the head, his first kill that had nothing to do with the Lincoln County War. In another version of their fatal encounter, Grant and Billy had been friends and fellow hardcases who never wanted honest jobs and instead just lounged around the saloons of Fort Sumner. One day, a drunken Grant started destroying the glassware on the bar before him and then drunkenly threatened to kill saloon patron James Chisum, the brother of renowned cattle baron John Chisum. A few minutes before the threat was made, Chisum ranchhand Jack Finan (in another version, it's Charlie Bowdre) playfully lifted the gun from the drunken Grant's holster and replaced it with his own. Fully aware of the switch, a playful Billy walked over and pulled the gun from Grant's holster, remarking on the pistol's craftsmanship. While examining it, he purposely rotated the cylinder so that it would fall on an empty chamber. After Grant returned to smashing glasses, an act that Billy joined him on, the drunken man pulled his gun and turned it on Billy. Fully knowing he was facing a man with an empty gun chamber, Billy pulled his own gun and shot Grant in the head.

In the film, Billy removes the last two bullets from Grant's gun. The conflict starts (and Newman's overacting increases) after Billy walks away and then spins around, drawing on Grant. In fact, at Penn's direction, Newman has the annoying habit of walking away from another character and then swiveling around and pointing a gun at this person; at other times, he's pointing with his finger, as if he's Monty Hall singling out a member of the audience for a big prize on *Let's Make a Deal*. Whether he's pointing with his finger or a gun, it doesn't matter; the future Oscar winner does this annoying gesture frequently throughout the film. However, the big gundown is averted when Billy is talked out of it by Garrett.

Somewhere during this mishegas, a derby-wearing little southerner named Moultrie (Hurd Hatfield) appears; not only is this giggling little slug following Billy around, but he inexplicably hero-worships the young hellraiser. At this point, the gay subtext in Vidal's TV play comes to the fore (though, since this is 1958, not too much). Even the title, *The Left Handed Gun*, according to Newman biographer Lawrence Quirk, translates as "an old-fashioned euphemism for homosexuality."[23] While not agreeing with this interpretation, but emphasizing Billy's role as a social outcast, *Time* magazine critic Cecil Smith commented on the film's title, seeing the Kid as "a left-handed gun in a *right*-handed world." Though that might be a stretch, the film *does* have its implications. Viewing Billy from afar, Tom asks Charlie, "Do you like him?" despite the fact that he met the outlaw only a few seconds ago. At another point, Billy seems to be having an awfully good time caressing Grant's .45. Then, of course, there's the slavishly adoring groupie Moultrie; Penn makes sure that Hatfield never fails to gaze lovingly at Billy during every scene the two characters share, with the outlaw responding to the adulation as if the little leech doesn't exist. When Billy is killed at the end, Moultrie bursts into tears.

Totally full of himself, Billy thinks he's unstoppable. ("I don't run. I don't hide. I go where I want. I do what I want.") Feeling his oats, he corners Celsa in a stable and attempts to seduce the reluctant Latina. After Celsa prompts him to "Stay," yet *again*, Newman's Billy walks away, whirls around and points his finger, this time completing her sentence with the words "With *you*." Obviously one of Penn's instructions was for the actor to latch onto a word or a phrase and keep repeating it, ad nauseam, as he's doing the scene. Then, in a fadeout that would have amused the Zucker-Abrams team, as Billy puts his arms around Celsa, Penn has a close-up of the flames in the blacksmith's forge.

In the meantime, Governor (and former Civil War general) Lew Wallace has called for amnesty for wanted felons, which includes Billy and his posse, as long as they stay out of trouble for a year. The film removes the real-life machinations behind the scenes, where a jailed Billy appealed to Wallace to hold up his end of the amnesty deal and the author of *Ben-Hur: A Tale of the Christ* ignored the outlaw's letters. Nevertheless, there are still more names on Billy's hit list, the next target being Brady's sad-faced second-in-command, Deputy Moon (Wally Brown of RKO's "Brown & Carney" comedy team). Backed out of the sheriff's office by the gun-toting Billy, the desperate Moons attempts to alert the town to his plight by ringing an iron triangle, but he is gunned down, not by Billy but by Charlie, thus breaking the amnesty.

On the day of Pat's wedding Billy, Tom and Charlie are along for the festivities, as well as Hill (Robert Anderson), a former member of the Brady-Morton outfit. Then, while Billy is getting his picture taken, the outlaw is forced to be absolutely still and show no reaction while Hill humbly apologizes for his part in Tunstall's death and insists he wants no trouble with Billy. Of course, we assume that this is the famous picture Billy took where he holds his rifle with his right hand on the barrel as it balances on the ground and his pistol is supposedly worn on the left side of his gun belt. Not only is Newman's Billy not wearing the battered stovepipe hat and worn jacket that was in the real picture, but the tintype that was taken (there were actually *two*, though one got lost) reversed Billy's image. He really was a *right*-handed gun, and his left was holding the rifle by the barrel. Nevertheless, Billy purposely allows Hill to walk the entire length of the courtyard and patiently waits for him to leave the front gate, *then* calls him out. Frightened, Hill turns around and fires, accidentally hitting Tom in the belly. When Hill turns to flee, Billy shoots him in the back. Needless to say, Billy's murderous little stunt ruins Pat's wedding. Newman's overacting returns when he (again) points at his victim and chortles, "It is *over*! *Killed* my last one!" When Garrett reminds Billy of his word not to attack Hill, Billy replies glibly that the killing didn't take place at the wedding site, but *outside*. As Billy and Charlie take the wounded Tom away, Garrett finally puts on the sheriff's badge that the dead Hill had offered him and vows to bring Billy in if it's the last thing he does. Billy the Kid, who had arrogantly proclaimed himself "the law" through most of the film, is now about to meet the *real* law.

A posse is formed and led by Garrett. Also joining him on the hunt, to the sheriff's eternal regret, is the arrogant Bob Ollinger (the ubiquitous Denver Pyle). As in practically every film featuring Billy the Kid (including Sam Peckinpah's *Pat Garrett and Billy the Kid*), there is a reenactment of the famous siege at Stinking Springs, in which Billy and what was left of his gang were trapped in a one-room rock-and-adobe house by Garrett and his men. In the film, both Tom and Charlie are killed by blasts from Ollinger's shotgun. Now alone, Billy is forced to surrender to Garrett. With manacles on both his hands and his feet, he is incarcerated in the Lincoln County Jail.

At this point, before discussing the most daring jailbreak of the 19th century, we must go into the personalities involved. Ameridith Robert B. Ollinger, after an upbringing as a Kansas farmboy, migrated to New Mexico Territory where he ended up on the side of the Murphy-Dolan faction battling Billy's "Regulators." In October 1880, he was commissioned a deputy U.S. marshal for Lincoln County where he assisted Pat Garrett in the capture of cattle thieves and rustlers. On April 10, 1881, Ollinger was appointed a deputy sheriff for Dona Ana County. A large, taciturn man, Ollinger carried with him a reputation for cruelty and arrogance that disgusted his fellow lawmen. Texas Ranger Jim Gillett said, "I knew him well and considered him a coward." Pat Garrett, whom Ollinger assisted in his duties, called him, "a murderer at heart. I never slept out with him that I did not watch him." Taking note that there there was little, if any, screening process for lawmen in those days, he added lamely, "Of course, you will understand that we had to use for deputies such material as we could get."

On the flip side of the coin was Deputy U.S. Marshal James W. Bell. Well-liked by all who knew him, Bell was a native of Georgia. Having tired of mining gold out west, he turned to law enforcement and, at the age of twenty-seven, seemed to have found his niche. A veteran of many posses hunting outlaws in the freezing wilderness, Bell was described by a White Oaks newspaper as "a very cool and daring man.... The citizens of White Oaks have full confidence in him and believe that he will conscientiously discharge his duties at any cost." Even outlaws came to respect Deputy Bell, with none more admiring the young lawman than the infamous, fun-loving hellion whom Bell helped transport to the Lincoln County Jail.

However, the arrogant Ollinger and the likable Bell had one thing in common: Both of them totally underestimated the resolve of Billy the Kid. In the excellent *To Hell on a Fast Horse: Billy the Kid, Pat Garrett and the Epic Chase to Justice in the Old West*, author Mark Lee Gardner wrote:

> In a pinch, William H. Bonney could be as ruthless and cold-blooded as any outlaw and thug who plagued New Mexico Territory. When life and death hung in the balance — Billy's, that is — that was the time to be the most cautious around the Kid. Everyone knew he was a killer. Everyone had heard about his flair for escaping tight spots. If you could read, all you had to do was to pick up one of the Territory's newspapers to see that Billy had been talking of escape ever since his confinement at Santa Fe. But Billy's real and deadly talent was fooling people. Time and again, they misjudged the diminutive outlaw's abilities and resolve. Billy joked and smiled, but his quick mind was always sizing up the situation, looking for a sign of weakness, a slight mental error, something that would give him an edge.[24]

In fact, this was the time when Billy was at his most dangerous; and, despite his immense wit and charm, he was still a cold-blooded killer. With this hard fact in mind, it can't be emphasized enough that, despite his affection for James Bell, Billy now regarded the likable deputy on the same level as the bullying Ollinger: a target for his guns.

While Ollinger went to the local café to get a meal, leaving his shotgun back at the jail, Billy told Bell that he wanted to go to the bathroom, which was the small water-closet outside. At this point, Billy knocked Bell down with his chained hands and, with great difficulty since his legs were manacled, quickly hobbled his way back into the jail (which was in the old two-story Lincoln County Courthouse), hopped up a flight of wooden stairs to the second floor, used his shoulder to break into the arsenal, grabbed a .45 still in its holster and shot Deputy Bell to death. Another version of this has the two men struggling over the gun at the top of the stairs where Billy won possession of the pistol, causing Bell to run down the stairs and escape in order to warn others that Billy had gotten loose, only to get shot in the back for his trouble. Either way, there *was* the possibility that Billy warned the young deputy *not* to come up after him; however, there is no guarantee that Billy had ever issued a warning of any kind since no one else was there when the killing took place. Witnesses had heard three shots, but only one bullet felled the deputy, and by sheer adrenaline, he staggered outside and collapsed in the arms of county employee Gottfried Gauss. Hearing the shots, Ollinger ran back to the courthouse and was stunned to look up at the balcony and see a still-manacled Billy standing there smiling and pointing his own double-barrelled shotgun at him. A second later, Ollinger was dead, his head and shoulders ripped apart by 36 heavy slugs of pure buckshot.

At this point in *The Left Handed Gun*, we are seeing the most honest moment in the entire overwrought, neurotic film; and that is Billy's escape from the Lincoln County Jail. Here, both Penn and Newman show us the Kid's feral energy, his cool, determined drive to do *anything* in order to survive, no matter the cost to anyone else. But we also see Billy's murderous need for revenge; like the real Billy who could have easily ignored Ollinger and just escaped, the Kid actually waited around those precious few minutes for his enemy to appear so he could kill him — and do it in such a way that would insult his dignity, killing Ollinger with his own prized shotgun.

Now hunted thoughout the west, Billy refuses to leave the vicinity of Lincoln County. As the real Billy had famously said, "I am not going to leave the country, and I am not going to reform. Neither am I going to be taken alive."

Knowing full well that the Kid sometimes saw Paulita Maxwell, the daughter of his friend Pete Maxwell, in Fort Sumner, Garrett showed up on his property with two deputies on the night of July 14, 1881. Waiting in Maxwell's pitch-black bedroom, Garrett heard a lone figure calling out "*Quien es? Quien es?*" Then the lawman fired two shots, the first hitting Billy in the chest right above the heart, killing him instantly; the second shot going wild and hitting the wall.

Unfortunately, Penn, Stevens and Newman don't make it that easy for the young outlaw. Paying a last visit to Celsa and Saval, Billy is resigned to the fact that Garrett is outside waiting for him. Drowning in maudlin self-pity (he gave his pistol to Saval and wanted him to kill him with it), Billy whirls and points his finger (yet *again*), pretending he's drawing a gun, which forces Garrett to kill him. Earlier, when Billy emerged from the cabin at Stinking Springs after being captured, Penn has Newman not raise his hands in surrender, but instead stretch them out as if he was being crucified. Now, after Garrett's bullet makes impact, Newman's Billy staggers forward and falls across a wagon tongue, rolling over with his arms outstretched, fully implying that the law enforcement officers of New Mexico Territory Know Not What They Do. Why director Penn and his mannered star actually thought of this neurotic little psycho as a Christ figure is anyone's guess.

After Billy dies, Garrett's bride appears and says, "Let's go home." And so John Dehner, a character actor known mostly for playing villains, walks off with the girl at the end of a film for the only time in his entire screen career.

Here, both Penn and screenwriter Stevens concentrate on Billy's vengeance quest. Though he kills all through the picture, his various victims were part of the Brady-Morton faction responsible for the murder of John Tunstall, thereby allowing the Kid to retain a certain measure of sympathy (though you wouldn't know that from Newman's horrible performance). Unfortunately, by concentrating on Billy's taking the law into his own hands, the film totally ignores his busy outlaw career; if nothing else, the Kid was first and foremost a robber and thief. The film never once mentions his many stage holdups or horse and cattle rustling; he was also a young man who would kill at the drop of a hat, as witness his murder of Joe Grant. The film has Garrett talk Billy out of shooting Grant, despite the fact that he wasn't anywhere near that saloon on that day; according to the film, when the Kid did kill, he killed only the "real" bad guys. It is only when he shoots Deputy Bell that the Kid kills a sympathetic character for the first time. The *real* Billy had no such qualms about pulling the trigger on anyone if it served his purpose.

In a letter to Jack Warner, dated May 3, 1957, new MPAA head Geoffrey Shurlock warned the mogul that, because of the "great number of personalized and quite brutal killings," as well as the "clear suggestion that Billy has had an adulterous affair with Celsa,"[25] the script for *The Left Handed Gun* could not be approved. Scenes between the two were promptly changed, though the focus on that blacksmith's forge certainly implied that *something* was going on. After the film was released on May 7, 1958, Philip K. Scheuer wrote in the next day's issue of the *Los Angeles Times*:

SOMEBODY UP THERE *DOESN'T* LIKE YOU. Director Paul Newman in *The Left Handed Gun* (1958). The actor and director Arthur Penn turned Billy the Kid's story into a comic opera of hysterical overacting and juvenile delinquency kitsch.

"[The cast] — Newman included — look a bit old for the parts, but they frequently act like the subnormal adolescents they are meant to be.... *The Left Handed Gun* is hardly for juveniles, deliquent or otherwise. Adults will find it erratic, uneven, coarse, agitating when it isn't irritating. It's certainly 'different.'"[26]

In fact, the film emphasizes the juvenile delinquent angle. In the taglines, Billy is referred to as a "juvenile tough from the back alleys of New York" and a "teenage desperado." Another tagline proclaimed: "Just for 'kicks,' Billy would slip down to Mexico."

Hollywood had always treated the Billy the Kid story as a lesson about what happens when a headstrong young man loses his only father figure and then takes the law into his own hands when the Law itself is either incompetent or corrupt. However, Vidal, Penn, Stevens and Newman turned Billy's story into that of a 1950s teen rebel who declares his own private war on adults. Drowning in the hand-wringing Method acting of the day, *The Left Handed Gun* enters film history as one of the most unintentionally funny westerns of all time. Or, as Gore Vidal acidly put it, Penn turned his script into "something only the French would love."[27]

In her *Los Angeles Times* column of September 4, 1956, long before Warners was preparing the script for *The Left Handed Gun*, Hedda Hopper wrote: "Paul Newman's slated as the next screen Billy. Hear this version's being done along lines of modern Greek tragedy. I can hear some readers groaning 'Say it isn't so!'"[28]

"I say, let's open 'em up and leave 'em here...." — *Claude Tobin*

By the early 1950s, Gary Cooper's career was in a slump. He was still a superstar making superstar money, but his box office was faltering. Turning 50 in a Hollywood that cherished youth, and opposite new tough-guy actors like Kirk Douglas and Burt Lancaster, he no longer seemed relevant. However, part of this "sudden" surge of unpopularity might also have been because of the actor's appearance before HUAC on October 20, 1947. It was the same week he had signed a lucrative contract with Warner Brothers that resulted in interesting misfires like *Task Force* and *Dallas*, and laughable abominations like *The Fountainhead*. Generally Cooper was a man whom very few in either Hollywood or Washington ever accused of being a mental giant on the politics of the day. However, when he was called before HUAC as a "friendly witness," he ended up fooling those on both the right and the left by cunningly refusing to name names of any alleged Communists during his testimony. Besides slamming Communism as a movement that wasn't "on the level,"[29] the actor was able to paint himself as a patriot, yet at the same time avoid mentioning any actual performer or behind-the-camera personnel as being a Party member.

Those on the left, still a powerful faction in Hollywood despite the Blacklist, were no fans of the actor, and many writers and directors who might have helped his career, stayed away from him during those years. A passionate affair with Warner contract starlet Patricia Neal didn't help his career either, and Jack Warner basically regulated him to B westerns that were indistinguishable from Randolph Scott's output at the studio; that is, until *High Noon*. Written (and in many cases, *overwritten*) by leftist screenwriter Carl Foreman and produced by Stanley Kramer (who, to his credit, didn't care about Cooper's politics), the low-budget, black and white western saved his career and subsequently won him his second Best Actor Oscar.

Thanks to *High Noon*, Cooper again appeared in big-budget prestige Hollywood films, though the actor always strove for something different. Even his mid-1950s westerns always had to have a certain amount of darkness or amorality in them. Repeatedly turning down scripts that had him again playing marshals like Will Kane, the actor instead chose material that accentuated the new realities of Hollywood, where the breaking of the Production Code inaugurated a brutal and bloody change to the westerns of the 1950s. *Garden of Evil* and *Vera Cruz* (the second directed by the mean-spirited Robert Aldrich) were violent and sleazy. Mr. Deeds wouldn't have gone anywhere near the sociopaths that populated these efforts. However, Cooper was smart enough to play a character who rose above it all, usually taking the role of a basically decent man who may be allying himself with brutes for the time being, yet the audience knew that "Coop" would set things right by the end. The actor was not an intellectual by any stretch of the imagination, but he was shrewd enough to know not to throw away a painfully crafted image just to give audiences a quick, violent thrill.

Anthony Mann's company, Security Pictures, was releasing their films through United Artists in the late 1950s. After a long run at Universal-International, and contracts of shorter duration with Paramount, Warners, MGM and Columbia, Mann's work perfectly fell into the category of the violent, amoral western which dominated the 1950s. In many ways, his heroes were as violent as his villains. Sometimes driven to the point of madness, these obsessed, usually vengeange-crazed men had to conquer the charming but psychotic villains, seen as the hero's darker self. A shrewd judge of good material (that is, if you forget his remake of *Cimarron*), Mann brought neurosis and mania to the standard cowboy hero. Now dealing with audiences who were well-acquanited with the atrocities of World War II, the helmsman was able to raise the kill factor in a way he never could in the 1940s (though he did a damn good job increasing the level of violence past the ever-watchful eye of Joseph Breen with *Border Incident*). Still, unlike Robert Aldrich, Mann never gave us violence-for-the-sake-of-violence; his heroes may have been brutal, but they always found their better selves by the end credits. During the years leading up to Security Pictures' formation, Mann had bought the rights to several properties, including Erskine Caldwell's *God's Little Acre*. One of those properties turned out to be a pulp western by a little-known author named Will C. Brown.

His real name was Clarence Scott Boyles Jr., and he was born in Baird, Texas, in 1905. He flooded the market with dozens of sagebrush stories and novels, mostly set in his native Texas (as Elmer Kelton would set his own books much later on). His efforts ultimately resulted in a much-deserved Spur Award in 1960 for his novel, *The Nameless Breed*. In 1955, Brown published a novel set in South Texas called *The Border Jumpers*. Under Mann and screenwriter Reginald Rose (the author of the hit TV play *Twelve Angry Men*, as well as the film version), the new film's structure was totally different from the novel; so would its title. Taking the focus off the villains (*The Border Jumpers*), the new title would put it squarely on the hero (*Man of the West*).

Lincoln "Link" Jones (Cooper) is married to simple prairie gal Lucy and is the father of two adorable children. About to board a train, he is carrying with him a carpetbag with $5000 contributed by residents of his town so that he can purchase the services of a teacher back east. After a con man named Beasley (Arthur O'Connell) makes Link's acquaintance on the Crosscut railroad platform, the sudden appearance of the marshal (Frank Ferguson) forces the grifter to quickly move away. However, when the suspicious lawman grills Link, claiming that he's seen him somewhere before, the innocent husband and father of two lies to the marshal and gives him a phony name. Here, Mann emphasizes the danger of exposure that Link faces by having the marshal's holstered gun fill the frame as Jones moves away from him. It will not be the last closeup of a gun in this film, as Mann emphasizes both the danger, and the power, of those who wear them.

On the train, Beasley attempts to pass off sultry saloon singer Billie Ellis as a schoolteacher. Here, the blonde, husky-voiced singer, Julie London, replaces the novel's black-haired Billie, also known as "the Girl with the Golden Voice." This is done in order to relieve Link of his carpetbag with the $5000. At a stopover, an outlaw gang appears and shoots up the train, forcing the engineer to quickly pull out, leaving exactly three passengers stranded: Link, Beasley and Billie. Beasley had sprained his ankle, and Billie is in high heels. In Brown's novel, Link's anger at being stranded with these two reveals the cruelty that was once in his character, since he sees them as too "soft" to travel miles in the wilderness. Almost by instinct, Link finds the old Alcutt cabin and wonders if it is abandoned. Now, had our hero done what many a cautious cowboy would have done and investigated the corral (or, if necessary, the barn), he would have discovered that horses were there and that the place was occupied, thus causing him and his reluctant companions to avoid the cabin. However, had Link done that one little thing, there wouldn't have been a book *or* a film, so....

No sooner does Link enter the house than he has guns pointed at him by members of the same gang that held up the train. The film drops the sombrero-wearing Mexican outlaw Ponch and replaces him with a white outlaw named Ponch (Robert Wilke, *the* baddest western henchman of the 1950s). Also pointing a gun at Link is the vicious mute Trout (Royal Dano); in the novel, he is a very talkative ex-convict who lusts after Billie. Third but not least is Coaley Scull. In the book, he is a young man of 22 or so with long dark hair; in the film, he becomes the 38-year-old Jack Lord. Missing from this gang of lovable rogues is the gang's surly cook, Henny.

In the novel, Link is forced to go back to his outlaw past in order to protect Billie, Beasley and himself:

> Somebody had to get top hand here before the girl came into the room. Them or him. Whatever bad blood had been in him at birth, he had worked ten years to get the stain out. Now it stirred again and he had felt the years slip back. He was among his own. The knowledge came and the decision wrote itself in the silence. *From now on, he had to be one of them.*

Soon, the familiar voice of an old man is heard and Link turns around to see his uncle, Dock Tobin, head of the ruthless Tobin gang. When Lee J. Cobb played Dock, he was 47 years old, which actually made him a full *nine years younger* than the man playing his nephew. To cover up this little embarrassing detail, the studio makeup department worked overtime to give Cobb a white-haired wig and thick scruffy white beard — quite different from the dirty brown-bearded mountain-man look that Dock had in the novel.

Playing for time, Link is forced to say that he's "come back." It seems that our stranded family man had once been running with his evil uncle and the rest of his lunatic family.

In the novel, Brown is specific on the backgrounds of his characters, a family history that goes out of its way to show Link as more victim than victimizer. After the death of his parents, the teenager was taken in by Uncle Dock. Unfortunately, the innocent youngster would soon find that his Uncle Dock acted more like Papa Doc. Forced to join his family on robberies where he seemed to do no more than hold the horses, Link was also the victim of his uncle's warped idea of manliness; at one point, the young man was tied up and forced to watch Dock and his gang rape two frightened Mexican women. Prominent among the outlaws was Link's cousin Claude, a big, hulking bundle of malevolence who always harbored jealousy against the youngster for being their uncle's favorite. In fact, for years, Link was terrified that Claude would murder him in his sleep.

Link is forced to bring in Billie and Beasley, all the time reminding these violent men that the saloon singer "is mine." It seems that the gang has been living in Mexico, with a base just over the border; this allows them to raid American banks and trains for money, then scramble back into Mexico, making them "border jumpers." In the novel, their next job is plundering the railroad's safe at a lonely stage stop named Lasso. In the film, Dock Tobin is under the impression that the bank in Lasso is one of the biggest in the west. "Lasso! The name rings like a bell!" shouts Cobb in a shameless piece of hamming.

Alcutt, mortally wounded during the robbery, had been placed on a table in the rear room. At Dock's orders, Coaley finishes the job, proving to the old man that his nephew has guts, even though he still blames him for screwing up the train robbery. Again, Mann focuses on a gun, this time Coaley's, as he smoothly puts it back into his holster.

Though Link is accepted as Dock's favorite, Coaley's hatred for him and the appearance of Billie make things very tense in the Alcutt cabin. Frantically, Coaley holds a knife to Link's throat and orders Billie to strip. As the knife digs into Link, he develops his own hatred for his cousin.

Also showing up at the cabin is Claude (John Dehner), in some ways the most dangerous Tobin, obviously because he's the smartest one. In the novel, Claude is a big, hulking bundle of energy and meanness. And, just like in the novel, Claude doesn't trust Link, refusing to believe his claims that he is back for good. However, there is a difference between the two Claudes; in the film, it is obvious that as a kid, he was close to Link. "What happened, Claude?" asks Link. "We used to be pals." Unlike the novel's Claude, Mann and Rose use Dehner's talent for playing shrewd, articulate characters and make this one a far greater danger to Link than even the backstabbing Coaley. Plainly skeptical of Link's intentions, Dehner's Claude is allowed to let his guard down and proudly announce that he "loves that old man [Dock]." It's actually a touching speech, and Dehner puts the audience in Claude's corner as he indicts his cousin for running out on Dock and making him cry. However, the killer in Claude comes to the fore when he quietly issues the threat, "You're not gonna make it, Link." In many ways, it's the film's best performance.

At a stopover on their trip to Lasso, Link prods a furious Coaley into a knockdown, dragout fight. Mann's fight scenes were usually brutal affairs, full of face-clawing, kidney punches and all manner of kicking and stomping on vital body parts. (In his underrated film noir *Railroaded*, Mann has Sheila Ryan fight Jane Randolph in a claustrophobic living room set.) Usually, the helmsman insisted on grueling close-ups of his stars as they go through their suffering, with Cooper and Lord being no exception. However, there are also many long shots for obvious reasons. Cooper was then 56, and had already been injured in fight scenes as a young lead at Paramount. Possessing a bad back and busted ribs, as well as ulcers, the aging actor may have been in shape for a fight scene with Lloyd Bridges in the hay-covered stable in *High Noon*, but *not* a fight scene in an Anthony Mann film.

A MAN'S GOTTA DO WHAT A MAN'S GOTTA DO. Gary Cooper reloads in Anthony Mann's *Man of the West* (1958), the film version of Will C. Brown's *The Border Jumpers*. Unfortunately, the actor was about thirty years older than Brown's tormented hero.

Mann changed the fight's location; in the novel, Link accuses Coaley of stealing the money from his bag and starts the fight as a delaying tactic so that Billie can escape the Alcutt ranch on a stolen horse. The fight is predictably long and violent as the two men battle all over the small cabin, breaking chairs and other furniture until they take the fight outside where Link triumphs. Expanding on his theme of using natural outdoor locations, Mann "opens up" the sequence, taking into account the creative use of swinging tree branches in an antagonist's face, or having one of his fighters get slammed into the side of a whinnying horse. In previous Stewart westerns, Mann had the fights near flowing rivers (*The Naked Spur*) and in them (*Bend of the River*). As Link is beating a tiring Coaley, he repeats what Link did in the novel, which was order the outlaw to remove his clothes. With Coaley half-naked, Link is strangling him until his better side causes him to stop. This bit is also in the novel, and it works perfectly for Mann, whose heroes had always stopped themselves before they committed murder. When Coaley grabs a gun and threatens to kill Link, Beasley finds his courage and jumps in the way, taking the bullet instead. Dock then guns down Coaley.

During the interim, Billie has fallen for Link, despite the fact that she knows he will return to Lucy and the little ones. "I love touching you!" says the formerly jaded saloon singer to her twice-her-age rescuer.

Since the folks at Lasso will know the Tobin gang on sight, Link convinces Dock to let him go in and check out the place; unfortunately, he has to take Trout along just in case. Lasso, now devoid of people, is a long dead ghost town. When Link and Trout meet a scared Mexican woman pointing an old pistol at them, Trout unnecessarily kills her. Link then grabs the dead woman's gun and kills him. Gut-shot, the mute finds his voice and utters a bloodcurdling scream as he tries to run from town, finally dying at the edge of it. Now armed, Link waits for the remaining members of the gang to arrive. When they do, Link quickly guns down Ponce and finally kills Claude.

Link's killing of Claude, as the wounded outlaw takes shelter under the porch of an adobe house, is reminiscent of James Stewart's shooting of villainous judge John McIntire under the boardwalk of a saloon in *The Far Country*; the killing enacted under a building's foundations is symbolic of its proximity to Hell. However, there are some inconsistencies here. Not only does the cool and calculating Claude start to panic when he sees that his leg is useless, but Link's shout to Claude that the outlaw had been waiting to kill Link all his life is odd since the two also "used to be pals." Still, Link is truly sorry he had to kill his former childhood friend, and in a gesture of respect, he folds Claude's arms over his chest.

When Link returns to the camp, he finds a half-naked and beaten Billie in the covered wagon; the girl has been raped. Finding Dock on a nearby hill, Link spitefully tells him that his gang is dead. Shocked, the old man asks, "You killed *Claude*?" The question again emphasizes how close the two cousins were, and how tragic it was for Link to have to kill his childhood pal. At this point, Link becomes the Gary Cooper of the movies and says the time-honored line, "I'm takin' you in, Dock!" Link does not take the law into his own hands and kill his evil uncle for raping Billie. With the need for due process in mind, they emphasize Link's desire to turn Dock over to the law, not commit murder. In the novel, Link comes to realize the responsibility he now has:

> Fate had given him the opportunity to avenge great evils, such as it had not given even to the lawmen who represented decent society and who had tried long and fruitlessly to track down the elusive Dock Tobin band. He'd better make up his mind — was he going to run away again and leave the snake crawling or stay put and cut off its head?

After hearing about Claude's death, the old man cries out that he has nothing to live for any more and fires on Link, causing his nephew to return fire and kill him. Mann's reminder that Dock was, in his own way, a king of his own domain, is underlined by the blare of ancient trumpets heard on the soundtrack as the outlaw tumbles down the hill. Link finds the stolen money on Dock, but unlike his respectful treatment of Claude's corpse, he contemptuously leaves his uncle's body as it is. It is certainly a far more cinematic death than in the novel. In *The Border Jumpers*, Dock, now without his family and belatedly realizing that his life has been a waste, pulls out his gun and blows his brains out in front of Link and Billie.

As they head back to civilization, Billie tells Link that she knows she cannot have him, but will always cherish the feeling of having loved someone. In the novel, Billie suffers a far different fate than she does in the movie. Being a pulp western author, Will Brown had to avoid the kind of tough issues that Mann enjoyed confronting in his own "adult westerns" of the 1950s. In the novel, Dock only *attempts* to rape Billie, but the attack is interrupted by the gang's return. The gorgeous saloon singer has picked up fans throughout the west, despite the fact that she wants to give up that life and find a good man to settle down with. Hot on the gang's trail, however, is Texas Ranger Ray Duncan, a man who has coincidentally developed a crush on "the Girl with the Golden Voice." At the end, as Link returns to Lucy and the kids, Billie ends up in the loving arms of her new Ranger beau. Rejecting the novel's pat ending, Mann forces the audience to confront the issue of how a rape victim, who also happens to be in love with a married father of two, must now go through life all alone.

Audiences stayed away from *Man of the West*, with the nation's exhibitors unceremo-

CABIN FEVER. Lee J. Cobb (left) plays the gang leader uncle of Gary Cooper's former outlaw in *Man of the West* (1958). Julie London is caught between them. As in Mann's other films, the hero must destroy the villains in order to save his better self.

niously putting it on a double-bill with the low-budget film version of Ed McBain's *Cop Hater*. The reason for this was pointed out by the critics, and that was the casting of 56-year-old Cooper to play the novel's Link Jones, a man in his late twenties. Had Link's relative youth been retained, it might have made the temptation of *really* sleeping with the attractive Billie much harder to resist. In the film, when the young woman announces her love for Cooper's aging Link, we cringe. It was said that Jimmy Stewart was set for the role, and it was true that the actor hoped that Mann would cast him. However, their falling-out over Mann leaving the filming of U-I's *Night Passage* worked against the actor. Certainly, one can understand a director refusing to make a film his lead actor wanted to appear in merely because it allowed him to play the accordion on screen. Consequently, *Night Passage* was stolen by Audie Murphy as Stewart's amiable outlaw brother.

Despite the critics' carping that Stewart should have played the role, it's highly doubtful that the actor, seven years younger than Cooper, would have been a better choice; he *still* would have been a full twenty years older than the Link of the novel. In the scene where Link reminds Claude what pals they were as kids, audiences had good reasons to laugh. John Dehner was a good fourteen years younger than Cooper. Casting Stewart in the role and making him *seven* years older than Dehner wouldn't have been much of an improvement.

Howard Thompson, in his *New York Times* review of October 2, praised the film for being "well-acted and beautifully photographed." Ending his review, he noted: "The plot is actually little more than a battle of wits between Mr. Cooper and Mr. Cobb's gang. The turning point, a three-way gun battle in a ghost town is a pip. This is a small picture, but it does have a cryptic defiance and an aura of snakelike evil that gets one."[30] However, another of the film's reviewers was not as kind. Carl Foreman, the now-blacklisted screenwriter who wrote Cooper's *High Noon*, said: "I thought it was appalling—one of the sickest films I've ever seen. This was obviously a psychological western, with pretensions of being an adult western, and actually it was only an exercise in pure sadism."[31]

Man of the West is considered a minor classic today. In spite of the horrible miscasting of its leading man, some consider it Mann's best work (though it most definitely *isn't*).

At the time *Man of the West* was released in October 1958, Universal-International was in the process of shooting a western that broke new ground for its star, a man who was a hero off screen as well as on....

"Mr. Gant, who have you come to see?"—*Ann Benson*

Audie Murphy himself had considered his first villain role to be the Utica Kid in *Night Passage*. Though he does not get the girl, and indeed dies in the film, his comments on the role are interesting for what they reveal about a certain period in his film career. Audie said that he was "tired of sweetness and light" and claimed that he "is playing a bad boy and I love it."[32] Off-screen, Murphy was a blunt man who did not suffer fools gladly, yet it's quite possible these comments might have been encouraged by the front office at Universal. Hoping to promote the Texan as an actor of versatility, the studio had put him in *Night Passage*, with the appropriate publicity that he was playing a villain. However, all one had to do was read Norman A. Fox's original novel on which the film is based and the studio's claim is blown out of the water. As written by Fox and then portrayed on-screen by Murphy, the Utica Kid is about as "villainous" as a housebroken puppy.

In the fall of 1958, Universal-International was still experimenting with giving the actor offbeat parts in unusual settings. In their new production *No Name on the Bullet*, the town of Lordsburg was not an unusual setting, but Audie's part certainly was. Audie would now portray a character who had no one else but himself to blame for his criminal actions. Even Universal didn't realize the leap their top western star had made as an actor. John Gant is as close to a villain as Murphy would ever play, with the actor giving a performance that surprised those who thought he could only play the hero.

A lone rider named John Gant (Murphy) enters the town of Lordsburg and registers at the local saloon-hotel. When the proprietor, Sid (Charles Watts), calls him "Mr. Grant," the cool young man corrects him and announces his real name, throwing an uncomfortable chill on Sid and the poker-playing regulars in the room. After Gant goes upstairs, Henry Reeger (Simon Scott) and Chafee (John Alderson) are aghast that they have finally seen the famous Mr. Gant. A shocked Chaffee refers to him as "that kid." By this time, the "kid" was thirty-three, but still looked younger.

Ordered by Reeger to tell the sheriff of Gant's arrival, Sid passes crooked town boss Stricker (Karl Swenson) and his clerk, Lou Fraden (Warren Stevens) and also tells them of the gunman's appearance. Both men are fearful and question the reasons for Gant's visit, with the final rhetorical question, "What does Gant want anywhere?" held forebodingly in the air.

Once Sheriff Buck Hastings (the always dependable Willis Bouchey) and his deputy (Jerry Paris) hear Sid's horror-story version of Gant's reputation, the sheriff responds, not without a hint of professional respect, that "a killer's one thing; Gant's another." Officially in a class by himself, the gunman instills fear in people despite his courteous manners and quiet appearance.

After this introduction to the central character's reputation, our gentle little killer (this is what John Huston admiringly called Audie in his autobiography) visits the blacksmith Asa Canfield (future Peckinpah player R.G. Armstrong) to check on his horse. It is there that he meets Asa's son, Luke (Charles Drake), the town doctor. In the cinema of Audie Murphy, the casting couldn't have been more appropriate; Drake had been Audie's co-star for five films. Luke is Gant's ideological opposite, and eventually opposes him but harbors admiration for the man.

The doctor is engaged to lovely Ann Benson (Joan Evans, Audie's leading lady in *Column South*). The actress had been doing Republic westerns in the past few years, including William Witney's evocation of torn loyalties and family betrayal, the underrated film version of Todhunter Ballard's *The Outcast*. In *No Name on the Bullet*, Evans rises to the occasion, particularly in two standout scenes with Murphy. Ann's father is Judge Benson (Edgar Stehli), a man who is dying of consumption.

At the Canfield house, Luke and Asa's dinner is interrupted by the sheriff's appearance. Explaining to the innocent physician that Gant is not the fun-loving gadabout he thinks he is, the lawman also pulls out his gun emphatically to show that Gant himself is a kind of physician who prescribes medicine dispensed out of a six-shooter.

Meanwhile at Sid's place, Gant does nothing more murderous than ordering a cup of black coffee from Sid. Throughout the film, the gunman will be drinking it like it's going out of style. In this case, screenwriter Gene L. Coon (future co-creator of *Star Trek*) wisely rejects the concept of the swaggering gunslinger constantly guzzling rotgut whiskey in his favorite watering hole. In *No Name on the Bullet*, Gant's preference for coffee is obviously tied to the professional killer's occupational hazard of having to keep alert in the event of trouble. In Robert B. Parker's *Gunman's Rhapsody*, the author's conception of Wyatt Earp has him *never* taking a drink, but instead, constantly ordering coffee. Cautious to a fault, Parker's Earp always plants himself in a seat where he has a commanding view of the room, even to the point of using mirrors if he happens to be seated at the bar. Of course, it's perfectly logical that John Gant would also sit in what we today refer to as "the Wyatt Earp Seat," while drinking his favorite caffeinated beverage.

As Sid heats up another pot, the gunman is visited by Stricker and banker Thad Pierce. Pierce is played with appropriate spinelessness by the excellent Whit Bissell, a friend of No Name director Jack Arnold's since the days when both were actors on Broadway in the 1930s. (One particular collaboration that stands out is Arnold's cold-blooded performance as a Nazi opposite Bissell's spineless young man in Kaufman & Hart's *The American Way*, produced on Broadway in 1939. Now under contract to Universal as a director, Arnold always found a role for his old friend, casting Bissell frequently in his sci-fis and melodramas.)

Believing that an offer of money will make Gant leave, Stricker and Pierce underestimate the killer's honest dedication to his employer and the love he has for his job. To the horror of these self-important men, they see that Gant is incorruptible, and that he has nothing but contempt for those who aren't. Audie is especially chilling in this scene, with minimum gestures and eyes that reveal more than the dialogue. When Gant rejects their offer, Pierce tells him he's making a mistake. Staring bullets at the bank president, the gunman replies, "You'll never know, banker ... unless *I have come for you!*" The blunt statement about "coming for" someone is in itself frightening, Murphy's eyes conveying a punishment that drives the fearful little banker out of the saloon but fast.

Scared to death, Pierce locks himself in his own office as Luke and Gant prepare for filmdom's most important chess game since Max von Sydow faced Death in *The Seventh Seal*. They cast brief but suspicious glances at each other between chess moves; it is the first time Luke is facing Gant with the knowledge that he is a killer. Expertly parrying with the physician, keeping up the appearance of "a game," the philosophical hit man reflects that the real ills of people "are seldom physical," explaining that he's had more experience with those "ills" than Luke has. When a gunshot is heard from the bank, Gant is clearly the only one around who's not surprised, and it is implied that he is no stranger to suicides being committed in his vicinity.

When Luke confronts Gant after the banker's suicide, the wily gunman turns Luke's personal indictment of him into an indictment of the doctor, deriding a man who prolongs the lives of those who would "rob and lie again." It is a wonderful scene, Audie playing the character with just the right touch of irony and more than a little conceit. Gant may be violating the law, but the actor who plays him makes his case so simply and honestly, one can't help but respect the man. In a later scene, Luke himself admits to liking Gant, and expresses the typical do-gooder's wish that he can reform him. As we see in this scene, Arnold added little details to the characters and their backgrounds without the use of dialogue. Though Gant is seated at a bar, he is once again drinking his mandatory cup of coffee. As Luke and Gant discuss morality and justice, it is done with the saloon's mirror in the background, another Ingmar Bergman reference.

When the town council, run by the vindictive Stricker, contrives to get rid of Gant, they dig up an ancient law for the purpose. However, after calling Gant a "public nuisance" and drawing on him, Hastings is wounded by the gunman. When asked why he didn't finish the job, Gant replies bluntly, "I wasn't paid to!"

Now forming a vigilante committee of the town's most important citizens, Stricker leads his group to Gant's hotel in order to force the gunman out of town. Joining the mob is Luke and Asa, but only in an effort to resolve the matter peacefully. Rising to the occasion, Gant tells the vigilantes that, yes, they could very well kill him, "if you're willing enough," but as he goes down he'll take the mob's leaders with him. The group, faced with the prospects that *their* names might be on Gant's bullets, quickly disperse. A dozen years later, the scene will be repeated, almost verbatim, by Audie's future co-star on *The Unforgiven*, Burt Lancaster, in the excellent *Lawman*.

Ann Benson is also caught up in the madness. The next morning, she is accosted at the general store by Gant. It is a brief, but memorable scene, with Gant expressing admiration for judges "who have the power over life and death." Watching Murphy and Evans deliver this dialogue, it is hard to believe the same two actors played a down-to-earth cavalry lieutenant and snotty eastern princess in *Column South*.

Later, searching through her father's old papers (obviously kept around so he could get back at old cronies), Ann finds that own father was a thief who had collaborated with local and state officials in some unspecified crooked dealings. *Now* she knows who Gant is after.

Ignoring Sid's warnings not to disturb Gant, Ann goes up to his room and the gunman soon finds himself facing the business end of a derringer. Easily fooling Ann into believing her gun is unloaded, he disarms the young woman. Ann may be deprived of a loaded gun, but she still attempts to hit him between the eyes. Telling Gant she has discovered who his target is, she also accuses him of having a love for killing, a charge the gunman doesn't even bother answering. She also informs him that her dying father will not attempt to defend himself, thereby making Gant's "hit" a murder in the eyes of the law.

Backing the suddenly fearful young woman up against the wall, he rips her blouse, exposing the petticoat covering her cleavage. Arnold quickly cuts the scene on Ann's startled look. For a man with Audie's heroic image, the scene was a shock for its day. The gunman heads for the Benson ranch, as Luke and Asa go up to Gant's room and free Ann, who was left unconscious in the gunman's closet. From her they learn where Gant is headed.

DEATH AND THE MAIDEN. Joan Evans is protected by a gun-toting Audie Murphy in this posed publicity shot for the underrated *No Name on the Bullet* (1959). Using Audie's reputation as a soldier who killed 241 Nazis during the war, director Jack Arnold had the actor give one of his finest performances as hired assassin John Gant.

Gant quietly enters the Benson home and then approaches his intended victim. The director purposely makes sure Audie's footsteps are silent, as Death's would be. When Gant sees that the old jurist is not afraid, his victim replies that he and Death are old friends, and that he has no intention of resisting him; this Bergman-like dialogue is not usually found in your standard western. Seeing the old man's will to resist, Gant breaks it in record time when he pulls out a piece of Ann's blouse, his remarks implying the rape that never happened. Recognizing the material, the judge angrily leaves his wheelchair and grabs a loaded Winchester off the wall rack. Once outside, Gant draws his gun when the judge is about to fire, but to the gunman's astonishment, the judge finally dies of his consumption before he can kill Gant.

Luke, accompanied by Asa, rides up just in time to stop Gant from leaving the grounds. Facing a raised blacksmith's hammer, the gunman wounds Luke in self-defense. The physician, however, returns the favor by throwing the hammer right at Gant's gun arm, permanently damaging it. Painfully Gant picks up his gun and aims it at Luke, but his obvious respect for his opponent stops him from going through with the murder. After Luke is told that Gant *didn't* kill the judge, the physician offers to fix Gant's arm, but, true to his principles, the gunman replies with the strangely moving line, "Don't worry about it, physician. Everything comes to a finish...." With this statement, John Gant rides away, knowing full well the fate in store for an assassin who can no longer use his gun.

From the film's first frame to the final shot, director Jack Arnold evokes an atmosphere of tension and foreboding, much of this demonstrated in the measured, controlled way in which his characters move. Gant's ride over the title credits at the beginning, his unhurried saunter into the hotel, Asa's pause before shaking Gant's hand and, much later, Gant's final walk towards his victim, would indicate that the director gave a lot of thought to evoking a certain mood in which a silent Death walks among us. At the time, Ingmar Bergman's films were being imported to the U.S., *The Seventh Seal* being the film's main point of reference. When Gant checks into his hotel, he is given room number 7. Significantly, when Gant and Luke walk down the dusty street, the two men agree to meet for a game of chess. It is only then that Luke shakes Gant's hand, with the latter remarking that Luke "will make an interesting opponent." The handshake is purposely delayed until the two agree to play a game. Luke doesn't yet knw that Gant is seeking to play a game much bigger than chess.

Further examples of dialogue freely compare Gant to the Grim Reaper, with Hastings himself calling the gunman "a disease without a cure." Returning the compliment in his own way, Gant never refers to anyone by name (with the exception of "Miss Benson"), preferring to call people by their *occupation*, as we assume Death would. He calls Luke "physician," Pierce "banker," the proprietor of the general store "storekeeper," and Lou Fraden "little friend," an obvious sign of contempt.

The film is filled with flawed personalities: fallen men who had cheated and "sold out." Yet it is paranoia that truly dominates the comings and goings of the people of Lordsburg, with Gant's appearance awakening long-hidden fears that secrets will now come out into the open. The gunman openly calls Reeger "Dutch," implying a necessary change of identity for some unknown discretion; Lou Fraden has stolen the wife of a powerful rancher (a small but moving cameo by Virginia Grey) and fears that Gant has been hired to kill him for it; town boss Stricker has been moving in on Chaffee's silver mine and thinks that Chaffee has hired Gant to kill him; similarly, Chaffee believes that Stricker has hired Gant to kill *him* and steal the mine; and Pierce believes that Gant has been hired to kill *him* because of his own crooked past. As the philosophical Hastings says, it's a rare man who doesn't step on someone's toes.

Also gracing the film are two old coots who seem to have escaped from a PRC film of the 1940s. These two senile old men are forever playing games with each other, particularly checkers and horseshoes, though their biggest sport seems to be head games. As one accuses the other of constantly lying, these two varmints are almost a microcosm of the film's obsession with those who hide behind lies — and the punishment to come later. Arnold and Coon wisely use them as people who compliment the proceedings, rather than two vaudeville comics who stop the film for a hackneyed routine. Even when Gant sits on a railing and literally casts a shadow on their checker game, one of the old coots accuses the gunman of blocking out the sun — a universal symbol of life.

Yet even with our knowledge that Gant is a murderer, we are almost rooting for him to get away with his crimes. His victims are the corrupt, the weak and the ethically challenged. Paid by unseen employers to make sure that the crooked accomplices of their pasts don't live to indict them in the future, Gant rides the west prodding these doomed individuals to draw first, making their executions legal. The film is a potpourri of the many distortions and abuses of the law in the old west: hired gunmen, mob rule, an ineffective sheriff, factions battling over property, systematic local corruption, and, of course, the use of witnesses to avoid prosecution for shooting someone during a gunfight. There is also the western's traditional contempt for lynch mobs. When the crippled Benson suggests ganging up on Gant, Luke flatly turns down the idea of mob rule. After Gant slyly suggests that most of his victims deserved to die, Luke firmly argues that he wouldn't give Gant or any other man the right to punish anyone, "except for the law!" After Stricker and Rieger organize others to drive Gant out of town, Hastings confronts them and shouts, "A mob is not the answer!" All through *No Name on the Bullet*, the workings of mob rule and the missions of hired gunmen all come to naught (the film never once shows Gant actually killing anyone; all his killings had already taken place before the film starts). Instead, Gant is literally stopped by the one man in town he admires and actually compares himself to.

Friendless, alone, yet carrying with him an almost unworldly serenity in the face of fear and controversy, Gant upsets the status quo of Lordsburg as much as a certain Medal of Honor winner prodded the pretentions of Hollywood. Audie was not friendless or alone, but his war-related post-traumatic stress certainly made him isolated. Fighting sleeplessness, various physical pains and the stigma of "being bored to death," for the first time, the star portrays a killer who uses his gun to cure the west of "moral ailments." Seeing his paid assassinations as "a mission," Gant's appearance brought hidden sins to the surface in an era that would popularize the investigations of HUAC and the Kefauver Commission.

From its gloomy beginning to its sad ending, *No Name on the Bullet* confused audiences and critics of 1959 with its strange portrayal of a west that owed more to Albert Camus than Zane Grey. Seen as a cult film today, it also shocked those who always cherished Murphy as a cowboy hero. With John Gant, the actor went outside the limits of his usual roles and proved his versatility by playing a gunman with his own twisted set of principles. Critics praised Audie's attempt at change but were generally not happy to see their hero now playing a villain, no matter how principled (the *New York Daily News* did take note that Murphy "plays the triggerman with calculated stolidity"[33]). Audiences, particularly kids, didn't know how to react to this new Audie either. The results can be seen in his future projects for Universal. Never again would the studio cast him as anything but the reluctant hero who righted wrongs and helped those in need. They felt that John Gant was an aberration, an existential stain on their western star's heroic portfolio.

Previously showing a Gant-like ironic detachment to the usually cliché-ridden roles Universal was giving him, the actor was now starting to regret renewing his contract with the studio. Famously, he would say that the studio always had him playing the same character and doing the same stories, adding wryly, "Only the horses have changed." Indeed, it seemed that every time Murphy attempted to expand as an actor, Universal ended up deeming the experiment a failure and went right back to limiting his roles again.

A straight-shooter off screen as well as on, Audie certainly had no use for Hollywood backstabbing. According to his friend and fellow war veteran, cartoonist Bill Mauldin: "Audie took the hard way, cutting a swath through the *Wehrmacht* and then trying to do the same in Hollywood. There, in twenty years as an actor and producer, he found himself outflanked by people he called 'phonies' who wouldn't fight his way."[34]

After *No Name on the Bullet*, he would have just twelve years left in his film career, a short period of time for an actor so young and still full of potential. A Hollywood has-been at forty-six, the talented Murphy would die in a plane crash in a mountain range outside Martindale, Virginia, ironically on Memorial Day weekend of 1971.

Everything comes to a finish....

> "Tom would kill himself for Blaisedell, but you would do it for that silly star on your chest!"—*Kate Dollar*

Very few western authors have striven to tear the genre away from the clichés of the pulps and their bastard children, the B movie and the low-budget TV show. Yet in the postwar era, some writers endeavored to change the playing field, and elevate what had always been considered a cliché-ridden, action-oriented genre to new intellectual heights. The 1950s originated that overused and ridiculous term "adult western," as if only those under the age of eight had previously enjoyed them; or the term "psychological western," as if the genre's fans had little or no brains at all.

Contrary to popular belief, the genre had far more depth than the high-brows gave it credit for. On the apex of the postwar movement for more reality in previously cliché-ridden genres (such as film noir adding psychological dimension, better characterizations and starker photography to what had previously been known as "the gangster film"), were the many war heroes who, upon returning to the States, used their experiences to become best-selling writers. Veterans Norman Mailer and Irwin Shaw both wrote groundbreaking war novels that made the top of the bestseller lists (*The Naked and the Dead* and *The Young Lions*, respectively). However, one particular war hero addressed his combat experiences by putting them into a different genre, the western.

Oakley Maxwell Hall was born in San Diego on July 1, 1920, and joined the Marines shortly after the Japanese bombed Pearl Harbor (his native Southern California was also on high alert at the time, with Japanese bombardment of the Pacific coast a very real danger). It was while he was stationed on the island of Maui in mid-1945 as his batallion prepared for an invasion of the Japanese mainland that Hall started to write. After he returned to the States, he ended up writing over two dozen novels, some under a pseudonym, and even a libretto. He became a professor of English at the University of California at Irvine, and would end up married to the same woman (Barbara Hall) for 63 years.

However, thirteen years after he returned from the war, Hall wrote a western novel that stretched the possibilities of the genre far beyond the accepted formula of the day. Published by Viking Press in early 1958, *Warlock* did not inject controversial elements in the genre as much as inject psychological dimension and epic tragedy into the time-worn sagebrush formula of good vs. evil. Intricately detailed, with sharp characterizations and intimate knowledge of time and place, *Warlock* turned the age-old story of the town tamer who battles the bad guys into a tale of an all-too-human hero and the dysfunctional citizens who both admire and fear him. Far from being about male witches, the town called Warlock is a place where the Devil doesn't steal souls; he just borrows them once in a while.

The citizens of Warlock are being terrorized by powerful rancher Abe McQuown and his gang of evil cowboys. Lawman after lawman has been chased out or murdered by the gang and a list of the departed badge-toters has been scratched into the adobe wall of the deputy sheriff's office. Realizing that duly appointed lawmen don't last long in Warlock (the job pays a meager forty dollars a month), the town council (a new plot element in the postwar western, symbolizing the growing role of politics in the genre) decides to pool their money and hire an outside enforcer, a professional gunman who can break the hold of McQuown and the cowboys. And that man is gunfighter Clay Blaisedell! Blaisedell is a blonde-haired and mustachioed killing machine who has carved his name across the west by taming towns and getting paid very handsomely for it. Accompanied by his gunfighter pal Tom Morgan, Blaisedell has made his gruesome but necessary work count; towns under siege have tasted freedom for the first time in years. However, as we will see in Warlock, there are lessons to be learned and prices to be paid for these very same freedoms. According to Oakley Hall, war veteran and witness to fascist atrocities, just desiring to dispense with evil doesn't necessarily mean that all will be right with the world in the end.

With the novel selling well, Twentieth Century–Fox bought the rights in late 1958 and the property was set to be filmed at some point the following year. Still under contract to Fox after making the film version of Shaw's *The Young Lions*, Edward Dmytryk was penciled in as the director of *Warlock*. In his autobiography *It's a Hell of a Life, But Not a Bad Living*, Dmytryk complained of his unhappiness while filming the Shaw novel. Squeezed between the egomaniacal demands of star Marlon Brando and the alcoholism of co-star Montgomery Clift, the helmsman accepted the western assignment, hoping that it would be like a vacation. A former member of the Hollywood Ten, he had betrayed his Communist "friends" to HUAC. After his testimony, opportunites magically opened up for him and the former B maven found himself directing major Hollywood films with big budgets and A-list stars. Though a duplicitous man, and one whose claims should be taken with more than a grain of salt, Dmytryk nevertheless bore witness to a dreadful time in Hollywood history. With both the extreme left and the extreme right seeking to control the film industry, Dmytryk was that rare individual who had repudiated the politics of his fellow Communists while at the same time continuing to make films that attacked capitalism and America's sacred cows. For instance, his post-blacklist films differentiated little from those he made while he was still a loyal Party member. His obvious portrayals of the rich in films like *The Carpetbaggers* and *Where Love Has Gone* as dysfunctional psychopaths and self-absorbed alcoholics could have easily been scripted by Party demogogues John Howard Lawson or Lester Cole. Another trait of Dmytryk's is his penchant for extreme violence which bordered on the crude, tasteless, and especially the misogynistic. Only the Production Code stopped the helmsman from going over the line into the gory; when the precepts of the Code were broken once and for all in the 1960s, his scenes of violence and gore repelled audiences in schlocky works like *Shalako* and *Bluebeard*.

However, that was years later; it was now 1959. Dmytryk wrote that he worked on the *Warlock* script with former TV writer Robert Alan Aurthur, who had written only one film (*Edge of the City* with Sidney Poitier). With obvious admiration for the novel's author, Dmytryk wrote that Hall was "still the best of the writers to treat the Old West as something more than mere grist for the pulp mills."[35]

Dmytryk also wrote that the novel was good enough for two westerns: One being the story of mining companies terrorizing the miners, as well as the town, and the victims deciding to hire a town tamer to protect them; and the other the story of the town tamer and his close friend, gambler-gunfighter Tom Morgan. Dmytryk claimed that he decided to concentrate on the latter element; what he doesn't say, however, is that an attack on mining bosses in the Old West would be considered an attack on capitalism barely a few years after HUAC cleared him. Trying to attack America's sacred cows while at the same time not wanting to remind others of his Communist past, Dmytryk played it safe. In the film, no one knows exactly *why* Abe McQuown and his cowboys bully and murder the citizens of Warlock. Though there are mines outside of town, Dmytryk and his camera never once go near them; consequently we never see any mine owners terrorizing anyone, nor do we see any exploited and angry miners. McQuown is considered a cattleman, yet we never see any cows. It's as if McQuown and his men came from another film, didn't like it where they were, and decided to take it out on the people of Warlock.

In the town of Warlock, somewhere in the southwest, Deputy Sheriff Roy Tompson (Walter Coy) is waiting in his office nervously for Abe McQuown and his toughs to ride into town and do what they promised, which was murder the deputy sheriff—which would be *him*. On the adobe wall, standing out like some macabre blacklist, are the names of deputy sheriffs who have been scratched off due to the fact that they've been murdered. When McQuown (Tom Drake) and his men arrive, they call Tompson out. Bravely, the lawman meets McQuown on the street. The rancher's usual modus operandi is to set up the time-honored showdown in the streets and then cheat by having his opponent shot in the back by one of his men. When Tompson realizes that he is about to die, he turns tail and runs for his horse, causing the men to laugh uproariously, smear dirt in his face and further shame him by sending him out of town tied to his horse.

That night, after lots of drinking and other rowdy behavior, one of McQuown's men murders the town barber for accidentally nicking him with his razor. Dmytryk's penchant for violence comes to the fore by showing the barber, having fallen against the side of a horse trough, suddenly slide down, thus revealing the trough spouting water from two bullet holes, the slugs having passed completely through the poor man's body. One man is disgusted by it all, Johnny Gannon (Richard Widmark), whose younger brother Billy (Frank Gorshin) is a hot-headed tough perpetually spoiling for a fight. After the gang vanishes, the town council, led by storekeeper Henry Richardson (Vaughn Taylor) insists that they hire a town tamer to take on McQuown and his trash. And that man is Clay Blaisedell.

In the novel, it's obvious that Hall was doing his own spin on Wyatt Earp, Doc Holliday and the Gunfight at the O.K. Corral. It is doubly obvious when it is claimed that much of the self-proclaimed town tamer's fame is based on his decimation of outlaws at the unusually named Acme Corral. Some are against the idea of hiring a town tamer, like the handicapped Judge Holloway (Wallace Ford). Dropping in on the meeting unannounced is the slyly insinuating Curley Burne (DeForest Kelley). Blaisedell (Henry Fonda) and Tom Morgan (Anthony Quinn) arrive and take a room at the Western Star. Jessie Marlow (gorgeous Fox contract starlet Dolores Michaels) is opposed to hiring Blaisedell.

That night, the saloon is visited by McQuown and his crew. As Blaisedell stands ready for a throwdown (and is prodded by a subtly condescending Curley), McQuown has placed one of his men (the barber-killer) at the bar behind the new marshal. When things look tense and the dry gulcher is about to pull his hogleg, Johnny steps in and grabs the man's hand, spoiling the backshooting ambush. Outside, McQuown berates Johnny for interfering and the gunman is officially thrown out of the gang.

The next day, based on the info from the slovenly Fen Jiggs (a man who would have a long future in the western: L.Q. Jones), Morgan learns that gambler Bob Nicholson (Sol Gorses) is coming to Warlock with his pal Lily Dollar (who in the novel was named *Kate Dollar*; Dorothy Malone). Hours later, as the stage is pulling in, two of the gang, one being Johnny's younger brother Billy, stop the stage at gunpoint. Hiding in the hills with a rifle, Morgan guns down Bob Nicholson after Billy orders him out of the coach. Now with a corpse on their hands, the two bandits are forced to watch the stage roll away, leaving them empty-handed. After Lily arrives in town, Nicholson's death and the wounded stage driver galvanize Blaisedell to form a posse and hunt the two "murderers," especially Billy, who was recognized. Though others blame the stage bandits, Lily clearly accuses "a third gunman," the one hidden in the hills with a rifle. Apparently, there is a history to the characters here. Morgan was sweet on Lily and prodded his pal Blaisedell to have a showdown with Ben Nicholson, Morgan's rival for the saloon gal's affection. After the killing, Lily has harbored hatred for the town tamer and his handicapped shadow. It seems that Morgan has had a dual reason for killing Bob Nicholson: He murdered another rival for Lily's affections, and he also suspected that Lily enlisted Nicholson's help in killing Blaisedell; thus, by the dry-gulching, Morgan was protecting his pal as well.

THROWDOWN. Quick-draw Henry Fonda is about to open fire in *Warlock* (1959), the film version of Oakley Hall's sprawling novel. The film took a stand against lynch mobs and using hired guns in place of duly appointed lawmen.

Now with Billy locked in jail, Johnny joins the council in protecting his brother and his friend from a lynching. Confronting the mob, Blaisedell quickly buffaloes the mob's leader with his pistol, a typical Wyatt Earp move. Here, Fonda is doing yet another scene in his long film career condemning lynch mobs. When Sheriff Keller (the sympathetic rancher in *Along the Great Divide*, Hugh Sanders) transfers the two robbers for trial, he gladly appoints Gannon as the new deputy sheriff when he is the only one to volunteer for the job.

The formerly sarcastic Jessie has gotten close to Blaisedell, and Lily has now romantically gravitated towards the new deputy sheriff. After Billy and his co-bandit are found innocent of the murder, the two men return to town where the hot-headed young man challenges Blaisedell. When Gannon fails to get his brother to leave, the new marshal tries to talk the young man out of the gundown as well. Unknown to Billy, Ed Calhoun (veteran cowboy star Don "Red" Barry, reduced to a walk-on here) has been sent to dry-gulch Blaisedell while Billy throws down on the marshal. Morgan guns down Calhoun, a service the crippled gambler had performed for Blaisedell in many a town, unbeknownst to the famed gunfighter. Not willing to turn tail, Billy wounds Blaisedell in the arm, forcing the marshal to gun down the young man to protect himself. Frightened, the other McQuown man runs for his life.

Things are now coming to a head. After Blaisedell tells Morgan that he will marry Jessie, the gambler does not take the news well; and his rage over the marriage causes Blasidell to dissolve their partnership. Now the marshal orders McQuown and his men not to enter the town on penalty of arrest, which can only mean a showdown.

Trying to avoid killings, Gannon rides out to McQuown's ranch to try to talk him out of a confrontation. Instead, the crazed rancher and the man who murdered the barber beat the lawman senseless, culminating in McQuown grabbing a knife and impaling Johnny's gun hand. Here, the violence-loving Dmytryk almost relishes the attack of Johnny. Though he judiciously keeps the impaling of his hand out of camera frame, there is no mistaking Widmark's painful cry or the agony on his face. In more than one postwar western, the mutilation of the hero's gun hand is looked upon almost as a Christ-like stigmata. Randolph Scott gets his trigger finger stomped on in Ray Enright's *Coroner Creek*; James Stewart is shot through the right hand in Anthony Mann's *The Man from Laramie*; and now Widmark gets his hand impaled. Outraged and disgusted by the mutilation, the formerly loyal Curley Berne promises Johnny that he will not let McQuown have him backshot when they ride into town the next day.

After a painful night's sleep, Gannon rises to face McQuown and his gang. Even though his hand is not anywhere near healed, Johnny is willing to die for the principle of law and order. Though Blaisedell tries to persuade Johnny to accept his help, the deputy sheriff says that in order for the law to work, *he* must handle the trouble, not a privately hired gunman. During the meeting, Blaisedell talks about the first man he gunned down, and how easy killing came to him afterwards, though he always adhered to the rules of the game. In fact, Blaisedell's recitation of "the rules of the game" closely parallel those of Marshal Jared Maddox (played by Burt Lancaster) in *Lawman* eleven years later.

To stop Blaisedell from helping Gannon, Morgan holds him up in their room at gunpoint. When the gang arrives, McQuown has the barber-killer throw down on Johnny, but the lawman dives to the ground and, despite his wounded hand, kills him. Then, as McQuown's backshooter is about to kill Johnny, Curley appears and buffaloes him, keeping the promise to his friend to keep the gunfight fair. Surprisingly, the townspeople show up with guns and back up their new deputy sheriff in a way they never had before. Now outnumbered, the raging McQuown draws on Johnny and is gunned down. Law has returned to Warlock.

All is not perfect now that the evil McQuown and his killers have been vanquished. Realizing that he has permanently lost his close pal to a woman, Morgan gets drunk and shoots his pistol off dangerously close to citizens (apparently, he's still an accurate shooter even when drunk). However, when Morgan fires at his friend, the marshal returns fire, killing him. Drowning in grief (a subtly effective performance by Fonda), Blaisedell turns his rage on the men who hired him, cruelly kicking the crutch out from under the handicapped judge (an act that also happens in the book) and setting fire to the saloon. Gannon orders Blaisedell to leave town in the morning, but the gunfighter refuses, saying he will be ready for the lawman.

Knowing that he can't outdraw Blaisedell, for the second time in 24 hours Gannon shows moral courage and faces the seasoned gunman. However, after he is outdrawn, Johnny is surprised to see Blaisedell throwing his precious golden-handled pistols in the dust. (They were provided by a famous pulp western writer, much in the same way legend has it Ned Buntline gave Wyatt Earp his extra long-barrelled "Peacemakers.") Then, with a little smile on his face, Blaisedell mounts his horse and rides out of town, leaving Jessie behind. Relieved, Lily runs out and joins Johnny as the famed gunfighter leaves Warlock forever. Duly appointed law and order has triumphed over the privately hired gunslinger.

The intricacies of Hall's novel are far too numerous to mention here. As previously mentioned, Dmytryk (who claimed in his autobiography to have trimmed Aurthur's overlong screenplay) cut out plot elements that he surely would have retained had he still been on speaking terms with Party ideologues. Hall's subplot of miners being exploited by the mining bosses had been removed; so was the character of General Peach, the fanatical territorial governor, wistfully hoping for a return to the days of Indian-fighting; and the character of storekeeper Henry Holmes Goodpasture, who keeps diary entries of various happenings in Warlock. In the novel, Blaisedell kills Curley Burne; in the film, Curley not only lives, but helps save the day for Johnny. In the book, Tom Morgan kills the evil McQuown from ambush; in the film, Johnny guns him down out in the open as they have their faceoff in the street. In the novel, Lily Dollar is called Kate Dollar, but it is inferred that her real moniker is "Big-Nose" Kate Williams, another tie-in to the Earp-Holliday story (she's supposed to be Big-Nose Kate Elder). In both novel and film, however, Billy Gannon is clearly based on the hot-tempered and tenacious Billy Clanton, the youngest of the Clanton-McClaurey gang to face the Earps and Holliday at the O.K. Corral. He was the only one who, while dying, kept firing at his enemies until he ran out of bullets. Those who admired this young fighter would always say that he "died game."

Central to the action is the figure of Clay Blaisedell. A tall, blonde-haired and mustachioed man in the novel, he is portrayed by the lithe, dark-haired and mustache-less Henry Fonda in the movie. Yet Blaisedell is much more in the novel than in the film. In the book, the town tamer is seen by the locals as more than a man; he is a symbol, a deity, a vessel of action and ironclad resolve put on a pedestal by citizens who cherish inaction and compromise. He fulfills their needs for a hero, and they project onto him the qualities of heroism they themselves lack (after all, his name is *Clay*). His pal Tom Morgan has contempt for those who think of Blaisedell "as only a name, a thing, a machine to which they feed their pennies and out of him came the same trick which they could then class good or bad for their amusement." Even Blaisedell realizes that he has become, not a human being, but "a damned, unholy *thing*!"

Morgan clearly relishes the attention his pal is getting, and vicariously lives through him; the more he literally watches Clay's back and adds to his reputation for invincibility, the more he enjoys the fame which comes with it. A Clay Blaisedell could not exist without towns like Warlock. He is not a hero of the wilderness, a pioneer carving whole cities out of forests; the gunfighter needs the adulation that only a thriving community can provide.

In *Playing Cowboys: Low Culture and High Art in the Western*, Robert Murray Davis points out the fact that the novel's characters regard Blaisedell as Hemingway regarded bullfighters. Both are men of action who crave the applause only a town full of people can give them:

> [C]onsidered purely as gunfighter, Blaisedell needs the arena because a gunman lives in a Berkeleyan universe. If his antagonist falls in the forest and there is no one to see or hear, then he may have conquered, but he has not triumphed — a point demonstrated cinematically in *The Man Who Shot Liberty Valance*. He needs the spectators to bear witness as much as they need him to remedy their deficiencies in skill and resolve. For this reason, many westerns — and the climax of *The Virginian* — are set in town, not merely because it represents burgeoning civilization, as Robert Warshow thought, but because it provides a clearly defined area of conflict, a turf, an audience, and a sanction or excuse for violence that can be seen by and limited to the ritual of the gunfight.[36]

In the novel, after Blaisedell throws down his guns and rides out of town, thus letting duly appointed law and order take control, he is headed towards a mountain range appropriately called "the Dinosaurs."

As Davis noted, Gannon "becomes the suffering servant, a Christ figure without cult, almost without recognition, because he is able to understand as well as to act, because he is able to move from the bondage of guilt to the freedom of responsible choice, and because he is able to embody the best impulses of the society that he serves and helps, if only for a time, to transform."[37] Even the cynical Tom Morgan compares Gannon's face to "one of those rude *Christos* carved by the Mexican Indio with more passion than talent." In both novel and film, then, it's not much of a surprise that Gannon's right hand would be mutilated by McQuown's knife, giving the principled lawman a kind of stigmata.

However, besides Christ comparisons and the veneration of Wyatt Earp clones, perhaps the most controversial element of *Warlock* was what many have seen as a gay relationship between the characters of Clay Blaisedell and Tom Morgan. Coincidentally, *Warlock* is not mentioned once in Henry Fonda's as-told-to autobiography, co-authored with Howard Teichmann (though he *does* talk about the inferior *Firecreek*). In his autobiography, Dmytryk wrote:

> There was an interesting relationship between the marshal (Blaisedell) and his right-hand man (Morgan). Many critics and viewers thought it might be homosexual (a no-no at the time). Actually, it wasn't — it was a good deal more complex than that, and of more than passing interest to the audience. The big duel in the street was not between the hero and the villain, but between the hero and his best friend — and not for reasons of hate, but of misdirected love.[38]

It is worth noting that while Dmytryk totally denied that there was a gay relationship between Blaisedell and Morgan, he still saw the climactic shootout as being caused by "misdirected love." Certainly, both Hall and Aurthor (if not Dmytryk) imply quite a bit. Besides Morgan's obvious talent for interior decorating, including getting those new curtains, the gambler has a bum leg (in the language of dime store psychologists, this means sexual frustration). Though the gambler did desire Kate Dollar (called Lily in the film), he has now apparently shifted his focus to his iconic gunfighting pal, and is possessive enough to threaten Dollar to keep her away from him. However, the dandified gunman really hits the roof when Clay tells him he wants to marry Jessie; and it is their subsequent argument over her that causes a break between them. After Blaisedell kills his friend, he orders the townsmen to "keep their hands of him," personally carries him to the saloon and sends him out, Viking-style, with a burning funeral pyre.

It is obvious that Hall based the character of Tom Morgan on Doc Holliday, with the author giving him a bum leg rather than TB. However, had anyone said to Doc that his friendship with Wyatt was based on suppressed homosexuality, it's a sure thing that individual would have had four or five bullets coming out of the back of his head.

Hall offers an interesting theory as to why his iconic gunfighter backed down to Gannon and let the law take over. In the book's afterword, he has Henry Holmes Goodpasture suggest the reason in a letter the storekeeper wrote to his grandson, Gavin Sands, in 1924. While guessing that Blaisedell ended up becoming a lawman and possibly being murdered in one town or another, one theory as to what happened to the gunfighter stood out: "The most common [rumor] has been that Blaisedell had been half-blind when he left Warlock, and soon completely lost his sight. Consequently, there were a number of tales, variously embroidered, concerning tall, fair, blind men represented as being Blaisedell." Here, Hall intriguingly merges the illness that befell an aging Wild Bill Hickok with that of the Earp legend. Unfortunately, Hall doesn't exploit this; it is just mentioned briefly by a supporting character near the end of the book.

In his May 1, 1959, review in the *New York Times*, Bosley Crowther called *Warlock* "good, solid, gripping western fare." Of the three leads, the critic wrote, "Mr. Fonda, as usual, is excellent — melancholy, laconic and assured — and Mr. Widmark is properly nervous but full of sincerity, and spunk. Mr. Quinn lays it on a little heavy in a slightly pathetic role, but he adds his measure of drama to the final rock-bottom goings-on."[39]

With *Warlock*, the 1950s westerns came to a close. The decade that started with a continuance of the Cold War, Stalinism and the Blacklist ended with further continuance of the Cold War, years of prosperity, and a new president waiting in the wings. During the Kennedy years, the western film, influenced by its lower-budgeted TV model, returned to Bs with a vengeance, though without any minor star to reprise the years of the series western. Only Audie Murphy, his career slipping as he made cheap western remakes of what were cheaply made Bs to begin with, survived to connect the 1950s western to the newer, more violent European-made model. With political assassinations and deeper involvement in Vietnam on the horizon, Hollywood tried to shoot westerns with all-star casts, wide screens and full color which lacked the cut-to-the-chase action and unpretentious charm of even the most minor Republic effort.

With the nation headed for turmoil, the preservation of law and order in the old west seemed minor opposite our incursion into the jungles of Southeast Asia where the Vietcong emphatically did *not* believe in "innocent until proven guilty."

In the following decade, with the censor's dictates on screen violence crumbling as rioting hit the nation's streets and campuses, vengeance-obssessed cowboys in these new westerns would bring a new dimension to the Unwritten Law.

5

Deadly Force: 1960–1969
Riding the Vengeance Trail as War Breaks Out at Home and Abroad

"He got carried away with a shiny tin star and all the good with it...."—*Nona Williams*

The westerns produced by A.C. Lyles and Paramount in the 1960s didn't exactly age like fine wine, though the films' atmosphere of over-the-top delirium certainly suggests that someone was on a bender while they made them.

Produced from 1964 to 1968, they were double, and sometimes triple-bill fodder at grindhouses across the country—especially that grindhouse mecca, Times Square. Steve Fisher wrote nine of these opuses. Fisher was a mystery and western novelist whose copious output almost, though not quite, put pulp maven Frank Gruber to shame. Unlike that old hack, Fisher was good enough to still be working almost to his death in 1980, turning out scripts for TV shows like *Fantasy Island*. With the Lyles westerns, the key word here was indeed *fantasy*. The scripts were drowning in clichés, with no discernable rescue effort in sight. This was surprising since Fisher was the author of the classic noir *I Wake Up Screaming*, written in 1940. He did the screenplays for dozens of '40s and '50s thrillers like *Dead Reckoning*, *Lady in the Lake*, *Tokyo Joe* and *City That Never* Sleeps; in the western genre, he had scripted Budd Boetticher's *The Man from the Alamo*, and for Republic he wrote *San Antone* and the feminist *Woman They Almost Lynched*. By the 1960s, however, most of Fisher's scripts were written for TV or the foreign film market; though still in demand, it looked like there would be no more *Lady in the Lake*s in his future. Nevertheless, thanks to Fisher's participation, as well as the producer's penchant for casting aging actors, the Lyles westerns took on a certain tone. Though one can easily laugh at Fisher's we've-seen-it-all-before plots, as well as the appearance of actors some might consider far too old for their roles, the films' lack of pretense and, in many cases, lack of intelligence, give them a kind of raw charm.

On the distaff side, many of them were just plain absurd. Apparently there are no saloon gals in these films younger than Jane Russell or Virginia Mayo; fistfights between middle-aged leading men and middle-aged bad guys happen at the drop of a hat, with the direction of a fading R.G. Springsteen or Lesley Selander doing little to hide the fact that they are doubled by stuntmen half their age; Native American characters (usually the Apaches) lost all their skill and cunning, as well as their admirable horsemanship, and openly presented themselves before the heroes so they could be shot. If there were any young people in these films (like the Fisher-scripted *Young Fury*), they were minor characters. Many of Lyles' grizzled actors were or had been alcoholics, and unfortunately, with the producer working on a low budget, there were no retakes when someone like Wendell Corey would blow his lines in *Buckskin*. Many of these westerns are reminiscent of the simplistic Bs made at Monogram or PRC, except that Lyles' efforts were longer and in color.

Yet, in 1966, Fisher wrote a script (based on a treatment by him, Lyles and Andrew Craddock) that stood out among the other Lyles-produced yarns. The acting was still either non-existent or over-the-top, and it was hard not to laugh at certain aspects of the production. Yet *Johnny Reno* stands out as a western that spoke up for the need for due process and took a stand against mob rule, its storyline quite pertinent in the mid-1960s since it also dealt with matters of race.

First we will hear the laughable title tune about the wonders of Johnny Reno, sung over the credits by a little-known vocalist named Jerry Wallace (trying to sound like Elvis) and his two unfortunate female backup singers (trying to sound like an angelic choir but sounding more like *Ted Mack Amateur Hour* rejects). U.S. Marshal Johnny Reno (Dana Andrews) is riding through the desert and being spied upon by brothers Ab Connors (Republic stuntman-actor Dale Van Sickel) and Joe Connors (Tom Drake). Believing that the lawman is chasing *them*, the quick-tempered Ab opens fire. A shootout commences and Reno kills Ab and wounds Joe in the arm. Then, to the wounded man's torment, he finds that Reno was not chasing them at all; he was just headed to the town of Stone Junction on a "personal matter." Apaches try to seize Joe, accusing the wounded man (and his dead brother) of having murdered the chief's son, Ed Little Bear, but Reno stands in their way.

When Reno arrives in Stone Junction with the wounded Connors, he finds a lynch mob atmosphere there, with the townsfolk happy to forestall an attack on the town by turning the wounded man over to the Apaches. Reno will not let them have him. He meets the town's cowardly Sheriff Hodges (frequent Lyles player and close friend, Lon Chaney Jr.) and bullies him into locking up Joe and not turning him over to the ruthless Mayor Jess Yates (Lyle Bettger) and the mob. Also prominent in the crowd of bloodthirsty citizens is storekeeper Jake Reed (Robert Lowery), Ed Tomkins (John Agar), Ned Duggan (frequent Paramount player Richard Arlen) and Yates' daughter Marie (Tracey Olson).

Handling that "personal matter" he spoke of, Reno visits the saloon run by his former sweetie Nona Williams (the former "full-figured gal" herself, Jane Russell), who has made herself scarce since she doesn't want to see Reno again. When Reno refuses to turn Joe Connors over to the mob, Mayor Yates attacks the lawman. This plot point is ridiculous; if Yates *really* wanted to force Reno to change his mind and use violence to do it, why didn't *all* the men gang up on Reno instead of just the mayor? Of course, this is done in order to give us yet another of Fisher's patented (and usually laughable) fight scenes. There is an increase on the laugh meter here when we can easily see Dale Van Sickel (who was killed in the first reel) doing the stunting for Dana Andrews, and a younger man with more hair on his head than Lyle Bettger doing *his* stunts. Still, director R.G. Springsteen (formerly of Republic) tries to make the fight more action-packed by taking it outside in the street and then having the victorious Reno dump His Honor soundly in the nearest horse trough. Reno, with some help from Hodges, thwarts the efforts of Reed and his mob to hang Joe.

Reno visits Joe in his cell to get the skinny on the murder of Ed Little Bear. It seems that when the Connors boys rode into Stone Junction, they were feted as if they were family, given free drinks and bid a fond farewell as they rode out of town. On horseback they were passing Ed Little Bear, apparently an Indian who spoke English and knew much of the white man's ways, and Ab noticed that the young man "already looked like a dead man propped up on his saddle." Then gunfire rang out and the Indian fell off his horse. Before the Connors boys knew it, they were being accused of having shot down the young man. Now the chief is looking to capture the Connors brothers. Yates and the townsmen want to deliver Joe Connors to the tribe as a *corpse*.

Yates and his saloon crew have sent their womenfolk and childrenfolk away because they heard that the Indians will ride in and burn the town. Nona, still pining for the aging, taciturn lawman, sticks around. That night, Yates and his men attack the jail. After Hadley is gunned down saving Reno, the beleagued lawman releases the innocent Connors and gives him a

JOHN LAW. Dana Andrews in the role of *Johnny Reno* (1966). Probably the best of producer A.C. Lyles' usually cliché-ridden Paramount westerns of the 1960s, the film not only took a stand against lynching, but its racial subplot added a note of urgency during the Civil Rights era.

gun. Reno even starts chucking lit sticks of dynamite at their attackers (what were sticks of dynamite doing in the sheriff's office?). In the explosions to follow, the vindictive Reed and several of Yates' men are blown to bits. During the siege, the usually brown-nosing Ed Tomkins leaves Yates.

The next morning after the bloodbath, Joe purposely knocks out Reno so that he'll be spared, believing that he's doing at least one honorable thing in his life. Surrendering, Joe finds that Yates will not keep his word; his men pull the groggy Reno out to the street besides Joe so that both men will be killed. But no one wants to pull the trigger on a federal marshal. All the time, Yates had treated his partners in the town's business community as willing collaborators; that way, when they kill someone, he'll always have something on them. Reno immediately sees this and says that Yates will have to pull the trigger himself for a change. While this is debated, the Indians ride in with the tortured Ed Tomkins on one of their saddles. With blood streaming down his face (Lyles was very big on gore), the dying man is forced to say that Yates had Ed Little Bear gunned down because he was seeing his daughter. It seems that Yates had married an Indian, and his dark-haired daughter is a result of that union; the mayor has been keeping it a secret that he's a "squaw man," a racist term meaning a white man married to an Indian woman. With Eddie Little Bear and his daughter falling in love, Yates saw his own interracial marriage repeating itself and had the young man murdered, then framed the Connors boys.

After this is revealed, Yates shoots Tomkins in the head and multiple fights and shootouts break out. Several of the Indians, including the chief, are killed, as well as Yates' few remaining men. When the murderous mayor tries to run away, he trips on the noose left at the tie rail and is gunned down by Reno.

Only Reno and Connors are left alive. After Nona returns, she decides to settle down with the lawman, and it is implied that Stone Junction, now rid of its racist mayor and his men, will become a real American town again.

Here is one of the few times Lyles brings up issues of race in his usually cliché-ridden works. At a time when southern blacks had to face police dogs and firehoses as the federal government tried to force racists to treat them as equals, *Johnny Reno* shows a federal marshal trying to enforce due process in a western town under the thumb of a racist mayor. Touting itself as "respectable," Stone Junction has several skeletons in its collective closet, just as the "noble south" kept feeding itself a "moonlights and magnolia" glorification while enacting the brutal laws of Jim Crow. Like the south, the town of Stone Junction finds its soul only after federal intervention, in this case personified by a U.S. marshal. And again, like many southern whites of the 1960s, Jess Yates fears the "horrors" of miscegenation, with the inference that his daughter, half-white and half-Indian, will marry the son of a chief and further "contaminate" the white bloodline. Further confusing the issue is the fact that Ed Little Bear has been accepted by the folks of Stone Junction, or, in white parlance, is considered "civilized." Even Joe Connors, when accused of having been spooked by the sight of Eddie Little Bear to the point of shooting him, insists that "that was no painted savage. We weren't scared." It is one of *Johnny Reno*'s saving graces that Fisher has enabled the audience to get a full picture of Ed Little Bear, the victim of the shooting, without that character actually appearing anywhere in the film.

However, the film still has its schlocky A.C. Lyles touches. One of these is Fisher's rather far-fetched detail in Ed Little Bear's murder that he was already a corpse propped up on a horse and that the Connors brothers didn't notice that they were riding past a dead man. (How did Yates get the body to sit upright on the saddle, Crazy Glue?) There's the bloody but laughable fight scene between Andrews and Bettger, with Springsteen clumsily revealing the faces of the stuntmen. Richard Arlen shows up long enough to show that he's Richard Arlen and then disappears. And, of course, the Indians are so respectful of Johnny Reno's name that they don't do what they realistically would have done, and that's blow away the monosyllabbic lawman and then take Joe Connors back to their camp for a memorable torture session.

There's much to say for Andrews' performance, with the word "asleep" being the one that most comes to mind. According to Lyles, Andrews, a former drinker, was having Alcoholics Anonymous meetings on the set (with the producer expressing fear that he'd be in deep trouble if his alcohol-loving cast went on a toot[1]). However, there was no denying that Andrews is sometimes slurring his words and sleepwalking through the film. In fact, the actor seems to go out of his way to make Reno the most dislikable lawman who's ever hit the west. He bullies the weakling Hodges, and when the sheriff finds his courage and loses his life to save Reno, the federal man makes a brief throwaway comment and that's it. Instead, it's up to John Agar's Ed Tomkins to issue Hodges' epitaph, "You never know about a man."

In a scene at Nona's ranch, Russell is the only one giving a performance, Andrews not showing even a *hint* of emotion. In the jail scene when Joe is telling Reno why the town is after him and his brother, Andrews tries little scene-stealing tricks, like purposely crossing in front of the camera as Drake is doing his monologue — an act which forces the actor, sitting on his jail cot, to uncomfortably shift his position so that he'll be seen.

Though Russell and Chaney try very hard, the film's best performance is probably Tom Drake's. If one can get past his anachronistic 1960s crewcut, as well as his strong Brooklyn accent, he's convincing as an innocent saddle tramp used as a pawn to justify Ed Little Bear's murder. Meanwhile, as Andrews barely gives a performance, Lyle Bettger overacts his role as the psychotic Jess Yates. He conveyed evil far more subtly in his 1950s westerns; here, the aging actor practically froths at the mouth while spouting Fisher's usually risible dialogue.

Though the film can be seen as a statement about racism against African-Americans in the 1960s, Lyles, Fisher and Paramount made sure that things didn't go *too* far (these films had frequent bookings in southern theaters). For instance, the wrongly accused man is *white*, not a person of color. The people of Stone Junction seem to have treated Ed Little Bear with respect, and the mayor pretends to be going after his murderers; it's only at the end when Yates and his men are about to kill Reno and Connors that the mayor admits to not caring about "a dead Indian" or "dead saddle tramps," as he extols the virtues of his "model community."

As A.C. Lyles continued to grind out the kind of western schlock that would be his trademark all through the 1960s, his home studio, Paramount, was preparing a western that repudiated the Steve Fisher formula of the aging lawman and his aging saloon gal sweetie fighting aging villains. The new film would feature a character created by a bestselling author, a young half-breed Indian in search of the murderers of his parents. And it would star one of the most iconic figures of the decade.

> "The kid's creepy, he ain't human! He doesn't kill people, he executes them!"
> — Tom Fitch

In 1964, Paramount had a hit with the film version of Harold Robbins' schlocky bestseller *The Carpertbaggers*, with its blistering portrayal of a dysfunctional movie mogul-aviator which closely resembled dysfunctional movie mogul-aviator Howard Hughes. As directed by Edward Dmytryk, *The Carpetbaggers* was another in the long line of over-the-top campfests which added to the auteur's decline; there would be no more Oscar-nominated *Caine Mutiny*s in his future, just the horrors of *Shalako* and *Bluebeard*.

However, *The Carpetbaggers* did introduce an interesting character who almost stole the attention away from the lunatic shenanigans of Jonas Cord: an ex-outlaw and gunfighter, but now, merely a silent film cowboy, Nevada Smith. The role gave the dying Alan Ladd his final bow on screen. For the most part, it was a dignified exit; that is, if you ignore Dmytryk's staging of the brutal and bloody fight scene near the end (Ladd vs. young George Peppard). Though Dmytryk clumsily shows us the doubles doing the stunts, when Ladd is in closeup, he's the same tough guy who beat up so many bad guys in his Paramount thrillers of the forties.

Paramount was going to do a prequel with the Smith character, set in the old west. It is said that Ladd was supposed to star in it (which would make the proposed project the first time he would star at his old studio since 1953), but the actor's death at 50 put a crimp in the studio's plans. This, of course, is the popular story. In fact, one wonders just how the studio, with all the makeup people on the planet, was going to turn the 50-year-old actor into a young man of sixteen who had his parents murdered and vows revenge. By 1964, the underrated Ladd was ravished by alcohol and physical illness; that he was able to still look good while beating up the much younger George Peppard in a knockdown dragout fight was in itself amazing. Still, to have various characters, including main villain Tom Fitch, refer to the middle-aged Ladd as a "wet-nosed kid" would have drawn laughter from audiences.

Ultimately, Paramount went to the actor who had starred in their cult classic *The Blob* (1958) and more recently, the studio's *Hell Is for Heroes* (1962). Certainly, things had changed a *lot* for Steve McQueen in the four years between his battling outer space jelly and his gritty work in the Don Siegel film. He had starred on TV as an old west bounty hunter in the hit series *Wanted: Dead or Alive*. Bounty hunters, as a rule, were mostly portrayed as money-hungry, cold-blooded murderers; McQueen made the character of Josh Randall immensely likable. His youth, charm and non-showy, realistic portrayal made him a star. His combination of toughness and innocence was rarely projected so successfully. At this time, only Audie Murphy had projected this quality on screen (ironically, both men had grown up in poverty and both had fathers who walked out on their respectives families). But Steve also had a background on Broadway and Lee Strasberg's Actor's Studio. This added some Method to his performances (until he grew out of it).

By the time Paramount offered him the role of Max Sand in *Nevada Smith*, he was a top star, with *The Great Escape* and *The Cincinnatti Kid* under his belt. A man who didn't have much schooling, rarely read anything, and didn't have decades of acting experience behind him, Steve was a genius at knowing what worked for him and knew exactly how to "edit himself" on camera. As a star (and even before he became one), he demanded that he be given *less lines*, an amazing thing for an actor in a vain business to demand, but McQueen knew best. Besides being a good judge of what worked for him onscreen, Steve could also be, to the suits at the studios and various people he'd worked with, a royal pain in the ass. Moody, sometimes paranoid, hard-driving, competitive and naturally ornery, McQueen was also a professional who went all the way for a project when he believed in it. After being offered the script to *Nevada Smith*, he was planning on making the studio wait while he made his decision; that is, until his wife Neile convinced him to take on the role before anyone else did.

Our story begins in the southwest in the 1880s. Young Max Sand (McQueen) is working on the range near his parents' home when three men ride up and ask him how to get there, since they want to see his father. Max is a half-breed, the son of a white father and an Indian mother (with blonde-haired midwesterner McQueen in the role, it's pretty hard to accept this). Still, Max knows something's wrong when the three suddenly scatter the family's horses, making it difficult for the young man to follow them. These three louts are Tom Fitch (Karl Malden), Bill Bowdre (Arthur Kennedy) and Jesse Coe (McQueen's fellow Strasberg alumni, Martin Landau). At the house, the three men beat and torture Max's father Sam (Gene Evans) and his mother to get their hands on Sam's gold (which apparently is not as much as the three thought). By the time Max is able to make it to the house on foot, the three men are gone and his parents have been mutilated and murdered. ("They don't even look like human beings any more," Max laments.)

The opening scenes drew the attention of the Production Code office. In a letter to Paramount executive Erwin Gelsey, dated June 22, 1965, PCA head Geoffrey Shurlock wrote:

> The first of these problems has to do with the questions of brutality and cruelty. We understand that it is necessary to have certain scenes of extreme cruelty to open up this story, so that [Max's] motivation throughout the body of the script would be intelligible. However, it is incumbent on your director to use prudence and good taste in the presentation of the killing of

Max Sand's father and mother, and to get as much of this over to the audience as possible by suggestion rather than photographing it in gruesome detail.[2]

Director Henry Hathaway almost crosses over into brutally violent Edward Dmytryk territory when Jesse starts slicing his knife down the mom's back. Being a proud Indian, she says, "I am not afraid." Part of her Native American pride, however, might have been prompted by the censor's warnings about showing too much. In a letter to Gelsey, dated July 14, Shurlock wrote "When her clothes are ripped off, her breasts should not be exposed, nor should there be a *full* nude shot of her from the rear. Also, we caution you regarding the use of the knife on her body."[3]

Following Shurlock's suggestions, the helmsman wisely pulls back on the crude violence, whereas Dmytryk probably would have extended the torture scene. When Max finds his parents' bodies, Hathaway makes sure we never see them; Max enters the dark house, his figure silhouetted in the open doorway, and then he backs away slowly. McQueen is excellent in this scene, purposely underplaying; no tears, no tantrums or rages. The young Method actor reacts quite differently here than he did when his hero discovers a victim of the ectoplasm *The Blob*; he had grown considerably as a performer.

Max ignores the warning of his uncle Ben McCandles (John Doucette) that revenge is against God's law, since his inclinations are more in line with his feisty aunt (Josephine Hutchinson) who says, "Go get 'em, Max!"

Max spies a camp with two strange men in it; he is about to gun down one of them when he is jumped by a third man. After a brief fight, he is accepted by them and bygones seem to be bygones. That is, until he wakes up the following morning and finds that the three men have relieved him of his horse and saddle and everything on it. Soon Max happens upon a traveling gun salesman and trader named Jonas Cord, the grandfather of George Peppard's character in *The Carpetbaggers* (and played by the wonderful Brian Keith). Feeling sympathy for the hungry youngster, Cord agrees to not only feed him, but teach him how to use guns to help him on his quest. Cord also tells the young man that, as he's tracking the three killers, he'll be forced to hang around in sleazy saloons, get a taste for rotgut whiskey and generally lower himself to their level, a deal with the Devil that Max is more than willing to make.

By the time Jonas leaves him, Max has become, under the older man's tutelage, a crack shot. Going from one town to another and taking odd jobs to live, Max finds Jesse Coe gambling in a saloon (the killer is stupid enough, after all this time, to still be riding the same horse he stole from Sam's spread). After being called out, Jesse plays for time and then breaks a chair over the head of the sympathetic bartender (veteran bad guy Ted DeCorsia, on the side of the angels for a change). Max chases Coe into a cattle pen where the two have a brutal knife-fight. When Max's blade guts the killer, it's one down, two to go.

Learning that Bill Bowdre has been sent to a Louisiana prison camp, Max pulls a gun on a bank teller and purposely gets himself locked in the bank's vault so that he'll be sent to the same prison. A bit extreme, perhaps; he could have just let him rot in prison, but no! Max has to do things *his* way, kinda like the actor playing him. The prison camp is surrounded by swamps filled with moccasins, crocodiles and other slimy creatures. When Bowdre is brought back after an escape attempt, he is whipped and left to drown until he is saved by—you guessed it—*Max*. Predictably, the scene prompted a complaint from Geoffrey Shurlock. ("This whipping scene seems in danger of being prolonged to an offensive degree. We urge much care in this regard."[4])

After hooking up with female prisoner Pilar (dark-haired Suzanne Pleshette tries, but doesn't quite make it as a Cajun), Max is able to get hold of a boat and the two of them, with Bowdre along, attempt to escape at night. Pilar is fatally bitten by a moccasin, but with her waning strength (and Max's rather sadistic prodding) is still able to guide the boat far away from the camp. Not dealing with the hardship of escaping in a rickety boat in a crocodile-laden swamp very well, Bowdre makes a racist remark about Indians to get at Max, and is shocked when his fellow escapee brings up the killings of his parents. Wallowing in the water, Bowdre claims that the others killed his folks and begs mercy, but Max isn't buying it. Possessing a gun he stole off prison trustee Big Foot (Pat Hingle), Max shoots him several times. Pilar then rejects Max, accusing him of using anyone, including her, on his quest for vengeance. Grasping her crucifix, she dies from the snake's bite and Max escapes his pursuers.

THE COOL COWBOY. The one and only Steve McQueen as *Nevada Smith* (1966). Though not looking one bit like the half-breed Indian youth Harold Robbins created in *The Carpetbaggers*, the actor excelled as a cowboy who rode the Vengeance Trail.

Now a wanted man with a price on his head, Max returns to the west where he tries to track down Tom Fitch. Thrown into jail by Sheriff Bonnell (Paul Fix), he is broken out by Fitch's men (Max purposely pretended he *was* Fitch to order to smoke him out). When they realize that they broke out the wrong man, the three men grab Max and sadistically drag him through a lake until he is saved by the appearance of Father Zaccardi (Raf Vallone). Max heals physically, but not spiritually, as Father Zaccardi tries to turn the young man from his vengeance quest.

Finding out where Fitch and his men are hidden, and calling himself Nevada Smith, Max is offered a chance to join them on the robbery of a gold shipment. When the robbery occurs, Fitch and his men murder the men guarding the shipment and help themselves to the gold. But when Fitch looks up and sees Max looking down on him from a hilltop, the killer suddenly realizes who he is. Max chases Fitch all the way to a stream where he fires three bullets into him, one in his arm and two at his legs (including a painful shot at his kneecap). In agony, Fitch challenges Max to finish him off, but the young man makes a sudden realization: "You're just not worth killing...." After throwing his pistol away, like many a western hero from years past, Max rides off with his honor intact.

When Henry Hathaway called for a first meeting with his star, he laid down the law;

basically, that he was the boss and that "I'm not nice not to be nice to." McQueen's response: "Listen hard and you'll hear my teeth chattering." Though McQueen did have a good professional working relationship with the usually sadistic helmsman, it didn't change the fact that he was still Steve McQueen, Ultimate Rebel and Champion Ballbuster. And so, to the director's horror, Steve would tear off his costume as soon as a scene was done and go out in the woods and do wheelies on his motorbike. Returning all sweaty and with a big smile, he'd say to his furious director, "Miss me?" Hathaway never once mentioned McQueen or his work with the actor on *Nevada Smith* in his own oral history (edited by Rudy Behlmer). When Paramount had a press party for the film on the studio backlot, a fire broke out on the adjoining soundstage. A man of action off screen as well as on, Steve pulled off his suit jacket and joined the firemen in putting out the fire.

Though *Nevada Smith* has the same old plot of the hero trailing the killers of his loved ones and learning that revenge is wrong, the film is also made in the 1960s, meaning this is not your typical western from the old days. Besides the sadistic scene when the three killers torture the Sands, the film is filled with brutal scenes; the whipping at the prison camp, Max being dragged through a lake, various beatings, Coe's stabbing (and his bloodcurdling scream afterwards) and Fitch's neurotic penchant for showing off his specially fashioned tobacco pouch supposedly made out of the dress worn by Max's mother. The sadism level would have been raised quite a bit had John Michael Hayes' screenplay kept what Robbins had originally written about the pouch: It's actually made of his mother's *skin*.

Besides the violence level, what used to be censorable just ten years before is seen here in all its adults-only glory. Janet Margolin's half-breed prostitute Neesa has the beginning of a makeout scene with Max in a rug-laden tepee; Max shooting an unarmed Bowdre in the swamp; Fitch's men cold-bloodedly murdering the riders guarding the gold shipment. (They apparently get away with it, as Hathaway turns our focus on Max's chasedown of Fitch in that stream.)

Max's "hookup" with Neesa was a lot more X-rated in its original form, with Shurlock's office warning against showing any scenes with nudity. And so, the filmmakers duly cut out a male shower scene in the prison camp, as well as a scene showing Neesa and Max bathing in a stream. Also, there were complaints about the scene "in which the Indian girl apparently undresses in preparation for love making...."[5]

Still, the traditionalists in the audience must have loved the appearance of Father Zaccardi as a reminder of the moral issues involved. When the padre brings Max into his church, we are reminded of another scene in a western of 1948, *Coroner Creek*. In that film, cowboy Randolph Scott vows revenge on the man who was responsible for his fiancée committing suicide. When he meets the heroine's religious father, the man says that there are those "who run away from the Bible"; it's a comment that could have been made about either Scott's character or Max Sand. After the villain in the Scott film is killed by accident, the soundtrack quotes the Bible: "Vengeance is mine, I will repay...."

Yet God seems to be missing in action in *Nevada Smith*. Max not only pays back his enemies, but his obsessive quest gets Pilar killed as well (and Bigfoot, who was not a nasty character, gets to serve out Max's sentence). Though pointing out that Max's quest for revenge is wrong, *Nevada Smith* withholds any moral judgment on the many sinners Max runs into on his episodic adventures. The three men who had a fight with Max and steal his belongings apparently get away with it since they're never seen again; and the riders who guarded the gold shipment are needlessly killed and the robbers are now rich. Ultimately, the connecting thread in the episodic story is Max and his three targets; once he leaves one scene and goes on to the next one, whatever threads there are left to the previous scene are left hanging, the various characters and their stories disappear forever. Even when Max stops himself from killing Fitch and rides away, he's *still* a wanted man. Is he planning to give himself up? Like all the other threads in the film, this also is left unanswered. (In Robbins' novel, the Fitch character is not wounded, but killed outright.)

Nevada Smith was released in Los Angeles on May 23, 1966, and opened wide on June 10. Within its highly charged story, we see a young man walk a moral tightrope between the law of the old west as dictated by law books and the Unwritten Law. It focused on the character of a 16-year-old half-Indian, half-white boy who was played by a 35-year-old blonde-haired white man who was a fine actor, but not exactly appropriate casting. This little detail was noted by the unnamed reviewer for *Time* magazine in its review of July 15, 1966:

> McQueen appears to have spilled the last of his Indian blood before the cameras began turning. Tightly wound, unmistakably modern, he looks as if he would be more at home in the saddle of a Harley Davidson than on a horse. He lends presence, but not substance to the simple, single-minded character....[6]

This review might be a little unfair, since Steve, who never liked animals, *does* make a conscious effort to ride his horse and move about like a westerner, including scenes of rolling his own cigarettes. The reviewer also seemed to forget how TV audiences accepted him completely as a cowboy for years on *Wanted: Dead or Alive*, as well as his convincing performance as a gunslinger in *The Magnificent Seven*. Still, the critic was right on target when he wrote that "Brian Keith rings true as an amiable peddler...."

On July 9, the unnamed critic of *Cue* magazine wrote: "Skeptics may be surprised, but when the film is making its reputation strictly as a western, it has strength in the tradition of that genre. However, the movie also strains for larger drama and a philosophical viewpoint on how hatred corrupts, and in this attempt, it founders badly."[7]

Nevada Smith was a worldwide hit, cementing McQueen's status as a superstar of the 1960s. Riot police in Trinidad were called in when patrons broke into a theater playing the film because they couldn't wait for it to open.

McQueen was a young man whose rebel image appealed to young fans during the tumultuous 1960s, just as Max Sand's determination to violate the letter of the law appealed to an international audience in nations that didn't necessarily follow the course of American-style due process.

In 1968, Warner Brothers would produce a film starring two veteran actors in a story that was a plea for law and order and civic responsibility. As a changing America saw riots break out in its streets, one western euphemistically demanded an end to the madness...

"When there is no law, you set your own."— *Bob Larkin*

By the mid-1960s, Hollywood was going young. The JD and youth films of the late 1950s had really only scratched the surface. The entrenched older stars of a previous day were still starring in blockbusters, but these expensive dinosaurs always seemed to be the last gasp of a faded studio system. (Decades later, does anyone *really* still find something relevant or entertaining in *How the West Was Won*, *The Greatest Story Ever Told*, *The Bible* or *The Way West*?) John Wayne was one of the few older stars who still dominated the western genre, and would continue to be among the top ten box office stars into the early 1970s. However, by 1975, even he would fall out of the box office top ten, another casualty of the new, youth-dominated Hollywood. Films with older, established stars began to be reduced to double-bill status at theaters around the country.

TOWN MEETIN'. James Stewart confronts unseen trouble in *Firecreek* (1968). Dean Jagger is seated on the left, Ed Begley is standing to the right of him, and unidentified women are seated around him. With very few exceptions, everyone in *Firecreek* seems to be over fifty.

As the Vietnam War continued to siphon away young lives in the jungles of Southeast Asia and young people were beaten and eventually shot to death in student protests around the country, Jack Warner, an elderly movie mogul from the Golden Days of Hollywood, was preparing a new western to fill double-bills in Stanley Warner theaters. In 1966, Calvin Clements Sr., a scenarist with plenty of TV work to his credit, including many episodes of *The FBI*, wrote a script called *Fury at Firecreek*. The story dealt with five killers-for-hire, men who had fought range wars for wealthy employers, riding into the tiny frontier burgh of Firecreek. It's such a tiny, isolated community that, for two dollars a month, they've hired a farmer as a part-time sheriff; this is because no outlaws have ever considered the town important enough to start trouble in. Cut off from the real world, they are totally unprepared when the five gunslingers ride into their lonely hamlet and, after promising to leave in a few hours, begin terrorizing the helpless citizens. Towards the end, the farmer realizes his responsibilities to the town and takes his ceremonial tin star seriously. In a blazing gundown, the farmer emerges triumphant.

Perhaps in a comment on his own age, Jack Warner always had fellow middle-aged man James Stewart in mind for the role of the farmer. Unfortunately, it was this pair of blinders worn by the aging mogul that ruined the film. With two lead roles that could have been played by young men, especially in a youth-dominated Hollywood, Warner harked back to an idealized past, cast actors his own age, and ruined a film that could have been a great one. *Firecreek* (as it would be called) would end up being sarcastically referred to by at least one critic as "a geriatric *High Noon*."[8]

Our story begins in Firecreek, a town whose closest neighbor is Sweetwater in Wyoming Territory. Five men on horseback are riding straight for the film's credits, led by Bob Larkin (Henry Fonda), who is nursing a bullet wound in his side. Beside him are the psychotic little hellion Earl (a pre–*2001* Gary Lockwood), the bearded Norman (Jack Elam), the perpetually giggling Drew (James Best), and the laconic Willard (Morgan Woodward). When Larkin orders Earl and Norman to ride ahead and find out where the nearest town is, the two outlaws discover young blonde bimbo Leah (Brooke Bundy, beating out Shelley Fabares, Mimsy Farmer, Tisha Sterling and Kim Darby for the role). Earl is about to rape her when he is stopped by Larkin.

Farmer Johnny Cobb (James Stewart), the father of two young boys, is about to get another child from his pregnant wife, Henrietta (the versatile Jacqueline Scott). The beautiful red-headed actress is made to look frumpy and disheveled throughout the film, not merely because she's a prairie woman who's about to have a baby, but so that she'll look closer in age to the man playing her hubby (Stewart was 59 years old when *Firecreek* was made; Scott only 32). Cobb has his wife watched by Leah's cold and distant mother, Dulcie (another outstanding performance by Louise Latham, who also played the cold, distant mom in Hitchcock's *Marnie*).

With his two little boys, Cobb takes the buckboard into town, where he runs into its various denizens. There is storekeeper Whittier (Dean Jagger), pain-in-the-ass Hall (John Qualen), traveling preacher Broyles (Ed Begley), the simple-minded Arthur (Robert Porter), boarding-house owner Pittman (frequent Anthony Mann player Jay C. Flippen), his granddaughter Evelyn (the gorgeous Inger Stevens), and Meli (Barbara Luna), an Indian woman taking care of a little blonde boy. Larkin and his gang are already in town. After Cobb rides up with his boys, he is just in time to save Drew from a horse-trough drowning by Earl. Seeing a man (Cobb) who could have been him at another time, Larkin orders the gang to have restraint around the farmer, whom he suspects has more guts than one would expect.

At Mr. Pittman's boarding house, Larkin is smart enough to be diplomatic and is able to find a room and have his wound cared for by Evelyn. It is soon apparent that the two are attracted to each other, but Evelyn, tormented by Larkin's resemblance to a past love murdered by Indians, has repressed her emotions in this dead-end town. She quickly deduces (and is honest enough to say it to Larkin's face) that the outlaw wasn't thrown from his horse, as he claimed, but was shot. Lonely for company, the intelligent gang leader admits that he and his gang were hired guns. Proud of his murderous accomplishments, in a rare boast, Larkin claims that men are waiting all over the country to "be Larkin men." The dialogue crackles between the two actors, and their lines point up the fact that both are lost souls who have suppressed what they could have been, just like every other character in *Firecreek*.

Meanwhile, Broyles holds services in Whittier's store (the town is not big enough to have a church). Earl and the gang enter, with the young hellion helping himself to a bottle of whiskey during the sermon. Told not to drink in church and angered by Broyles' stare during a sermon on those headed for Hell, Earl orders the preacher to shut up. Outside, after Broyles mounts his horse, Earl fires his gun at the church bell. The noise causes Broyles' horse to panic and the preacher is thrown to the ground. With Earl still waving his gun around, Cobb and the preacher back down.

As Larkin gets some much-needed rest and he and Evelyn get to know each other, the gang starts getting rowdy. As they get drunk in the local cantina, the gang members, especially Earl, are amused by the crude tin star Cobb still carries (made by his sons) which says "Shareef." However, as time goes on, amusement will turn to rage.

Hearing noises coming from Meli's house, Arthur arrives just in time to see Drew raping the Indian woman. The outlaw beats up the mentally challenged young man but Arthur pulls the gun out of Drew's holster. Warned by the outlaw that it has a hair trigger, Arthur is horrified when the gun goes off and sends a bullet into the rapist's back, killing him.

Calling for Larkin to "protect his own," Earl insists that they get a rope and hang Arthur. Afraid of more trouble, Cobb is forced to lock up the young man in the ramshackle jail. Believing his wife is ready to give birth, Cobb returns to Dulcie's cabin where he is stunned to hear that his own wife had always thought that the couple had settled for less in life. Earlier, storekeeper Whittier had revealed to Cobb that he was a failed lawyer; and that he, like the other denizens of Firecreek, are nothing but losers.

Returning to town, Cobb is horrified to find Arthur's body hanging from a beam in the stables. "How can you let it happen?" he screams to the townspeople, who are too ashamed to show themselves. After Larkin appears and claims that Arthur had been tried and found guilty, Cobb threatens to pursue the gang and have a real court of law charge them with murder. (Stewart's threat to pursue Larkin and his men is reminiscent of his threat to Arthur Kennedy and his bunch in Anthony Mann's *Bend of the River*.) Larkin's response is to fire a bullet into Cobb's leg. As a final gesture of contempt, Earl tosses Cobb some coins to pay for his leg. ("There ain't nothin' that five dollars won't buy in this town!" he says with a smile.)

Limping, Cobb makes it over to Whittier's store where he demands a .45 and a box of shells. Here, actor Stewart, after giving a good performance reacting to others, comes perilously close to ham as he delivers a long monologue about fighting for what's yours, and declaring that "the day a man stops facing the world is the day he better step out of it!" It is a powerful message about fighting back against bullies, and it is actually reminiscent of the message in *Destry Rides Again*, but the star's overacting almost makes one laugh at his words, rather than be stirred to action.

After said pistol is procured, Cobb bursts through Whittier's door into the street, firing at the outlaws without warning. It is a much-needed burst of action that puts the film back on track. Considering the evil modus operandi of the gang, Cobb's "sneak attack" is perfectly reasonable, and just what these bullies deserve after their various outrages. Willard falls out of his saddle but his foot is caught in the stirrup, and his panicked horse runs out of town with Willard sure to meet a painful death on some rocky surface.

Taking cover, the three remaining outlaws decide to kill Cobb. (Henry Fonda delivers one of my favorite lines in his laconic Nebraska drawl: "A man worth shootin' is a man worth killin'!") Knowing his way around town, Cobb escapes their attack. Hoping to lure Cobb out, Larkin threatens to burn the town. When Norman tries to set fire to the stable, he is stopped by Cobb. A fight ensues between the two (Stewart and Elam had already tangled in Universal's *The Rare Breed* in 1965) and, though beaten up, the farmer is still able to impale the outlaw in the stomach with a pitchfork. Ignoring Larkin's call for restraint, Earl stalks the farmer and is about to ambush him until a warning from Cobb's son saves him. The part-time sheriff riddles the young psycho with bullets. Now there's just one man left.

Larkin appears and shoots Cobb in the shoulder, but the wounded man *still* continues to reach for bullets to reload his gun. "What are you trying to prove?" the outlaw leader cries out, reminding the farmer that he is a fool to die for a lousy two dollars a month. Cobb reloads the gun and aims it, but then Larkin is shot by Evelyn, firing a rifle from the hotel window. Larkin has enough time to look up at her in stunned disbelief before he dies. The wounded Cobb is now reunited with his family.

THE LAST SHOT. Henry Fonda (back to camera) is about to finish off the wounded James Stewart in *Firecreek* (1968). Though a plea for law and order amidst chaos, the film could also be seen as a defense of the status quo in the turbulent 1960s.

Though *Firecreek* is a film with a powerful message, top-notch direction and mostly good performances, the film falls far short of the very similar *High Noon*. Where it does succeed is in its passionate belief in law and order, and how ordinary citizens sometimes just have to say "enough!" and fight against outlawry. Unfortunately, its message of backing those in authority did not have a receptive audience in that tumultuous year of 1968. At the time the film was made, anger against the LBJ administration for the country's growing involvement in Vietnam was rising. Coupled with the racist murders of civil rights activists down south and the revelations of chicanery within the nation's intelligence community (complimented by rampant political assassinations), these events galvanized young people to protest the powers-that-be en masse. For them, it was pretty hard to respect law and order when those in charge seemed to be breaking it on a daily basis. Another reason for the film's failure was Jack Warner's cynical ploy of dumping it on a double-bill program in neighborhood theaters (not first-run houses). This was typical behavior for Warner in his final years at the studio he helped to build. (*Bonnie and Clyde* was thrown onto double-bills in local theaters until Warren Beatty pressured Warners to re-release it, and it was eventually "discovered.")

However, a major reason for its failure was the team behind the film itself. Calvin Clements, Sr., was a TV writer, and a prolific one too; yet two of his assignments call into question his impartiality on the subject matter of his scripts. Previously he had written episodes of *Wagon Train* and was the head writer for *Gunsmoke*, as well as other family-oriented TV series of the times. However, after his work on *Firecreek*, between 1972 and 1974, Clements wrote seven episodes of *The FBI*. In 1975, he wrote the teleplay for *Attack on Terror: The FBI vs. the Ku Klux Klan*. It would not be made public until many years later that J. Edgar Hoover insisted on investigating everyone involved in any Hollywood project where the Bureau was mentioned. All actors playing FBI agents, as well as other performers, all behind-the-scenes personnel, and even the extras were investigated.[9] (Paranoid to a fault, Hoover had expensive reshooting done when he discovered that one of the extras in the training academy scene in *The FBI Story* was gay.[10])

Promoted by the media as portraying the Bureau's valiant fight against the KKK, *Attack on Terror: The FBI vs. the Ku Klux Klan* was based on a book by Don Whitehead, the Bureau-approved author of *The FBI Story*, and its teleplay was written by Calvin Clements Sr., a man who had to have been investigated and given a clean bill of health by the Bureau itself. (Hoover died in 1972, but many of his dictates continued for years afterwards.) Therefore, it shouldn't be a surprise that Clements' work on both the FBI-themed TV movie, as well as the weekly series, met certain guidelines approved by the Bureau.

Which brings us back to *Firecreek*, a film that was, like the Bureau-sanctioned projects of the day, a gung-ho cry for more law enforcement. Its villains are uncompromisingly evil. As the nation's young people saw hypocrisy and moral corruption in the adults who ran the country, *Firecreek* concentrated its villainy on outlaws who were acting like wild young hellions. Particular attention was paid to Earl, the youngest of the group and the most deranged (his hatred of parental authority figures is obvious in his defiance of the elderly Preacher Broyles).

The pro-authority James Stewart certainly had no problem with the film's message of a complacent citizenry fighting back against "troublemakers." The actor had backed the nation's involvement in Vietnam, and it wouldn't be revealed until many years later his own racial bias *vis-à-vis* the civil rights movement.[11] It would not be farfetched to deduce that the actor might have seen *Firecreek* as a pro-authority film that depicted 19th century killers-for-hire as those young people of the time who rejected the status quo. Fonda, however, probably saw Larkin and his gang as some kind of fascistic entity whose outrages defied due process and the rule of law; for instance, the gang's lynching of Arthur (this is yet *another* anti-lynching film on Fonda's résumé). As previously mentioned, many of the actor's films, particularly his westerns, deal with the repudiation of privately hired gunmen who enforce the law over duly appointed lawmen, like *The Tin Star* and *Warlock*. However, in *Firecreek*, it is his friend Stewart who will wait till the last minute before he puts on the tin star (albeit with the word sheriff misspelled).

In a backhanded way, Fonda would tweak his good friend's "nice guy" image in his as-told-to bio, *Fonda: My Life*: "[In *Firecreek*] I played a bad guy who tried to kill Jim Stewart. Now, any man who tries to kill Jim Stewart *has* to be marked as a man who's plain rotten. You can't get much worse than that."[12]

Besides the script's pro-authority message, Stewart might have also been attracted to the perks, like a salary of $250,000 and ten percent of the gross above $2.5 million. Fonda would receive exactly half of this, $125,000 for ten weeks' work. Stewart was also to receive top billing above the title, with no one else being above the title without his approval.[13]

In a September 14, 1966, letter to Stewart's agent Arthur Park of the powerful Chasin-Park-Citron Agency, longtime Warner honcho Walter MacEwen wrote:

> Mr. Stewart has certain approvals. He has pre-approved Vincent McEveety as director. He has approved Robert Burks as cameraman. He has approval of the roles of Larkin, Earl and Henri-

etta—and has pre-approved Richard Widmark for the role of Larkin. He has pre-approved Philip Leacock and John Mantley as producers. He is to be consulted on important members of the cast other than the three previously named.[14]

The above excerpt from MacEwen's letter is significant if one is to understand just why the town of Firecreek seems to be populated by mostly old people. Though the script implies that these folks are burned-out losers, it's obvious that the various actors playing them were also cast because they made the film's star more comfortable that they wouldn't look younger than he was.

Indeed, Firecreek is a town with absolutely no young men (with the exception of the not-too-bright Arthur). Like Columbia's *The Wild One* of 1954, there are no young men to either identify with or defy Marlon Brando's (quite overage) motorcycle gang leader; all their victims are old people, even the sheriff, played by Robert Keith. Stewart, who approved most everything else in *Firecreek*, also approved the film's now-ancient character actors Dean Jagger (67), Ed Begley (68), John Qualen (68), and Jay C. Flippen (68). With the possible exception of Arthur, this makes Stewart, at 59, the youngest adult male "good guy" in the film.

Most of the villains of the piece also show their age. Fonda, Woodward and Best were all World War II veterans; Elam was old enough, but was exempt because of his glass eye. Also reinforcing the "geriatric *High Noon*" critique, the film pairs the 59-year old Stewart with the 32-year old Jacqueline Scott, as well as the 62-year old Fonda with the 33-year old Inger Stevens.

One wonders why the prematurely silver-haired Richard Widmark didn't make the cut. As it turned out, according to studio files, the actor had complaints about the role of Larkin. In a letter to Walter MacEwen, dated October 3, 1966 (when the project was still known as *Fury at Firecreek*), studio executive Robert H. Solo wrote:

Widmark met with [Philip] Leacock and [Vincent] McEveety this afternoon and feels very strongly that the role of Larkin, in its present form, is a little too passive. He feels that the two scenes should now be given to the Larkin character.

They are: Scene No. 198—which Larkin now plays with Evelyn; Widmark would like to play the same scene with the Cobb [Stewart] character.

Scene No. 280—now played by Cobb and Whittier; Widmark would like it to be a Cobb and Larkin scene.[15]

Leacock was against altering the Cobb-Whittier scene, which the producer felt would be "very damaging" to the picture. There might have been another reason for the rejection of Widmark's casting: Stewart might have had serious concerns that the hands-on Widmark might alter the script to his (Stewart's) disadvantage. The star of *Kiss of Death* and *Pickup on South Street* was *out*; the star of *Young Abe Lincoln* and *The Grapes of Wrath* was *in*. Another loser in the *Firecreek* sweepstakes was the husky-voiced star of *All About Eve*. In the same September 14 memo to Robert Solo, Walter MacEwen wrote, "Stewart's agent Arthur Park has asked that we give special consideration to Anne Baxter for the role of the girl Larkin [the heavy] falls for. I believe the character's name is Evelyn. According to Arthur, the price would be right."[16] But the former Eve Harrington didn't make the cut.

With its title officially changed to *Firecreek* on December 8, 1966, by Jack Warner himself, the film debuted across the country in late 1967. In his review in the *Chicago Sun-Times* of January 1, 1968, Roger Ebert wrote:

Firecreek was obviously conceived with high aims. I have the feeling that the people involved thought they were making a pretty good movie. And they almost did. Several scenes, including one between Stewart and his pregnant wife (Jacqueline Scott), and another between Fonda and Miss Stevens, are filled with tenderness.

But somehow the parts don't quite come together. Despite the presence of character actors like the legendary Ed Begley, despite the dust-blown photography, despite Stewart and Fonda, something is missing.

The tension we need to draw us into the story isn't there; things move at too leisurely a pace, and the movie, like the Jimmy Stewart hero, has to be dragged into the excitement against its will.[17]

The *New York Times*' Howard Thompson gave the film an unrestrained bravo. In his review of February 22, the critic wrote:

Firecreek is a good, sturdy and occasionally powerful little western. James Stewart is plain wonderful and Henry Fonda almost matches him.... In a cold light, the film is a kind of vest-pocket *High Noon*, with Mr. Stewart as a part-time sheriff and the culprits, led by Mr. Fonda, arriving in town at the outset.... But the beauty of this picture is its professional and genuine simplicity, the way nearly every line of dialogue has been made to count, either limning a characterization or edging the action forward. Calvin Clements, the scenarist and a man who knows people, is attacking complacency head-on.[18]

The critic also praised the film's direction: "[Vincent] McEveety starts at a deliberate, casual pace, whips up a chilling crescendo and stages a shoot-'em up climax that's a graphic beaut. This sequence is something to see, with the wounded, hobbling Stewart almost berserk with righteous rage."

"Righteous rage," a feeling expressed quite often in the western that called for enforcement of the Unwritten Law, would be a major character in a film MGM was making in Durango at the same time *Firecreek* was shooting in Burbank. Originally planned for television, the film was deemed too violent by studio executives and released theatrically.

Not since the works of Anthony Mann would the western show good men cross over into such darkness...

"It's what I call an *evil gun*. I'll never know how one man can kill another."
— Mr. Willford

By the late 1960s, opposite a new, younger crop of male actors, Glenn Ford may have been starting to feel his age. He was one of the most natural actors in Hollywood; audiences never tired of seeing his familiar, sometimes craggy face because he usually portrayed good guys in such a non-flamboyant, realistic manner. It was this honesty in his acting that added to his popularity.

However, by 1969, though still constantly hired by the studios for both films and TV, Ford's work was becoming second-feature fodder; this included westerns which were almost always released theatrically with another film. His choice of genre scripts were always interesting, though, and the actor aggressively looked for something within them that stood out from the TV-influenced oaters then flooding the theaters before the release of *The Wild Bunch* changed the playing field forever. One of these was Columbia's appropriately titled *A Time for Killing*, in which his Union officer leads his men into Mexico to kill the Confederate prisoners who kidnapped his wife, his obsessive quest indirectly causing tragedy for all.

Situated between his performance in MGM's *The Last Challenge* and the King Brothers' *Heaven with a Gun* came *Day of the Evil Gun*, the most fascinating of this trilogy. In all of these films, Ford played an aging gunfighter. There was a good reason for this: Ford was reportedly one of the fastest-drawing actors with a gun anywhere in Hollywood.

Yet in all the above-mentioned films, despite the fact that Ford was a pro-gun conservative off-screen, the actor obviously approved of the message that the Way of the Gun is wrong. In *Day of the Evil Gun*, we will see how exposure to violence affects the lives of two men with different personalities, and how they use the Unwritten Law of the frontier to rescue a woman that each man claims as his own. It was expertly directed by Jerry Thorpe.

The film's credits are run over the figure of a blacksmith creating sparks while striking metal with his hammer, an image of fire and steel, of forging something through violence. This hellish imagery gives viewers a foreshadowing of what's to come. *Evil Gun* was originally set as a movie for television. It was violent imagery like this, as well as the acting which went for realism rather than melodrama, that caused MGM to release the film theatrically.

It is 1869 in the southwest. Gunfighter Lorn Warfield (Glenn Ford), tired of killing, has returned to the wife and two little girls he walked out on years ago, after he won a gunfight in the town's main street. But the man's reputation precedes him: When a big-mouthed teenager calls him out in the street and even tosses the unarmed gunfighter a pistol, Warfield dismissively kicks the gun into a mud puddle. It is just the beginning of the low-keyed, realistic approach of Jerry Thorpe, working from a screenplay by Charles Marquis Warren and Eric Bercovici. Instead of teaching the young loudmouth a lesson, Warfield simply shows his contempt by kicking the proffered gun into the mud, knowing full well that the young man won't be stupid enough to dry-gulch him (and get an unwanted reputation as a backshooter). Ford revels in this approach, rejecting excessive dialogue in favor of subtle facial expressions, especially his eyes, to convey his character's feelings.

When Warfield returns to his family home, he is shocked to find that his wife and little girls were kidnapped two months before by the Apaches. This info is conveyed to him by his wife's new beau, Owen Forbes (Arthur Kennedy), a New Hampshire man who tells the gunfighter that his wife Angie (Barbara Babcock) has forgotten him. While in town, Warfield learns that the reverend's wife was kidnapped along with Angie and the girls, but the warriors released her because the experience has disturbed her mentally. After getting past the reluctant Reverend Yearby (Ross Elliott), Warfield tries to crack Lydia's shell by asking where the tribe took his family. When he asks what the women might have been wearing (to ascertain what the weather was like where the tribe had camped), the traumatized woman responds with "*I was naked!*" Some critics have dismissed this film as a copy of *The Searchers*; however, *Day of the Evil Gun* lacked the sophomoric humor of Ford's work, playing it grim and violent all the way. Made in the more permissive 1960s, Thorpe's film goes into territory where Ford in the 1950s couldn't go; a good example of this is Lydia Yearby's scene-ending shock line quoted above.

Warfield finds Jimmy Noble (third-billed Dean Jagger in his one and only scene in the film), a giggling peddler with the mind of a child. It was Jimmy who found Mrs. Yearby and brought her home. Realizing that the giggling man is shamming (Apaches consider mental illness a sign that a person possesses evil spirits, which is why they released Mrs. Yearby), Warfield sets fire to Jimmy's wagon. The suddenly lucid peddler admits to helping the reverend's wife.

Unfortunately for Warfield, the gunfighter has to deal with the persistant Owen Forbes, who follows him on his mission. At one point, Warfield jumps him and the two roll into a narrow stream and duke it out. Taken captive by the Apaches, the two men are about to die when Warfield bluffs Mexican Comanchero Jose DeLeon (Nico Minardos) into believing that the two men had buried a cache of money somewhere in the hills. Warriors stake the two men to the hot desert sands (where either the sun or the vultures will kill them), but the greedy DeLeon later appears and releases them. Through more bluffs and conning, Warfield turns the tables on the bandit. When DeLeon makes a grab for Forbes' rifle, the easterner accidentally shoots him dead.

When the two men make it to the next town, they find that people there are dying from cholera. The disillusioned Dr. Prather (the always-reliable Royal Dano) is setting fire to all the buildings. When Forbes purchases supplies from a sleazy storekeeper (James Griffith), he's able to make the man tell him where the Apache camp is (he'd been selling them guns and booze) by threatening to set fire to both him and his store.

Coming upon a ramshackle town, the two men run into a garrison of soldiers including Sergeant Parker (Harry Dean Stanton) and their commanding officer, the southern-accented Captain Addis (the wonderful John Anderson). They're really a group of deserters who have stolen a wagon of guns so that they can trade them to the Apaches for a stolen payroll. However, as everyone soon finds out, the Apaches don't make deals. After warriors run off the horses, they attack the town, and many are killed during the battle. Warfield allows the warriors to steal the wagon of guns so that they can be tracked back to their camp.

After their wounded horse dies, Warfield and Forbes slog through the desert until they finally find the Apache camp. While Forbes stabs to death one of the Apache lookouts, Warfield sees that the easterner is a little *too* enthusiastic in his grisly work. With incredible daring, Forbes is able to grab Angie and the two girls and escape with a buckboard while Warfield runs off the tribe's horses and blows up the wagon of guns.

Back in town, a doctor tells Warfield that Angie and the girls are all right, but it will take patience to get them back into society again. Meanwhile, the vindictive Forbes is demanding that the gunfighter leave the family. Warfield pays storekeeper Willford (Parley Baer) for groceries with his own cherished pistol, a symbolic gesture (the gunfighter hopes to finally give up the way of the gun). Outside, the now kill-crazy Forbes fires his gun at the unarmed Warfield and is about to finish him off when Willford shoots the easterner dead with the same weapon he had referred to only moments before as "the evil gun."

From the opening titles to its ironic denouement (where a small-part player actually saves the day), *Day of the Evil Gun* is a bleak journey into a west physically ablaze with sunshine, but in reality covered in darkness. Tracking the Apaches through the wilderness is bad enough, but the misery that seems to follow these two men is relentless. Screenwriters Warren and Bercovici and director Thorpe create a dismal west where the only laughter comes from either Apache captors or the feigned giggling of a man pretending to be insane. The atmosphere is relentlessly grim; this is reinforced by the film's lack of music. There is nothing glorious in the quest to rescue the females; and it is through bum luck and happenstance that the two men don't die without being able to rescue them.

Wherever Warfield and Forbes go, they encounter either death or lies. Nothing in *this* west is as it seems: the sleazy storekeeper who acts as if he's respectable, but is in reality selling guns and booze to the Apaches; Addis and his men pretending to be dedicated soldiers when they're actually deserters, etc. Hoping to get supplies, Warfield and Forbes find a town where people are dying of cholera; this includes a heartbreaking scene where Dr. Prather tells a dying little boy to just let go and accept his own death. No one wants to help the two men find the Apaches' camp unless they're physically threatened, coaxed by greed or paralyzed with fear. Lydia Yearby's outburst about being naked was done not to give Warfield information but to emphasize her own suffering; Jimmy Noble cooperates only when his beloved wagon is threatened with arson; DeLeon provides information at gunpoint (and had rescued the two men only when promised money); the storekeeper who sold guns to the Indians gives Forbes information only when he and his store are threatened with fire; Addis cooperates (temporarily) with the two men only when the Apaches attack and he needs the two extra guns to help fight them off; and Willford allows Warfield to purchase supplies (despite owing him money previously) only when the gunfighter gives him his prized pistol. Ironically, the only truly selfless act in the entire film where no one expects anything in return is when the storekeeper kills Forbes in order to save Warfield's life.

Thorpe fills the picture with ugly and violent imagery, of a western landscape where honesty and fair play are useless and only duplicity, violent action and a cruel, unforgiving nature win out. During the staking-out of the two men in the sands, Thorpe inserts close-ups of the hungry vultures waiting to attack; the shots of these ugly birds are unsettling. When Warfield and Forbes finally come to civilization, the town is ravaged by cholera, taking even the town's children; the town's physician is now forced to be a destroyer, going from house to house and setting fire to them to prevent the spread of the disease. When the two men are chased down by the Apaches, the warriors sadistically increase their quarry's humiliation by stripping them of their weaponry and taunting them with their raised lances before finally stopping their mounts. Certainly, after their own brush with the Indians, the two rescuers have no problem cruelly knifing the Apache lookouts and then blowing up the warriors with the gunpowder-filled wagon.

However, the grim and prairie-smart Warfield has seen enough killing to last him a lifetime; to him, the rescue of his family was a necessity, not an adventure. Sick of killing, he has no problem selling his gun to Willford. (When Forbes fires at him, he uncharacteristically hides behind a buckboard, now knowing what it's like to be the target of a swaggering man with a gun.) Yet it's the naive easterner who takes the wrong turn, both psychologically and ethically. Warfield tells him how, after the first killing, it'll be easier for him to kill from then on.

By the time Forbes has threatened to burn the storekeeper and his wares, we are reminded of Warfield's use of fire to make Jimmy Noble talk. But Warfield never doused Jimmy himself with kerosene, just his wagon; the difference being that the grim gunfighter, sickened by death, couldn't kill a defenseless person, but there is definitely something deep inside Forbes that now makes a man's murder frighteningly permissible. By the end, his family returned, the gunfighter who had spread death, now embraces life; however, the man from the pampered and civilized east who had embraced refinement (we first saw Forbes smoking a pipe) now lets his gun do his talking for him. This metamorphosis alone, where one of the rescuers turns psychotic, sets this film far apart from (though not above) *The Searchers*. The John Ford film also has many breaks between scenes of tension, as well as the obvious use of soundstages standing in for outdoor locations. *Day of the Evil Gun* has no breaks for comedy relief or anything else; the film just goes from one bleak scene to the next, with dialogue kept to a minimum (partly thanks to Glenn Ford's input) and not one soundstage substituting for actual outdoor locations.

In fact, because of Thorpe's insistence on shooting in Durango the production did *not* go, shall we say, smoothly. Before the cast and crew assembled on location, the region's powerful rains had washed away the western town MGM built, and it had to be rebuilt at a cost of $40,000. Notice that both the town Warfield returns to and the one where Addis' men hide are sparse, with mostly ramshackle barns and cabins. Virna Lisi was supposed to play Angie, but the time spent in rebuilding the town took too long and the actress went on to another film; Barbara Babcock stepped in. Despite the fact that we see the two main characters going through their search on clear, sunny days, this was largely an illusion. According to Glenn's son Peter, in his biography of the actor, it rained every day they were on location, forcing a production slated for 34 days to extend its schedule to two months. Both cast and crew got sick, with the actor's son admitting to being so "gravely ill" he thought he would die in Duango (with the village "doctor" giving him an injection which reportedly made him feel *worse*). Dean Jagger took ill and had to be flown back to the States to receive some *real* health care.[19]

However, all the misery and frustration Ford was going through came out quite well in this film. The actor gives one of his best performances in the genre. Indeed, Warfield's refusal to answer Forbes' many questions, with Ford effectively showing disdain with his eyes alone, was more an acting choice than a scripted bit of business. The actor once said, "I had input on my scripts on most of my films after I became established. If you look at the notes on the shooting scripts, you'll see I was always cutting dialogue. I hate dialogue."[20] This little fact didn't escape A.H. Weiler in his *New York Times* review. After mentioning that "Glenn Ford again outlasts the competition," Weiler wrote, "The dialogue has been kept to a minimum and the fighting to a maximum."[21]

TRIGGERMAN. Glenn Ford as the aging gunfighter tracking down the Apaches who kidnapped his wife and daughter in *Day of the Evil Gun* (1968). This dark film was unfairly compared to *The Searchers*.

Evil Gun was considered too violent for TV so MGM released the film theatrically, which probably pleased Ford, even if it was shown in double-feature houses. Even more than *The Searchers*, this grim little film showed the psychological changes a rescue attempt can have on the rescuers, as well as the rescued. Using the Unwritten Law to even the odds against Apache marauders and a harsh wilderness, two men succeed in their rescue mission, but at the cost of what they had been before.

Three months after the Ford film, audiences witnessed the starring debut in a Hollywood film of a man who would not only become an icon for the western film, but American film itself...

> "When you hang a man, you better get a good look at him."— *Jed Cooper*

As the American western evolved during the 1960s, it often remained attached to its prime-time TV influences. In movie theaters, there were either all-star super-westerns complete with CinemaScope or Cinerama or the typical second feature western which was nothing more than *The Virginian* or *Laredo* stretched to feature length.

Then, from 1964 to 1966, Sergio Leone made his famous spaghetti western trilogy *A Fistful of Dollars*, *A Few Dollars More*, and *The Good, the Bad and the Ugly*. When I was about 12, my father took me to see these films when they played as a triple feature in Times Square and my world was changed forever; so was my father's. A concentration camp survivor who

WAITING FOR HIS BIG CLOSE-UP. Clint Eastwood in *Hang 'Em High* (1968), the first American film in which he starred.

had witnessed man's savagery up close, Harry Herzberg was usually appalled by the sunny optimism of so many Hollywood films, particularly its westerns. When the Man with No Name rode into view on that Times Square movie screen, we both experienced a revelation.

This serape-wearing misanthrope with the dirty, flat-crowned Stetson captured our imagination in a way few screen characters had. At no time did this gunslinging killer elicit our admiration for his noble deeds; in fact, he performed no noble deeds. Nor did he save women in distress, thwart bank robberies, stop stagecoach holdups, bring outlaw gangs to justice or talk to his horse.

Instead, the Man with No Name was an ornery, slimy and at times, unearthly individual so cut off from other human beings that to this day one might still be mystified by his wide appeal. Instead of having a girlfriend or fiancée, as any upright cowboy hero would (the usual rancher's daughter or proprietress of the local dress shop), he screwed the local whore; instead of fighting fair and square, he was not beyond shooting opponents in the back, or, if he felt like it, tossing a homemade bomb at them; instead of riding into a town to "clean it up" and make the place safe for women and children, his prime motivation in life was in looking out for number one. In the old westerns, the hero usually regretted the taking of life, even that of the bad guys; when the Man with No Name killed, the audience was invited to laugh at his grisly work (as for instance, telling an undertaker to get three coffins ready; then, after the shootings, saying he made a mistake and actually needed *four*). When he did destroy the villains, he didn't do it because he was on some lofty mission or on behalf of law and order, but for lots of money.

Smoking a rancid-looking cigarillo (which, in loving imitation, yours truly used to smoke openly in the halls of Erasmus Hall High School) and scanning a town he had nothing but contempt for, the Man with No Name seemed to symbolize the cynicism America displayed shortly after the assassination of President John F. Kennedy, and our deepening involvement in Vietnam.

For those who had seen Clint Eastwood on *Rawhide* every week, it was not a surprise that he was cast. (He got the part after several American actors, fearful that playing such a seedy character would ruin their images, turned it down.) According to Sergio Leone, as he watched a *Rawhide* episode, he was intrigued by the actor's catlike movements, as well as his presence, which projected, in his words, "indolence and menace."

Few film actors, especially in the western genre, personalized the emotional need for vengeance and retaliation, or lived by the Unwritten Law, more powerfully than Clint Eastwood. His distinctive film persona rejected every cowboy hero cliché Hollywood or the pulp western ever created. Taking advantage of the loosening of censorship restrictions on violence, Eastwood's characters *never* suffered fools or villains gladly; ignoring the rule of law, he was a law unto himself; when attacked, he struck back in kind, caring little, if at all, for the legal ramifications. Hitting the bad guys (and the audience) with his now-patented ugly sneer, he said what he wanted and did to others what he pleased. He was a cinematic safety valve for all of us, doing everything we always wanted to do, and without having to worry about any penalties for his behavior (which, if not always legal, always seemed to be right nevertheless).

In 1968, after the phenomenal popularity of the Leone films in both Europe and America, United Artists and Leonard Freeman Productions offered Eastwood the script for *Hang 'Em High*, about the lynching of a cowboy wrongly accused of stealing cattle and murder, and how this man survived to become a town marshal sworn to bring in the hanging party legally. At the time, studio executives were realizing that Eastwood was not merely a TV star any more. In short order, Columbia Pictures and formerly blacklisted director and screenwriter Carl Foreman offered Clint the lead role of the marshal pursuing Omar Sharif's Egyptian-accented half-breed Apache outlaw in *Mackenna's Gold*. Based on Will Henry's rather tiring and overblown novel (the Apaches are all wonderful and the whites are all villains who crave gold), the film would have cast Eastwood as a stiff-necked and upright, cliché-ridden lawman nowhere near his usual screen persona. In fact, in the novel, the character isn't really a lawman at all, but a red-bearded Scottish-American geologist in his thirties who speaks fluent Apache. Written by the left-leaning Foreman, the film slammed materialistic greed (all the white characters who desire gold, even when they were not the bad guys, die horribly, while the Indians who have murdered folks throughout the film are seen as inherently good). It would have been a film with an all-star cast and a big paycheck for Clint, but he turned it down. Instead, *Mackenna's Gold* starred the always limited Gregory Peck as the stiff, frozen-faced marshal (far more appropriate casting). Atrociously directed by Foreman, this laughable film bombed at the box office.

Far more to Clint's liking was the script for *Hang 'Em High* which, he was smart enough to realize, was a continuation and even an enhancement of his film persona that began with the Man with No Name. Referring to *Hang 'Em High* as a "much more modest project" than *Mackenna's Gold*, Eastwood said in a 1984 interview with Michael Henry: "I liked the idea of weighing the pros and cons of capital punishment in the setting of a western. That gave me the idea of starting my own company to share in the production of this small film."[22]

The "my own company" was known as Malpaso, which meant "bad step" in Spanish. Hardly a bad step, the company survived and flourished for the next 40 years. In another interview, Eastwood said, "I felt it was time, even though it was a smaller film, to challenge myself that way."

In his biography of Eastwood, author and film critic Richard Schickel surmised, pretty accurately as it turns out, that *Hang 'Em High* "took up and extended the main theme of a favorite picture of his, *The Ox-Bow Incident*...."[23] Indeed, in an interview with French film critics Thierry Jousse and Camille Nevers in the October 1992 issue of *Cashiers du Cinema*, Eastwood praises the Henry Fonda classic:

> One of my favorite pictures was a film by William Wellman from the forties called *The Ox-Bow Incident*. I worked with him once, not one of his best [Warners' *Lafayette Escadrille*, the helmsman's last film]. And I asked him quite a few questions about *The Ox-Bow incident*, which I thought was a great film. He told me that at the time, the wife of one of the studio bosses had hated the film at its first screening—she thought it was the worst crap a studio had ever financed—and then the producers had more or less gotten rid of it by distributing it as a B film. But when it was released in France, the critics were very appreciative of the film, they emphasized the value of its point of view, of what it had to say about capital punishment, about mob violence, about justice; Wellman's picture had a right to excellent reviews. Then it came back to New York by way of France, and the Americans began to see its qualities too, but it was already too late, the film was at the end of its run and was taken out of distribution. It was a terrible fiasco—and totally unmerited. Today, people see it with a different eye, and I hope, in the U.S. as well as elsewhere....[24]

For Eastwood to admire this movie, was, to say the least, an enormous surprise. In his films, Eastwood had promoted a vigilante's idea of enforcing justice that was seriously at odds with the innocent-until-proven-guilty ethics of his favorite film. However, I believe that the star was totally sincere about tackling the ambiguities and complications dealing with the subject of capital punishment. Amoral though the character was, the Man with No Name (or Dirty Harry Callahan, for that matter) never lynched anyone. I believe it was abuse of the law, as well as a lack of enforcement, that Eastwood was against.

Nevertheless, the rising new star decided to use his power to help old friends and collaborators, as he would do for decades to come. The distributor of the film, United Artists, as well as Leonard Freeman, wanted a seasoned western movie director, someone like John Sturges or Robert Aldrich; Eastwood wanted the Brooklyn-born and -bred helmsman who directed him on TV in *Rawhide*: Ted Post. Needless to say, between what the studio wanted and what Eastwood wanted, Dirty Harry won. When Freeman tried to interfere with Post's direction, Eastwood threatened to shut down the production unless the producer kept away from the set. This intimidation, as well as a thoughtful script and good cast paid off. The film continued Eastwood's rise in status to western film icon, while at the same time making a pointed comment on the complexities involved in enforcing the law in a lawless landscape.

Cowboy Jedediah "Jed" Cooper (Eastwood) is guiding a small herd of cattle across a stream until he dismounts and helps a young calf stuck in the mud. "I'm not going to have to carry you, am I?" the future Dirty Harry asks the bawling heifer. It's a cute bit, and was symbolic of the evolution that would take place in Clint's screen character (the scene is reminiscent of his performances on *Rawhide*). Despite the box office success of the Man with No Name trilogy in the U.S., he fully realized that he had to introduce Americans to his anarchic screen persona gradually. Even the name of his character, Jed Cooper, harks back to old cowboy movie legends like Gary Cooper. Still deeply influenced by the tried-and-true portrayal of the western hero as depicted on TV every week, the American public had to "get to know" Eastwood first as a cowboy who worked for the law; that is, *sans* dirty Stetson, cigarillo and black humor. Therefore, Clint had to display kindness towards wounded calves before taking the proverbial eye-for-an-eye.

After crossing the river with the future beefsteak, Cooper is surrounded by several mounted men accusing the cowboy of stealing the cows and murdering their owner. The so-called "bill of sale" that he shows the mob doesn't deter them since it was fraudulently made out by the man who originally stole the cattle and murdered the owner and his wife. The riders are a varied but ruthless lot, led by Captain Wilson (Ed Begley), and consisting of men like Miller (then premier movie psycho Bruce Dern), Matt (Alan Hale, Jr.), Loomis (L.Q. Jones), Reno (Joseph Sirola) and Jenkins (old western veteran Bob Steele), the only posse member against hanging the poor cowboy. Despite Cooper's protestations of innocence, Wilson gives the now-famous order: "Hang him!" Cooper is hanged from the nearest tree; then right over Cooper's booted feet dangling in air, Post throws on the credits.

Fortunately for Cooper (and the cause of Eastwoodian vengeance), Marshal Bliss (one of the genre's best actors *ever*, Ben Johnson) happens along. After cutting down Cooper, he tells the wounded man that he'll have to join the prisoners in his wagon, but if he's innocent, Judge Fenton will release him. Not only does this statement fortuitously underline the strength of American due process, but it further emphasizes the kind of decent screen westerner Johnson would almost always portray. Even in a slasher film, 1980s *Terror Train*, Johnson's screen character still had the fairness and decency of the old west lawman. When a gang of young passengers want to kill the murderer who has been targeting them, Johnson, as the train's head conductor, confronts the mob's leader. After handing him an ax to supposedly use on the murderer, he says in his quiet but firm Oklahoma drawl, "Now, son, do you *really* want to do that?" Johnson shames the young man into abandoning his vigilantism and letting due process run its course. It's the best moment in the whole film, and reminds one of the western tradition of justice and fair play coming from a man who had played a number of sheriffs and marshals for decades.

Bliss next stops to pick up a bearded and manacled lunatic named "The Preacher" (appropriately played by bearded off-screen wild man Dennis Hopper). The maniac attempts to escape; though egged on to kill the escapee by some of the bloodthirsty prisoners in his wagon, Bliss merely wounds him in the leg. The Preacher continues running, and Bliss gives him repeated warnings to halt. Finally, the marshal is forced to kill him.

When the prisoners arrive at Fort Grant, a young woman named Rachel Warren (the beautiful and tragic Inger Stevens) is allowed to view them. In the chambers of Judge Fenton (a wonderful performance by Pat Hingle), Cooper is released since the real cattle thief-murderer was caught; Fenton invites Cooper to watch the man hang. Fully aware that he had been a lawman, the wily judge offers the cowboy (who now has a deep rope-burn around his neck) the job of marshal for his court.

Forced to treat lawbreakers fair and square, including the men who tried to hang him, the newly minted marshal goes out on his hunt. Accosting Reno in a saloon he has no choice but to kill the robber-murderer (he had stolen Cooper's wallet before hanging him) when he draws. However, the three bullets he fires into the felon serve to remind us that the man doing the shooting is still *quite angry* about the attempted hanging. In fact, during this scene, Clint is showing us the kind of take-no-prisoners anti-hero he was becoming even as he decided to bridge the gap by still playing, essentially, a by-the-book lawman. Even after killing this hated enemy fairly, Cooper insists that the saloon's patrons put down what they witnessed in writing. Such an act would have elicited derisive contempt from the likes of Josey Wales. Still, it's another bit of business emphasizing the fairness of American justice and due process.

After being sent hundreds of miles to catch some cattle rustlers and murderers, Cooper fortuitously finds Miller as the one leading two youths in the theft of several hundred head. Again, due process is emphasized when Cooper draws his gun on the sons of the ranchers Miller murdered (they were attempting to lynch the three outlaws). After Cooper takes charge of the prisoners (and beats up the psychotic Miller when he attacks him), the marshal returns them to Judge Fenton and the hangman's rope. The vengeance-filled lawman did his job bringing his enemy in alive, meriting Fenton's respect.

However, Cooper is so disgusted by the sight of the massive hanging in the town square (complete with carnival atmosphere and concessions being sold), that he grabs whore Jennifer (*Mayberry RFD*'s Arlene Golonka) and takes her back to her room. The circus atmosphere here is darkly satirical, but at a time when there was no television and no movies, hangings *were* considered entertainment. Modern audiences are appalled by this cruel spectacle, but to the denizens of the old west, this was prime-time. The portrayal of children being brought over to gleefully watch a hanging is a scene which *never* would have been allowed under the Breen office. Yet by the 1970s, the spectacle of small children watching men being shot or hanged would be revisited most cruelly in Sam Peckinpah's *Pat Garrett and Billy the Kid*, as well his earlier *The Wild Bunch*, where children witness the Bunch's bank robbery and shootout near the beginning of the film. Even in 1958's *The Left Handed Gun*, Arthur Penn has some little boys playing with a scaffold noose as if they were swinging from a treehouse.

After his time with Jennifer, Cooper goes to the local saloon (now empty since everyone is watching the hanging). Suddenly, Captain Wilson, Maddow and Loomis open fire on him as he's taking a drink. Brought to the local whorehouse to recuperate, the fallen lawman is tenaciously looked after by Rachel. After Cooper is well enough to go on a picnic with her, the tormented woman tells him of the murder of her husband and her rape by three men months before; it is why Fenton allows her to view the faces of new prisoners when they arrive. Stevens is excellent as she recites what happened to her; even with her blonde hair blowing in her eyes, she wisely continues her monologue. After a thunderstorm starts, the two go to an abandoned cabin where Rachel uses her body warmth to help the freezing Cooper. During the night, the two wounded people consummate their relationship.

Now back on his feet again, Cooper defies Fenton's order to bring the men in alive and, predictably, reverts to doing things the Clint Way. That night, Cooper storms the Wilson property; if he has a warrant, he doesn't bother to serve it. After Loomis attempts to stalk Cooper with a knife, the ranch hand's body is soon found by Maddow with the blade in his chest. Then, after gunning down Maddow (in self-defense), Cooper heads for Wilson's house. The old man is so terrified of Cooper's retribution that he ultimately hangs himself — a poetic justice ending if there ever was one.

FEELIN' LUCKY, PUNK? Clint Eastwood as the marshal in *Hang 'Em High* (1968). The film skillfully bridged the gap between the anarchic mayhem of his spaghetti westerns and the more conventional plot elements of American westerns.

Meanwhile, the compassionate Jenkins, after having confessed his part in Cooper's hanging, is set for the scaffold by Fenton's orders. Cooper demands the old man's release. Though Fenton acquiesces, the wily jurist bargains with his ace lawman: The old man will be released, but only if Cooper keeps his badge and returns to work (he wants him to go after the two remaining members of the hanging party). Ultimately, Jed Cooper, former victim of a lynch mob, will now ride the trail of John Law. The last we see of him is not a final romantic clinch with Rachel, but riding out of town to hunt his next quarry for Judge Fenton's court. (Reportedly, Post and Eastwood had cut a final scene with Rachel so that the film would stay on track with its important theme.)

In his entertaining (and sometimes infuriating) *Western Films*, Brian Garfield goes on a lengthy tirade about the film. Here's an excerpt:

> Intriguing complexities were implied in the character of Jedediah Cooper, but the writers, the director, nor the star could bring these complexities to life. The end result is that the film *Hang 'Em High*, like Clint Eastwood's voice, was a thin expressionless whisper that left many audiences dissatisfied because of what it might have been. It failed to provoke any emotion. Several scenes potentially were quite moving, but they passed too quickly to register ... *Hang 'Em High* started as a first-rate idea and ended as a superficial oater that went through the motions, but left one with a feeling of having wasted two hours: We hadn't been stirred, we hadn't enjoyed it, we hadn't seen enough to think about, and we hadn't been entertained.[25]

Audiences apparently disagreed with Garfield. On an estimated budget of $1,800,000, *Hang 'Em High* grossed $6,778,000 in the United States alone.[26]

Now, an American western movie star as well as a European one, Eastwood would continue with the twin themes of resurrection and enforcing the Unwritten Law. The decades ahead would be his for the taking; indeed, at times it would seem that he was the *only* one to continue making theatrical westerns into the 1990s. Expanding on the Man with No Name, Eastwood eventually took his screen persona into Oscar territory with 1992's *Unforgiven*.

Meanwhile, over at Universal, the studio shot a western that depicted one lawman's use of deadly force, and how "civilization" would be bought at the point of a gun...

"Fear's the only goddamn thing they understand!"—*Marshal Frank Patch*

Lewis Byford Patten was born in Denver, Colorado, on January 13, 1915. A graduate of the University of Denver, Patten became a rancher in 1944, and five years later he began his writing career. His birthplace alone would give him the "required" credentials to be a western author. A man who had grown up listening to stories of the famed lawmen and outlaws who roamed Colorado and the surroundings territories, Patten had a remarkable facility for producing a sheer volume of western stories and novels which few in the profession could match. He lacked the originality and historical scope of a Les Savage Jr. or Ernest Haycox; his heroes were not the authoritarian strongmen of Louis L'Amour novels, nor did his characters have the heart and soul that Elmer Kelton brought to his works; his heroes and heroines were even devoid of the romantic conflicts that were characteristic of Luke Short. Indeed, one wonders why the works of Lewis B. Patten were printed and reprinted into the 1990s. Perhaps it was because of the man's prolific output; like Wayne D. Overholser and Marvin H. Alpert, Patten banged them out with regularity from the early 1950s almost to his death in 1981, entertaining millions of western fans. Perhaps it was because of his versatility in western subject matter: He did the homesteader vs. cattleman story (*The Homesteader*, among many others), Custer vs. the Indians (*Red Sabbath*), Indians-on-the-warpath stories (*Cheyenne Drums*), tales of Indian vengeance (*Death Stalks Yellowhorse*), Civil War novels (*Trail to Vicksburg*), the Mexican Revolution (*Villa's Rifles*), and town lynchings (*The Gallows at Graneros*).

Some of Patten's novels have a great many variations on the same story, with none used so often as that of the beleaguered lawman guarding a prisoner, whether that prisoner be a rapist or murderer (*Guns of Grey Butte* is a good example), and fighting off lynch mobs and indifferent town elders and keeping the accused alive so he can get a fair trial. In 1968, on the heels of angry street protests all across the country, as well as a rise in urban crime, Patten wrote *Death of a Gunfighter*, a parable about a tough lawman who finds that his violent methods no longer fit a country ready to leave its frontier past behind. As the cry of police brutality could be heard throughout America's big cities, Patten gave us a law enforcer who killed when he had to, not caring whether self-proclaimed social activists in the local government or the town itself were shocked by the violence.

Universal had already filmed one of Patten's books way back in 1956. Based on the novel *Back Trail*, *Red Sundown* is another story about a gunfighter trying to hang up his guns, only to have to use them again to fight an evil cattleman. Starring Rory Calhoun and directed by cult director Jack Arnold, *Red Sundown* provided the usual action elements that distinguished the studio's western output in the 1950s. However, *Death of a Gunfighter* was a different animal altogether. Coming at a time when the western was still going strong, the film was also influenced by the cynicism and downbeat atmosphere of the late 1960s, a time of turmoil for America.

At the turn of the 20th century, Cottonwood Springs, Texas, is a growing metropolis.

It is a western town with saddled horses at the tie-rails and where men are still wearing their hog-legs tied low on their respective hips, but there are also automobiles in the streets and telephone poles in the background (not the usual glitch made by inattentive western filmmakers). In fact, the town brings to mind the usual Republic B with Roy or Gene which mixed old west conventions like horses and six-guns with airplanes and telephones. But *Death of a Gunfighter* emphatically does *not* conjure up the fantasy worlds of *Melody Ranch* or *Phantom Empire*.

In the film, we see Claire Quintana (Lena Horne) in widow's weeds, accompanying a coffin containing the body of her late husband on the night train as it leaves Cottonwood Springs. This scene is a "wraparound" put in by the film's second director, Don Siegel. After the helmsman focuses on a lone kid following the train as he toddles along the tracks, he fades into a shot of teenage Dan Joslin (Michael McGreevey) sauntering around town. At this point, we begin to see the work of the film's *first* director, Robert Totten. Dan visits his friend Dan Patch (Richard Widmark), a tough marshal of the old school.

That night, while Patch makes his rounds on horseback, he is spied on from the second-floor window of the local whorehouse by local pipefitter Luke Mills (Jimmy Lydon), who suspects that his wife is having an affair with the lawman. When Patch rides into a darkened stable, he is shot at from the hayloft by Luke. Though the lawman pleads with Mills to give himself up, the pipefitter's reply is more gunfire. Patch is then forced to kill him.

The shooting inspires controversy in the town; apparently Patch has blown away quite a few lawbreakers in the twenty or so years he's been on the job. Previously grateful that he's cleaned up their town from outlaw elements, the citizens of Cottonwood Springs and their civic leaders now regard their marshal's use of deadly force as detrimental to their town's growth. Not only that, but as the local saloonkeeper-loudmouth Lester Locke (a pre–Archie Bunker Carroll O'Connor) says, because he had been marshal of Cottonwood Springs for over twenty years, Patch knows everyone's secrets, embarrassing and scandalous details about even the hifalutin town elders that they would like to forget. The most vindictive city council member is Ivan Stanek (Morgan Woodward), who prods Mayor Sayre (Larry Gates) and the council to get rid of Patch one way or the other. Other council members include Andrew Oxley (Kent Smith), Arch Brandt (Royal Dano), Father Sweeney (James O'Hara), Doc Adams (the wonderful Dub Taylor) and the council's only Jewish member, Edward Rosenblum (former comcentration camp survivor David Opatoshu). There was also the character of an old religious woman named Mary Elizabeth, played by Kathleen Freeman, but either Totten or Siegel cut her scenes out, and we just hear her voice briefly at the beginning of the film as she harangues a crowd. This is a shame since Freeman was a talented actress-comedienne whose character probably could have added to the story.

After Luke dies, Patch visits his widow Laurie (the always reliable Jacqueline Scott); when Patch tries to embrace her in her grief, there is certainly an implication that Luke's fantasies about an affair between his wife and the marshal might not have been drunken ravings after all. Having had enough of Patch's violent methods of law enforcement, Stanek prods the council to write an edict officially dismissing him from his post. Taking their Model As to the outskirts of town where they find Patch fishing with Dan, the mayor and the senior council members serve the damning paper (Rosenblum and Father Sweeney are not there). Patch contemptuously rips it to shreds, reminding the council that they promised him the job for as long as *he* wanted it. When Andy argues with Patch, the lawman knocks him down. Also witnessing this skirmish is Andy's son Will (Mercer Harris), who is ashamed of his father for not fighting back. It is soon revealed that Patch has something on the old man.

Realizing that he has to win back his son's respect, Andy decides to kill Patch. Trying to talk him out of his desperate act, Patch is horrified when the tormented man shoots himself. Over his dead body, Patch lamely says, "Andy, I wouldn't have talked...." The death of his father only makes Will hate the lawman even *more*.

At the next city council meeting, Stanek proposes that this august body of cultured men should now kill their stubborn marshal. This not only drives Father Sweeney from the room, but enrages Rosenblum; this triggers an anti-Semitic outburst from Stanek. Ultimately, the town elders decide to send for lawman Lou Trinidad (John Saxon), who will officially fire Patch. Apparently, the two have had a history. Trinidad was once Patch's deputy, with the older man insisting on his appointment despite racist opposition from council members to a Latino lawman. (One wonders where these men have been, since Texas was full of Latino lawmen after the Civil War; they were even in the Texas Rangers.) Stopping himself from calling Trinidad a "greaser," the angry Patch still knocks down his former friend and then tosses him out of his office.

As Doc patches up Lou, the council members decide to go ahead with Stanek's plan to murder the marshal. As Trinidad prepares to leave by train, Patch gets himself hitched to Claire by Reverend Rork (the ubiquitous Harry Carey Jr.). However, at Locke's saloon, the vindictive barman and his two lackeys, Miller (Victor French) and Hogg (Robert Sorrells), are propping up Will's courage with booze and phony compliments. But when the young man actually does attempt to kill Patch, the marshal guns him down. But before he dies, the lawman tells him that many years ago, he had dropped charges against Andy for shooting a man in the back if he would raise the man's son.

Since Will has botched the job of rubbing out Patch, Locke, Miller and Hogg quickly open fire on the lawman and wound him. After Patch kills Hogg, Locke shoots Miller in the back when he tries to turn tail. Attempting to flee on the departing train, Locke is lassoed and throwned in jail by Patch.

But it is too late for the proud lawman. At a signal from the mayor, Stanek and other members of the city council (*sans* the compassionate Rosenblum and Father Sweeney) open fire on Patch and kill him. The film returns to the beginning when we see the widowed Claire accompanying her husband's casket out of town.

Though the film had all the time-honored elements, the stubborn lawman, the nasty villains, and plenty of shooting, it reflected great changes in the genre. Unlike the westerns of previous years, not everyone in the film was white and Christian. In fact, this turn-of-the-century Texas town acknowledged the presence of ethnicities in important positions. Lou Trinidad is a respected lawman, and the only one making a racist crack is Locke (Carroll O'Connor already starting to sound like Archie Bunker). We are told that Lou has a wife and family and is a man who is proud of his job, a wonderful acknowledgment of the possibilities for minorities living the American dream. However, we do not forget (and this is what makes Trinidad's visit so ironic) that Lou's first crack at being a lawman was made possible by Marshal Patch, the man he was supposed to dismiss.

For the first time in the history of the American western, a Jew is now serving as a respected member of the lawmaking body of a western town. However, like Lou Trinidad, Rosenblum is still the victim of bigotry. When Stanek proposes to have Patch killed, the compassionate Jew is one of only two council members to be against the idea. After Rosenblum sarcastically suggests that they burn Patch at the stake (conjuring up imagery of per-

TRAPPED. Richard Widmark as the stubborn marshal whose excessive use of deadly force leads to his finish in *Death of a Gunfighter* (1969). Off-screen, Widmark had director Robert Totten fired and replaced him with Don Siegel. Then, after Siegel refused credit on the film, Universal credited the direction to the non-existent Allen Smithee, the first time that the *nom de shame* was ever used.

secution that his people were all too familiar with), he gets everything but the word "kike" thrown at him by Stanek.

However, the greatest step forward for this western was the appearance of an African-American woman as the marshal's girlfriend. Apparently, this was a casting choice insisted upon by the film's star, a man who always believed in integration. In fact, the saloon owner-madam is *not* African-American in the novel. However, the role of Claire would have one glaring difference from out-in-the-open minority figures like Rosenblum and Trinidad: Claire's skin color is never alluded to once in the entire film. Locke and Stanek can freely call Trinidad a "greaser" and heap anti–Semitic remarks on Rosenblum, yet somehow forget to use the N word when Claire is around? Rather strange.

Though Lena Horne liked the fact that Claire's race is never mentioned, she hesitated about accepting the job, insecure about returning to movies after so many years. Widmark flew out to visit her in New York to convince her to take the role. In her biography *Stormy Weather: The Life of Lena Horne*, author James Gavin wrote: "'Richard [Widmark] was a sensitive man, I think,' recalled Horne. 'He didn't frighten me.' She tested his racial attitude in their conversation, and was relieved that he responded 'in the correct way.'"[27]

One wonders what Horne, a world-class diva who had her own problems with tolerance, thought was the "correct way" (she was reportedly upset that her daughter was marrying white director Sidney Lumet[28]). But the singer was ultimately sold on the project; she not only accepted the role, but she sang the sad title song, "Sweet Apple Wine," which was also heard over the end credits. (It was also rumored that she and Widmark were lovers.)

In Don Siegel's self-serving autobiography *A Siegel Film*, the auteur relates how the problem on the movie began. He claimed that Widmark pressured Universal to hire him (Siegel) and fire Robert Totten. A TV director of many years, Totten was also a westerner and even rode his own horses (according to Siegel, anyway). Completely at ease directing dozens of TV western shows, Totten does a commendable job keeping up the film's pace. During the scene where Patch, on horseback, is roping and dragging Locke through the cattle pen, Siegel wrote that it was Totten himself who shot the scene on horseback with a handheld camera (it *is* a well-shot sequence). Siegel wrote that Widmark disliked Totten because "I don't like his thinking. We don't speak the same language." Despite the box office magic Siegel had with Widmark on *Madigan*, the auteur rejected his former star's offer.[29]

Then Universal-MCA president Lew Wasserman called—and when Lew Wasserman called, Hollywood listened. Siegel would always claim that most of the film was Totten's work; he had simply filmed the "wraparound" scenes of Horne the widow accompanying her husband's casket. However, Siegel also did pickup shots and pared down any scenes that went on too long. He might have been instrumental in cutting out Kathleen Freeman's role; Jacqueline Scott, who was prominent early in the film as Luke Mill's wife, suddenly disappears midway through the film. Talking about the film years later, Horne maintained that she liked the fact that Claire's whorehouse is integrated, yet after Siegel's cut we don't see any black women in the place.

Patten's novel, like much of his work, builds up the many conflicts among his townspeople until the story hurtles to a climax. Joseph Cavelli's screenplay continues Patten's breakneck pace, though it soon becomes obvious that there was some directorial tampering, especially when two directors were at work on the same film. After Totten's firing, Siegel took over, but he would claim that he refused credit because it was really Totten's film. However, since Siegel had no enthusiasm for the project to begin with, and probably sensed that it would be a bomb, it's highly doubtful that the usually self-serving helmsman had altruistic motives for having his name removed from the film. Ultimately, the Directors Guild created that mythical auteur Allen Smithee. And so, Allen Smithee has remained the stubbornly iconoclastic ghost helmsman who has confounded critics and alienated audiences with his works to this very day.

Some critics felt that the film deserved some credit. In his review in the May 12, 1969, *Chicago Sun-Times*, Roger Ebert wrote:

> *Death of a Gunfighter* is quite an extraordinary western. It's one of those rare attempts (the last was *Will Penny*) to populate the west with real people living in a real historical time. But in this one we're given a loving portrait of a western town in transition.... Against this background, we begin to meet the townspeople. And this is an amazing town, for a Western. It had Italians, Negroes, Jews and Greeks in it.[30]

Besides taking note of the groundbreaking changes the film made in the genre, Ebert called Marshal Patch "one of Richard Widmark's best, most fully realized performances." However, the esteemed critic added, "Director Allen Smithee, a name I'm not familiar with, allows his story to unfold naturally. He never preaches and he never lingers on the obvious. His characters do what they have to do."[31]

Death of a Gunfighter demonstrated the limits of deadly force to be used by lawmen in a now-dying west. As civilization settles in, those badge-toters who had perpetuated the rule of law by "Judge Colt and his Jury of Six" now found themselves as passé and irrelevant as the once proud warriors of the plains whose vastness only ended with the horizon. According to other characters in the film, the problem with Dan Patch was not the lack of due process and the rule of law, but in the way he enforced it. Stubborn, proud, and far too angry, Patch doesn't grow with the land around him (the villainous town elders ride around in cars; Patch is still riding his horse). As shown in Peckinpah's *The Wild Bunch*, when tough men do not grow with the times, they are destroyed by the new west that now considers them sad anachronisms.

The 1960s began in relative peace and ended in turmoil. Racism, rioting, political assassinations, Vietnam and soon Watergate were going to dominate the news for quite a while. Not since the Civil War would the nation be so divided. Its residual effects would be reflected in "with it" entertainment like *Easy Rider* and the underrated satire *Wild in the Streets*. Even the western would give us its first hippie gunslinger (though since he was a hippie, he wasn't what you'd call an expert pistolero) in *Zachariah*. The posters cried, "The first electric western!" *Groovy* it wasn't.

However, in the years ahead, more grounded filmmakers used the western to deliver their own messages about the state of the country. As young Americans died in Southeast Asia, the landscape of the old west would also become a killing field....

6

Bloodbath: 1970–1976
Vietnam, Race Riots and Abuse of the Law in the Old West

"You know what they call you, Jared? The Widow-Maker!"—Laura Shelby

Michael Winner began as a TV director in his native England in the 1950s. He had written British B movies since the late '50s and worked his way up to becoming a director of films, most of them featuring English pop stars and comedians. Nothing in his past seemed to even imply that this man would be responsible for making three *Death Wish* movies (as well as three other exercises in screen violence using his favorite star, Charles Bronson), the more crude and violent remake of *The Big Sleep*, and the convoluted revenge actioner *Firepower*. The days when he would use Billy Fury and Frankie Howerd were over; his films now featured tough-guys like Bronson, James Coburn and Burt Lancaster.

Even when Lancaster performed in films featuring multiple shootings and a high body count, he was the Thinking Man's action star. Not once did the actor do a film featuring violence and mayhem unless a comment could be made on just *why* there was violence and mayhem. In 1973, he and Winner collaborated on one of the best films *ever* made about double-crossing intelligence agencies, the underrated *Scorpio*.

Shooting in Durango, Mexico, in early 1971, actor and director focused their attention on the old west and gave us *Lawman*, a film centering on a straight-as-an-arrow marshal whose adherence to the letter of the law results in tragedy for all. This is quite a change from the westerns of the past where the lawman who deals in fair play (Randolph Scott is an excellent example) was a voice of calm and reason in a sea of civic hysteria and rampant outlawry. In *Lawman*, everything seems to be going well until that very same voice of "calm and reason" arrives in someone else's town merely to do his duty.

Our story begins in the town of Bannock, circa 1887. Members of the Bronson outfit are in town along with their aging boss, Vincent Bronson (Lee J. Cobb). These cowboys do what liquored-up cowboys usually do on their night off: They shoot up the town. This includes firing their Colts into shop windows, resulting in much broken glass and fires being started. Seeing his men going out of control, Bronson calls them together and the whole outfit rides out. Unfortunately, an old man is lying on the ground with a bullet in his skull.

Marshal Jared Maddox (Lancaster) rides into the neighboring town of Sabbath. In a scene that recalls the consternation of the citizenry when Henry Fonda rode into town with a corpse on the back of his pack horse in Anthony Mann's *The Tin Star*, Maddox enters Sabbath with a dead man on the back of his pack horse. The outraged Sabbathians, led by the vindictive Luther Harris (Walter Brooke) already think that Maddox is a bounty hunter. However, it turns out that Maddox is a strictly-by-the-book lawman; he enters the office of aging Marshal Cotton Ryan (played by the aging yet still powerful, Robert Ryan).

Maddox has a list of the seven men responsible for the fracas that killed the old man in Bannock, and he wants Ryan's help in arresting them. However, Ryan is sad and disillusioned about the way things have turned out. Refusing to help Maddox, he honestly admits that he is a bought-and-paid-for lawman put in his job by the powerful Bronson. One must compliment the two actors for making every scene between them work; the literate dialogue crackles between them as they comment on the law and how the two had enforced it during their lives. It was obvious that Lancaster admired Ryan and vice versa. They had worked together in Richard Brooks' excellent *The Professionals* and would work together again, unfortunately, in Communist screenwriter Dalton Trumbo's paranoid fantasy on the Kennedy assassination, *Executive Action*. It seems that the man Maddox killed was one of the men rioting in Bannock the night the old man was killed; the man's big mistake was calling Maddox out.

Of course, Ryan rides out to the Bronson Ranch to tell the cattleman about Maddox's arrival. Again, one must give credit to screenwriter (and frequent Winner collaborator) Gerald Wilson for an intelligent screenplay which flies in the face of genre clichés. Vincent Bronson is not an evil man; unlike the cattle barons of 1950s movies and TV shows, Bronson doesn't rant and rave. Instead, after calling his hands together, Bronson democratically asks them for their opinions on the matter. His men are played by a veritable potpourri of early 1970s character actors: Bronson's right-hand man, ramrod Harvey Stenbaugh (Albert Salmi), small rancher Vernon Adams (Robert Duvall), Jack Dekker (Ralph Waite), his hot-tempered son Jason (John Beck), Hurd Price (J.D. Cannon), Choctaw Lee (William Watson), and a young man who was *not* involved in the trouble in Bannock, Crowe Wheelwright (Richard Jordan in his film debut). Retaining (at least for now) his portrayal of Bronson as a sober-minded rancher, scenarist Wilson gives the cattleman's righteous rage to his foreman, Stenbaugh. The angry ramrod wants to throw down on Maddox personally, especially for having already killed one of their own (the fact that the cowhand had called out Maddox is barely mentioned). Bronson counsels restraint and hopes that simply paying for the dead man's funeral and helping out the widow will suffice. Maddox hears the offer and refuses; he doesn't want their money, he wants them under arrest.

The irony here is that, even if Maddox brings all the accused men back to Bannock, it's a sure thing that the town's judge will be bought by Bronson and that the men will be found not guilty. However, to Maddox, the law is the law; his job is to bring them in, their sentencing is not his problem.

Maddox is visited by his old sweetheart, Laura Shelby (the still-lovely Sheree North). The actress was a long way from the 1950s when Fox was promoting her as a possible replacement for the troublesome Marilyn Monroe, and since then, she had done far too many Bs and lots of TV. In *Lawman*, she gives a fine performance. Her casting compliments the similarly aging Lancaster. Having apparently gotten over Maddox, Laura has taken a husband. Unfortunately, it's the cowardly and plainly no-good Hurd Price, one of the men Maddox is after.

Accosting Maddox in the local saloon, Luther Harris and the town elders, including its deaf mayor Sam Bolden (played for laughs by the ubiquitous John McGiver), order the marshal to leave "their" town. Maddox calls Harris a "big mouth" and challenges the men to take him if one of them has the guts to start shooting. Everyone, including the loudmouthed Luther, meekly leaves. This scene is *highly* reminiscent of the one in *No Name on the Bullet*, starring Audie Murphy. In fact, like John Gant, the gunfighter who always has to stay alert, Maddox is at the bar drinking coffee.

GOING BY THE RULES. Burt Lancaster as the by-the-book marshal in *Lawman* (1971). It was the first and best of the actor's trilogy of early 1970s westerns in which he used the genre to make euphemistic comments on twentieth century racism and the Vietnam War.

After Maddox leaves the saloon, he is called out by Stenbaugh, but the lawman outdraws him and guns him down. Furious, Bronson changes his tune and calls for Maddox's execution; however, unlike previous cattle barons, he does calm down long enough to see if violence can be avoided. Still, Stenbaugh was like a son to him. The next one to call out Maddox is the youthful Crowe. But the wise lawman sees that he is a boy and simply walks up to him and plants himself two inches from his face. (It's hard to do a fast-draw on your enemy if he's close enough to touch. See John Wayne's wonderful reaction to Harry Woods' throwing down on him in *Tall in the Saddle*.)

During this time, Maddox has reacquainted himself with whorehouse owner Lucas (an unusually restrained Joseph Wiseman). When Maddox is *again* braced by Crowe (trying to prove that he's not scared of Maddox), the marshal gently chides the boy, then walks away. Just then a shot is fired at Maddox that barely misses him. Suddenly accusing Crowe of setting him up (which the boy denies), Maddox knocks him down. It is the first time we see the always-in-control lawman crack. He is brave and steady under pressure when he is called out, but when someone tries to backshoot him, Maddox becomes paranoid and violent.

Cotton leads Maddox to Lucas' establishment where the shot came from. Bursting into the building (Lucas cooperatively points out Jack Dekker's room), the two apprehend the Bronson man and, after Cotton roughs him up, he is thrown in jail. Still angered over the attempted backshoot, the lawman even opens the cell door, pulls his gun and prompts the gunman to make an escape attempt. It's Robert Ryan as his best.

The next day, while Maddox is riding out on the prairie, he is dry-gulched by Vernon Adams and Hurd Price. After capturing and wounding Adams, Maddox ends up taking him to the closest place around, Laura's cabin. During the night, the two ex-lovers decide to relive old times. (Unlike the youth-obsssessed films of the 21st century, the films of the 1970s had no problem showing middle-aged characters still being attracted to each other enough to do a bedroom scene.)

The revival of Maddox's love affair with Laura softens the marshal, and for the first time, he loosens up enough to entertain thoughts of leaving law enforcement and settling down with her on some plot of land. Bronson, and especially his men, have other ideas. After Maddox throws the wounded Adams in one of Ryan's cells, Bronson and his remaining men appear on the street waiting to open fire. When Maddox does appear, he shocks all of them by getting on his horse and riding away. He is about to be dry-gulched by Luther Harris until the storekeeper is shot in the back by Lucas.

The shot literally triggers a massacre. Maddox dives off his horse and Choctaw takes advantage of it to fire at the lawman. Returning fire, Maddox kills him. Still, the marshal announces "It's over," and attempts to leave town, but Bronson's son Jason wants the marshal's hide. Shoving his father away, Jason throws down on the marshal and is blown away for the attempt. In total despair, Bronson shoots himself in the throat. Frightened, Price turns tail and runs down the street. Maddox raises his Colt and fires, sending a bullet into Price's back right in front of the newly widowed Laura as she enters town on her buckboard. (When Lancaster asked his director just *why* Maddox shoots a fleeing man in the back, Winner simply replied, "Because he's a *bastard*, Burt!") Knowing that it is too late for him to stop killing men, Maddox rides past Laura, out of town and out of her life.

From its shoot 'em-up beginning to its bleak ending, *Lawman* is, in its own way, a minor classic. The climactic gundown, filled with Winner's sweeping camera movements, perfectly compliments a story where misinterpretation and mixed signals result in tragedy. It was the second in Lancaster's early 1970s western trilogy; every one of them commented euphemistically on the twin obsessions of those years, racism and the Vietnam War. The other two are *Valdez Is Coming* and *Ulzana's Raid*; *Lawman* is easily the best of the three. As in the Vietnam War and many other conflicts, what is at first thought to be a limited battle quickly gets out of control and the killings mount, and what was originally the routine enforcement of some doctrine or principle turns into a mindless bloodbath. As we see in *Lawman*, just because one side quits the fight doesn't mean the other side will. Maddox's remark to Cotton and Lucas that even when a man wants to quit, someone will pull him back in foreshadows Michael Corleone's famous line in *The Godfather, Part III* about wanting to quit, "but they pull me back in!"

In Vietnam, Americans tried to "roll back Communism"; lawman Maddox tries to roll back what he considers rampant outlawry and goes after Bronson's men. As he says to Laura, if he didn't enforce the law, the next time, they could kill those close to him. Echoing this talk, hawks in our government always claimed that if we didn't draw a line in Southeast Asia, a domino effect would occur and other nations would go Communist. Seeking to merely enforce the law, never drawing unless the other guy draws first, and repudiating lynch mob rule, Jared Maddox is a decent man. But as Laura says to him, just making sure he doesn't draw first is not enough; men are still dying. Just because someone plays fair and square is not enough. Good men can still kill each other unnecessarily despite good intentions. Very few westerns effectively commented on, not only the foibles of the law, but the international conflicts of the time.

However, there is another school of thought on this that repudiates the film's philosophy. Would it have been better had Maddox been *slow* on the draw and allowed himself to be murdered? Aren't folks allowed to defend themselves? Would the murder of the by-the-book lawman actually *stop* the killing? Obviously, without men like Maddox to enforce the law, widow-maker or not, outlawry and crime would most likely *increase*, as would the body count of innocent people.

In his review in the *Chicago Sun-Times*, dated August 31, 1971, Roger Ebert wrote:

> [Lancaster] plays a hard, cold, sullen law-and-order type who sides with justice against mercy at every opportunity, and he causes a lot of unnecessary grief before the movie's over. Still, he's the marshal, and we're supposed to be on his side.... In the meantime, Lancaster alienates everyone in town and does nothing to prevent a climate for violence. He doesn't do any of the things a sensible marshal would do; he just talks about the law and provokes confrontations.[1]

Of course, Maddox *didn't* provoke any of the confrontations; he played it fair and square right down the line. Rather, throughout the film he was provoked by others. (Were Winner and Gerald Wilson saying that the old man's killing should be forgotten?) It was only at the end, when he shot a fleeing Hurd Price in the back, that Maddox crossed the line from lawman to murderer. All in all, Lancaster, Winner, Wilson and the cast should be applauded for creating a western that is as thought-provoking to this day as when it was released in 1971.

Meanwhile, as urban crime continued to rise and the Vietnam War reached its zenith, liberal filmmaker John Huston and conservative screenwriter John Milius gave us a film in which a perpetrator of rope justice would also be facing a changing west. Focusing on a legendary old west justice of the peace, the film was a black-humored tribute to a man who thought of himself as the Law West of the Pecos....

> "The only lynching around here will be done according to the law!"—*Judge Roy Bean*

A lot had happened to the western in the 31 years after *The Westerner* was released in 1940. Most of all, there was an increase of violence in the genre. In 1940, when Walter Brennan dispensed justice as Judge Roy Bean, Samuel Goldwyn always had Joseph Breen's Production Code Office looking over his shoulder. This made Brennan's version of Bean a wily rascal whose evil was based on his oppression of the local farmers, rather than personal acts of brutality. However, by 1971, as urban crime increased and Hollywood gave us rightist wish-fantasies like *Dirty Harry*, *The Life and Times of Judge Roy Bean* became a tart commentary on both the need for and the excesses of the death penalty. However, unlike Walter Brennan's old jurist, Paul Newman's version of Bean dispensed with oppression of poor farmers and focused instead on bringing law and order to the west, one hanging at a time.

The film was a First Artists Production, a company with Newman, Steve McQueen, Sidney Poitier and Barbra Streisand as its figureheads. Their films were released by National General Pictures (whose facilities and completed films were eventually bought up by Warner Brothers). By 1971, Newman was at the top of his game; no longer the mannered and annoying young Brando imitator of *The Left Handed Gun*, Newman had finally found his own voice. One wonders why the liberal actor and the equally liberal helmsman decided to hook up with right-wing, pro-gun scenarist John Milius, though it was obvious that they all agreed to make a euphemistic comment on the death penalty by using an old west icon of rope justice as their central figure.

Seedy outlaw Roy Bean (Newman) stops off at a saloon-brothel in the middle of the South Texas desert. The denizens there promptly attack him, steal his money, put a rope around his neck and tie him to the back of a horse, which is sent galloping into the night. Forunately, for Ben, the rope breaks. He is lying in the desert when a Latina named Maria Elena (played by non-Latina Victoria Principal), used as a slave by the gang back at the house, sneaks a loaded gun to Bean as he revives. Bursting into the saloon, Bean guns down all the men and sends the few women there fleeing in terror into the desert. Now with a permanent rope burn around his neck and his head bent sideways, Bean grabs hold of an old lawbook and morphs into a parable of frontier justice, believing that his attack on the outlaws was successful because "God guided my bullets." However, in just a few minutes after he becomes a judge, Newman drops the head-bent-to-the-side look and the rope burn around his neck miraculously disappears. Must be that South Texas air.

When an outlaw gang arrives, Bean enlists the amiable ex–train robbers as "marshals of the court," along the lines of Judge Isaac Parker's court at Fort Smith, Arkansas. One of the ironclad rules of Bean's court, besides upholding the law of the state of Texas, is to respect the image of stage star Lillian Langtry, who just happens to look like film star Ava Gardner, and whose poster is prominently hung up behind the judge's bar. When a pimp arrives with a wagon full of whores, Bean has the man kicked out of town and then "confiscates" the women and orders them to marry his marshals. One night, a traveling wagon driven by mountain man Grizzly Adams (John Huston, never at any time as good an actor as he was a director) breaks down near the Vinegaroon. Bean orders Adams to move on, but the smelly old coot leaves behind his black bear, an awesome but mostly harmless creature who follows the judge around like a rather large terrifying puppy. In due time, the lumbering animal becomes another distinct character in his upside-down world. (Andy Williams recorded a song played over a scene in which Bean, Maria and the bear have a picnic and romp in the woods.)

As time goes on (it is 1899), Bean's law continues unabated, with more hangings of "lawbreakers." However, the judge's initiatives have also helped build up the town, and now there is a Bean Hotel to go along with the stores and businesses coming to Langtry. When crazed albino killer Bad Bob (Stacy Keach) shoots up the town (including shooting off the toe of one of Bean's men), and calls out the judge (going out of his way to insult Lily Langtry as well), the judge dry-gulches him with a shotgun. At this point, screen violence was becoming cartoonish, with the judge's shotgun blast literally blowing a hole through Bad Bob that is so huge that the audience can see through it. After the killing, happy music is played and Maria Elena runs into his arms.

Frank Gass (Roddy McDowall) arrives, claiming to be a representative of the previous owner of Bean's property, and high-handedly questions the judge's authority. A big mistake; Bean puts him into the bear's cage. Eventually Gass and Bean come to an agreement which allows Gass to stay in town and drop the property claim. But as time goes on, the wily lawyer will take advantage of Bean's hospitality and usurp the judge's authority. In the meantime, the former whores, now established women of the town, have become snotnoses and are susceptible to Gass' flattery and his plans to take over. After an assassin tries to kill Bean, the bear fatally mauls the gunman but is shot and killed in the fight. In mourning, Bean and his men bury the animal with full civic honors.

Hearing that Lillian Langtry is appearing in San Antonio, Bean goes up there in top hat and tails and a bouquet of flowers, but never meets her. Instead, he is mugged by two men in the theater's alley. After he returns to Langtry, Bean not only sees his beloved Maria Elena die while giving birth to their baby girl, but finds that Gass has effectively taken over the town and squeezed him out. With Bean's methods now considered barbaric, the system of justice instituted by him will be replaced by corruption and the rule of an expanding bureaucracy run by the town's new mayor, the crooked Gass. When his marshals fail to support him, a disillusioned Bean gets on his horse and rides out of town.

Cut to the 1920s. According to the narrator, Teddy Rossevelt is elected president, which was good, but then "women got the vote and everything went to hell." It is inferred that, through their evil influence, the Volstead Act came about, meaning that "drinking and gambling and whoring were declared unlawful." Bean's town has now become a wealthy enterprise, thanks to the discovery of oil. However, Gass' corrupting influence has also opened up the town to gangsters who are effectively bleeding the former bastion of law and order dry. Bean's old marshals are now has-beens and drunks. Even Bean's daughter Rose (Jacqueline Bisset) is disgusted by it all. Having grown up reading about her ornery dad and admiring him, she has his tendency to shake things up. When Gass threatens to evict her from her father's house, she drives the gang boss out with a shotgun.

HUSTLER. Paul Newman's not playing with a full deck as Judge Roy Bean in *The Life and Times of Judge Roy Bean* (1972). The liberal actor and his director John Huston gutted conservative screenwriter John Milius' serious script and turned it into sloppy comedy.

Then one night, Bean rides back in town and reorganizes his marshals and his daughter into a fighting force. Defying Gass' gunmen, they start a shootout and set fire to much of the town, meaning Gass' properties. Riding his horse hell bent for leather, Bean chases Gass into a building that goes up in flames. The last Rose will see of her father is as he's rearing his horse on its balcony and proclaiming, "For Texas and Miss Lily!"

Years later, after the town has been cleansed of Gass' evil influence, Lillian Langtry (the still stunning Ava Gardner) visits Bean's home (now a museum) to learn more about her admirer. She is told that Rose is now happily married to a military pilot. Lily is saddened to hear that the judge "cashed in his chips," and reads a letter that he never mailed to her, a final declaration of love from "the Law West of the Pecos."

In his autobiography *An Open Book*, John Huston referred to *The Life and Times of Judge Roy Bean* as "not exactly a failure, but you could hardly call it a roaring success." He then went on to explain just why he did the film:

> I was intrigued in the first place by John Milius' script, which showed a splendid feeling for the old west. *Roy Bean* was in the fine old American tradition of the Tall Tale, the Whopper, the yarn peopled with outrageous characters capable of prodigious and highly improbable deeds. At the same time, it said something important about frontier life and the loss of America's innocence.[2]

Huston was in ill health and at 70, the usually beneficial effects of a Tucson visit eluded him, causing him to down huge gulps of vodka all day (very dehydrating in the hot Arizona location). Added to this, he brought along his fifth wife CiCi, a hot-tempered woman who was less than half his age.[3] Further on in his autobiography, without actually naming her, he compares her mouth to that of a "sea snake." Huston's homophobia also made itself known, with Anthony Perkins openly complaining to Newman that the director was mercilessly picking on him because of his sexual orientation.[4] (Perkins may have had a good point. Huston contributed to Montgomery Clift's being blacklisted for four years in the early 1960s after he blamed production problems during the filming of *Freud* on Clift's alcoholism. However, it was also well-known that the helmsman hated working with Clift after he discovered the actor's homosexuality before the start of shooting.[5] This is an interesting sidenote in the life of a director who had protested HUAC's use of the blacklist.)

Not that the helmsman was the only one on the bottle. The dazzling but aging-fast Ava Gardner was allegedly drunk much of the time. And she had no good things to say about the film's star either: "I can't stand that man [Newman]. He's one of my unfavorite actors. He's an egomaniac and so false. He's 'on' all the time."[6]

Reinforcing the "egomaniac" part, Newman gave directions to the young

AND THAT'S MA RULIN'. Paul Newman as the judge in *The Life and Times of Judge Roy Bean* (1972). The production had to deal with the director's alcoholic binges as well as Ava Gardner's drunken behavior. Ultimately, it failed at the box office.

Victoria Principal. Of course, there may have been good reason for this; Huston was either off in his trailer with his young bride or he was drunk out of his gourd — or both. When the perpetually inebriated helmsman eventually told Victoria to do something a certain way, she replied that Newman told her to do it another way, causing the two-faced actor to chew her out in front of the company and insist that *Huston* was the film's director, not him. We can only assume that the young actress recalled acts of betrayal like this when she eventually played opposite the backstabbing characters of her hit series *Dallas*.

As for the film's conservative screenwriter, his role on the set was reduced by Huston to making sure that the drunken Ava, who had a tendency to wander off into the brush, was back on the set for her shot. Another version of this story is that Milius refused to go after Gardner and just told those who demanded that he do so to "go screw themselves!" The screenwriter was paid $300,000 by Newman's company.[7] Wanting to direct the picture himself, he was reportedly furious that the film Huston was making from his script was turning into a "caricature." Huston arrogantly retorted that he had "to make a turd smell sweet," and Newman called Milius' original "boring" and said that Huston had given it "class."[8] It was soon obvious to Milius that, mainly due to his politics, he was not going to be treated fairly.

"It was a joy to make," Huston outrageously claimed. "Altogether, I had a wonderful time."⁹ Unfortunately, audiences didn't. Thanks to the drunken director's cartoonish approach, a script that made a euphemistic comment on the death penalty in the twentieth century by cloaking it in the days of the old west failed badly at the box office. Milius' scripts would find more positive response with conservative stars like Clint Eastwood, especially since both actor and screenwriter believed in characters who enacted the Unwritten Law on screen, whether they were Dirty Harry or figures in the old west. In fact, to correctly gauge Huston (and co-director Newman's) influence on Milius' screenplay, witness *Jeremiah Johnson*, where the script is hardly changed. Despite Robert Redford's total miscasting as Johnson (Clint Eastwood was originally considered for the part and *should* have played it), we see the central character take the law of the wilderness into his own hands and revenge himself on the Native Americans who murdered his wife and the child he found; then both sides, having had their fill of needless killing, call a truce. Milius' script had the lead character in essence deliver his own "death penalty" to those who broke the law (even if that law was broken in the wilderness, far from the courts of big cities).

Exactly one year and three days later, Warner Brothers released a western which again emphasized the need for law and order to triumph over those who rode the Vengeance Trail. However, the film's message became buried beneath gratuitous violence and gore.

> "If you force me to watch you kill this man Brand, I will hunt you down...."
> —*Sheriff Gutierrez*

In 1969, Sam Peckinpah's *The Wild Bunch* had literally changed the face of the western and, along with the so-called "spaghetti westerns" of Sergio Leone and Clint Eastwood, rescued it from the purgatory of television. In fact, as the 1960s progressed, most new theatrical westerns looked very much like feature-length versions of prime-time TV westerns.

However, if the westerns of Anthony Mann raised the sadism factor in the genre, Peckinpah, Leone and company increased the sleaze factor. In some ways, this was good since it showed the west as a dirty, brutal place where goodness and virtue were realistically left in the dust, and only aggressive behavior backed by force of arms won the day. Maybe it wasn't the optimistic world of Louie B. Mayer or Joseph Breen, but then, history was not written with a Production Code in mind.

Warner Brothers, having botched the release of *The Wild Bunch* (like, for that matter, their other groundbreaking works which Jack Warner had no faith in), continued to make westerns featuring John Wayne, whose positive values helped make them box office winners. At the other end of the scale were things like *The Deadly Trackers*.

Based on the short story *Riata* by cult director Samuel Fuller (Riata is the name of his hero), *The Deadly Trackers* was the story of a formerly peace-loving sheriff who, after witnessing the deaths of his wife and little son, pursues the four murderers into Mexico, and descends into a world of sleaze, violence and ultimately (it is implied) madness. The film's central character, Sheriff Kilpatrick, can be seen as a more brutal and violent updating of the typical Fuller iconoclast hero of *Underworld U.S.A.*, *Shock Corridor* and *Pickup on South Street*. Though touted today as a father of the independent film movement, Fuller actually worked most of his career for major studios (Columbia, Fox and Warner Brothers). What Fuller did put into his films was originality, giving new life to many a tired genre film (and inventing new ones, since *Shock Corridor* and *The Naked Kiss* can hardly be categorized as belonging to any certain genre). His westerns *I Shot Jesse James*, *Run of the Arrow* and *Forty Guns* had innovative touches and various twists in their plots, but did not make you forget the works of Anthony Mann, John Sturges, Budd Boetticher, Delmer Daves or John Ford.

However, the auteur was *not* an easy man to get along with. Boasting of his ability to tell the truth to everyone ("If they're offended by the truth, why waste my time on them?"[10]), Fuller's my-way-or-the-highway style was not going to work forever in a collaborative medium like filmmaking. After a productive heyday in the 1950s and early 1960s, things started to fall apart. Having been fired from one production after another through the years, it was getting pretty hard for him to keep blaming ignorant front-office personnel who didn't understand his work.

Which brings us to *The Deadly Trackers*. Certainly, what Warner Brothers put on film was *not* what Fuller had in mind. Still, the rumor mill would continue to grind out stories in the wake of the film's box office failure.

It is said that Fuller shot half the film in Spain, then Warners, dissatisfied with the footage, had it entirely reshot in Mexico with Barry Shear replacing the cantankerous auteur. Co-star Rod Taylor claimed that Fuller did not get along with star Richard Harris; others claim that Fuller did not get along with producer Fouad Said. Either way, Fuller admirers should take note that it was that plain-speaking truth-teller *Fuller* who was the fly in the ointment in both tellings. The talented Harris, certainly no friend to directors who were self-proclaimed truth-tellers, could also be an on-set pain in the ass. Torn between Harris and Fuller, and probably remembering the decent box office returns of another Harris western, *A Man Called Horse*, Said chose to fire the eccentric auteur. The producer also junked Fuller's screenplay and hired Lukas Heller to rework it. All these changes severely affected not only the direction and the screenplay, but even the film's score. Lost in the shuffle was a quite valid tale on the dangers of vengence trumping due process and trial by jury. Made at a time when the antiwar movement was at its height, *The Deadly Trackers* gave us a story about a lawman reluctant to use deadly force who, twisted by revenge, becomes a murdering brute.

Our story begins in an old west town run by Sheriff Kilpatrick (Harris). Never wearing a gun, the well-liked Kilpatrick has apparently trained the townsmen to be prepared in case of trouble; his precautions have usually meant that outlaws can be captured without bloodshed. However, when four felons ride in, the reluctance to use force will vanish.

The four are Schoolboy (William Smith), Choo Choo (Neville Brand), Jacob (Paul Benjamin) and their leader, Brand (Rod Taylor). (This is a reunion of Brand and Smith after playing heroic Texas Rangers in the TV series *Laredo* in the mid–1960s.) Apparently, robbing the bank in a more or less quiet way and not calling attention to their crime was *not* the way of the Brand gang as they literally go out of their way to murder or assault anyone who has the misfortune to cross their path. Still, it looks like the gun-toting townsmen are going to capture the gang until Brand invades a schoolhouse and coincidentally uses Kilpatrick's son as a shield. At the sheriff's plea, the townsmen reluctantly put down their guns and the gang starts to ride out of town.

Unfortunately, the boy's mom runs out to the street to prevent Brand from taking her son and gets shot in the head for her trouble by the outlaw leader; then, shockingly, the boy is dropped to the street where the gang's horses graphically trample him to death. Violence upon children was rare in an American film, particularly a western.

After sadly saying a prayer over the bodies of his wife and child, Kilpatrick leads a posse after the felons. But the gang crosses the border into Mexico where Kilpatrick will have no jurisdiction. At this point, the posse hangs back while the grieving lawman forges on ahead. After crossing the Rio Grande, Kilpatrick is within sight of the knife-wielding

GETTING EVEN. Richard Harris as the tormented sheriff who rides the vengeance trail in *The Deadly Trackers* (1973). The film was started by Samuel Fuller, but disagreements arose and he was replaced by Barry Shear. Whoever directed it, this patchwork western is a bloody mess.

Schoolboy, who had lingered behind while the other three outlaws rode on. The sheriff tackles him and, after a brutal fight, pushes Schoolboy's own knife into the psycho's throat.

From atop a hill, Kilpatrick has a bead on Brand and is about to kill him until his rifle is shoved aside by Gutierrez, a Mexican sheriff (Italian-American actor, Al Lettieri). Gutierrez is one those few 19th century pre-revoluntionary Mexican lawmen that actually cares about the due process of law. Apparently, Brand is wanted for murder in his country and the lawman has a witness against the outlaw leader. Therefore, he pushes away Kilpatrick's rifle so that the mass murderer of women and children can get away so that one day he can stand trial. After the two lawmen fight, they come to an understanding: Kilpatrick promises to ride back home and let Gutierrez arrest Brand. Suddenly, in a symbol of the mean-spiritedness of this film, the Irishman plows his rifle barrel into the pit of the lawman's vital regions and knocks him out. In fact, though the two lawmen eventually bond, they also assault each every time it looks like one will thwart the other one's plans. And the violence they inflict on each other is nothing compared to the multiple shootings, beatings, clubbings, stabbings, pistol-whippings, near-hangings, throwing bodies through saloon windows, drownings, and incidents of rape throughout the film.

The other three outlaws take over the home of an old Mexican couple, with Choo Choo (who has a section of iron rail sewed onto his right stump where his hand should be) crushing the skull of an old peon. They gorge themselves on their food, with Choo Choo and Brand's disgusting gobbling up of a watermelon one of the grossest moments in film history.

Knowing that Kilpatrick is on their trail, Brand convinces the rather stupid villagers that the Irishman murdered an old couple (who were actually murdered, of course, by Brand & Co.). When Kilpatrick arrives, he is mercilessly clubbed by villagers wielding long sticks. Then, the blood-soaked lawman is strung up and actually hanged. After the screen goes black, Kilpatrick awakens in a jail cell with Gutierrez on the outside looking in, explaining that he arrived just in time to save him. Apparently, the Latino lawman *must* be a crack shot because if he didn't expertly shoot the noose apart, in all liklihood, Kilpatrick should have either had his neck broken by the impact of the drop or quickly strangled to death. After Gutierrez leaves to pursue Brand's gang, the imprisoned sheriff tempts a priest to get closer to his cell door and then grabs him; he threatens to kill him unless the jailer releases him, which he does. The attack on the man of God is just another example of the meanness and repulsive behavior that permeates this film.

At that point, Kilpatrick appears on Choo Choo's trail riding a horse with a full rig and firearms. In another missing moment in the picture, we never see just *how* the sheriff obtained the horse or the weaponry. Soon, after a stalk-and-shootout around an ancient fortress, the angry lawman is able to knock the iron-handed fiend into a quicksand bog. Kilpatrick is using his rifle to pull Choo Choo from the quicksand, but after the outlaw lamely apologizes for the deaths of his wife and son, the lawman angrily pulls the gun away, letting the killer drown in the bog.

Out in the hills, Brand dry-gulches the Mexican lawman. Again, after the shooting and a terrific fall down the side of the hill that would have killed normal human beings, Gutierrez is still alive (in the language of film clichés, he probably just received a scratch). However, Kilpatrick soon arrives and reluctantly rescues him.

In another sleazy village, Brand and Jacob hold court in the local cantina, with the outlaw leader visiting his prostitute wife Maria (iconic Mexican actor-writer-director Isela Vega). Bitter that the Latina wants to split up with him, Brand beats her and, for a thousand dollars, has Jacob sell her services to slimy saloon patrons. This scene of rape and other forms of female degradation is par for the course for this horror show of a western.

Brand rides off to visit his and Maria's daughter in some convent. When Kilpatrick and Gutierrez arrive outside the cantina, the Irishman decides to accept Gutierrez's offer of help by flinging his body through the large window as a decoy, then bursting in to riddle Jacob with bullets.

Still feeling his oats, the sheriff pistol-whips and punches several helpless bystanders until someone mentions that Maria is "Brand's woman." When he bursts into her room, the maddened lawman shoves her head into her wash basin and almost drowns her until she tells him where Brand is. Blinded by the flash of a gun from an angry patron (who is immediately punched out by Gutierrez), Kilpatrick begs the prostitute to help him find Brand, promising her all the stolen bank money which had belonged to the people who were once his friends.

Soon, Kilpatrick's sight returns and yet again he knocks out Gutierrez and then pursues the outlaw leader to his daughter's convent. There, Brand visits the little girl he obviously loves, even though she is justifiably scared of him. When Kilpatrick shows up, in a shocking move, he grabs the outlaw's daughter and uses her as a shield. Now with the shoe on the other foot, Brand is forced to go through the same agony Kilpatrick had gone through when the outlaw had a loaded gun pointed at his son's head. After Brand steps out from behind a column, he is shot and wounded by Kilpatrick, but the lawman finds that he can't finish the job. Instead, he drags the killer back to Gutierrez's village where he presents him to the lawman.

Gutierrez's witness has died, meaning that Brand will have to be let go (apparently, Guitierrez seems to have forgotten Brand's dozens of other crimes committed on Mexican soil). However, when Brand laughs at the lawmen and mocks the town, Kilpatrick suddenly shoots the outlaw dead with his rifle. Riding away, the Irishman is ordered by Gutierrez to stop or he'll shoot. Now having descended into madness and despair, Kilpatrick rides on, purposely prodding his friend to shoot him in the back. Kilpatrick falls from his horse and his body lands in a puddle of mud, an appropriate comment on just how low this film has gone.

Certainly, the various opinions, statements, complaints, reviews and vindictive attacks over the controversial film were numerous. In the words of the fired Sam Fuller, "They completely lobotomized my story, yet left my name on that piece of garbage as a co-writer."[11]

Echoing the "piece of garbage" theme, Brian Garfield, in his *Western Films: A Complete Guide*, wrote,

> The film is a tawdry, unforgivably brutal, obscenely moronic bloodbath. In those respects, it is not atypical of Fuller's earlier movies—it is simply more explicitly violent than they were, because the restraints of decency had been abandoned by Hollywood by 1973. The characters are cardboard, the shock effects cheap and the plot puerile.[12]

Talking to Harris biographer Michael Feeny Callan, Rod Taylor claimed:

> I didn't start with the production. In the beginning it was Richard and Sam, and it just didn't hold together because Richard hated the script. All I heard was that Sam had been impossible. Richard couldn't stand it, and then Fouad Said, the producer, took the whole deal back to Mexico, changed the story and put the "boy genius" director Barry Shear to direct and save our bacon.[13]

Taylor also gave credit for "saving" the film to production manager Sam Manners and his good pal Harris, whom, he claimed, had *a lot* of input on the final cut of the film. The star of *The Time Machine* also claimed that he rewrote some scenes (Taylor was a writer as well).

According to an article in the February 7, 1974, *Village Voice*, titled "Death by Word of Mouth," Michael McKegney wrote:

> Fresh from the disaster of *Shark*, Samuel Fuller began shooting a western called *Riata* in Spain about a year ago. After ten weeks, there were reports of disagreements between Fuller and the producer. Fuller was fired and the shooting was completed by Barry Shear. The result, titled *The Deadly Trackers*, has now been released on showcase and though its claim to the award of Worst Movie of the Year might be challenged by *Steelyard Blues* and *Executive Action*, its reputation as a complete disaster is rapidly spreading by word of mouth. Although Fuller gets credit for the original story and Lukas Heller for the dialogue, both have reportedly disowned the finished product and understandably so.[14]

Indeed, what exactly was it that Fuller was supposed to have filmed? According to the auteur in his self-serving autobiography *A Third Face: My Tale of Writing, Fighting and Filmmaking*: "*Riata* is one of the best scripts I ever wrote. It hit on all the themes I loved telling stories about. Father-Son relationships. Outlaws and lawmen. Revenge and forgiveness. Fidelity and betrayal. Violence and peace. Love and rancor. Sacrifice and satisfaction."[15]

In Fuller's retelling, Riata is an implacable Texas lawman who is tracking a barbaric killer, Brubeck, across Mexico to avenge his son's death. Riata is assisted by Paco, "a Mexican magistrate who's chasing the same killer." Riata also crosses swords with Pompy, "the smart French temptress who's Brubeck's lover." In the filmmaker's own modest words: "My opening was guaranteed to grab any audience by the balls."[16]

To reinforce the auteur's attack on our lower regions, Fuller wrote the scene where the gang invades the schoolhouse. Only *this* time, the outlaw kills the lawman's son inside the building and throws him out of the window. Riata had been trained by Chiricahua Apaches and is an expert tracker. As he and Paco hunt Brubeck, they encounter banditos, Indians and the "double-crossing Pompy." During all this scintillating action, Paco finds time to get shot. Before he dies, he makes Riata promise he'll bring Brubeck in alive. "He does," wrote Fuller, "winning hard-won revenge for his son and making peace with himself."[17]

The project was supposed to start shooting at MGM, but somehow the deal fell through. A reason for this might have been the reign of production head James Aubrey, aka "the Smiling Cobra," who delighted in taking the ax to many MGM projects in order to save the studio money. It was Aubrey who had large parcels of MGM land sold, including the sets for the studio's most famous films. He also ruthlessly cut Sam Peckinpah's *Pat Garrett and Billy the Kid* into an unrecognizable mishmash. Confronted with the choice of using another ornery, iconoclast director with his own ironclad cinematic vision, Aubrey quickly took a pass.

The project ended up at Warner Brothers. Harris was cast as Riata, Latino actor Alfonso Arau was cast as Paco, and Bo Hopkins (straight from *The Wild Bunch*) was cast as Brubeck. (At one point, Fuller had even suggested Mick Jagger as Brubeck.) Filming was set to begin in Almeria, Spain. Then things started to go horribly wrong.

When the project was at MGM, Fuller claims to have met a hotshot producer "whose first name was Barry and whose last name I had forgotten on purpose," referring to him as "a double-crossing wheeler-dealer."[18] Later, when the project went to Warners, according to Fuller, Barry what's-his-name insisted on staying with the film because he had a wife and two kids to support. Still, this mysterious Barry person insisted on casting a French gal "whose only qualifications as an actress were her oversized breasts and her willingness to sleep with whomever would help her 'career,'"[19] according to the miffed helmsman. He also claimed that Harris said she couldn't act her way out of a paper bag. It was this particular casting choice, Fuller insisted, that ultimately destroyed his involvement in the project: "I figured I'd cut the French floozy's role down to a minimum in the editing room. Her involvement, however, triggered a violent reaction from studio executives back in Hollywood. After the boys at Warner Brothers saw some of the latest rushes, they decided to shut the movie down."[20]

Fuller claimed that his agent Mike Medavoy told him the studio was "seriously in the red" thanks to bombs like the John Huston-Paul Newman collaboration *The Mackintosh Man* and that it was merely a matter of "cost-cutting."[21] Warners then sold the footage he shot to Fouad Said, who continued shooting the film in Mexico "with another director" (whose name the fiery Fuller apparently couldn't remember either).[22]

Somehow, it's highly unlikely that a studio would actually shut down a production, especially one with a major star like Richard Harris, simply because a supporting player's scenes were not good, or even as a matter of "cost-cutting." Firing one director and replacing him with another is not a decision to be taken lightly. Replacing the director in the middle of a production will ultimately cost a bundle in time and money.

Yet one must also see other factors involved here. At no time in his autobiography does Fuller mention that he and Harris weren't getting along (Harris died in 2002, the same year Fuller's autobiography came out), and he even claimed that Harris was trying to raise money to help him finish the film. However, Rod Taylor claimed that Harris couldn't stand the helmsman. Fuller also fails to address Taylor's assertion that Harris hated his script.

There might have been others who had problems with the iconoclast director. After the debacle of *Caine* (eventually released as *Shark*) in 1969, Fuller didn't work as a director in Hollywood until *Riata* in 1973. Then, after Warners fired him, and with the exception of his writing the screenplay for that schlock classic *The Klansmen*, Fuller wasn't involved in any Hollywood project, certainly not as a director, for seven long years until *The Big Red One*.[23] Why? Because a graduate of the casting couch couldn't read her lines?

Perhaps a word or two about "boy genius" Barry Shear. Referred to rather dismissively as a "TV director" far too many times by reviewers like Brian Garfield, as compared with the God-like Samuel Fuller, Shear obviously came into the project at a severe disadvantage. First of all, it couldn't have been easy for him, after a lucrative TV career, to almost find himself in the same position as another TV director, Robert Totten, when he was replaced by Don Siegel on *Death of a Gunfighter*—though Shear was the replacer, not the replaced. Besides a huge volume of TV credits, Shear had also directed several outstanding films. They included the action-packed *Across 110th Street* with Anthony Quinn and Yaphet Kotto and two films whose cult reputations continue to grow: the darkly satirical *Wild in the Streets* and the suspenseful *The Todd Killings*. Shear would be dead by the end of the decade, his life cut short by cancer at the age of 56.

Fuller never once mentioned the name of the man who replaced him as director, but somehow *did* remember the first name of the "wheeler-dealer" whose evil machinations may have led to his firing as *Barry*. Odd coincidence, isn't it?

Michael McKegney wrote in his review that Richard Harris was "laying on the sub-Brando masochism much too thickly" and that Taylor was "snarling, sneering and swaggering around to little effect." However, McKegney, a reviewer for the liberal *Village Voice*, also mistook one Latino actor for another (and that other actor was not Latino, but Italian-American) when he wrote that "Pedro Armendariz Jr. states the case for due process, ad nauseam."[24] As the Mexican sheriff, *Lettieri* spoke about due process throughout the film; Armendariz played the small role of the blacksmith he deputizes in order to return Choo Choo to his village.

All in all, despite its blood-soaked shenanigans, *The Deadly Trackers* at least tried to present a case for due process and the rule of law rather than vengeance. Perhaps the reason that this theme is still front-and-center in the film is due to Al Lettieri, who gives the film's best performance. However, his role is a total fantasy; the crookedness of Mexican law enforcement, especially at that time, was legendary. What 19th century Mexican lawman in his right mind would make a plea for American-style due process and trial by jury in a land teetering on the edge of revolutionary chaos and rampant banditry?

In the meantime, with the end of the Vietnam War in sight and the Watergate scandal casting doubt on the integrity of our leaders, the western was taking its last gasps. With those in charge of our laws permanently viewed as crooks, our most optimistic genre became darker and far more pessimistic. This dour point of view was seen in films depicting the Indian Wars; in films attacking formerly venerated American leaders; and finally in westerns portraying the efforts of lawmen to enforce justice in the old west. Only now, those in charge of the law were the bad guys and those whom society deemed as outcasts would be seen as heroes.

"A 44.40 in the brain pan would be my sentence for him...."— *Calvin*

Beginning in the 1960s, Thomas McGuane was a prolific author of novels dealing with the New West and often the New South. Born in Wyandotte, Michigan, on December 11,

1939, the author found his greatest inspiration for material far from industrialized, crowded urban conclaves and focused on dysfunctional males from places like Key West, Florida, and Livingston, Montana. His central characters were losers who often broke the law (*92 in the Shade, Rancho Deluxe*, etc.). However, his novels were not steeped in the language of pulp noir as were those of Jim Thompson, a man who practically owned the sub-genre of Southern Noir in the postwar years. McGuane, however, had his own particular style: the penchant of his vain, yet sometimes doomed, characters to make bitter observations, their crisp dialogue, and the sharply drawn surroundings in which they existed.

Based on the success of the film version of McGuane's novel *92 in the Shade*, which the author also directed, producer Elliot Kastner hired him to do a screenplay for a western, *The Missouri Breaks*. (The title means certain points in the Missouri River where stolen horses are ferried across.)

After sealing the deal with United Artists as distributor, Kastner sought to lower the film's budget by casting an older unknown character actor as the horse rancher and instead concentrate the budget on paying for two superstars to play the horse rustler and the "regulator." McGuane had written the role of the assassin for his good friend Warren Oates, who had given such a superb performance in *92 in the Shade*. A talented but underrated performer, Oates practically cornered the market on playing rural losers. Graduating from playing western henchmen and comical cowpokes, he brought an understated power to the country-born and -bred low-lives he portrayed, particularly his underdog gunman in Sam Peckinpah's *Bring Me the Head of Alfredo Garcia* ("No loser loses all the time!" he defiantly proclaims, a line that could be seen as a coda for most of the characters he played). With Jack Nicholson cast as the horse rustler and Oates envisioned as the regulator, the odds were that the collaboration would have resulted in a fine western.

According to Thomas McGuane, "When we did *Missouri Breaks*, I had written the bad guy in the cowboy movie as the equivalent of a 19th century contract killer, and my friend Warren Oates was going to play him, and he was going to play him right from his Kentucky roots."[25] Unfortunately, in order to boost the film's box office, Kastner went about casting the man who had just made a comeback with his performances in *The Godfather* and *Last Tango in Paris*. *The Godfather* is a classic; *Last Tango* isn't. Still, the incongruity of casting Marlon Brando in a western never became an issue with the producers. Thinking of the box office, they never looked back at his résumé and found that the actor usually fell flat on his face every time he appeared in the genre, which wasn't often. His ridiculous performance and over-the-top direction of himself in the bloated and pretentious *One-Eyed Jacks* almost bankrupted Paramount; and *The Appaloosa* was a total emasculation of Robert MacLeod's Mexico-set novel that was neatly stolen from the star by the performance of John Saxon. In the book, the hero is a clean-shaven and youthful 21-year-old who was half-white and half-Latino; when the film version was made, the very Anglo-Saxon Brando was forty years old, fat and covered with a wig of sloppy matted hair and a thick beard.

Now Brando was returning to the genre that he had never succeeded in, and indeed, usually stayed far away from. In another stroke of unconventional hiring, Kastner signed Arthur Penn to direct. Penn's westerns had always been quirky, unconventional and, for the most part, downright ridiculous. A decade before Peckinpah, he originated the act of people being shot down in slow-motion in the over-the-top *The Left Handed Gun*, but the hammy performances of Paul Newman and the rest of the cast, as well as historical inaccuracies and pseudo-Freudian symbolism, prevented it from being taken seriously. Penn's

Little Big Man was an overblown (and *again*, historically inaccurate) film version of Thomas Berger's book that turned the Indian Wars into a pathetic slapstick comedy, and featured a hysterical performance from Dustin Hoffman as a frontier loser who apparently can't make up his mind whether he wants to live with whites or Indians. Penn's lack of control over his stars, his inability to curb even the *least* of their fantastic acting choices, did not bode well for the McGuane film. Rather predictably, Penn later called the *script* the real reason for the production's failure, something the helmsman had also done with the ridiculous *The Left Handed Gun*.

Our story begins in beautiful northern Montana, near the Missouri River, some time in the 1880s. Rancher David Braxton (John McLiam) has hundreds of horses on his spread. His wife got fed up with the old man's ruthless domination and fled; this leaves him with his feisty and emancipated daughter Jane (Kathleen Lloyd) as his only family. Tom Logan (Jack Nicholson) and the middle-aged Calvin (Harry Dean Stanton) head a gang of youthful horse rustlers who have been robbing the rancher blind. Capturing one of the gang, the ruthless Braxton and his foreman lynch the young man.

With the stolen money from a train robbery, Logan is able to pose as a homesteader and purchase four sections near Braxton's spread in order to build a cabin and grow crops—and, of course, have his gang near the soon-to-be-stolen horse-flesh. When he meets Braxton, Logan hides his contempt for the old man and pretends to favor the lynching of horse rustlers. However, his supposed pro-death penalty stance infuriates the old man's daughter. As in the films of old, especially westerns, two people of the opposite sex who start to hate each other will ultimately fall in love.

YOU DON'T KNOW JACK. An unusually pensive Jack Nicholson as the horse rustler-turned-farmer in *The Missouri Breaks* (1976). The actor's performance was subtle and restrained compared to his co-star, Marlon Brando. Because of the hefty actor and Arthur Penn's quirky direction, the film failed at the box office.

Angered by the horse thefts, the rancher hires a frontier "regulator" named Robert E. Lee Clayton (Brando). Despite the fact that McGuane wrote the part as someone who was a former Confederate guerrilla, Clayton speaks with a heavy Irish brogue. Though this was accepted as another one of the actor's many eccentricities, there might have been a method to Brando's accent madness: Irish actor Richard Harris was compared many times to Brando, and was said to *resemble* the Oscar-winner in *The Deadly Trackers* (both had longish blonde hair of the same shade, and even their profiles, accentuated by prominent noses, were similar). Brando and Harris had detested each other since Harris wouldn't stand for Brando's scene-stealing tricks on the set of the 1962 remake of *Mutiny on the Bounty*. It's possible that Brando was purposely aping Richard from the recent *The Deadly Trackers*. Obviously, the mimicry was *not* a compliment.

Brando also made sure that his entrance stood out. Not since William S. Hart appeared in the far distance at the desert location of *Billy the Kid* was an entrance so purposely audacious—or egocentric: Brando rides up to the front of the house while hanging, Indian-style, off the side of his horse.

Brando shaped his every scene to call attention to himself (looking at his entire overrated career, what else was new?). Associate producer Marion Rosenberg said that Brando

> had decided to push the limits. Like his dumb Irish accent. That came out when he said his first line. Once he established it, he had to keep using it, but nobody had the courage to say, "Hey, wait a minute, what are you doing?" And it went on from there. Behind his back, people were saying, "Is he crazy? We can't use this shot!" But nobody stood up to him.[26]

At one point, Brando just stopped in the middle of a scene and rode away on his motorbike, causing Nicholson to shrug his shoulders and remark, "Oh, well. Another day, another twenty thousand...." When the regulator first meets Logan, there is a cat-and-mouse game going on, as if both of them know the real reason for the other's presence. Logan bluntly interprets "regulator" to mean *dry-gulcher*, meaning a backshooter and assassin, and a major insult to any man of the west.

Gradually, the cat-and-mouse game disappears and Clayton speeds up his killing. Pretending to be a preacher (Brando's Irishman suddenly and inexplicably speaks with a western twang), he lures gang member Little Tod (Randy Quaid) out to the middle of the Missouri River. When Little Tod refuses to answer Clayton's questions about Logan, Clayton drowns him. Furious, Logan corners the regulator in Braxton's upstairs bathroom while he is taking a bubble bath. Prompted by Clayton to shoot him, the inherently decent Logan cannot bring himself to do it and instead puts a hole in the tub.

With his temper pushed to the limit by Clayton's insults, Braxton fires the regulator, but the assassin decides to *still* go after Logan and his friends. In quick succession, Clayton murders the rest of the gang. One rustler is shot in the back while making love to a rancher's wife (the beautiful Luana Anders, Nicholson's friend and former co-star at AIP, probably cast through his influence).

One of the weapons in Clayton's arsenal is a combination mace-spear-Ninja star to throw at his victims. In one truly hideous scene, the fat hit man rides through the prairie screaming like some ancient warrior, then throws the thing and impales a helpless rabbit. Why Penn decided to shoot this repulsive scene can only be attributed to his total kowtowing to his mammoth star. Eventually, Clayton, wearing a huge gingham dress, sets fire to Calvin's cabin and then impales the old man with mace-spear thingie.

Clayton is alone with his horses after his murderous triumphs (there are kissing scenes with them and other unhealthy implications of beastiality). The fat regulator is asleep when Logan sneaks up on him and cuts his throat. Though Clayton was clearly ahead of the game all through the film, one wonders how Logan was able to sneak up on the professional killer in dense foilage without snapping at least one twig.

Now having finished off the assassin, Logan comes after the man who hired him. (Having fallen in love with Jane, Logan had previously been against Calvin's plan to kill Braxton.) But the rancher has supposedly suffered a stroke, and Logan finds that he cannot murder an invalid. When the old man hears that Jane is planning to leave him, he quickly grabs a gun and wounds Logan. Returning fire, the rustler kills him.

At the end, Logan and Jane leave in different directions, but there is an implication that, after she settles her estate and he starts another homestead nearby, that the two will get back together.

In his May 20, 1976, *New York Times* review, Vincent Canby unfavorably compared *The Missouri Breaks* to McGuane's *Rancho Deluxe* (the film version of his novel) where good-hearted thieves in 20th century Montana steal cattle. To the *Times* critic, the film was "funny and moving partly because they emphasized the disconnection between a romantic past and a motorized present that's lost all ideals, all purpose." Then, after pointing out that "the anachronisms in *The Missouri Breaks* too often seem like camp," the incisive Canby lowers the boom on the film's hammy star:

> This, I suspect, is principally because of the out-of-control performance given by Mr. Brando. He enters the film hidden behind a horse, which he at last peeks around, and spends the rest of the movie upstaging the writer, the director and the other actors. Nothing he does (affecting the Irish accent he used earlier in *The Nightcomers* and wearing odd costumes, including frontierswoman drag at one point) has any apparent connection to the movie that surrounds him. He grabs our attention and does nothing with it.
>
> In their earlier films, both Mr. Penn and Mr. McGuane have demonstrated a fondness for eccentric characters whose impulses have a kind of grandeur about them. There's no grandeur in Mr. Brando's character. Not much mystery. He behaves like an actor in armed revolt.[27]

Canby went on to praise the rest of the movie, including a funny sequence where a captured felon (wonderfully played by comic actor Steve Franken) mockingly refers to himself as the Lonesome Kid. He continued, "The film conveys a fine sense of place and period, of weather and mood and the precariousness of life, which are things that Mr. Nicholson responds to as an actor. Yet the plot, along with Mr. Brando, keeps intruding and throwing things out of balance."

The esteemed critic didn't know just *how much* Brando intended to throw things out of balance. According to Thomas McGuane:

> When they cast Marlon Brando, they came back and told me he wanted to be an Indian. Moreover, he had a pet wolf, and he wanted the wolf in the movie. And they said, "Marlon doesn't like the character of the girl's father," and I said, "Meaning *what*?" And they said, "He wants the wolf to kill the girl's father." Anyway, they sent me out there to talk him into being something other than an Indian, because it didn't make any sense — the Indian kills everybody in the movie.... Anyway, he ran amok, and the last thing I saw of him, he was in a dress burning down somebody's barn. I had no idea what that was for. You really get the sense of having created a monster.[28]

During the shoot, the former Oscar winner dove into a lake and reportedly ate half of a live frog; stuffed live grasshoppers into Randy Quaid's open mouth while he was sleeping (this was done *before* the scene shot for the cameras); insisted that producer Elliot Kastner ignore his own busy schedule and appear on the set whenever Brando worked; ordered the costume department to create his Las Vegas-style fringe buckskin outfit for his 19th century killer to wear; and insisted beyond all reason that he wear a gingham dress while going after Calvin, the last of Logan's gang. (Brando's insistence on wearing the dress infuriated Harry Dean Stanton, who played Calvin.)

After hearing about Brando's stipulation that he play an Indian, even Arthur Penn complained (though not too loudly) that the actor was "fantasizing that we would change the script — lock, stock and barrel." Meanwhile, as Brando was figuring out how to play a scene, a process that reportedly took hours, crew members broiled in the Montana heat, and there were reports that several of them fainted.

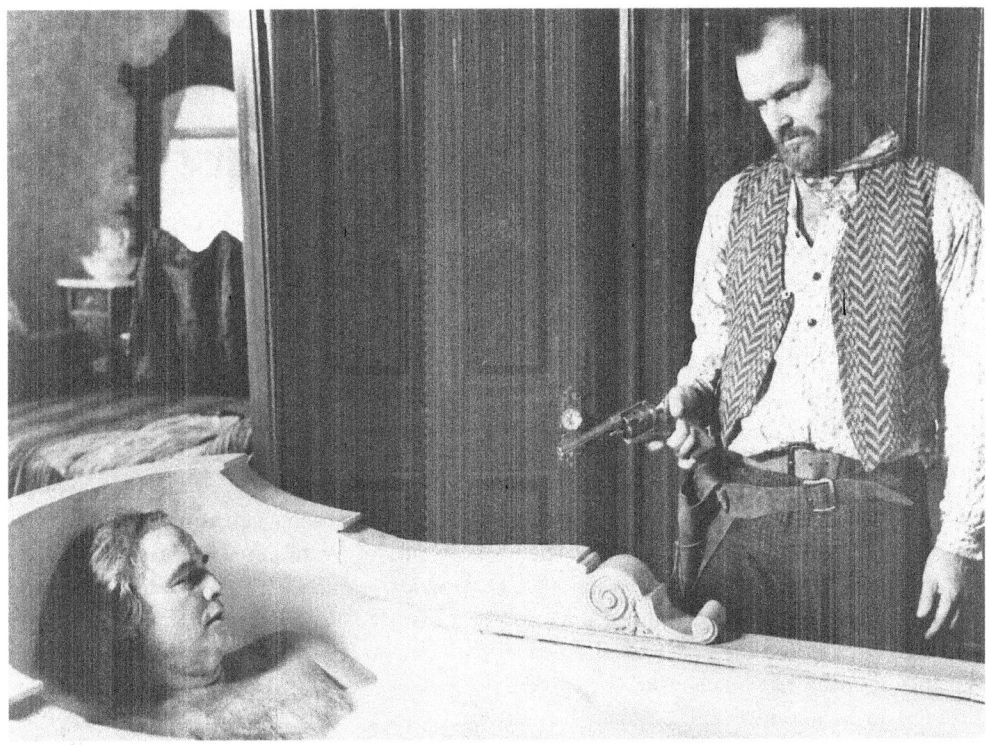

DON'T FORGET THE CALGON. Marlon Brando's girth barely fits the tub as Jack Nicholson has him in his sights in *The Missouri Breaks* (1976). Screenwriter-novelist Thomas McGuane originally wrote Brando's role for Warren Oates. Unfortunately, Arthur Penn let Brando do anything he wanted, except play the role as written.

However, it would be *Brando* on the hot seat when he was visited on the set by two FBI agents looking for Native American activists Leonard Peltier and Dennis Banks for the murders of two FBI agents in the Pine River Reservation. It had long been suspected that the actor actively helped the fugitives escape justice, a violation of federal law. Though Brando would shrug off the meeting and refer to the agents as "nice men,"[29] it was obvious that the visit threw a scare into him. Coincidentally, the actor's dedication to the Indian cause started to wane and, eventually, fugitives Peltier and Banks couldn't even get him on the phone.

Despite his overweight co-star's inflated opinion of himself, Nicholson deserves credit for giving a fine performance and holding the film together. Throughout *The Missouri Breaks*, you get the impression that Nicholson is acting in a western, and doing quite well at it too; but it must have been hard for him take it seriously when the actor who was supposed to be playing his bitter enemy was turning it all into a clown show. Nicholson's Tom Logan may be a horse rustler, but he's still a decent person; he is truly in love with Jane Braxton, not just using her to get back at her father. He feels a commitment to avenge the murder of his buddies, but restrains himself until pushed too far. Given an opportunity to kill Clayton in his bathtub, Logan cannot bring himself to do it (he shoots low and then claims that the bubbles obscured his aim); and again, when he goes after Braxton with a rifle, Logan cannot shoot a helpless invalid. Indeed, for a horse rustler, Logan seems to believe, like the good guys of old, in fair play. Thanks to Brando's antics, however, the film tanked. Penn never seemed at home in the genre, and *The Missouri Breaks* became his final western.

Of all the brickbats heaped on the film, however, one stood out; and it was made by a man who *definitely* knew how to direct a western. Clint Eastwood didn't like *The Missouri Breaks*, calling the film "ridiculous." However, ignoring the obvious lack of professionalism of one of its leads, the actor-helmsman instead unfairly criticized McGuane's script: "It wasn't a good script and they obviously felt so, too—why else would a guy dress up like his own grandmother?"[30]

In fact, barely a month after the release of the Penn film, Eastwood expanded his Man With No Name persona by portraying a character who was an implacable foe of federal law and the Union government that enforced it. However, even the usually shrewd Eastwood had no idea that this character, one of his greatest roles, was created by a man whose own past was immersed in evil...

"Dyin' ain't much of a livin', boy...."— *Josey Wales*

There are those who see *The Outlaw Josey Wales* as Clint Eastwood's best film, as well as a classic western. Released in the United States on June 30, 1976, the film grossed $31,800,000, a tidy figure for Warner Brothers and the Malpaso Company.[31] Vietnam was now a recent bitter memory, as were the shenanigans of Watergate. Released nationally within days of America's bicentennial, *The Outlaw Josey Wales* kept the western alive and brought a message of hope and reunification to a country divided by war and racial strife.

The film would also be a focal point of controversy, not for its story or its message, but for the machinations behind the camera, and one particular individual whose reputation was tarnished forever.

Its final message of reunification doesn't quite blunt the film's growing rage at federal authority during the Civil War and its aftermath — an obvious euphemism for rage at the various administrations running the country from the 1960s up to then. In *The Outlaw Josey Wales*, an outlaw is portrayed as the Last Angry Man who rises up against a growing federal bureaucracy. Unfortunately, forgotten by the filmmakers is the uncomfortable fact that the "hero" is not only a robber and a killer, but a guerrilla who fought for the cause of a slave state.

In 1863, farmer Josey Wales (Eastwood) and his wife and son are on their property in Clay County, Missouri (coincidentally, the home of the James brothers), when they are attacked and their home burned to the ground by Kansas Redlegs (also known as Jayhawkers—pro-Union guerrillas who terrorized pro-southern Missouri) led by a man named Terrill (Bill McKinney). Josey's wife is murdered and his little son is trapped inside the burning house. When Josey attempts to get to the house, he is struck in the face by Terrill's sword, giving him a permanent scar. At this point, the desperation and anxiety on Eastwood's face is *too* convincing; this may have been because the boy is played by the actor's own son, Kyle. After he revives, the Redlegs are gone, Josey's home is in ruins and he buries the bones of his wife and son. When a gang of Bushwackers (Confederate guerrillas) arrive, led by Bloody Bill Anderson (John Russell, former star of TV's *Lawman* series), they invite Josey to join them. Though Russell's cameo performance is good, the actor was also in his fifties, making him far too old to play the twenty-something Anderson, a man who was not known as "Bloody Bill" for his people skills.

Time goes by and Josey rides with Anderson and his men. The film takes pains *not* to show Josey committing atrocities; for certainly it was impossible *not* to commit them while riding with the psychopathic Anderson. Though Union soldiers were the official target, anti-slavery Kansans were attacked with impunity. At Centralia, Missouri, Anderson and his men decapitated Union soldiers and then played a sick game of putting one head on another headless corpse. Anderson also joined in the Lawrence Massacre, a genocidal act (led by William Clarke Quantrill) where over a hundred men and boys were murdered, and the town, a bastion of anti-slavery sentiment, was burned to the ground. The James boys were part of the massacre as well. Are we to believe that Josey was on sabbatical when all this madness occurred?

Finally the war ends. Anderson is no longer there (he was eventually shot down by Union troops), and the group's leader Fletcher (John Vernon, Eastwood's superior in *Dirty Harry*) wants to lead the demoralized boys into the federal camp to sign the oath of allegiance to the Union so they can all go home. Only one man refuses, partly since he has no home to return to: Josey Wales. His young, wet-behind-the-ears pal Jamie (Sam Bottoms) also decides to surrender. When the southerners arrive at the Union encampment, things are not what they seem. While surrendering their weapons, the guerrillas see that the bluecoats are acting like arrogant bullies. When Fletcher goes to the tent of Senator Lane (Frank Schofield), he also sees Terrill, now in the uniform of a Yankee captain. Fully expecting Union officers to handle the disarming of the guerrillas, Fletcher is arrogantly told by Lane that Terrill is the "regular federal authority."

A word on Jim Lane: He was a Kansas senator and ruthless Jawhawker leader, a kind of Bill Quantrill, though working for the other side. His murderous activities alongside the Jayhawkers should have branded him as a hated figure for all time, but Lane had never committed an atrocity on the scale of a Lawrence Massacre. In fact, Lane narrowly escaped Bushwacker vengeance during the massacre by hiding naked in a cornfield. Ironically, the hate-filled Lane is probably the only historical character in the film who's portrayed accurately; a vicious double-cross under the pretext of a peaceful surrender would be right up the Jayhawker's alley.

Predictably, as a bluecoat sergeant is administering the oath of allegiance, a soldier opens up on the guerrillas with a Gatling gun. Even during this act of duplicity, Eastwood couldn't help injecting a bit of black humor. He has the sergeant end his recitation of the oath by backing out of the way and screaming, "You Missouri trash!"

Josey rides in, kills the soldier firing the Gatling and turns the weapon on the bluecoats, mowing them down as they fire at him uselessly. The wounded Jamie, the only survivor of the guerrillas, joins Josey as they make their escape. Now they are pursued by Redleg soldiers led by Terrill and accompanied by Fletcher, whose motivations seem to change back and forth as the film progresses. After getting a ferry across a river, Terrill and his men try to take the same ferry across, but Josey shoots apart the rope guiding the boat with a Sharps rifle (complete with sniperscope). There is a cute vignette with a ferryman who sings "Dixie" when dealing with guerrillas like Josey, but switches his tune to "The Battle Hymn of the Republic" when he has to ferry Union men across.

Soon, the two head for the Nations (Indian Territory; today part of Oklahoma), but it is too late for Jamie, who dies of his wound. In his travels, Josey meets an old Cherokee man named Lone Watie (Chief Dan George in a scene-stealing performance), a relation to Cherokee chief-Confederate general Stand Watie. The old man claims that he never surrendered to the Union; however, "They took my horse and made him surrender. They have him pulling a wagon in Kansas, I bet."

Stopping off at a lonely general store to purchase a horse for Lone, Josey is just in time to stop two frontier louts from raping a Cherokee woman named Little Moonlight (Geraldine Keams). Figuring on shooting Josey for the bounty money, they dare him to draw, not realizing that Bushwackers always kept *many* loaded guns on their person. In fact, during their raids, there was always the chance that the favored Navy Colt could get wet (while riding through rivers) and not fire. The penchant for carrying many guns also precluded the need to reload, a time-wasting procedure (especially with Civil War-era cap and ball weapons). Guerrillas had to ride fast and shoot fast; therefore, their garments were fashioned to carry multiple pistols. In this case, the extra guns allow Josey to kill the two would-be rapists even after he's "disarmed" by them.

THIS IS THE .44 NAVY COLT, THE MOST POWERFUL HANDGUN IN THE WORLD (IN 1865). Clint Eastwood in *The Outlaw Josie Wales* (1976), one of the actor-director's greatest films. However, it was based on a novel by an author who had more than a few skeletons in his closet.

After obtaining the horse, Josey and Lone are somewhat dismayed to find the grateful Little Moonlight tagging along. Abused by her own tribe, as well as the white store owner, she has nowhere to go, but she turns out to be a powerful ally when trouble comes. Even an old red hound follows the three as they make their way south.

Finding a town to pick up supplies, Josey sees a stuck-up old Kansas grandma named Sarah (Paula Trueman) and her granddaughter Laura Lee (in the prime of her willowy phase, Clint's then squeeze, Sandra Locke) in a general store. A carpetbagger-slick oil salesman (Woodrow Parfrey) outs him as Josey Wales, and four Union-backed Redlegs stare at him. With little ado, Josey kills three of them and Lone shoots down the fourth.

Stopping at a huge valley, Josie, Lone and Little Moonlight see Grandma Sarah and Laura Lee manhandled by Comancheros who have already murdered the rest of their family. After the Comancheros capture Lone Watie, Josey suddenly appears before them, forcing the Comancheros to face the sun. Effortlessly he guns them all down with his endless pistols.

After arriving on the spot where Grandma's son built a new home (which happens to be on Comanche territory), all of them, including a few folks from the town's saloon, help them in tending the land. When Terrill and his Redlegs attack the house, all are killed except for their leader. Chasing the wounded Terrill, Josey traps him near a barn and then pulls out all of his empty guns and pulls their triggers, taunting the murderer of his wife and child. Terrill attacks with his sword, but Josey quickly impales him on it.

Afterwards, in order to free two of Josey's new friends from the Comanches, he rides out to meet with their chief, Ten Bears (Will Sampson), a Quanah Parker clone. The chief agrees with the ex-guerrilla that those who run the government talk in "double tongues" and that it is only "the word of iron" from two warriors that will count. Slicing their own hands and then pressing the bleeding palms together, they become blood brothers and opt for peaceful co-existence.

When Josey returns to the saloon, he is shocked to see Fletcher there with two Texas

Rangers. To protect Josey, the patrons call him Mr. Wilson, and the Texans accept him as that. (There is an implication that the Rangers know exactly who he is, but decide to let him go.) However, to Josey's surprise, Fletcher also calls him Mr. Wilson and says that if ever he runs into Josey he'd tell him "the war's over." No longer a wanted man, and living in a territory where he will be protected from the intrusion of big government, Josey rides back to Laura Lee and his new family.

Though Eastwood had directed before, this film, considered by many to be a classic, was not supposed to be directed by him in the first place. The original director was co-screenwriter Philip Kaufman. However, Kaufman's penchant for "exploring" the material and experimenting with scenes severely clashed with the budget-conscious, let's-just-shoot-the-crap Eastwood. With Malpaso (as well as Warner Brothers) money sunk into the project, Eastwood knew he had to seize control from Kaufman if a profit was to be made. (This was just a few years before UA gave Michael Cimino his head and let him do whatever he wanted on another western, *Heaven's Gate*; the upshot of UA's kowtowing to Cimino's "artistic vision" was the end of UA itself.) To Eastwood, exploring the scene meant an indecisive director, and hundreds of feet of film used for this "exploration" translated into time, which translated into money. Consequently, if his films didn't make a profit, the Man with No Name would soon become the Star with No Name.

The "Captain Queeg incident," as Clint liked to call it, began when the cast and crew were ready to shoot the scene where Josey confronts the Comancheros, with the sun partially blinding his antagonists to "gain an edge," according to the original novel. The sequence had to be shot during "Magic Hour," when the sun was setting, but still bright enough to light up the valley. Days before, Kaufman had explored the terrain and found an ideal location to mount the camera for the shot; therefore, he planted a container of some kind to mark the spot and return in a few days and shoot the scene. Unfortunately for Kaufman, the desert's shifting sands effectively buried the container and when the crew arrived for the shot, Kaufman couldn't find it. Therefore, he proposed that they spend time looking for it. It was plainly ridiculous; any ridge would do, a fact that Eastwood realized immediately. Time was growing short; "Magic Hour" wasn't going to last forever and the budget was rising fast. When Kaufman refused Eastwood's suggestion that they shoot from any available ridge, the star suggested that he take a car and driver and search for the container. When they were gone, Eastwood turned to assistant director Jim Fargo and said, "Get the camera. Let's shoot it."

The controversial move infuriated Kaufman and, after the star called him aside days later, the helmsman was unceremoniously fired. After Eastwood took over the direction, the Directors Guild protested and soon stipulated in their rulings that no member of a film's cast or crew could take over the direction of a film after the original helmsman was fired; to this day, it is known as the Eastwood Rule, which was *not* meant as a compliment. Eastwood respected Kaufman enough to not to radically change the screenplay (which the canned helmsman had written with Sonia Chernus). But the whole gist of the film, the character of Josey Wales, his friends and antagonists, and his violent fight against the scourge of big government, all came from the man who created them. As it turned out, he was a character himself, and not at all a pleasant one either.

The Outlaw Josey Wales was based on the novel by a little-known southern author named Forrest Carter. There are different tellings as to just how the novel came to Eastwood's attention. The most common story was that Carter, lacking an agent, sent the novel to Malpaso with a letter commenting on Eastwood's "kind eyes." Eastwood's assistant, producer Bob Daley, wondered who would describe the Man with No Name's eyes as "kind." Curious, he read the book in one sitting. Late at night, he called Clint and insisted that he buy the rights. After Eastwood read it, he agreed with his aide's verdict and authorized the purchase. The next move was to contact the author, who was reportedly living in Alabama. When Carter got Daley on the phone, he cheerfully said that he just happened to be in the neighborhood and could drop in; as it turned out, the "neighborhood" he was calling from was Dallas, a bit of a walk to L.A. If this didn't set off alarm bells in Daley, another incident clinched it for him.

It was arranged for Carter to meet Daley at Malpaso's production offices in Hollywood the next day, with company driver-security man Art Ramus sent to meet him at the Los Angeles airport. Carter was not on the arriving plane, and the author soon called Daley to tell Ramus that he would be on the next one. It seems that the esteemed writer got drunk with his pals the night before and had been thrown in jail. When Carter did arrive, Ramus was shocked to find him drunk and peeing on the carpet of the classy Satellite Lounge. Ramus saved the author from arrest, hustled him over to his hotel and, through a magical combination of hot coffee and cold showers, got him sober. The next day, as soon as he arrived, Carter reportedly wanted to leave (the author also turned off Daley by purposely speaking in Josey's hillbilly dialect). A meeting was arranged for the following day in a popular Hollywood lounge with Ramus and two Malpaso secretaries. *Again*, Carter showed up drunk. During the subsequent meal, Carter drew a knife, put it to the throat of one of the secretaries, told her he loved her and would kill them both if she didn't promise to marry him. Though Carter had inexplicably got himself signed with the William Morris Agency, he soon soured on Eastwood and Malpaso, demanding more money from the star's company. To keep peace, Eastwood advanced Carter $15,000 out of his own pocket even *before* the film pulled in a profit. (Clint would be reimbursed more than ten times over after its release.)

Carter had also written a novel called *The Education of Little Tree* which also interested Malpaso. The book was supposed to be somewhat autobiographical, telling the story of a Cherokee boy and the bigotry he encounters. Meant to be a plea for tolerance, the novel was reprinted and found a readership of millions years after the author's death. Yet the movie sale was not to be. Something happened that soon stopped Carter's joy ride for all time.

Little Tree was selling fast, quickly making the *New York Times* bestseller list the same year as the successful release of *The Outlaw Josey Wales*. Drunk or sober, Carter apparently craved the limelight and quickly got himself booked as a guest on *The Today Show* where he was interviewed by Barbara Walters. Practically the moment the interview ended, the phones at NBC rang off the hook, with most of the callers situated in Alabama. It seems that Carter had a totally different identity that he had not revealed to Malpaso, Warners, William Morris, NBC or anyone else. The real name of the author of *The Outlaw Josey Wales* and *The Education of Little Tree* was actually *Asa* Carter, a native Alabaman who was once a speechwriter for George Wallace. However, this was just the tip of the iceberg.

In 1976, the same year that Carter received praise and had phenomenal literary success, historian and future Wallace biographer Dan Carter (no relation) wrote a devastating piece for *The New York Times* outing the fledgling author. On the heels of this exposé, Alabama journalist Wayne Greenshaw went one better in another piece for the *Times*. It seems that Carter's background was far more colorful than he had originally let on.

For those who had lived through racial segregation in the south, it was hard not to shake off the existence of George Wallace. Elected the governor of Alabama, he physically used his own body to block two African-American students from entering the University of Alabama. This aberrant behavior from a governor of the state was backed up with the remark that he "hereby denounce the illegal and unwarranted actions of the central government," meaning, of course, the *federal* government. After this confrontation with federal law, in an angry response to the speeches of Dr. Martin Luther King Jr., Wallace thundered: "In the name of the greatest people that ever tread the earth, I draw the line in the dust and toss the gauntlet before the feet of tyranny. And I say, 'Segregation now! Segregation tomorrow! Segregation forever!'" The above words were written, with heartfelt enthusiasm, by the author of *The Outlaw Josey Wales* and *The Education of Little Tree*, Asa Carter.

Born in Anniston, Alabama, in 1925, Asa Earl Carter joined the Navy during World War II in order to fight the Japanese. He reportedly refused to join the Army and fight the Germans in Europe because he considered the Nazis "racial kin." As a radio announcer in the 1950s, he was fired from one station in 1954 for his rampant Jew-baiting. By 1958, Wallace, desperate to win the governorship, heard about the inflammatory Carter and hired him as a speechwriter. By 1968, however, Wallace had decided to run for president, which meant, quite plainly, that he had to change his tune and ramp down his racist rhetoric. And so, with absolutely no guilt or regrets of any kind, he cut Carter loose. In the years ahead, Carter also ran for governor and was widely seen on Alabama TV. Standing before a Confederate flag, Carter attacked the specter of "race-mixing," as well as "Communists in Hollywood" and the "guv'ment in Washington." Times were apparently changing; Carter lost in a landslide.

However, it seemed that Carter was not only a speechwriter, radio personality and gubernatorial candidate, but also took an active hand in the southern racial politics of the day. He was a leader of the Alabama White Citizens Council and a member in good standing of the local Ku Klux Klan. With fellow Klanner Jesse Mabrey, he had even started a racist scandal sheet called *The Southerner*. Though this may have been the fledgling author's first published work, his other activities were far from literary. In an 18-month period during the early 1960s, Carter's followers participated in the stoning of Autherine Lucy, a black student trying to register at the University of Alabama; attacked Nat King Cole as he performed on a Birmingham stage (warned not to perform, the courageous singer did so anyway); beat civil rights leader Fred Shuttlesworth and even stabbed his wife. Yet even these acts of racist terror didn't match the castration of a slightly retarded 34-year-old black handyman named Edward Aaron as a warning to "black trouble-makers." Not finishing there, the assailants poured turpentine on the poor man's wounds. Four of Carter's men, including his "good buddy" Mabry, were indicted for the attack and sentenced to twenty years in prison. To this day, it is uncertain whether Carter was with them that night or joined in on other attacks, though his violent background certainly point towards his active, and probably enthusiastic, participation. And even if he didn't join them, it was pretty obvious that he knew about them and, by his refusal to turn his pals in to the law, tacitly approved of their acts. Dan Carter blatantly called him "a psychopath."

Yet somehow, such a man had actually written the source material that became a classic western film and one of Eastwood's all-time best works, apparently finding an accommodation with those so-called "Communists in Hollywood" that he used to rail against. His racial attitudes, however, never really changed, and there were reports that he shouted anti–Semitic epithets at William Morris' agents when he demanded more money from them. One can even read between the lines on just why Carter, reinventing himself as a writer, started calling himself "Forrest." As it turned out, he was naming himself after Confederate general Nathan Bedford Forrest, who had founded the Ku Klux Klan.

Though one is certainly impressed by the film's final message of reconciliation, the director also coupled it with a vicious slam at all federal authority. This is no surprise since the author held these very same beliefs (though there were changes from the book, Eastwood retained Carter's anti-government stance). Even during Josey's meeting with Ten Bears, the chief is ready to let Josey go free merely because, as "the Gray Rider," he has fought against the victorious Union. This was ridiculous since a great many tribes had contempt for both the North *and* the South (excepting, of course, those members of the Creek, Choctaw, Chickasaw, Seminole and Cherokee tribes who fought for the Confederacy). With troops fighting the Civil War in the east, the western tribes, particularly the Comanches (and without a hint of guilt either), used those four years to massacre and burn out every settler they could.

Certainly, if one took a close look at the novel, one can plainly see the inflammatory, anti-government politics of speechwriter Carter being transferred, euphemistically, to the story written by author Carter. It was almost as if the same ugly language Carter had written for George Wallace attacking the "tyranny" of the federal government as he physically blocked the doorway to black students in Alabama somehow made its way into *The Outlaw Josey Wales*. There are no black people in the novel. Instead, Carter attacks the hated North who won the war, the "Northern aggressors" and "Reconstructionists" who supposedly oppressed the south after the war and "forced" on them all those nasty little civil rights laws. This is symbolized by the almost iconic figure of Josie Wales who, as portrayed in both novel and film, is God in weeks' old stubble and dirty Stetson who uses .44 Colts to cleanse the world of evil rather than a sceptor. Eastwood, who apparently liked to play God in his films, had no trouble with this portrayal — that is, if you believe ousted director Philip Kaufman. In an interview with author Allen Berra, Kaufman said: "'Fascist' is an overworked word, but the first time I looked at that book, that's what I thought: 'This was written by a crude fascist.' It was nutty. The man's hatred of government was insane. I felt that that element in the script needed to be severely toned down. But Clint didn't and it was his movie."[32]

It must be pointed out that this quote does *not* appear in Richard Schickel's worshipping biography of the auteur. In Marc Elliot's biography of Eastwood, however, it was claimed that he fired Kaufman because both married men wanted to take Sandra Locke out for dinner on the same night, and that Clint was merely disposing of a romantic rival. This is also a little far-fetched, but anything's possible in Hollywood.

Though Kaufman probably said the above quote in bitterness years after his firing, it jibes perfectly with Eastwood's love of portraying mavericks who stand against those who represent the workings of the law, particularly federal law. To Clint, the Lone Wolf Unwritten Law of the fast-draw gunslinger seemed to make more sense than the words of a government bureaucrat. And Carter's hero, plainly depicting the Confederate guerrilla as a noble symbol of a master race cleansing the prairie of inferiors working for an all-consuming federal bureaucracy, cannot be dismissed as just the central character in "a cowboy movie." In fact, Carter's depiction of Josey reminds us of Louis L'Amour's rather hateful portrayals of his own heroes as Aryan supermen of the west. With little variation, these "good guys" arrogantly ordered folks around, heaped contempt on all human weakness, were physically flawless, won every fistfight, drew their guns faster than anyone on earth, and had absolutely *no* faults.

To Carter, Josey was "the fighter, natural born." Lone Watie sees him as "a fighting man who carried himself as a warrior should, with boldness and without fear." There are other examples of the author's rather passionate love for his own creation:

> And despite the cool cunning he had learned, the animal quickness and the deliberate arts of killing with pistol and knife, beneath it all there still rose the black rage of the mountain man. His family had been wronged. His wife and boy murdered. No people, no government, no king could ever repay. He did not think these thoughts. He only felt the feelings of generations of the code handed down from the Welsh and Scot clans and burned into his being. If there was nowhere to go, it did not mean emptiness in the life of Josey Wales. That emptiness was filled with a cold hatred and a bitterness that showed when his black eyes turned mean.

Somehow, it didn't seem far-fetched for KKK man Asa Carter to admire such a man, a tenacious warrior for the southern Aryan way. In fact, Nazi propaganda films made in the 1930s and early '40s would refuse to portray the German as a rich aristocrat who never worked a day in his life. Under the dictates of propaganda minister Joseph Goebbels, the Nazi film industry made so-called "documentaries" like *The Eternal Jew*. Besides its vicious anti–Semitism, the film portrayed Germans as hard-working men and women who toiled in the fields and the factory. Far from living soft and cushy lives, the Germans in these films were portrayed as thriving on physical activity, loving hard physical labor and, because they're pure Aryans, fearlessly confronting all hardships and triumphing in the end.

However, Kaufman and Eastwood injected some much-needed humor into Carter's rather pompous depiction of Josey. Certainly there were changes from book to film. To perhaps minimize Josey's hatred of the government, Kaufman personalized his hatred by creating the Redleg leader, Captain Terrill, who burns down Josey's home and murders his wife and boy. The character of Fletcher was also created for the film as a symbolic pursuer. However, Fletcher's motives change back and forth during the movie. At first he openly hates Terrill, then he joins the hated Terrill in pursuing Josey, expressing the hope that he'd like to see Josey dead; then, after Terrill is killed, he meets Josey at the end of the film and lets him go. The entire scene in the Union camp where the guerrillas are mowed down by the Gatling gun and then Josey mows down the Redlegs, was written for the film. In the novel, Jamie is wounded during a bank holdup he and Josey take part in; in the film, Josey never once robs a bank, an act which would have reduced any sympathy we might have had for him.

And, of course, there are the numerous gaffes. The Gatling gun in the film fires as fast as a twentieth century machine gun, when in reality Civil War-era Gatlings were much slower. Josie rarely cocks the hammers of his weapons, something that *had* to be done years before the invention of the double-action Colt. After Josey and Lone shoot the government-sanctioned Redlegs in town, the very same dead men, apparently now very much alive, walk into the street and watch them ride away. After Josey finds that Jamie has died, the boy is still apparently blinking his eyes. When Laura Lee tells a joke about why Missouri is called the "show me state," she is using a state nickname that didn't come about until 1899.[33]

One line in the film would echo down through the years and be repeated almost verbatim in 1992. Grandma Sarah criticizes those from Missouri, particularly Josey, as "murderers of innocent men, women and children"; the same canard would be used to describe gunfighter William Munney, also from Missouri, in Eastwood's Oscar-winning *Unforgiven*.

Lone Watie, who is sixty years old in the book, is played by the 77-year-old Chief Dan George in a semi-improvised performance. Too old to remember his lines, he was reportedly encouraged by Eastwood to ad lib. Though some of his lines are amusing, there are times when one does want him to just shut up (in the book, the character is no clown).

The Outlaw Josey Wales was a box office winner, and Eastwood cemented his reputation as the number one western star (with very few rivals at the time) by again portraying a man who defies due process and follows the Unwritten Law.

As for Asa Carter, the revelation of his evil activities was growing, and his fear that he would finally pay for it all turned him into "a bundle of nerves," according to friends. Added to the revelations of his racist past, his claim that he was designated "the official tribal storyteller for the Cherokees" was repudiated by the Cherokee Tribal Council who vociferously denied having ever heard of him.

In the late 1970s, Carter wrote a book lionizing Geronimo, the mass murderer of whites and Latinos, as a great hero. He also wrote a sequel to his Wales book called *The Vengeance Trail of Josey Wales*. In this one, a female friend of Josey's (barmaid Rose, who appeared in the Malpaso film) is raped and murdered and a friend is kidnapped by Rurales and taken to Mexico. Throughout the book, Carter shows sympathy for the poor peons who are victimized by their oppressive government and heaps contempt on the Rurales, who, of course, happen to be representatives of (Mexican) federal law.

One night in June 1979, while visiting his son, Asa Carter died at the age of 53. It was reported that the author, drunk again, got into a violent argument with his offspring over the treatment of his mother, whom Carter had abandoned. Supposedly, there was a fight and Carter fell against a counter and cracked his skull; some say it caused an embolism in his brain, some say he died of a heart attack right then and there. However, all sources basically agree that the drunken author ultimately choked on his own vomit.

Then, in 1980, Warner Brothers released a film made by a fading Hollywood superstar. Depicting the last few years in the life of a man who became a hired assassin, the film was considered a final bow from an iconic actor who was living out his last years...

7

Reload: 1977–1992
American Cynicism and
Revisionist Western History

"Riding hard, drinking hard, fighting hard, so passed his days until he was crushed between the grindstones of two civilizations." — *Glendolene Myrtle Kimmel*

By 1903, the man known as Tom Horn was in bad shape.

He was the last legendary figure to come out of the Wild West. He was both angel and devil, hero and villain, protector of the law and wanton murderer. Caught in the midst of a changing America that was gradually swallowing up a rowdy, undisciplined west and replacing it with urbanized law and order, Tom Horn symbolized the era's final days. One does wonder about this legendary figure's bad timing of birth in 1860. Had he been born ten years earlier, Horn probably would have been considered, like Wyatt Earp, Bat Masterson and other gunfighting enforcers of the law, one of the great figures of the west with a take-no-prisoners style that fit the wild times in which he lived. Instead, in the glare of the early twentieth century, with industrialization and civic order on the horizon, he became a notorious pariah and an anachronistic embarrassment to the powers-that-be.

Thomas Horn Jr. was born in Scotland County in northeast Missouri on November 21, 1860. He was the son of German immigrants who were also the parents of eleven other children (one Tom Horn website says twelve, another knocks down the number to eight). Any way you look at it, Tom was not an only child. Unfortunately, being born to highly religious immigrant parents sometimes meant the always controversial use of violence to instill in a child a fear of God (and, more likely, a fear of the parents) as the little one is led down the path of the righteous. In fact, it is now accepted, as it never was in previous biographies of the man, that Tom Horn was an abused child. One can only guess at how this deeply seated psychological trauma affected the character of the adult killer, but that would be years later. Craving adventure rather than living a pious life, young Thomas ran away from home at 16 (some sources say 14), to either join a wagon train, join a freighter's outfit, join a gold-mining camp, join up with the cavalry in Arizona Territory or join in the construction of the Union Pacific Railroad as it reached its end-of-steel to California; again, depending on what website or biography you're looking at. Either way, young Tom *was* a packer and teamster for a freighting company, *did* join a wagon train, *did* work on the railroad, *did* prospect for gold, and definitely *did* join up with the cavalry. In fact, Horn was hired by the army as a scout and tracker, and worked under the tutelage of famed scout Al Sieber as the army was tracking down Geronimo and his band. Adept with languages (he knew German from his parents and also picked up Spanish in the southwest), Horn quickly learned the Apache dialect. It is said that he helped negotiate Geronimo's surrender, but it's more likely that the capture of the famed Apache murderer was a group effort rather than a one-man show (Sieber, Lt. Charles Gatewood, General Nelson Miles, etc.). Besides these various occupations that would have filled the lives of ten hellraising men, he even won a rodeo championship.

At some point in time, Horn was even a deputy sheriff in Colorado (yet another website says Arizona). Without a doubt, Horn was a very effective lawman and, in his pursuit of wanted outlaws, was already developing a reputation as a tenacious and deadly adversary. From Sieber and the army, he learned how to be an expert tracker, but from something far deeper within him he also became an expert killer. While wearing the tin star, this was accepted, especially in the late 19th century when the use of deadly force was never an issue. Though Tom was a fair man who accepted peaceful surrenders from his quarry, he was never more than a split second from pulling the trigger if there was even a smidgen of resistance. In fact, it was his success rate as a lawman that impressed C.W. Shores, an operative for the Pinkerton Detective Agency. With the possibility of earning more money (and the possibility of more adventure), Horn soon became a Pinkerton agent, working out of their Denver office under Superintendent James McPartland. He officially worked for the agency from 1890 to 1894 and, periodically, in an "unofficial" capacity from 1894 to 1898. For years, Horn was a tenacious investigator and, in a much darker vein, a man who ended up killing 17 men while working for the agency. However, there were constant examples of his bravery, one being his capture of the notorious Peg-Leg Watson, suspected in the robbery of the Denver & Rio Grande Railroad, without firing a shot.

While working on undercover assignments, Horn was arrested several times under suspicion of robbery or murder (as he pretended to be an outlaw or member of a gang). However, one incident called into question whether Horn was performing his roles a little too well....

During the time he was with the Pinkertons, Horn supposedly pulled a robbery in Nevada, though details seem to be sketchy. He was still employed by "the Eye that Never Sleeps," and superintendant William A. Pinkerton was furious over the adverse publicity that would result from Horn's conviction and reportedly pulled strings to get him off. According to fellow operative Charlie Siringo in his book *Two Evil Isms*: "William A. Pinkerton told me that Tom Horn was guilty of the crime, but that his people could not let him go to the penitentiary while in their employ."

But the cat was now out of the bag: The Pinkertons were employing a lawbreaker. After a meeting with District Supervisor McPartland, Horn was told that he'd be quietly let go (though the agency would still use him on a freelance basis if the need arose, and depending on where he was at the time). It didn't matter anyway. In 1894, he received an offer to work as a "range detective" for the Wyoming Stock Growers' Association. Washington had authorized homesteaders, including immigrant families and Civil War veterans, to claim for themselves 160 acres of land apiece and "prove up" on them, meaning put in irrigation, grow crops and make other improvements, and fully own this land after five years. However, the territory's cattle barons had other ideas.

Horn fell into his new job all too easily: gunning down cattle rustlers and "invading" homesteaders (though scaring the homesteaders out was usually tried first before gunplay). Using a Winchester '94 .30–30 rifle, Horn roamed the vast cattle lands killing anyone he suspected of being a cattle thief or an encroaching "nester." Whether shooting his victims in the front or the back didn't matter. The job paid well, $600 for each rustler or other alleged miscreant killed. Thus, in the space of a month, he was earning thousands of dollars from his kills (as compared to $40 a month for a deputy sheriff, not including the lawman sometimes providing his own horse, gun and ammo).

After taking time out to join Teddy Roosevelt's Rough Riders in the Spanish-American War (he served as a packer and teamster), Horn returned to Wyoming. (There were reports that Horn had contracted malaria before he could make the trip.) Another big cattle concern, the Swan Land & Cattle Company, soon employed him. Supposedly his job was as a "stock detective" and "horse-breaker," but he didn't fool anyone, especially those homesteaders trying to start new lives on their 160 acres of land. To them, Horn was a hired assassin who killed without mercy and who worked for folks who wanted their land. Horn himself had no qualms about his job either: "Killing men is my specialty. I look at it as a business proposition, and I think I have a corner of the market."

A profit motive might have been just the tip of the iceberg. According to Don Patterson, a former chief of police in Cheyenne who had studied criminal behavior: "Psychopaths are unable to feel remorse or guilt. They would be ideal stock detectives.... A body count would be nothing more than an example of a job well done."[1]

Also on Horn's list of targets were sheepherders (sheep consume the grass also coveted by herds of cattle). One Kels Nickell, a particularly nasty piece of defiant sheepherder, was grazing his sheep on cowman James Miller's land. On July 18, 1901, as Nickell's 14-year-old son Willie, in his well-worn shirt and trousers, his head topped by a floppy Stetson, was opening the tie-gate to the family corral, he was shot from behind by a rifle (some sources say he was riding a pony, some say the rifle slug penetrated the boy's chest). Either way, someone using Horn's modus operandi murdered an innocent boy.

In an article in the *Cheyenne Leader*, dated July 19, 1901, the unnamed reporter gives us a general idea of the rage that such a crime inspired in the public: "The killing of the boy who was only thirteen [sic] years of age was, of course, deliberate and unprovoked murder, and whoever is guilty of this heinous crime should pay the full penalty of the law."[2] "The full penalty of the law" in the old west was the noose.

Horn's involvement in the Willie Nickell murder was, so far, based on rumor. What would happen next pushed rumor into accepted fact. Joe LeFors was a deputy marshal (or, more likely, the less impressive-sounding "office worker" for the U.S. marshal). A former Texas cowpuncher, he was just five years younger than Horn. After coming up north with a Texas herd, LeFors stayed around Wyoming and aided in the pursuit of cattle rustlers and train robbers, including the Hole in the Wall Gang and the men who robbed the Union Pacific train outside Wilcox, Wyoming. His work prompted U.S. Marshal Frank A. Hadsell to appoint the ex-cowboy to the lawman position. Next the marshal appointed his "office worker" to investigate the Nickell murder. However, LeFors had other irons in the fire; around the same time, he was appointed by Montana cattle barons as an inspector for livestock in northeast Wyoming, concentrating his activities around Newcastle. Though his job was to aid in the apprehension of cattle thieves and recapture stolen stock, it also clearly had him in the employ of the powerful cattle interests. Therefore, when LeFors met with Horn in a Cheyenne bar and got him to talk about the Nickell murder, "Deputy" LeFors was literally working for two masters, though one paid a lot better than the marshal's office.

A further connection to the cattle barons was revealed when W.D. "Billy" Smith, a brand inspector for the Montana cattlemen, made a lucrative job offer to Horn and had LeFors meet with him to feel him out on the matter. Tom had been working in the meantime for cattleman John Coble but on August 9, after his testimony at the coroner's inquest on the Willie Nickell murder, the bored range detective entered a Cheyenne rodeo competion and handily won the calf-roping competition. Pretty soon, however, the poor calf would not be the only one who found himself hog-tied.

On January 11, 1902, after Horn had spent all night drinking in the saloons of Laramie, he caught the train to Cheyenne. After his trip, and hardly feeling any pain, he met with Joe LeFors, who took him to the marshal's office on the second floor of the Commercial Building on 16th Street, arriving at 11:20 A.M.

Horn was usually a reserved man when he was sober. However, when drunk, he revealed a startling capacity for boasting and blowing his own (sorry about this) horn. He had already had the left side of his jaw punched in when his big mouth annoyed boxing champ Johnny "Young" Corbett (no relation to Jim) in a Cheyenne bar. Now, as Joe LeFors fed him whiskey after whiskey, the drunken range detective spilled more than just his drinks. Unbeknownst to the now-sloshed Horn, two men were situated in the next room: court reporter Charles J. Ohnhaus and Deputy Sheriff Les Snow. LeFors had even gone to the trouble to have the adjoining door redone so the two men could hear the conversation easier and watch Horn's reactions. When asked about Willie Nickell, Horn said: "It was the best shot that I ever made, and the dirtiest trick I ever done."

After this interview, the two repaired to Harry Hynds' saloon down the block. Then they returned to the office (with rebuilt door) and continued the conversation. Certainly, during the interlude while the two men were away, it was strongly suspected that Ohnhaus and Snow, might have edited or "doctored" Tom's words.

However, whether the words were altered or taken down verbatim, it looks like the range detective was talking hypothetically, as if he were concocting a scenario that *might* have happened. After making several suppositions on how the murder occurred, including an educated guess that someone was waiting in the draw by the creek below Nickell's home, Horn actually says: "That's the way I think it occurred."

LeFors purposely baited Horn into "admitting" that he had run across the field barefoot before the killing (in order to stifle any sounds), and that he had ten days to nurse his cut-up feet after the murder. At this point, Horn mentions his friendship with Glendoline Kimmel, certainly implying that he could have stayed with her while he "healed." Today, it's pretty certain that, had a proud, boastful man been prodded with booze into loosening his tongue and then hauled into court on a charge of murder, the jurist would promptly toss the case out of court. However, in the Wyoming-Montana region at the turn of the century, bigger forces were at play. Horn became a kind of western version of the Man of La Mancha; only now the windmills he was battling were the machinations of the powerful cattle barons, the same ones who failed to come to his aid after he was arrested, tried and sentenced to hang for the murder of Willie Nickell. Curiously, no one really bothered to bring into court as witnesses those individuals who could swear that Horn was fifteen or so miles north of Iron Mountain that fateful day, tracking down another cattle rustler. The prosecuting attorney at Horn's trial, again using the range detective's vanity against him, prodded him to admit that, yes, he *was* a good enough horseman and so knowledgible of the area that, yes, he *could* ride back to Iron Mountain in record time — and *yes*, could have been in the vicinity when Willie Nickell was killed.

Horn had tried to break out of jail after assaulting a guard and seizing an automatic pistol. (In his review of the Steve McQueen film *Tom Horn*, Brian Garfield ridiculously claimed that Horn wouldn't have known how to work an automatic. Horn, an avid gun hawk, definitely would have figured it out fast enough.[3]) Deputies quickly recaptured him.

And so, on November 20, 1903, one day before his 43rd birthday, Thomas Horn Jr. was hanged on the contraption known as the Julian Gallows. Invented by a Cheyenne architect named James P. Julian, this weird-looking device allowed the accused to literally hang himself. To relieve hangmen of any feelings of guilt, Julian created the only gallows in the world that was powered by water. Once the condemned man stepped onto the platform, the man's weight triggered a lever which released water from a barrel, and then, through a complicated system of weights and pullies, another lever soon opened the trap door beneath the doomed man's feet and he dropped into eternity.

Reportedly, Horn's last words were either, "I never saw such a pasty-faced bunch of deputies in my life" or "Hurry it up, I got nothing more to say."

However, one thing is certain: Tom Horn faced his death with courage and dignity, cool under fire all the way to the end.

By 1978, the man known as Steve McQueen was in bad shape.

After many years of physical abuse, his first wife (and perhaps his one true love) Neile finally divorced him, and the actor went on to marry younger women Ali McGraw and Barbara Minty. The Hippie Era introduced the actor to hard drugs. Under their influence, he was known to beat his "one true love" whenever his will was thwarted or if his day just wasn't going well. He was a lifetime smoker and drinker, and his manic obsession with racing cars and motorcycles and his continued exposure to their exhaust fumes caused the actor to accumulate carcinogens in his lungs. He had already busted the eardrum of his left ear thanks to his deep-sea scuba-diving and, with cocaine and pills sapping his body's resistance to disease, was totally unprepared for the malignant cancer that was spreading throughout him. After the worldwide box office success of the early 1970s films *The Getaway, Papillion* and *The Towering Inferno*, McQueen decided to branch out and abandon the tough anti-hero image that pleased so many and brought him international fame. He pressured Warner Brothers into making a film version of Henrik Ibsen's *An Enemy of the People*; his performance wasn't very good, but he deserved an A for effort. Horrified by the film, Warners held up its release until 1978; and even then, its bookings were sparse.

During the mid-1970s, Steve moved far away from Hollywood with last wife Barbara Minty and settled on a property in the Montana wilderness. He had gotten fat, his hair had grown wild and his beard was thick and fuzzy. Feasting daily on candy bars and Cokes (allegedly the sugar fix choice of drug addicts, like Lenny Bruce), McQueen's health was failing, with colds and shortness of breath frequent companions. But he needed work. Though he was still receiving offers from Hollywood (*Apocalypse Now, The Bodyguard* and *The Driver*, to name but a few scripts that were sent to him and immediately returned unread), the suits were clearly frightened of him, and one wonders how seriously they were taking their own efforts to obtain his services.

By late 1978, with the help of Barbara, Steve put himself on a vigorous regimen of daily physical exercize and a healthy diet. He lost many of his extra pounds, got a haircut, trimmed his scraggly beard and found himself talking to the suits at Warner Brothers about one of his pet projects, *Tom Horn*. Steve would later say that he drove to Tom Horn's gravesite in Cheyenne and spent a night there under the stars. Lying face down on the slab, the actor claimed that he felt movement below him, as if the dead man was saying "Please do my story. Please do my story."⁴ This is an interesting claim since Horn's grave was in the Columbia Cemetary in Boulder, Colorado, which means that Steve was communicating with the wrong corpse.

Robert Redford also wanted to make a film version of the Horn story. However, the not-very-macho actor was always frightened of Steve McQueen, and when he heard that the star was determined to play Horn, the one-time Jeremiah Johnson timidly dropped the project. David Carradine didn't drop *his* project, and would portray Horn in a barely watched TV movie called *Mr. Horn*.

McQueen was one of the owners of First Artists, the independent production company in which he was partnered with superstars Sidney Poitier, Barbra Streisand, and his friend (and friendly rival) Paul Newman. First Artists had produced Newman's *The Life and Times of Judge Roy Bean*, and now it was McQueen's turn to portray another figure of the old west whose activities were a corruption of due process and the letter of the law.

McQueen had been in a personal war with First Artists president Phil Feldman, and therefore yearned to break away from the company and never see his mortal enemy again. A tough ex-Marine who had fought in World War II, Feldman was the producer who insisted that his studio, Warner Brothers, give a troublesome director named Sam Peckinpah a chance at a comeback and make *The Wild Bunch*. Now it was ten years later. National General Pictures, which had distributed First Artists' productions, was long gone, and the star-owned company had now taken up residence on the Warner Brothers lot. However, with very few exceptions, First Artists' efforts were bombing with the audience, and Warners was impatient to end its association with the company. Feldman, who had battled the suits at Warners to get *The Wild Bunch* in the can, had now morphed into one of those hated suits himself. McQueen, who hated studio honchos no matter what decade it was, had to deal with Warners' cynical slashing of *Tom Horn*'s budget from $10 million to $6 million. It was obvious that the studio saw McQueen as a pathetic has-been, a wild-man relic of the 1960s who had blown his own fame with his rages, his drug-fueled paranoia (and McQueen didn't necessarily need drugs to be paranoid anyway) and his general contempt for those who ran the Hollywood studios, meaning, of course, *them*.

But this was no longer the Steve McQueen of 1965, the same McQueen who had defied the vindictive Henry Hathaway on the set of *Nevada Smith* and did wheelies with his dune buggy while the director seethed. This was a physically tired, drained and pathetically exhausted man, with the physique of a man twenty years older than his current age of 48. The cool young stud of *Bullitt* who insisted on doing his own stunt-driving on the streets of San Francisco now could hardly mount his own horse without feeling pain. In a chilling portent of things to come, just as Humphrey Bogart coughed up a storm on the set of his last movie *The Harder They Fall*, so to would McQueen, in *his* last film, cough up a storm on the set of *The Hunter*, which began shooting a few months after *Tom Horn* wrapped.

However, he was still Steve McQueen, Hollywood rebel and champion ballbuster. He interviewed and either fired outright or totally rejected director after director. Perhaps with the cancer ravishing him and with Death hovering over the Arizona set like an unwelcome fan, the intense pressure he was under might have distorted his judgment. In mid-1978, over the objections of producer Fred Weintraub, Steve hired James W. (Jim) Guercio, ex-manager of the rock group Chicago and the director of the offbeat cop film *Electra Glide in Blue*. Soon enough, Steve unceremoniously fired him as well. Next on the hit list was Elliot Silverstein, the director of *A Man Called Horse* and *Cat Ballou*. Then Don Siegel quit after two weeks, a fact the helmsman doesn't bother to mention in his autobiography *A Siegel Film* (nor the fact that Steve had previously turned down offers to star in Siegel's *Dirty Harry* and *The Beguiled*). In fact, Siegel would complain to his good friend Lee Marvin about what it was like working for Steve McQueen: "Every meeting he was late. Every fucking meeting he'd freak out. Where does he get off treating people this way?"⁵ However, even the disgruntled helmsman had to make this admission: "That shit's a great actor."

The new director's chores would be split between (until *his* firing) the little-known William Wiard and the star himself.

Producer Phil Parslow was either replaced or quit, depending on whom one asks, and Fred Weintraub became the new producer. At one time, Communist screenwriter Abraham Polonsky was involved with the project. His script concentrated on Horn's time with the Apaches, giving the anti–American scenarist a chance for a withering portrayal of the U.S. military.

YOU WORK YOUR SIDE OF THE PRAIRIE AND I'LL WORK MINE. Steve McQueen in his second-to-last film, *Tom Horn* (1980). The iconic actor, already dying of cancer, portrayed the famous Apache scout and Pinkerton detective in the last years of his life. Though he looked nothing like Horn, McQueen expertly captured the gunslinger's melancholy as he faced his last days.

According to Polonsky's script, titled *I, Tom Horn*, and dated May 1, 1978, General Nelson Miles tells an officer to order his men to chase down a 12-year-old Apache boy. At another point, Miles has a scene with a Lieutenant Lawton that implies a rather brutal military agenda: "He will lead you to a final solution of the Chiricuhua Apache under Geronimo. I say you men are our best. You are the equal in activity and endurance of any Apache warrior. [*Then, in voiceover*:] You'll outsmart him, you'll outlast him, and you'll outfight him...."⁶

With the buzzwords "final solution," the Communist screenwriter was obviously comparing the cavalry to Nazi troops about to commit genocide. McQueen had no problem firing the vindictive screenwriter. Years later, when ex-Communist helmsman (and friendly witness) Elia Kazan was to receive a special Oscar, Polonsky publicly hoped that someone with a rifle would shoot him dead.

Polonsky's script also featured Mickey Free and Al Sieber, but Thomas McGuane (who reportedly wrote a 450-page blockbuster script) and Bud Shrake now shifted the emphasis to Horn's later years, effectively removing any need for the studio to construct Indian camps.

Fresh off *The Missouri Breaks* fiasco, McGuane now had to deal with another eccentric actor, though at least McQueen cared about his work far more than the contemptuous

Brando. Still, in an interview with writer Judson Kinger, the author complained rather bitterly about his experience on *Tom Horn*. After mentioning that that the range detective was "an abused child with a Pennsylvania Dutch family" (abused he was, Amish he wasn't), McGuane said what a great story it would be to film and that McQueen was the perfect actor to play the part. Though praising McQueen as "a terrific actor," he also admitted that he "was not any fun to work with at all as a producer." After praising McGuane's script and urging him not to change a thing on it, McQueen said he didn't like anything in it. Declaring that McQueen's word was no good, the scenarist also said he "just smoked dope 24 hours a day" and "there was a side to him you absolutely couldn't trust."[7]

McGuane's misgivings about working for the erratic actor were finally verified when he received a call at his home at 3:00 A.M. According to the author: "[And] this voice said, 'You can take your macho bullshit and go back to Montana!'"[8]

Through process of elimination, Bud Shrake now became the sole surviving screenwriter of *Tom Horn*. However, according to cinematographer John A. Alonzo, McQueen would have both McGuane's script and Shrake's revisions before him and would consult *both* scripts, choosing from each just what he needed for that particular day's shoot, a good indication as to who probably set up most of the camera shots on *Tom Horn*.

Our story begins in Wyoming Territory in 1901. Tom Horn (McQueen) sits on a hill near his horse and holds one of the Indian charms given him by the Apaches during his time with Geronimo. The opening titles tell us of his accomplishments as Pinkerton agent, Rough Rider, cavalry scout and shotgun guard. After putting his wild-natured horse in the local stable ("Don't put 'em with any other horses, he'll kill 'em!"), an obvious comparison to his own wild nature, Horn goes to the local saloon for a "morning whiskey." During the stable scene, we not only see the usually taciturn McQueen uncharacteristically blabbering away, but if you look real quick, you can actually recognize Elisha Cook Jr. in a thankless role as the stable man (the darkness of the place makes it hard to even see Cook's face). At the saloon, several dudied-up gents at a table call Horn "Tex" and insist that he join them in toasting Jim Corbett as the next heavyweight champ. (Jim Corbett wasn't anywhere near Wyoming and never met Tom Horn; it was another fighter whose last name happened to be Corbett.) Instead of toasting the fighter, Horn sees the picture of an aged Geronimo brandishing a rifle over the bar and suggests that they toast *him*. (And what bartender would be insane enough to have a picture of Geronimo, whose murders of innocent people still resounded in the west, over his bar? This script connivance literally smells of Polonsky's doing.) When asked how Geronimo compares to Jim Corbett, Horn replies that the fighter would have to stand on a chair to kiss the Apache's ass, a remark that obviously infuriates the boxer. Horn leaves the place with his breakfast, but Corbett follows, only to get Horn's platter smashed in his face. Cut to a beaten-up Horn recuperating in the stable. Cattleman John Coble (Richard Farnsworth) shows up to offer the fallen scout an opportunity of a lifetime.

Coble brings Horn out to his spread where the cattlemen are having a feast. At this point, they offer him the job of killing off rustlers at $200 (not 600 a pop). Also at this soiree, he meets the lovely schoolmarm Gwendolene Kimmel (Linda Evans) and U.S. Marshal Joe Belle (Billy Green Bush). It's pretty obvious that Belle is a stand-in for U.S. Marshal Joe LeFors, the cattlemen's lackey who set up Horn with that alleged "confession." Horn asks Belle the pointed question: "What's the difference between a U.S. marshal and an assassin?" Unfortunately, as his enthusiastic participation in *An Enemy of the People* proved, by the late 1970s, Steve might have been influenced by the political paranoia of the

LAST CALL. Steve McQueen is about to be entrapped by marshal Billy Green Bush in *Tom Horn* (1988). Steve ended up firing five directors and then taking over the direction himself. With the budget cut down by Warners, and the script revised constantly, the film ultimately failed.

times. His question to Belle is an outright insult to U.S. marshals throughout history who have bravely fought against outlawry.

As the film progresses, we see Horn blasting rustlers out on the prairie with his ubiquitous .45–60 Winchester '76. This is rather amazing in and of itself since that model was obsolete by 1900. The real Tom Horn had actually used the .30–30 Winchester '94 while assassinating rustlers and homesteaders in Wyoming. However, Horn shoots nothing else but this ".45–60" all through the film, and never even wears a handgun.

At the same time he is committing his killings, Horn's romance with Gwen grows. Taking a page out of the B westerns of the past, there is even a scene where the hero's horse pushes the two into a clinch.

But Horn's killings have aroused anger. In town one day to buy a present for Gwen, he is shot at by a bearded assailant. Helpless without his .45–60, Horn gets to his horse in time to get the rifle and kill the man. No one knows who this bearded man was; he just showed up in town and started shooting at Horn. It would have been nice had the filmmakers given us some background here. Nevertheless, the shooting occurs right in front of the horrified cattle barons.

Cut to: a lonely hilltop somewhere out on the prairie where the cattle barons, including John Coble, are having a meeting. The opinion is expressed that Horn might be "a little bit too protective." Fearful of exposure, the cattle barons now prod Coble to reluctantly go along with their scheme to "divest ourselves of this Mr. Horn." Though we see Horn engaging in killing rustlers (who always fire on him first), the film neglects to mention any passage of time where the range detective piled up *dozens* of killings on his résumé. For all we know, by the time of Horn's hanging, it's still 1901. This failure to show any passage of time not only works against the film, but makes it look like the cattlemen are getting rid of Horn after just a *few* killings.

A young boy sits on a fence near some penned-in sheep. He is shot from behind and falls into the flock in a way Willie Nickell never did. Horn is immediately suspected since the boy has had a rock placed under his head in the same way that Horn has done this to dead rustlers as a warning (though the film never shows this), and the weapon used was the same kind that Horn owns. U.S. Marshal Belle invites Horn to his office. With a bottle on his desk and a court transcriber in the next room, he tricks the plastered range detective into delivering the evil line about the worst shot he had ever done and so forth. Horn is arrested for the boy's murder.

Whereas the first part of the film moved at a good pace, the second half grinds to a crashing halt as Horn awaits his trial. The Nickell boy is killed at the 48-minute point and the film lurches ahead for the next 49 minutes into either pure boredom or the absolutely unbelievable. At some point, Horn escapes (with Steve doing an admirable 200-yard dash across the fields that must have been painful for him) and he is promptly chased down by Sheriff Creedmore's (Slim Pickens) deputies. The deputies *were* friendly to him; they now want to whip him to death with their lariats (of course, Horn's assault on two deputies during his escape might have something to do with their anger). Even more incredible is that Horn runs right past some horses, one of which he could have stolen, but *no*, he had to foolishly hot-foot it across the desert with riders after him. Go figure.

And so, being a persecuted victim of "the System," Horn refuses to answer questions about whether he did or he didn't kill the boy (on the witness stand, he refers to the duplicitous U.S. marshal as a "sell-out son of a bitch"). His supposedly principled stand costs him his life as the jury votes for a guilty verdict.

Horn is led up the gallows steps and put on the platform. We hear that no one wanted to pull the lever on Horn and it is even heavily implied that Mr. Julian invented his water-powered gallows for the sole purpose of hanging Tom Horn. And so, Tom Horn is hanged, the cattlemen get away with their crimes, and life goes on. If the audience learned anything, it was that this could have been a truly great western had the star himself not given up on its possibilities. And yet, what was he supposed to do when he himself probably realized that he was a dying man?

Certainly, Horn's fame would resonate with the studios, even its research departments. Discovered in Paramount's pressbook for *The Tin Star* was some of the detailed research the studio was doing for background into Henry Fonda's role as a bounty hunter. At one point, the studio claimed: "El Paso's sheriff's office wired Paramount's publicity shop that 'Tom Horn, last known bountyman in these parts, was hung here in 1905 [sic].' Horn, the wire said, got carried away with himself and shot a sheriff.[9]" Reading this fantasy, one can easily come to the conclusion that *someone* got carried away.

At another point in the same pressbook, the studio claimed to have searched for any surviving bounty hunters who could help them in their research. Again, a familiar name is mentioned: "Tom Horn, a heartless stalker with a tendency towards cruelty, was hung from the gallows that year (1903). He carried his killing too far. He shot a 14-year-old boy."[10] In the original correspondence, the unknown publicist, after writing the words, "He shot a," crossed out "marshal after an argument" and replaces it with "14-year-old boy." Though the publicist's correction was hardly more accurate than what had originally been written, it signaled what the studios thought of the legendary Tom Horn, and that, outside of George Montgomery playing him once in a long-forgotten Fox B (*Dakota Lil*), Hollywood would rarely use the old range detective as the hero in their westerns.

The critical and box office failure of *Tom Horn* is a shame since McQueen is excellent in the role. In the film's opening shot, we see a tired McQueen, with every bit of his lined face emphasizing the years of Hollywood battles, fast cars, chemical dependency and countless affairs. Even more than *Nevada Smith* where Steve was supposed to be a 16-year-old half-breed, *Tom Horn* fit the actor playing him. It was a portrait of the hellion in decline, the natural man of the wild now hemmed in on all sides and forced to do what the "suits" tell him to do. And even though Steve didn't look like Horn, he quickly grasped what the man represented, someone who had plainly outlived his time and was now expendable to those in charge. If the film has one major fault (and it has many), it's that Steve only played a *part* of Tom Horn, not the whole man. The controversial range detective was certainly not the complete victim the film makes him out to be. Horn was a murderer, though the film takes great pains *not* to show him dry-gulching anyone, nor actually terrorizing any homesteaders' families. His enemies *always* fire at him first before he kills them. His scenes with Gwen are clearly done in order to sentimentalize the range detective, though there is one scene where even she is shocked when he's forced to kill an assailant. Therefore, the film shows Horn as being damned when he kills for his job, and, damned when he kills in order to defend himself.

On November 7, 1980, McQueen died of cancer in Chihuahua, Mexico, while searching in vain for some unconventional cure for his illness. In his last two films, he played bounty hunters, the same type of character that enabled him to skyrocket to fame. Whether seeking vengeance (in *Nevada Smith*) or enforcing the Unwritten Law of the privately hired gunman, the actor proved, besides his many other accomplishments, that he could make a pertinent comment on due process in the old west and how some tried to circumvent it.

> "And I looked, and behold a pale horse: and his name that sat on him was Death, and Hell followed with him."—Revelation, *Chapter Six, Verse 8, as read by Megan Wheeler*

By the mid-1980s, the western was in decline. Eclipsed by "B" science fiction and violent urban thrillers, the genre was now considered passé with contemporary audiences. In the post–Vietnam, post–Watergate era, the public's cynicism with the American political scene would be reinforced by revelations that the history of the old west that we read in schoolbooks and avidly followed in movies was probably *not* as accurate as the powers-that-be wanted us to believe. Suddenly, Wyatt Earp was *not* an honest, upstanding lawman who tamed the west; Pat Garrett killed Billy the Kid, not to preserve law and order, but because he was prompted by the crooked Santa Fe Ring (see Peckinpah's *Pat Garrett and Billy the Kid*); Indian tribes, whether they were inherently peaceful or whether they had butchered whole families, were now collectively seen as innocent victims; and the Union government that triumphed over the South and freed the slaves was now considered every bit as corrupt and racist as their Confederate opponents. Even the George Washington whom we were taught chopped down a cherry tree and refused to lie about it would grow up to own slaves.

In the midst of this cynicism, Hollywood would behold the one man, the one cinema icon who could ride into town and save the western from total extinction ... and a hellish box office gross followed with him. When asked about his new film, said icon (Clint Eastwood) replied to Tim Cahill in a 1985 interview for *Rolling Stone*:

One of the earliest films in America was a western: *The Great Train Robbery*. If you consider film an art form, as some people do, then the western would be a truly American art form, as jazz is. In the sixties, American westerns were stale, probably because the great directors—Anthony Mann, Raoul Walsh, John Ford—were no longer working a lot. And then the Italian western came along and we did very well with those; they died of natural causes. Now I think it's time to analyze the classic western. You can still talk about sweat and hard work, about the spirit, about love for the land and ecology.[11]

And let's not forget about all that shooting.

Screenwriters Michael Butler and Dennis Shryack told Eastwood they always wanted to write a western. As Richard Schickel related in his *Clint Eastwood: A Biography*:

> The genre might be in general disfavor, but [Eastwood] thought that if they could find a middle course between dull archetype and the revisionism that he had himself pioneered, they might have a viable project. Or, as he put it in a pre-release interview: "Basically, I wanted to have contemporary concerns expressed within ... the classical tradition."[12]

What Eastwood and his screenwriters *didn't* say in that pre-release interview, however, was that they were going to re-do *Shane*.

Pale Rider begins in Idaho Territory. Hull Barrett (Michael Moriarity) and his adopted family members Sarah Wheeler (Carrie Snodgrass) and her daughter Megan (Sydney Penny) are part of a group mining for gold. They are supposedly trespassing on land owned (though not legally filed on) by the appropriately named Coy LaHood (Richard Dysart) and his son Josh (Christopher Penn). LaHood and his son are in charge of a group of bully boys who have other ideas about how to use the land the miner families are on (the miners are contemptuously referred to as "tin pans"). LaHood's posse rides into their camp randomly shooting at anything that moves and totally wrecking the place. In the process, the band leader cruelly shoots and kills Megan's dog. As the saddened girl buries her pup, she looks heavenward and prays for "a miracle." Before you can say "This is a .357 Magnum, the most powerful handgun in the world," Clint Eastwood's figure is super imposed onto the screen riding a white stallion (a pale horse, get it?).

When Barrett takes the buckboard into town to replace supplies destroyed by the gang, the miner predictably meets the same gang that ruined their camp. After they beat the living daylights out of him, they are about to set fire to his buckboard until the would-be arsonist is doused with a bucket of water. "You shouldn't play with fire," says the man called Preacher (Eastwood). In no time at all, Preacher grabs a hickory stick from a barrel and beats the snot out of the five evil henchmen and then accompanies the injured miner back to his camp. Though the folks at the camp are grateful for his intervention, Sarah has serious reservations that Barrett's tall and taciturn new friend is a gunfighter—an assumption quickly dashed when the stranger removes his coat and reveals a reverend's clerical collar. Preacher has an almost Shane-like cool; and the usual underplaying by the actor portraying him is clearly reminiscent of the traditional style of underplaying of the actor who portrayed Shane (the underrated Alan Ladd).

Though Barrett is against it, Preacher insists on doing some work. The two men take sledgehammers to an irritating boulder which has been an impediment to something or other in the same way Shane and Van Heflin's farmer tackle that huge tree stump. Josh LaHood rides into camp with one of the gang's larger henchmen, Club (the always huge Richard Kiel). When Club is about to hit Barrett, Preacher is quicker with his own sledghammer. Josh and Club ride away with the miners *not* terrorized by their appearance, thanks to Preacher.

The laconic Man of God (who apparently has no problem with using violence to reinforce the Word) imbues the downtrodden miners with renewed spirit to continue their quest for gold despite LaHood's attacks. Obviously impressed with more than just the Preacher's encouraging words, Sarah becomes attracted to the tall stranger, yet it is her daughter who tries to get first dibs. One night out in the woods, Megan admits to Preacher that it is *she* who really loves him; and when he gently rebuffs her advances, being a teenage girl, and a bit of a twit to boot, she loudly declares that she now *hates* him. Preacher certainly knows more than he's telling; in the privacy of his cabin, after he removes his shirt and collar, we clearly see six bullet holes in his back.

Meanwhile, there is trouble in LaHood. The evil land-raper angrily complains about his efforts to get backing for his schemes from the California governor ("Sacramento is *moose piss!*" he memorably proclaims). One does wonder why he seeks the help of the California governor when his operation is in Idaho, but we won't dwell on that right now.

Still in a snit about Preacher rejecting her, Megan stupidly rides into the camp of LaHood's mining operation. To the amusement of the men, Josh grabs the teenager, throws her to the ground, and is prepared to rape her. Preacher fires a shot through the young man's hand, giving him a sort of *stigmata*. The Man of God quickly takes the girl back to her mom and Barrett.

LaHood realizes that Preacher is giving the miners the spirit of community — as well as defiance. Working fast, the town boss contacts the evil Marshal Stockburn (Bloody Bill Anderson of Eastwood's *The Outlaw Josey Wales* and the memorable star of TV's *Lawman*, the talented John Russell). In fact, we see Stockburn come riding over the hills with five of his equally evil deputies. With Russell in the role, it's almost as if Marshal Dan Troop had gone rogue, ditched his deputy Johnny, and hired some hardcases to take his place.

When cynical miner Spider Conway (Doug McGrath) discovers a large chunk of gold, the deliriously happy man decides to get drunk and rather stupidly announces his find in the street outside LaHood's office. With little hesitation, Stockburn and his deputies step out onto the boardwalk, pull out their guns and riddle the frightened man into Swiss cheese. Eastwood films the sequence almost as a ritual killing; the ex-lawmen are seen as warriors executing their king's (LaHood) enemy as an example to the town and as a demonstration of their power (the coup de grace final bullet is delivered to the victim's head by Stockburn himself). And despite the clever and disciplined way the six men line up and repeatedly shoot bullets into their helpless victim like some kind of psychotic chorus line, it's the equivalent of the *Shane* scene in which Elisha Cook Jr.'s character gets killed by Jack Palance's Stark Wilson.

The film implies a history between Stockburn and the Preacher ("That man is dead," the murderous ex-lawman insists). After Conway's son returns to camp with his father's body, Barrett and the Preacher resolve to take matters into their own hands. Somehow obtaining dynamite, the two ride over to Josh's camp and freely throw the burning sticks at the tents (giving the men a chance to flee just before the dynamite explodes). When Josh tries to shoot Preacher, he is oddly saved by Club, much in the same way Ben Johnson's character saves Shane. Not wanting Barrett to accompany him back to town to take on LaHood's men as well as Stockburn's deputies, Preacher shoos away his friend's horse. He seems to have forgotten that Josh and his miners, also afoot, can easily kill Barrett.

Back in town, after Preacher slaughters LaHood's gang, he slyly plays a game of stalk-and-shoot with Stockburn's deputies, gunning them down one by one. When Preacher finally has his face-to-face showdown with Stockburn, the ex-lawman realizes who his

MAKE MY DAY. Clint Eastwood riddles John Russell in *Pale Rider* (1985). It was the actor-director's return to the western after nine years. The film was a box office success for Warners, despite the fact that the script freely pirates *Shane*.

opponent is and goes for his gun — a big mistake. Effortlessly, the Man of God fans the hammer of his gun and riddles Stockburn, the bullets coming out of the ex-lawman's back looking very much like the holes in Preacher's own back. Again, Stockburn's final bullet fired into Conway's head earlier is replicated by Preacher as he fires his own bullet into Stockburn's skull.

When LaHood is about to shoot Preacher from his office, Barrett, who obviously walked all that distance, returns just in time to kill the town boss. His job done, Preacher rides off into the mountains as Megan runs after him and shouts "I love you, Preacher! Thank you!" Under the circumstances, this might sound better than "Shane, come back!"

Filmed in Sun Valley, Idaho, and Columbia State Park in Columbia, California (the same location where RKO shot *Rage at Dawn*), the film was Eastwood's return to the western after nine years. However, in all that time, one wonders just why the versatile Eastwood decided to film, of all things, *Shane* (one also wonders why Paramount Pictures didn't sue).

Certainly, Jack Schaeffer's classic novel *Shane*, written in 1949, gave us one of the most iconic figures of western literature. Shane was a god in a Stetson and worn buckskins; he could fight, shoot, ride, was flawlessly handsome, always seemed to make the right decisions, had the ability to stand back and gauge the situation perfectly and follow through without any fear or hesitation, had the quality of mercy when it was called for, was the best friend you can have in a scrape, won the admiration of a worshipful little boy who wished to emulate him and, through no fault of his own, even attracted the farmer's wife. Obviously familiar with the novel, Louis L'Amour must have been gnashing his teeth in frustration that someone far less prolific than he (but far more talented) created such a classic figure of the west. Rather frenetically, L'Amour knocked out book after book for the next thirty years trying to copy Schaeffer's perfect hero, and failing each time. For unlike Shane, L'Amour's heroes were handsome but cruel bullies who lacked Shane's natural grace and compassion for others.

In *Pale Rider*, Eastwood puts his own spin on *Shane*, transferring Shane's existential calm into Eastwood's unearthly cool. If Alan Ladd's Shane was a savior who equaled the odds, Eastwood's Preacher, a variation of the Man with No Name, was the embodiment of an eye for an eye. Shane would never throw dynamite at anyone; on the other hand, Eastwood's Preacher would never let himself be attacked by several men in a fight sequence where he has to be rescued by the Van Heflin character. Instead, replacing Ladd's fight scene with Ben Johnson, Preacher strikes Club a quick one-two with a sledgehammer. Instead of Shane being chased around by a worshipful little boy, Preacher is the recipient of a teenage girl's crush. Instead of the evil Stark Wilson, we have the murderous Marshal Stockburn; instead of one man, Eastwood and the screenwriters have Preacher face six evil bad guys for the climax (this is not counting LaHood's gang of thugs).

Resurrecting the Resurrection Theme from *High Plains Drifter*, Eastwood also revises the mistrust in governmental authority, whether federal or local, that is prevalent in much of his work. In *The Outlaw Josie Wales*, the Reb guerrilla wipes out a group of bullying Redleg soldiers; in *Pale Rider*, a badge-wearing marshal and his deputies, symbolizing state power, are portrayed as professional killers. In many of Eastwood's films, whether they're Dirty Harrys or his westerns, Man's law has become an arrogant and stifling bureaucracy; and only a lone gunman who embodies God's eye-for-an-eye retribution can set things right. In an interview with Christopher Frayling shortly after the film's release, Eastwood said:

> *Pale Rider* is kind of allegorical, more in the *High Plains Drifter* mode; like that, though he isn't a reincarnation or anything, but he does ride a pale horse like the four horsemen of the apocalypse, and he could maybe be one of those guys. It's a classic story of the big guys against the little guys, little guys versus big guys....[13]

In the interview, the actor-helmsman criticized corporate mining and again claimed that his film made an "ecological statement"; however, as we watch Preacher go about his various killings, it's highly doubtful that the preservation of the rain forest actually comes to mind.

In his June 28 review in the *Chicago Sun-Times*, Roger Ebert praised the film, but also pointedly wrote, "In its broad outline, *Pale Rider* is a traditional western, with a story that has been told, in one form or another, a thousand times before."[14] Not once did the esteemed critic mention *Shane*.

In his review in the *New York Times*, Vincent Canby justifiably praised Eastwood as an actor "who has continued to refine the identity of the western hero by eliminating virtually every superfluous gesture," but chided him on including "a final, shameless quote from George Stevens' *Shane*."[15]

There are those who claim that *Pale Rider* was a bomb, just another example of the western's slow fade to box office death. However, nothing could be further from the truth. It won no prizes at the Cannes Film Festival when Eastwood entered the film a month before its release (he didn't think it would win). However, on an estimated budget of $6,900,000, *Pale Rider* had a box office gross of $41,900,000, becoming one of the most successful films of 1985. Eastwood biographer Richard Schickel wrote that the film took in $9,000,000 in the first week and "close to $50,000,000" in the United States alone.[16]

Eastwood's next cinematic foray into the Unwritten Law of the West would be his greatest western triumph and finally land the actor/director a much-deserved Oscar.

And it would come about because it actually questioned Clint Eastwood's entire film persona...

"You'd be William Munny out of Missouri. Killer of women and children."
— *Little Bill Daggett*

Since 1976, a script had been kicking around the studios of the new, with-it Hollywood. It concerned out-of-control violence in the old west. Unlike the usual western where shooting and other forms of chaos were considered justified, *this* tale rejected the vicarious release that the genre always gave its fans and replaced it with horror at the violent acts perpetrated. Written by a little-known screenwriter named David Webb Peoples (usually credited as David Peoples), a former director, editor and all-around techie (he also wrote the cult film *Blade Runner* and the decidedly *non*-cult *Ladyhawke* and *Leviathon*), the script was called *The Cut-Whore Killings*, a title which seriously impeded any chance for its box office success. Yet the script was eventually bought in 1976 by Malpaso; Clint Eastwood liked the script's possibilities and was hoping to keep it around for a rainy day. By 1991, that rainy day had not only arrived, but so had the serious threat of storm clouds.

Signed with Warner Brothers, the actor had made the studio a pretty penny with the *Dirty Harry* series, not to mention his last western dealing with enforcement of the Unwritten Law, *Pale Rider*. However, after box office duds like *The Dead Pool* (his last performance as Dirty Harry), *Pink Cadillac*, *White Hunter, Black Heart* and *The Rookie*, one critic referred to him as Warners' "fading house star."[17] Eastwood knew he couldn't do Shaw or Ibsen (action maven Steve McQueen learned the mistake of performing in the latter), but at age 61 he definitely had to put away his .357 Magnum. For over a quarter of a century, Clint Eastwood had weaved a path of chaos and destruction to those bellicose bad guys and bloated bureaucrats who had the misfortune to cross his path; in the western, the genre he truly loved and in which he had first gained fame, he was the personification of the Unwritten Law. Despite its disturbing title, *The Cut-Whore Killings* seemed to be the way out of his box office slump. After the script's purchase by Malpaso, the title was changed to *The William Munny Killings*. However, Eastwood simplified the title by calling it *Unforgiven*. In reality, *Unforgiven* is a perfect title for Eastwood's new film, a violent tale in which the major problem of its various revenge-crazed characters is that none of them will ever forgive or forget a transgression made against someone close to them.

The story begins in the bleak and briskly cold burgh of Big Whiskey, Wyoming. As one can tell from the name of the town, its citizens are having a perpetual moral hangover; they are a complacent bunch, whose mundane existence will soon be shaken to its core. The fuse to this tinderbox will be lit when two cowboys, just off the cattle trails, visit Greeley's Saloon, the home of Strawberry Alice (the red-haired Frances Fisher) and the other whores in the oppressive employ of their weasel of a pimp Skinny Dubois (Anthony James). The ladies of the evening are going through their routines when a scream is heard from the room of the youngest and newest whore, Delilah (Anna Thomson). As Eastwood cuts to a burly cowboy named Quick Mike (David Mucci), he is cutting Delilah's face with a razor. His younger and more decent partner Davey (Rob Campbell) tries to stop him, but fails; only when Skinny points a gun at him does the madman stop his assualt. Apparently, all the young woman did to provoke the assault was giggle when she saw the small size of Quick Mike's ... um, *pistol*.

After the two men are tied to a column downstairs, Greeley's is visited by Marshal

"Little Bill" Daggett (an outstanding Gene Hackman) and his army of deputies. Complaining bitterly that his "merchandise" was ruined, Skinny insists on some kind of repayment. Daggett, a brutal lawman, uses his position to justify his own sadism; at first, he tells one of his deputies to get a whip, but then forgoes the whipping and negotiates a deal with Skinny and the two men. The pimp will receive a string of ponies in exchange for the charges being dropped. "That's it!?" cries Strawberry Alice. "They don't even get a whippin'?" Justifiably outraged at this deal between men of dubious ethics, the women know that their demands are ignored simply because they're whores.

The men return the next day and the decent Davey offers his best pony to Delilah, but Strawberry Alice heaps contempt on the young man's offer. The outraged redhead accuses him of cutting up Delilah's face and trying to make amends by giving her a horse. At that point, Eastwood wisely cuts to a closeup of the victim in the background. It is obvious that Delilah is somewhat moved by the offer; Davey had nothing to do with the slashing and he feels guilt over his partner's savage attack. Instead, it is Strawberry Alice who is the vindictive one; not slashed herself, she is in a position to play the righteous, angry woman though she was not victimized. As director Eastwood will incisively demonstrate, it is this kind of stubborn righteousness on the part of the various characters which will spark the tragedies to come.

In the beginning, we read a title card that tells us of a comely young woman who married William Munny, "a known thief and murderer, a man of notoriously vicious and intemperate disposition." That woman, Claudia, died of small pox in 1878. Two years later, we see a hard-working Kansas pig farmer named William Munny (Eastwood), covered in mud, being knocked to the ground yet again by his wild and rambunctious stock. Off to the side are his two cute young children. The brood is suddenly visited by an arrogant young man on horseback outrageously calling himself "the Scofield Kid" (Jaimz Woolvett). Apparently, led by the vindictive Strawberry Alice, the whores have pooled their meager savings and offered a huge reward for the killings of Quick Mike and Davey. The Scofield Kid offers Munny a chance at this bounty if he will join him on this job. At first, Munny turns the Kid down, but after being knocked into the mud by yet another future plate of sausages, he tells the kids to stay with their nearest relative. Grabbing a nag whose main function was to plow the land, Munny falls off the rebellious animal before his foot can settle into a stirrup. In fact, like being dragged through the mud by a wild hog, Eastwood's many pratfalls while trying to mount a horse is a sly parody of his well-established image as the ultimate cowboy hellion, a man who is a demon on a horse as he uses his equine to carry him on to the next killing.

Munny rides over to the home of his former partner in wildness, Ned Logan (an actor Eastwood liked using, Morgan Freeman). Ned is reluctant to leave the happy domestic life he has with his Native American wife. Director Eastwood gives the woman a good moment when she goes to put away Munny's horse and, eyeing his saddle-scabbard, reaches up and touches the butt of his Winchester. The woman is no fool; having seen Munny with her husband years before, she *knows* the reason for his ex-partner's return.

Ned is reluctant to join Munny, but when the pig farmer tells him that the whore was cut up all over, Logan decides to join him. (Similarly, when the Scofield Kid told Munny what happened to Delilah, he *also* exaggerated her injuries.) Out on the prairie, they are shot at by an unknown assailant; it is the Kid, firing at those he thinks are following him. As it turns out, though he can aim and fire his Colt well enough, the terrifying Scofield kid is near-sighted with a rifle.

With Strawberry Alice's lucrative offer making the rounds up and down the entire Texas Panhandle and beyond, Little Bill intends to keep *his* town free of "bad elements." Therefore he has instituted the rule of no firearms in town, Wyatt Earp-style, and has erected a huge, badly written sign on the outskirts of town to alert malefactors that he's not kidding. One of the men responding to the whores' "contract" is English Bob (one of our most dynamic actors, Richard Harris), who arrives by train. English Bob and some American cowpokes are discussing the July 2, 1881, assassination of President James Garfield, with the Englishman proclaiming that no one would kill a king or queen because of the sheer awe that royalty inspires, but an assassin would have no trouble shooting an elected president. Attaching himself to the British gunfighter is the bespectacled pulp writer W.W. Beauchamp (Saul Rubinek). It seems that the writer has penned a "biography" of the gunfighter called *The Duke of Death*. After the two men transfer to a wagon for the ride to Big Whiskey, Beauchamp sees the sign put up by Little Bill warning of no guns in town, but the pompous Englishman is so caught up in telling one of his tales that he fails to notice it.

Once in town, the two men are surrounded by Daggett and his deputies. After removing English Bob's guns (including a hidden revolver), the sadistic lawman proceeds to kick the stuffing out of him and tosses him in jail. It soon becomes apparent that, as the Englishman's fortunes go down and Daggett exudes triumph in his sadism, the fickle Beauchamp will switch allegiances and soon become enamored of the *marshal's* adventures. The next morning, English Bob is ridden out of town as he indicts the watching whores and Americans in general as "savages" (the town will soon be celebrating the 4th of July).

Riding through raging thunderstorms, Munny develops a fever. While entering the town's limits, he and his two companions also fail to see Daggett's sign about no firearms in town. Arriving at Greeley's, Ned and the Scofield Kid help themselves with "freebies" from the whores while Munny sits alone downstairs.

When Daggett and his deputies arrive, they surround Munny with guns drawn and then, once the fever-stricken man is disarmed, the marshal kicks the living daylights out of him and throws him out into the mud-covered street. Warned by the whores, Ned and the Kid barely escape out the back window with their lives and then pick up Munny on the way out of town. Munny must then recuperate for next three days, during which he has terrifying nightmares about his dead wife.

After Munny's fever breaks, the three men ride over to where Davey and his friends are herding cattle. From a hilltop, Ned kills Davey's horse, pinning the young man beneath it, but finds that he cannot fire the killing shot. Munny takes the rifle and kills the young man. Realizing he can't kill anyone any more, Ned decides to return home; Munny will make sure that he still gets part of the money. Traveling to the ranch Quick Mike is working for, the two men see the slasher go into the outdoor privy. The Kid quickly pulls open the privy door and, with Quick Mike pathetically shouting "No, no!" he riddles his victim while his pants are still down. With Munny covering him, the two men escape.

Ned, the only one of the three who didn't kill anyone (at least *this* time), is captured by the cowboys and then given over to Little Bill and his big whip. After one of the whores rides out to the appointed spot to pay off the the two assassins, she reveals to Munny that Ned has been tortured to death by Daggett. There is a good moment when the young woman, whose own fear grows as she speaks, tells them that Daggett knows he is the infamous William Munny, a wanton murderer of women and children. As the Kid stares in shock at the man he had previously derided, Munny shows absolutely no reaction to the young whore's words. Clint the director shoots himself in profile. Munny does nothing to reveal what's going on inside of him at that moment; he just keeps taking huge swallows from a whiskey bottle. It's one of the more unsettling moments in an already disturbing film.

After telling the Kid to hold onto the money for Ned's wife and his own kids, Munny rides into Big Whiskey during the night as a thunderstorm rages. Seeing Ned's body displayed in an open coffin out-

"WE'VE ALL GOT IT COMIN'." Clint Eastwood in what could be his final western, *Unforgiven* (1992). This classic film was a smash hit and finally won the iconic filmmaker a much-deserved Oscar for Best Director. The film powerfully rejects the black humor of Eastwood's spaghetti westerns and makes a man's death a tragedy.

side Greeley's, Munny enters the place and confronts Little Bill and all his deputies. By the time he makes his entrance, a metamorphosis has taken place. The fumbling pig farmer known as William Munny has disappeared and in his place we now see the Man with No Name, unrestrained Maker of Mayhem.

Munny shoots dead the ruthless pimp Skinny. But when his shotgun jams, the reenergized gunfighter pulls his Colt and guns down Daggett and all his deputies, as if Josey Wales had returned in all his glory. With a mortally wounded Little Bill on the ground spitting defiance, Munny puts the shotgun to the sadist's head and pulls the trigger, the director keeping the camera on his own face and not showing us the mess at his feet. When Beauchamp tries to ingratiate himself with Munny, the gunfighter points the shotgun barrel at him; unlike the others whom Beachamp curried favor with, Munny is the genuine article, the gunfighter who commits his acts of violence and *doesn't* want fame.

As he leaves the saloon, to forestall an attack, Munny threatens to murder everyone in town, including their families and friends; and if they don't give Ned a decent burial, he threatens to burn down Big Whiskey altogether. Though the threats are obviously bluff to deter any backshooting as he rides out of town, Munny has definitely changed. Eastwood wisely cuts to a close-up of Strawberry Alice and the whores, especially the redhead, as he makes his threats. It is *she* who has initiated the vendetta, and now she is forced to witness the results. The chain of events which began with the giggling of a young whore has ended in a bloodbath. Righteous in her wrath, Strawberry Alice has not only gotten her revenge, but she has indirectly reawakened a monster.

In an almost brutal indictment of his previous characters, especially the Man with No Name, Eastwood shows us death as the final word for its victims, but perhaps the beginning of insanity for those who deliver it. After these killings, there are no glib wisecracks from any cigarillo-smoking bounty hunter, only a grim scene out of a horror film, filled with its clichés, a raging thunderstorm and a frightened populace. In this final scene, no one will be joking about needing four coffins instead of three; the tableau is filled with terror and despair. In fact, as if reinforcing this dictum, as Will makes his bellicose threats, he sees Ned in his open coffin and looks down sadly.

After Munny rides out of town, the title card comes up revealing that the ex-gunfighter took his kids and probably settled in San Francisco, making a good living in dry goods. Though it's hard to picture this now-revived killer behind a counter selling bustle-wearing old women bolts of cloth, remember that many of us couldn't picture Eastwood as a hog farmer who keeps falling off his horse either.

The film is filled with self-righteous folks who proclaim that certain individuals "had it coming." Ned says the two cowboys (only one of whom slashed Delilah) "have it coming" for what they did; the vindictive Strawberry Alice shouts to the dead men's pals who have thrown a rock through the whores' window, "They had it coming!" And finally, when the Scofield Kid tries to validate his killing of Quick Mike with "Well, I guess they had it coming," Munny responds with the cynical "We *all* got it coming, Kid." Earlier, both Will and the Kid purposely exaggerate Delilah's wounds to justify their own involvement in the vendetta.

Written right after our involvement in the Vietnam War, the script could be seen as a parable of how righteousness and the defense of principles quickly spiral out of control into a bloodbath (*Lawman* of 1970 could be seen as a western euphemism on the then-current Vietnam War). However, by the time of its release on August 7, 1992, *Unforgiven* was seen as a comment on the Rodney King beating by the LAPD. Though this was emphatically *not* Eastwood's intention, neither the director nor the actor who played Little Bill Daggett rejected this theory (with Daggett being seen as racist LAPD Chief Darryl Gates and African-American actor Morgan Freeman standing in for Rodney King).

Almost ten years after its release, in an online reappraisal of the film on July 21, 2002, Roger Ebert found special meaning in the film's final scene:

> There is one exhange in the movie that has long stayed with me. After he is fatally wounded, Little Bill says, "I don't deserve this. To die like this. I was building a house." And Munny says, "Deserve's got nuthin' to do with it." Actually deserve has everything to do with it, and although Ned Logan and Delilah do not get what they deserve, William Munny sees that others do. That implacable moral balance, in which good eventually silences evil, is at the heart of the western, and Eastwood is not shy about saying so.[18]

The final scene of *Unforgiven* resonates in other ways too. When Eastwood rides out of Big Whiskey, the audience is also saying farewell to an icon of the western genre; it is the last hurrah for the Man with No Name and all his various reincarnations that have thrilled us for more than a quarter of a century. And with the character's exit from the screen, we're saying a final goodbye to the last actor to consistently star in the genre. *Unforgiven* grossed $44.4 million in the U.S. alone and won the Oscar for Best Picture, Best Supporting Actor (Gene Hackman) and Best Director for Eastwood. In 2005, Eastwood again won the Oscar for Best Director and Best Picture for *Million Dollar Baby*. Still going strong at age eighty-three, the icon has not signaled that, at his advanced age, he wishes to return to the genre where he first made his fame. Never again would Clint Eastwood, an actor whose characters enforced the Unwritten Law, ride the old west as he dealt justice on his own frequently homicidal terms.

I know that Harry Herzberg would have been saddened by this news.

Forty-six years after my dad took me to see my first Clint Eastwood film, I sadly realize that there's no one around who will ever replace him in the western genre. The little boy in me cries out, "We don't deserve this!"

But then again, deserve's got nothin' to do with it....

8

Back Trail: 1993–2013
The Last Twenty Years

"We come for justice, not vengeance.
Now them is two different things." — *Boss Spearman*

As we moved towards the twenty-first century, the western film seemed to pull a vanishing act, only to return, like a visiting in-law, at the most unexpected times. Despite the success of *Unforgiven* and other westerns released sporadically in the following two decades, Hollywood did not endeavor to give us sagebrush sagas on a consistent level alongside, say, the cop thriller, the computer-generated sci-fi or the youth-oriented sex comedy.

With the western's lack of favor all but verified as a new digital age came upon us, so too would disappear the film that insisted on due process and the rule of law. With Hollywood's move towards gross violence and mean-spiritedness, the rule of law, whether in the old west or the present day, was considered old-hat. Those who represented the law were considered corrupt and those who were selfish and dishonest criminals were considered the heroes. Doing things by the rules was out; to the New Hollywood, the size of your gun was what counted.

However, a year after *Unforgiven*'s much-deserved success, director George Cosmatos (who directed the Rambo movies) gave us *Tombstone*. Just as the first talkie Earp brothers movie *Law and Order* was a success during the gangster-dominated Depression years, *Tombstone* also became a box office hit at a time of rampant crime. (*Law and Order* was based on the novel *Saint Johnson* by W.R. Burnett. The characters were *not* called Earp, but it was obviously "inspired" by their legendary town-taming.) *Tombstone* had little to do with distortions of the law or lynch mob rule, but at least it had a refreshing "take back the streets" philosophy which promoted duly appointed law, not vigilantism or private justice (even if Wyatt and his friends *did* end up going on their famous "Vendetta Ride" against the remaining cowboys who murdered Morgan Earp and wounded Virgil).

Still, *Tombstone* was shorter (by an hour) than Lawrence Kasdan's somewhat bloated *Wyatt Earp*, released practically on the heels of *Tombstone*. Kevin Costner liked doing westerns, and single-handedly tried to get the studios to shoot more of them. There were historical inaccuracies, suspicions of plagiarism and a distorted portrayal of the Lakota Sioux in the Oscar-winning *Dances with Wolves*, but at least his heart was in the right place when attempting to film the west. (Author Michael Blake reportedly wrote the novel *Dances with*

Wolves because he was angered by the less-than-flattering [but far more honest] portrayal of the Sioux in *A Man Called Horse*. Indeed, when one reads Blake's novel and views Costner's film, practically every situation seems to be a comment on some scene in the Richard Harris film. Harris reportedly confronted Costner and accused him of stealing *A Man Called Horse*.)

Yet, in many respects, *Wyatt Earp* was better than *Tombstone*, if only because it tried to get into the head of its subject and portray, quite accurately in many respects, the figures around him and the times in which he lived. It dealt honestly (if somewhat briefly) with Wyatt's relationship with Bat Masterson, with one scene showing that Bat was a natural lawman who knew exactly when to buffalo a troublemaker, whereas his less aggressive brother Ed is slow to use his gun as a deterrent. The upshot of Ed's hesitancy is his being shot to death by a drunken rowdy (this is historically true). In a later scene, Wyatt makes an unruly lynch mob stand down; brandishing a rifle, he shouts at the mob with the spirited, "It all ends now!" This incident actually did happen, though it was in Dodge City, long before the Earps had come to Tombstone. Unlike Cosmatos', Kasdan and Costner bring Wyatt's lover (and later wife) Josephine's Jewishness front and center. At one point, the drug-addicted Matty Earp even calls Josie a "Hebrew whore," an example of old west anti-Semitism not seen often in the typical Hollywood western.

Despite the Costner version of the Earp saga being far more historically accurate than *Tombstone*, *Wyatt Earp* failed at the box office. Then in 1994, director Sam Raimi gave us *The Quick and the Dead*. In the little western town called Redemption a Best Gunslinger contest is being held. Biblical references abound, with Gene Hackman playing a black-suited gang leader and champion pistolero named Herod; and a pre-stardom Russell Crowe as a former gunslinger-turned-preacher who has rejected violence. And the most implausible of all, the always limited Sharon Stone as a gunslinger. Though against violence, Crowe's preacher will change his tune after multiple sadistic beatings by Herod's men and some moral persuasion by the blonde one. At the end, after she and Crowe kill off all the villains, she tosses a marshal's badge towards Crowe (who expertly catches it in slow motion) and delivers the final line: "Law has come to Redemption!" Not the usual moral drama that is the element of the traditonal western, the film still ends with the triumph of the Law, and with the knowledge that a good man (even one now re-accepting violence) will use force only to serve the law and due process. Symbolically, Stone blows up the town's big clock which signaled when the gunfighters opened fire on each other; thus, the credo of the private pistolero is subplanted by the rule of law.

Raimi fills the picture with action that borders on the cartoonish. Bullets rip through tummies and eyeballs are blown out of skulls with visceral energy. Raimi certainly does bow low to Sergio Leone's spaghetti westerns, with Stone's entrance in a saloon (with a laughable closeup on her boots stomping on the wooden planking) a comic highlight. The director also gives a nod to Leone's *Once Upon a Time in the West* with the little girl (who grew up to be Stone) in a flashback scene watching her father hanged by a younger Herod plainly reminiscent of a young Charles Bronson watching *his* dad being hung in a flashback scene in the Leone film. However, despite its high energy level and great visuals, *The Quick and the Dead* was a financial flop.

On August 15, 2003, Touchstone released *Open Range* starring Kevin Costner; though playing the nominal hero, the actor very graciously gave top billing to co-star Robert Duvall. Based on the novel *The Open Range Men* by the prolific Lauran Paine, the film dealt with more distortions of the law. The town Kostner and Duvall (and their small cattle outfit) pass through is run by a crooked Scottish town boss whose gang consists of the town's lawmen. Despite his having reportedly written, under various pseudonyms, over 700 novels, stories and magazine pieces, Paine's only other novel that was filmed by Hollywood was *The Quiet Gun* for Fox's B unit in 1957, and starring Forrest Tucker as the heroic marshal. By the end of *Open Range*, Kostner, Duvall and the townspeople turn against the ruthless Scotsman and his lackies and blow them away. Costner's cowboy is realistically not the brightest bulb on the prairie, but the actor makes the cowpoke immensely likable. His relationship with Annette Bening's mature ranch woman is quite touching, as well as refreshing in its old-fashioned simplicity and sunny optimism. On an estimated budget of $26,000,000, *Open Range* made a disappointing $14,047,781 its first weekend. However, by the end of November 2003, with the addition of its video release, the film had an impressive gross of $58,328,680 in the U.S. alone.[1]

In 2007, American audiences were graced with the release of *3:10 to Yuma*, the remake of the celebrated cult film made by Columbia in 1957. Starring the ubiquitous Russell Crowe as the wily outlaw and Christian Bale as the farmer-turned-lawman, the film perfectly encompassed Hollywood's mean-spiritedness masquerading as "realism." It also continued somewhat of a tradition in westerns (see Errol Flynn and Richard Harris) where its central figures would be portrayed by actors from the British Isles (Crowe was Australian and Bale was Welsh). It was a long way from the time when Texans like Audie Murphy and Nebraskans like Henry Fonda carried a western. Still, Elmore Leonard's characters (which were actually expanded and improved upon, to the property's advantage, by original scenarist Halstead Welles) have now become sad losers. Bale's farmer husband has a wife and son who hate him for being a failure. Crowe's outlaw is highly intelligent, but cruel and homicidal, committing violent acts that Ford's Ben Wade would never even *think* of doing. Certainly, Crowe stabbing one of his guards in the throat with a fork, even while tied up, should have alerted Bale and his cohort that Crowe was dangerous; in order to stop him from killing again, they had the right to defend themselves. This is verified when the outlaw tosses Peter Fonda's lawman over a cliff, again while his hands are tied up, for an insult to his mother. "Even badmen love their mamas," he righteously claims. The climactic gun battle is not only a radical departure from the ending of the original, but cartoonish as well. Though inside the compartment of a moving locomotive, Crowe can still whistle for his horse to follow the train; was the equine blessed with super hearing? Though making money, the film's ending reportedly left a bad taste in the mouth of at least one man, its author, who said dismissively, "Yeah. They had that ending, with the whistling for the horse. But the actors were good."[2]

The film version of Robert B. Parker's *Appaloosa* was based on the first book in the Marshal Virgil Cole-Deputy Everett Hitch series; the fourth book turned out to be the last novel the prolific author ever wrote before his 2010 death (at his word processor). Cole and Hitch are the traditionally laconic lawmen of years past. However, in the novels, the two men have long, *long* discussions on the rule of law and how, as lawmen, they have to follow the rules. Despite discussing the rule of law, there are times throughout the novels when one man or the other *does* violate it, even though they do it for allegedly good reasons. As directed by actor Ed Harris, who also stars as Cole, the film version of *Appaloosa* was pathetically slow. Though it was filmed competently enough and the acting and screenplay (which was loyal to Parker's novel) were good, the pace was dreadful. It didn't make enough to merit a sequel based on the other Parker novels.

Then, in Christmas of 2010, Paramount released the remake of *True Grit*. It was an enormous risk for the filmmakers. The original 1968 version of the landmark Charles Porter novel starred the iconic John Wayne. Porter's fat, drunken lawman was a mustachioed man with one eye, the other eye covered by an eye-patch. The Duke refused to grow a mustache, but he did concede on the eye-patch. The performance, seen as the Duke's good-humored parody of his own heroic image, won him a much-deserved Oscar for Best Actor. The film's screenplay was written by the formerly blacklisted western scenarist Marguerite Roberts (who did the screenplay of *The Sea of Grass*). This film demonstrated a spirit of forgiveness for blacklisted Communists by the conservative Wayne; less vindictive and fanatical than other right-wingers, the actor had always admired Roberts' talent for writing western screenplays. At another point, the Duke cheerfully threw his arm around formerly blacklisted Communist Jeff Corey (cast as the murderer Tom Chaney) and said, "Jeff, it's been too fucking long!"[3]

In the remake, Rooster Cogburn is still fat and one-eyed, but this time he's also a bearded lout as well (and played by Jeff Bridges). The actor tries, but can't erase the memory of the Duke as Cogburn. (Wayne also had the advantage of playing the role again in a sequel, *Rooster Cogburn,* co-starring Katharine Hepburn.) Though the performances were relatively good, with young Hailee Steinfeld a standout as Matty Ross (she should have won the Oscar), the film couldn't escape the ghost of John Wayne.

In the trial scene in the 1968 original, where an outlaw's attorney tries to indict Cogburn for being a little *too* quick to use deadly force on the men he pursues, the Duke parries with the lawyer, mocking the quality of mercy he would have for armed felons and murderers. This scene is taken practically verbatim from the novel, and obviously met with Wayne's approval. (The author had the actor in mind for the character to begin with.) For his conservative, pro-gun, anti-coddling-of-criminals politics, Wayne *was*, in essence, very much like the brave, quick-triggered law enforcer he would win an Oscar for. It was this reality, this ideal merging of actor and role, that made Porter's take-no-prisoners lawman Wayne's possession for all time.

Still, Bridges' performance was very good; he was gruff and crude, yet ultimately likable, and he eventually warms to Steinfeld's Mattie. You could see his marshal carrying the girl on his back for miles in the cold night to get her some help after she was bitten by a rattler (an episode that was in the book). Ironically, one could also easily see Wayne doing the same thing had Roberts chosen to keep that scene from the novel in her screenplay. Nevertheless, whoever was better in the role of Cogburn, audiences responded enthusiastically to the film. With a promotion that used the tagline, "Justice is Coming!" the film was an enormous success. On an estimated budget of $38,000,000, the film ended up with a worldwide box office gross of over $244,000,000.[4]

Despite this, Hollywood hesitated to make more westerns. When it did come out with a western in the summer of 2011, they merged the genre with science fiction. Based on a graphic novel, *Cowboys and Aliens* was released. It starred Daniel Craig as Jake Lonergan and Harrison Ford as the brutal rancher who at first opposes him, then allies with him in destroying the alien menace seeking world conquest. The film was entertaining, but it lost money, barely making back its original budget of $163,000,000.[5] And though due process of the law had little to do with the film's story, it's to be commended for showing whites and Indians working together (even white outlaws) to destroy a common enemy, not only to their country, but to the world.

And so we come to an end of this massive tome.

One of the reasons of why the western was so successful in both literature and film was that the law always won out. When the American western evolved in the 1970s and beyond to include cynicism and mean-spiritedness, with those who represented the law portrayed as being no better than the outlaws they were after, the genre lost its moral thrust; it became as brutal and violent as the urban cop vs. psycho thriller, where the violent cop "hero" had to be as crazy as the felon he was chasing in order to catch him (and, presumably, kill him in an appropriately bloody manner). In essence, this development meant that lawmen of the old west stopped being heroes and the admiration of millions that were once commanded by the Wild Bill Elliotts and Roy Rogers of the world disappeared. The cowboys they portrayed were fantasies, but they were fantasies that promoted the workings of the law and due process. As of this writing, it doesn't look like there will be any more Marshal Will Kanes fighting the good fight against overwhelming odds in the near future.

Yet stubbornly, the western genre keeps coming to the fore again and again, constantly making its many "comebacks" in movie houses, TV screens and literature. For over one hundred years, the western film and novel have been our country's greatest cultural salesmen. With lynchings, hired gunmen, the need for vengeance and other distortions of the law challenging our cowboy or lawman hero, the principles of due process, the rights of the accused, trial by jury and, above all, Innocent Until Proven Guilty, taught the rest of the world that America had something great and inspiring that they should have also.

Emphasizing the need for due process and *not* rush to judgment, we're reminded of a line the great Henry Fonda said in *Warlock* in 1959. While his Marshal Clay Blaisedell faces the men who are about to storm the jail, he says something that could be meant for any group that uses violence in place of freedom and democratic law:

"All of ya go home! And while you're doin' it, think how bein' in a lynch mob is about as low a thing as a man can do...."

Chapter Notes

Chapter 1

1. Jon Tuska, *The Filming of the West*. p. 189.
2. Ibid., p. 189.
3. Ronald L. Davis, *William S. Hart: Projecting the American West*. p. 50. Article by Lutz White in Aurora Beacon News, June 30, 1929, which takes quotes from earlier interview with John Scheets soon after the publication of Hart's autobiography, *My Life East and West*.
4. Ibid. p. 50.
5. Loren D. Estleman, *The Wister Trace*, p. 27.
6. Jon Tuska, *The Filming of the West*, p. 193.
7. Jon Tuska, *Billy the Kid: His Life and Legend*, p. 190; C.L. Sonnichsen, *From Hopalong to Hud: Thoughts on Western Fiction*, p. 19.
8. Ronald L. Davis, *William S. Hart: Projecting the American West*, p. 50.
9. Jon Tuska, *Billy the Kid: His Life and Legend*, p. 190.
10. Ibid., p. 190.
11. Richard D. Jensen, *The Amazing Tom Mix: The Most Famous Cowboy of the Movies*, p. 144; Robert S. Birchard, *King Cowboy: Tom Mix and the Movies*, p. 250.
12. Mark Lee Gardner, *To Hell on a Fast Horse: Billy the Kid, Pat Garrett and the Epic Chase to Justice in the Old West*, p. 240.
13. *The Oklahoma Kid* file, University of Southern California, Warner Brothers Archives.
14. Ibid.
15. Ibid.
16. *New York Times* film review, March 12, 1939.
17. *New York Herald Tribune* film reviews, March 11, 1939.
18. Ibid.
19. Michael Munn, *Jimmy Stewart: The Truth Behind the Legend*, p. 101.
20. *New York Times* film reviews, November 30, 1939.
21. Ibid.
22. Michael Munn, *Jimmy Stewart: The Truth Behind the Legend*, p. 100–101.
23. IMDb, *Destry Rides Again*, Trivia.

Chapter 2

1. Ten Things You Always Wanted to Know About Judge Roy Bean, wwwtexasescapes.com.
2. Ibid.
3. Jeffrey Meyers, *Gary Cooper, American Hero*, p. 156.
4. Ibid.
5. Ibid.
6. Ibid.
7. Ibid.
8. *New York Times* film review, October 25, 1940.
9. Found in Commentaries in *The Ox-Bow Incident* by Walter Van Tilburg Clark, the Modern Library Classics, 2004 edition, p. 245; Clifton Fadiman, *Make Way for Mr. Clark — The O'Neill Family, Afloat and Ashore*, published in the New Yorker, October 12, 1940.
10. Ibid.
11. *Memo from Darryl F. Zanuck: The Golden Years at Twentieth Century–Fox*, editor, Rudy Behlmer, February 15, 1944, p. 75.
12. *New York Times* film reviews, May 10, 1943.
13. Ibid.
14. IMDb, *The Sea of Grass*, Trivia.
15. IMDb, Marguerite Roberts, Biography
16. Elia Kazan, *A Life*, p. 306–314; *Directed by Elia Kazan: The Sea of Grass*, www.tcm.com.
17. Ibid., p. 312.
18. *The Man from Colorado* file, Margaret Herrick Library.
19. Ibid.
20. Ibid.
21. Ibid.
22. Ibid.
23. Ibid.
24. Ibid.
25. Ibid.
26. Letter from Joseph I. Breen to Harry Cohn, May 7, 1946, *The Man from Colorado* file, MHL.
27. Ibid., December 9, 1946.
28. Lawrence Grobel, *The Hustons*, p. 332.
29. Paul Buhle, *Hide in Plain Sight: The Hollywood Blacklistees in Film & Television, 1950–2002*, p. 110.
30. Letter from Breen to Harry Cohn, December 9, 1946, *The Man from Colorado* file, MHL.
31. *Hollywood Reporter* film reviews, November 18, 1948.
32. *Variety* film reviews, November 18, 1948.

Chapter 3

1. *Colt .45* file, USC-WB Archives.
2. Letter from Breen to Jack Warner, August 17, 1949, *Colt .45* file, USC-WB Archives.
3. Austin Statesman, p. 11, Randolph Scott Interview with Bob Thomas, January 30, 1951; info found in *Shooting Stars: Heroes and Heroines of Western Film*, editor, Archie P. McDonald, p. 47, *The Western Heroism of Randolph Scott* by John H. Lenihan.
4. Ronald L. Davis, *Zachary Scott: Hollywood's Sophisticated Cad*, p. 142.
5. Bridges actually initiated his meeting with the FBI in April 1951, and told them he wanted to testify before HUAC. His testimony before the Committee took place behind closed doors on October 22, 1951.
6. Ronald and Allis Radosh, *Red Star Over Hollywood: The Film Colony's Long Romance with the Left*, p. 84–86.
7. The *New York Times* film reviews, June 8, 1950.
8. Letter from Breen to Jack Warner, November 15, 1949, *Colt .45* file, USC-WB Archives.
9. *New York Times* film reviews, May 6, 1950.
10. Letter from Cannon to Jack Warner, May 29, 1950, *Colt .45* file, USC-WB Archives.
11. Kirk Douglas, *The Ragman's Son*, p. 160.
12. Letter from Steve Trilling to Anthony Weiller, May 9, 1949, *Along the Great Divide* file, USC-WB Archives.
13. Kirk Douglas, *The Ragman's Son*, p. 117.
14. Ibid., p. 160–161.
15. Letter from Breen to Jack Warner, September 22, 1950, USC-WB Archives.
16. *Los Angeles Herald Express*, Harrison Carroll, December 2, 1950; *Along the Great Divide* file, USC-WB Archives.
17. Letter from K. Douglas to Anthony Veiller, September 8, 1950, *Along the Great Divide* file, USC-WB-Archives.
18. Ibid.
19. Michael Munn, *Jimmy Stewart: The Truth Behind the Legend*, p. 214–215, undated 1979 inteview with Munn.
20. An Interview with Joan Leslie by Mike Fitzgerald for *Western Clippings*, www.westernclippings.com, undated.
21. Letter from Breen to J.E. Baker, October 6, 1952, *The Woman They Almost Lynched* file, MHL.
22. Synopsis by Steve Fisher, October 28, 1952, MHL.
23. Ibid.
24. Letter from Breen to J.E. Baker, October 6, 1952, *The Woman They Almost Lynched* file, MHL.
25. An Interview with Joan Leslie by Mike Fitzgerald, *Western Clippings*, www.westernclippings.com, undated.
26. Peter Bogdanovich, *Allan Dwan: The Last Pioneer*, p. 152–153.
27. Ibid.
28. *Variety*, film reviews, "Brag," March 30, 1953.
29. Dan Rottenberg, *Death of a Gunfighter: The Quest for Jack Slade, the West's Most Elusive Legend*, p. 146.
30. Ibid., p. 146–147.
31. Ibid., p. 217.
32. Buffalo Bill Cody, *The Life of Buffalo Bill*; from back cover of *Slade: The True Story of the Notorious Badman* by Bob Scott.
33. Dan Rottenberg, *Death of a Gunfighter: The Quest for Jack Slade, the West's Most Elusive Gunfighter*; letter from Dr. John DeShazo to Rottenberg, October 7, 2009, in Postscript, p. 516.
34. Ibid., p. 347.
35. Letter from Breen to Vincent Fennelly, April 6, 1953, *Vigilant Terror* file, MHL.
36. Ibid.
37. Letter from Andre DeToth to Ted Sherdeman, December 10, 1952, *Riding Shotgun* file, USC-WB Archives.
38. Ibid.
39. *DeToth on DeToth: Putting the Drama in Front of the Camera*, editor, Anthony Slide, p. 101.
40. Letter from Steve Trilling to Ted Sherdeman, December 12, 1952, *Riding Shotgun* file, USC-WB Archives.
41. IMDb, *Riding Shotgun*, Box Office/Business
42. Bob Herzberg, *The FBI and the Movies: A History of the Bureau on Screen and Behind the Scenes in Hollywood*, p. 159.
43. Ibid., p. 160.
44. *The Army-McCarthy Hearings*, Wikipedia, www.wikipedia.org
45. *New York Times* film reviews, Oscar Godbout July 24, 1954.
46. *Hollywood Reporter* film reviews, unknown writer, May 12, 1954.
47. *Motion Picture Daily* film reviews, unknown writer, May 12, 1954.
48. Letter from Breen to Benedict Bogeaus, December 10, 1953, *Silver Lode* file, MHL.
49. Ibid.
50. Ibid.
51. Breen letter to William Feeder, October 5, 1954, *Rage at Dawn* file, MHL.

Chapter 4

1. Bob Herzberg, *Savages & Saints: The Changing Image of American Indians in Westerns*, p. 180–183.
2. C. Courtney Joyner, *The Westerners: Interviews with Actors, Directors, Writers and Producers*, p. 237–238.
3. Peter Ford, *Glenn Ford: A Life*, p. 175.
4. C. Courtney Joyner, *The Westerners: Interviews with Actors, Directors, Writers and Producers*, p. 20.
5. Ibid., p. 244.
6. Ibid., p. 18.
7. Letter from Geoffrey Shurlock to Harry Cohn, October 5, 1956, *3:10 to Yuma* file, MHL.
8. Ibid., November 27, 1956, MHL.
9. *New York Times* film reviews, August 29, 1957.
10. *Village Voice* film reviews, J. Hoberman, Aug 28, 2007.
11. Pressbook, *The Tin Star*, unknown writer, undated, MHL.
12. Charles Winecoff, *Split Image: The Life of Anthony Perkins*, p. 132.
13. Pressbook, *The Tin Star*, MHL.
14. Pressbook, unknown writer, undated, *The Tin Star* file, MHL.

15. Personal Injury Report, Paramount Pictures, November 6, 1956, *The Tin Star* file, MHL.
16. Pressbook, *The Tin Star,* MHL.
17. Charles Winecoff, *Split Image: The Life of Anthony Perkins,* p. 128–129.
18. *Hollywood Reporter* film reviews, October 15, 1957, the *Tin Star* file, MHL.
19. *New York Times* film reviews, October 24, 1957.
20. Lawrence Quirk, *Paul Newman,* p. 87.
21. Shawn Levy, *Paul Newman: A Life,* p. 123.
22. Ibid., p. 123.
23. Lawrence Quirk, *Paul Newman,* p. 88.
24. Mark Lee Gardner, *To Hell on a Fast Horse: Billy the Kid, Pat Garrett and the Epic Chase to Justice in the Old West,* p. 142–142.
25. Letter from Shurlock to Jack Warner, May 3, 1957, USC-WB Archives.
26. *Los Angeles Times* film reviews, May 7, 1958, USC-WB.
27. Lawrence Quirk, *Paul Newman,* p. 89.
28. *Los Angeles Times,* Hedda Hopper column, September 4, 1956.
29. Jeffrey Meyers, *Gary Cooper: An American Hero,* p. 226.
30. *New York Times* film review, October 2, 1958.
31. Jeffrey Meyers, *Gary Cooper: An Amercian Hero,* p. 304.
32. Bob Larkins and Boyd Magers, *The Films of Audie Murphy,* p. 113.
33. Robert Nott, *The Films of Randolph Scott, Joel McCrea and Audie Murphy,* p. 112.
34. *Life Magazine* article by Bill Mauldin, June 11, 1971.
35. Edward Dmytryk, *It's a Hell of a Life, But Not a Bad Living,* p. 231.
36. Robert Murray Davis, *Playing Cowboys: Low Culture and High Art in the Western,* p. 37.
37. Ibid., p. 46.
38. Edward Dmytryk, *It's a Hell of a Life, But Not a Bad Living,* p. 234.
39. *New York Times* film review, May 1, 1959.

Chapter 5

1. C. Courtney Joyner, *The Westerners: Interviews with Actors, Directors, Writers and Producers,* p. 118.
2. Letter from Shurlock to Erwin Gelsey, June 22, 1965, *Nevada Smith* file, MHL.
3. Ibid., July 14, 1965, MHL.
4. Ibid.
5. Ibid.
6. *Time* magazine film reviews, July 15, 1966, *Nevada Smith* file, MHL.
7. *Cue* magazine film reviews, July 9, 1966, ibid.
8. *The Overlook Film Encyclopdia: The Western,* edited by Phil Hardy; critique of *Firecreek,* p. 307.
9. Bob Herzberg, *The FBI and the Movies: A History of the Bureau on Screen and Behind the Scenes in Hollywood,* p. 196–198.
10. Ibid., p. 199.
11. Donald Dewey, *James Stewart: A Biography,* p. 453–455.
12. *Fonda: My Life,* as told to Howard Teichmann, p. 328.
13. Letter from Arthur Park to Walter MacEwen, September 14, 1966, *Firecreek* file, USC-WB Archives.
14. Ibid.
15. Letter from Robert Solo to Walter MacEwen, October 3, 1966, *Firecreek* file, USC-WB Archives.
16. Letter from Walter MacEwen to Robert Solo, September 14, 1966, *Firecreek* file, USC-WB Archives.
17. Roger Ebert, *Chicago Sun-Times* film reviews, January 1, 1968.
18. *New York Times* film reviews, February 22, 1968.
19. Peter Ford, *Glenn Ford: A Life,* p. 240–243.
20. C. Courtney Joyner, editor, *The Westerners: Interviews with Actors, Directors, Writers and Producers,* p. 24.
21. *New York Times* film reviews, April 26, 1968.
22. *Clint Eastwood: Interviews,* edited by Robert E. Capsis and Kathie Coblentz; interview with Michael Henry, undated, 1984, p. 96.
23. Richard Schickel, *Clint Eastwood: A Biography,* p. 186.
24. *Clint Eastwood: Interviews,* interview with Thierry Jousse and Camille Nevers, undated, 1992, p. 183.
25. Brian Garfield, *Western Films: A Complete Guide,* p. 82–83.
26. IMDb, *Hang 'Em High,* Box Office Gross.
27. James Gavin, *Stormy Weather: The Life of Lena Horne,* p. 371.
28. Ibid., p. 336–337.
29. Don Siegel, *A Siegel Film: An Autobiography,* p. 316–321.
30. Roger Ebert, *Chicago Sun-Times* film reviews, May 12, 1969.
31. Ibid.

Chapter 6

1. Roger Ebert, *Chicago Sun-Times* film reviews, August 31, 1971.
2. John Huston, *An Open Book,* p. 339.
3. Shawn Levy, *Paul Newman: A Life,* p. 268.
4. Ibid., p. 268.
5. Robert LaGuardia, *Monty: A Biography of Montgomery Clift,* the filming of *Freud,* p. 228–251, Huston's and Universal Pictures' efforts to blame Clift for the increase in budget of *Freud,* p. 252–254, p. 260–262.
6. Shawn Levy, *Paul Newman: A Life,* p. 268.
7. Lawrence Quirk, *Paul Newman,* p. 221.
8. Ibid., p. 222.
9. *John Huston: Interviews,* Robert Emmet Long, editor, p. 32.
10. IMDb, Samuel Fuller, Biography.
11. Samuel Fuller, *A Third Face: My Tale of Writing, Fightin and Filmmaking,* p. 461.
12. Brian Garfield, *Western Films: A Complete Guide,* critique, *The Deadly Trackers,* p. 145–146.
13. Michael Feeney Callan, *Richard Harris: Sex, Death & the Movies, An Intimate Biography,* p. 223.
14. *Death By Word of Mouth, Village Voice* film section, February 7, 1974.
15. Samuel Fuller, *A Third Face,* p. 456.
16. Ibid., p. 456.
17. Ibid., p. 458.
18. Ibid., p. 459.
19. Ibid., p. 460.

20. Ibid., p. 460.
21. Ibid., p. 460.
22. Ibid., p. 460–461.
23. IMDb, Samuel Fuller, credits.
24. *Death by Word of Mouth, Village Voice* film section, February 7, 1974.
25. Conversations with Thomas McGuane, editor, Beef Torrey; *The Novelist in Hollywood,* interviewer — Leonard Michaels, p. 32.
26. Peter Manso, *Brando: The Biography,* p. 811.
27. *New York Times* film reviews, May 20, 1976.
28. Conversations with Thomas McGuane, p. 32–33.
29. Peter Manso, *Brando: The Biography,* p. 815.
30. *Clint Eastwood: Interviews; Eastwood on Eastwood,* interviewed by Christopher Frayling, unknown date, 1985.
31. IMDb, *The Outlaw Josie Wales,* Box Office Gross.
32. *The Education of Little Fraud,* Allen Barra, December 20, 2001, www.salon.com.
33. IMDb, *The Outlaw Josie Wales,* Goofs.

Chapter 7

1. Chip Carlson, *Tom Horn: Blood on the Moon, Dark History of the Murderous Cattle Detective,* p. 50.
2. Cheyenne Leader, unknown writer, July 19, 1901, article found in *The Tin Star* file, MHL.
3. Brian Garfield, *Western Films: A Complete Guide,* critique of *Tom Horn,* p. 323.
4. Christopher Sandford, *McQueen: The Biography,* p. 369.
5. Ibid., p. 123.
6. *Tom Horn* file, MHL.
7. Conversations with Thomas McGuane, interviewer — Judson Klinger, p. 117.
8. Ibid., p. 117.
9. *The Tin Star* pressbook, unknown writer, unknown date, MHL.
10. Ibid.
11. *Rolling Stone,* July 4, 1985, interviewer — Tim Cahill, found in *Clint Eastwood: Interviews,* p. 126–127.
12. Richard Schickel, *Clint Eastwood: A Biography,* p. 403.
13. *Clint Eastwood: Interviews,* Chistopher Frayling, p. 135.
14. Roger Ebert, *Chicago Sun-Times,* June 28, 1985.
15. *New York Times* film reviews, June 28, 1985.
16. IMDb, *Pale Rider,* Box Office Gross.
17. Richard Schickel, *Clint Eastwood: A Biography,* p. 451.
18. Roger Ebert, July 21, 2002, *Unforgiven,* www.Rogerebert.com

Chapter 8

1. IMDb, *Open Range,* Box Office Gross.
2. C. Cortney Joyner, *The Westerners: Actors, Directors, Writers and Producers,* p. 244.
3. Kenneth Lloyd Billingsley, *Hollywood Party: How Communism Seduced the American Film Industry in the 1930s and 1940s,* p. 271; originally from an interview with Jeff Corey in *Tender Comrades: A Backstory of the Hollywood Blacklist,* written and edited by Patrick McGilligan and Paul Buhle, p. 197.
4. IMDb, *True Grit* (2010), Box Office Gross.
5. IMDb, *Cowboys and Aliens,* Box Office Gross.

Bibliography

Adams, Les, and Buck Rainey. *Shoot-Em-Ups.* New Rochelle, New York: Arlington House Publishers, 1978.
Arce, Hector. *Gary Cooper: An Intimate Biography.* New York: William Morrow & Co., 1979.
Barra, Allen. *Inventing Wyatt Earp: His Life & Many Legends.* New York: Caroll & Graf, 1998.
Behlmer, Rudy, editor. *Inside Warner Brothers: 1935–1951.* New York: Simon & Schuster and Warner Brothers, 1985.
_____. *Memo from Darryl F. Zanuck: The Gold Years at Twentieth Century–Fox.* New York: Grove Press, 1993.
Bergman, Andrew. *We're in the Money: Depression America and Its Films.* Chicago, Illinois: Ivan R. Dee, 1971.
Billingsley, Kenneth Lloyd. *Hollywood Party: How Communism Seduced the American Film Industry in the 1930s and 1940s.* Rocklin, California: Prima Publishing, 1998.
Blottner, Gene. *Universal-International Westerns, 1947–1963.* Jefferson, N.C.: McFarland, 2000.
_____. *Wild Bill Elliott: A Complete Filmography.* Jefferson, N.C.: McFarland, 2007.
Bogdanovich, Peter. *Allan Dwan: The Last Pioneer.* New York: Praeger Publishers, 1971.
Brand, Max. *Destry Rides Again.* New York: Dodd, Mead & Co., 1930.
Brough, James. *The Prine and the Lily: The Dazzling Provocative Story of Lillie Langtry.* New York: Ballantine Books, 1975.
Brown, Will C. *The Border Jumpers.* New York: E.F. Dutton & Co., 1955.
Buford, Kate. *Burt Lancaster: An American Life.* Cambridge, Massachusetts: Perseus Books, 2000.
Buhle, Paul. *Hide in Plain Sight: Blacklistees in Film and Television, 1950–2002.* New York: Palgrave Macmillan, 2004.
_____, and Dave Wagner. *Blacklisted: The Film Lover's Guide to the Hollywood Blacklist.* New York: Palgrave Macmillan, 2003.
Buscombe, Ed. *The BFI Companion to the Western Film.* New York: Macmillan Publishing Co., 1988.
Callan, Michael Feeney. *Richard Harris: Sex, Death & the Movies, An Intimate Biography.* London: Robson Books, 2003.
Carlson, Chip. *Tom Horn, Blood on the Moon: Dark History of the Murderous Cattle Detective.* Glendo, Wyoming: High Plains Press, 2001.
Chadwick, Bruce. *The Reel Civil War: Mythmaking in American Film.* New York: Random House, 2001.
Clark, Walter Van Tilburg. *The Ox-Box Incident.* New York: Random House, Inc., 1940.
Clinch, Minty. *Burt Lancaster.* New York: Stein & Day, 1984.
Corbett, Christopher. *Orphans Preferred: The Twisted Truth and Lasting Legend of the Pony Express.* New York: Broadway Books, 2003.
Crivello, Kirk. *Fallen Angels: The Glamorous Lives and Tragic Deaths of Hollywood's Doomed Beauties.* New York: Berkley Books, 1988.
Darby, William. *Anthony Mann: The Film Career.* Jefferson, N.C.: McFarland, 2009.
Davis, Robert Murray. *Playing Cowboys: Low Culture and High Art in the Western.* Norman, Oklahoma: University of Oklahoma Press, 1992.
Davis, Ronald L. *Duke: The Life and Image of John Wayne.* Norman, Oklahoma: University of Oklahoma Press, 1998.
_____. *William S. Hart: Projecting the American West.* Norman, Oklahoma: University of Oklahoma Press, 2003.
_____. *Zachary Scott: Hollywood's Sophisticated Cad.* Jackson, Mississippi: University Press of Mississippi, 2006.
Dewey, Donald. *James Stewart: A Biography.* Atlanta, Georgia: Turner Publishing, 1996.
Dmytryk, Edward. *It's a Hell of a Life, But Not a Bad Living.* New York: NYTimes Books, 1978.
Doherty, Thomas. *Hollywood's Censor: Joseph Breen*

and the Production Code Administration. New York: Columbia University Press, 2007.

Douglas, Kirk. *The Ragman's Son.* New York: Simon & Schuster, 1988.

Easton, Robert. *Max Brand: The Big Westerner.* Norman, Oklahoma: University of Oklahoma Press, 1970.

Estleman, Loren D. *The Wister Trace: Classic Novels of the American Frontier.* Ottawa, Illinois: Jameson Books, 1987.

Everson, William K. *The Hollywood Western.* New York: Citadel Press, 1969 and 1992.

_____. *A Pictorial History of the Western Film.* New York: Citadel Press, 1971.

Eyman, Scott. *Print the Legend: The Life and Times of John Ford.* New York: Simon & Schuster, 1999.

Fonda, Henry, and Howard Teichmann. *Fonda: My Life.* New York: New American Library, 1981.

Ford, Peter. *Glenn Ford: A Life.* Madison, Wisconsin: The University of Wisconsin Press, 2011.

Fraser, George McDonald. *The Hollywood History of the World: From One Million Years B.C. to Apocalypse Now.* New York: Ballantine Books, 1988.

Fuller, Samuel. *A Third Face: My Tale of Writing, Fighting and Filmmaking.* New York: Random House, 2002.

Gardner, Mark Lee. *To Hell on a Fast Horse: Billy the Kid, Pat Garrett and the Epic Chase to Justice in the Old West.* New York: HarperCollins Publishers, 2010.

Garfield, Brian. *Western Films: A Complete Guide.* New York: Da Capo Press, 1982.

Gavin, James. *Stormy Weather: The Life of Lena Horne.* New York: Simon & Schuster, 2009.

George-Warren, Holly. *Public Cowboy #1: The Life and Times of Gene Autry.* New York: Oxford University Press, 2007.

Graham, Don. *No Name on the Bullet: A Biography of Audie Murphy.* New York: Penguin Books, 1989.

Gussow, Mel. *Don't Say Yes Until I Finish Talking.* New York: Doubleday & Co., 1971.

Hall, Oakley. *Warlock.* New York: Viking Press, 1958.

Hardy, Phil, editor. *The Overlook Film Encyclopedia: The Western.* Woodstock, New York: Overlook Press, 1984 and 1991.

Herzberg, Bob. *The FBI and the Movies: A History of the Bureau on Screen and Behind the Scenes in Hollywood.* Jefferson, N.C.: McFarland, 2007.

_____. *Savages & Saints: The Changing Image of American Indians in Westerns.* Jefferson, N.C.: McFarland, 2008.

_____. *Shooting Scripts: From Pulp Western to Film.* Jefferson, N.C.: McFarland, 2005.

Horwitz, James. *They Went Thataway.* New York: E.F. Dutton & Co., 1976.

Huston, John. *An Open Book.* New York: Alfred A. Knopf, 1980.

Jarlett, Franklin. *Robert Ryan: A Biography and Critical Filmography.* Jefferson, N.C.: McFarland, 1990.

Jenson, Richard D. *The Amazing Tom Mix: The Most Famous Cowboy of the Movies.* New York: iUniverse, 2005.

Johnson, Dorothy M. *Western Badmen.* New York: Ballantine, 1970.

Joyner, C. Courtney. *The Westerners: Interviews with Actors, Directors, Writers and Producers.* Jefferson, N.C.: McFarland, 2009.

Kapsis, Robert E., and Kathie Coblentz, editors. *Clint Eastwood: Interviews.* Jackson, Mississippi: University Press of Mississippi, 1999.

Kazan, Elia. *A Life.* New York: Da Capo Press, 1997.

Kitses, Jim. *Horizons West: Anthony Mann, Budd Boetticher, Sam Peckinpah, Studies of Authorship Within the Western.* Bloomington, Indiana: Indiana University Press, 1969.

_____, and Gregg Rickman, editors. *The Western Reader.* New York: Limelight Editions, 1999.

LaGuardia, Robert. *Monty: A Biography of Montgomery Clift.* New York: Avon Books, 1977.

Larkins, Bob, and Boyd Magers. *The Films of Audie Murphy.* Jefferson, N.C.: McFarlnd, 2004.

Lenihan, John H. *Showdown: Confronting Modern America in the Western Film.* Urbana and Chicago, Illinois: University of Illinois Press, 1980.

Levy, Shawn. *Paul Newman: A Life.* New York: Random House, 2009.

Linet, Beverly. *Star-Crossed: The Story of Robert Walker and Jennifer Jones.* New York: G.P. Putnam's Sons, 1986.

Long, Robert Emmet, editor. *John Huston, Interviews.* Jackson, Mississippi: Univerity Press of Mississippi, 2002.

Mackay, James. *Allan Pinkerton: The First Private Eye.* New York: John Wiley & Sons, 1996.

Manso, Peter. *Brando: The Biography.* New York: Hyperion Books, 1994.

Marx, Arthur. *Goldwyn: A Biography of the Man Behind the Myth.* New York: Ballantine Books, 1976.

Mayo, Virginia, and L.C. Van Savage. *Virginia Mayo: The Best Years of My Life.* Chesterfield, Missouri: Beach House Books, 2001.

McDonald, Archie P., editor. *Shooting Stars: Heroes and Heroines in Western Film.* Bloomington, Indiana: Indiana University Press, 1987.

Metz, Leon Claire. *The Shooters: A Gallery of Notorious Gunmen from the American West.* New York: Berkley Books, 1976.

Meyers, Jeffrey. *Gary Cooper: American Hero.* London, England: Robert Hale, Ltd., 2001.

Morella, Joe, and Edward Z. Epstein. *Rebels: The*

Rebel Hero in Film. New York: Citadel Press, 1971.

Moss, Marilyn. *Raoul Walsh: The True Adventures of Hollywood's Legendary Director*. Lexington, Kentucky: University Press of Kentucky, 2011.

Mountcastle, Clay. *Punitive War: Confederate Guerrillas and Union Reprisals*. Lawrence, Kansas: University Press of Kansas, 2009.

Munn, Michael. *Jimmy Stewart: The Truth Behind the Legend*. Fort Lee, N.J.: Barricade Books, 2006.

Nott, Robert. *The Films of Randolph Scott*. Jefferson, N.C.: McFarland, 2004.

_____. *Last of the Cowboy Heroes: The Westerns of Randolph Scott, Joel McCrea and Audie Murphy*. Jefferson, N.C.: McFarland, 2000.

Porter, Charles. *True Grit*. New York: Simon & Schuster, 1969.

Quirk, Lawrence. *Paul Newman*. New York: Taylor Publications, 1997.

Radosh, Ronald, and Allis Radosh. *Red Star Over Hollywood: The Film Colony's Long Romance with the Left*. San Francisco, California: Encounter Books, 2006.

Reasoner, James. *Draw: The Greatest Gunfights of the American West*. New York: Berkley Publishing, 2005.

Richter, Conrad. *The Sea of Grass*. New York: Curtis Publishing Co., 1936.

Roberts, Randy, and James S. Olson. *John Wayne, American*. New York: The Free Press, 1995.

Rosa, Joseph G. *The Gunfighter: Man or Myth?* Norman, Oklahoma: University of Oklahoma Press, 1969.

Rottenberg, Dan. *Death of a Gunfighter: The Quest for Jack Slade, the West's Most Elusive Legend*. Yardley, Pennsylvania: Westholme Publishing, 2008.

Sandford, Christopher. *McQueen: The Biography*. New York: Rowman & Littlefield, 2001.

Schickel, Richard. *Clint Eastwood, A Biography*. New York: Random House, 1996.

_____. *Elia Kazan: A Biography*. New York: HarperCollins, 2005.

Scott, Bob. *Slade! The True Story of the Notorious Badman*. Glendo, Wyoming: High Plains Press, 2004.

Siegel, Don. *A Siegel Film: An Autobiography*. London: Faber & Faber, Ltd., 1993.

Sklar, Robert. *City Boys: Cagney, Bogart, Garfield*. Princeton, New Jersey: Princeton University Press, 1992.

Slide, Anthony, editor. *DeToth on DeToth: Putting the Drama in Front of the Camera*. London, England: Faber & Faber, Ltd., 1996.

Swindell, Larry. *Spencer Tracy*. New York: New American Library, 1969.

Terrill, Marshall. *Steve McQueen: Portrait of an American Rebel*. New York: Donald I. Fine, 1993.

Thomas, Bob. *King Cohn: The Life and Times of Hollywood Mogul Harry Cohn*. New York: G.P. Putnam's Sons, 1967.

Torrey, Beef, editor. *Conversation with Thomas McGuane*. Jackson, Mississippi: University Press of Mississippi, 2006.

Tuska, Jon. *Billy the Kid: His Life and Legend*. Albuquerque, New Mexico: University of New Mexico Press, 1994.

_____. *The Filming of the West*. Garden City, New York: Doubleday & Co., 1976.

Walker, Dale L. *The Calamity Papers: Western Myths and Cold Cases*. New York: Tom Doherty Associates, 2004.

Wallis, Michael. *Billy the Kid: The Endless Ride*. New York: W.W. Norton & Co., 2007.

Whiting, Charles. *Hero: The Life and Death of Audie Murphy*. Chelsea, Michigan: Scarborough House, 1990.

Winecoff, Charles. *Split Image: The Life of Anthony Perkins*. New York: E.F. Dutton, 1996.

INTERNET SOURCES

Arnold, Jeremy. "The Sea of Grass," http://www.tcm.com/this-month/article/374045%7C145268/The-Sea-of-Grass.html.

Barra, Allen. "The Education of Little Fraud," December 20, 2001, Internet Movie Database, http://imdb.com.

Internet Broadway Database. http://ibdb.com.

Legends of America. "Old West Legends: The Notorious Reno Gang of Indiana," http://www.legendsofamerica.com/we-renogang.html.

New York Times Movie Review Archives. http://www.nytimes.com/ref/movies/archive_a.html.

PBS. "American Experience: George Wallace, Settin' the Woods on Fire; Asa Carter," http://www.pbs.org/wgbh/amex/wallace/peopleevents/pande01.html.

Roger Ebert's Film Reviews. www.rogerebert.com.

Ron's Texas Page. "Judge Roy Bean, 'Law West of the Pecos,'" http://www.qsl.net/w5www/roy-bean.html.

Spartacus Educational. "Marguerite Roberts," http://www.spartacus.schoolnet.co.uk/USArobertsM2.htm.

The Thrilling Detective. "Tom Horn, 1860–1903," http://www.thrillingdetective.com/eyes/horn.html.

"Tom Horn: Misunderstood Misfit," June 12, 2006, http://www.historynet.com/tom-horn-misunderstood-misfit.htm.

Troesser, John. "Ten Things You Should Know About Judge Roy Bean," http://www.texasescapes.com/They-Shoe-Horses-Dont-They/Ten-Things-You-Should-Know-about-Judge-Roy-Bean.htm.

True West Magazine. "The Renegade Reno Brothers," wwwtruewest.com. http://www.salon.com/2001/12/20/carter_6/.
Wikipedia. "Army-McCarthy Hearings," http://en.wikipedia.org/wiki/Army-McCarthy_Hearings.
Wikipedia. "Johnson County War," http://en.wikipedia.org/wiki/Johnson_County_War.
Wikipedia. "Marguerite Roberts," http://en.wikipedia.org/wiki/Marguerite_Roberts.
Wikipedia. "Owen Wister," http://en.wikipedia.org/wiki/Owen_Wister.
Wikipedia. "Tom Horn," http://en.wikipedia.org/wiki/Tom_Horn.

Index

Ace in the Hole 69
Across 110th Street 202
Adams, Julia 33
Agar, John 70, 156, 158
Albert, Marvin H. 182
Aldrich, Robert 135, 178
Along the Great Divide 69–72, 104
Anderson, "Bloody Bill" 208, 229
Anderson, James 69
Anderson, John 173
Andrews, Dana 45, 48, 156, 157
Andrews, Robert Harry 59, 62
Ankrum, Morris 69, 104
Apache Uprising 156
The Appaloosa (film) 203, 240
The Appaloosa (novel) 203, 240
Arlen, Richard 9, 10, 20, 156, 158
Armstrong, R.G. 142
Arnold, Jack 141, 144, 145, 182
The Asphalt Jungle (film) 143
Attack on Terror: The FBI vs. the Ku Klux Klan 168
Auer, Mischa 29, 30
Autry, Gene 18

Bacon, Lloyd 24
Baer, Parley 174
Bale, Christian 240
Bardette, Trevor 50, 112
Barret, Robert 20, 25, 52
Barrier, Edgar 104
Bean, Judge Roy 35–38
Beery, Wallace 12
Begley, Ed 165–166, 170, 179
Bend of the River 74, 138
Best, James 128, 166
Bettger, Lyle 156, 157
Billy the Kid (1930) 11–14
Billy the Kid (1941) 14
Birth of a Nation 22–24
Bissell, Whit 142
Blackburn, Tom (Thomas W.) 66, 100, 103
The Blob (1958) 160, 161
Bluebeard (1972) 148

Boetticher, Budd 82–83, 197
Bogart, Humphrey 25, 28, 222
Bogdonovitch, Peter 82–83
Bogeaus, Benedict 104
Bond, Ward 25
Bonnie and Clyde 168
The Border Jumpers 136, 137, 139
Borgnine, Ernest 64
Bouchley, Willis 141
The Bounty Hunters 116
The Boy from Oklahoma 127
Brand, Max 14–15, 17, 29, 32
Brand, Neville 122, 123, 197
Brando, Marlon 148, 170, 203, 204–208
Bray, Robert 93
Breen, Joseph I. 47, 57, 59, 63, 71, 72, 81, 107
Brennan, Walter 21, 38, 40–42, 69, 72, 192
Brian, Mary 10, 12
Bridges, James 241
Bridges, Lloyd 65, 67
Bring Me the Head of Alfredo Garcia 203
Bronson, Charles 100, 101, 118, 188, 239
Brooke, Walter 189
Brown, Harry Joe 99
Brown, Johnny Mack 12, 13, 34, 127
Brown, Will C. 135–138
Buchanan, Edgar 41, 112
Buckskin 156
Burnett, W.R. (William Riley) 238
The Burning Hills (film) 71
Burns, Paul E. 47
Burns, Walter Noble 12, 14
Busch, Niven 38, 40

Cagney, James 24–28, 63–64
The Caine Mutiny (film) 148
Calhoun, Rory 182
Carey, Harry, Jr. 104, 184

The Carpetbaggers (film) 159, 161
The Carpetbaggers (novel) 159
Carradine, David 222
Carter, Asa (Forrest) 211–216
Castle, William 127
Chaney, Lon, Jr. 156, 159
Chapman, Marguerite 96
Chase, Borden 55–57, 59–60, 62
Chief Dan George 209, 215–216
Chief Thundercloud 65
Christine, Virginia 80
The City of Trembling Leaves 44
Clark, Walter Van Tilburg 17, 42–44
Clemens, Calvin, Sr. 165, 168–169, 171
Clift, Montgomery 148, 195
Cobb, Lee J. 137, 140, 188
Coburn, James 63, 188
Cohn, Harry 57, 91, 120
Cohn, Roy 103–104
Colt .45 63–69, 99–100
Column South 143
Conroy, Frank 47
Coon, Gene L. 142
Cooper, Ben 79
Cooper, Gary 9–11, 32, 38, 40–41, 64, 69, 134–136, 138
Corby, Ellen 78
Corey, Jeff 241
Corey, Wendell 156
Coroner Creek (film) 64, 68, 151, 163
Costner, Kevin 238–239
The Covered Wagon (film) 19
The Covered Wagon (novel) 19
Cowboys and Aliens 241
Craig, Daniel 241
Crisp, Donald 25–26
Crowe, Russell 119, 240
Cummings, Robert 20
Curtiz, Michael 24, 69, 100, 127
Custer of the West 61

Dallas 39

Dana, Leora 117
Dances with Wolves 238–239
Dano, Royal 136, 173
Darwell, Jane 45
Davenport, Doris 39
Daves, Delmer 118–121, 197
Davis, Jim 79
Day of the Evil Gun 171–175
The Deadly Trackers 196–202
Dean, James 127–128
Death of a Gunfighter (film) 183–187, 202
Death of a Gunfighter (novel) 182
DeCorsia, Ted 161
Deep in the Heart of Texas 35
Dehner, John 129, 133, 137, 140
Dell, Claudia 17
Denning, Richard 20
Destry Rides Again (film, 1932) 16–17
Destry Rides Again (film, 1939) 26, 29–34, 74, 80, 167
Destry Rides Again (novel) 14–15
DeToth, Andre 99, 102–103
DeWolf, Karen 104–106
Dietrich, Marlene 29–30, 33–34
Dirty Harry 179, 192, 208, 223, 232
Dixon, Thomas, Jr. 22
Dmytryk, Edward 148, 152–153, 159, 161
Dodge City 24
Doniger, Walter 72–73
Donlevy, Brian 30, 79
The Doolins of Oklahoma 68
Doucette, John 161
Douglas, Kirk 69–73, 134
Douglas, Melvyn 48, 52
Drake, Charles 142
Drake, Tom 148, 156, 158–159
Drew, Ellen 58
Drums Across the River 98
Duryea, Dan 104, 106
Duvall, Robert 239–240
Dwan, Allan 80, 82–83, 104

Earp, Wyatt 148, 238–239
Eastwood, Clint 77–78, 176–179, 181, 195, 208, 211–215, 227–228, 232, 235–237
Easy Rider 187
The Education of Little Tree 212–213
Elam, Jack 166–167
Elliot, Ross 172
Elliot, "Wild Bill" 91–93, 95
Enright, Ray 79, 151
Estavez, Emilio 14
Evans, Gene 160
Evans, Joan 142–144
Evans, Linda 224
Executive Action 189
Eythe, William 45

The Far Country 41, 139
Farr, Felicia 118
Fessier, Michael 78
Firecreek 165–170
Fisher, Frances 232
Fisher, Steve 78, 83, 155–156, 158–159
Fix, Paul 162
Flippen, J.C. 166, 170
Flynn, Errol 24, 240
Fonda, Henry 45–48, 121–122, 124–126, 149–150, 154, 166–168, 204, 242
Ford, Francis 45
Ford, Glenn 58, 60–61, 117–119, 121, 171–172, 174–175, 225, 240
Ford, Harrison 241
Ford, John 73, 121, 174, 197
Ford, Peter 119, 174
Ford, Wallace 149
Foreman, Carl 101, 135, 141, 177
Fort Apache 121
Fowley, Douglas 52
Franken, Steve 206
Freeman, Morgan 233, 236
Fuller, Samuel 196–198, 200–202

Gable, Clark 12
Gardner, Ava 194–195
Garrett, Sheriff Pat 11–12, 127, 129, 131–132
Gene Autry and the Mounties 62
Goddard, Paulette 30
Goldwyn, Samuel 38, 41, 192
Golonka, Arlene 180
Gorshin, Frank 149
Grey, Virginia 145
Grey, Zane 15–16, 146
Griffith, James 127, 172–173
Gruber, Frank 51, 111
Gunman's Rhapsody 142
Gunsights 116

Hackman, Gene 232, 236, 239
Hale, Alan, Jr. 104, 179
Hale, Alan, Sr. 65
Hall, Oakley 45, 147, 148, 150, 152–154
Hang 'Em High 42, 176–181
Harris, Richard 197–198, 200–201, 204, 238–239
Hart, William S. 8, 12–13, 16, 31, 64, 91
Hatfield, Hurd 130
Hathaway, Henry 64, 161–163, 222
Hatton, Raymond 21
Haycox, Ernest 64, 88, 114, 182
Healey, Myron 93, 111
Heaven with a Gun 171
Heflin, Van 117–119, 121, 228, 231
Hell Bent for Leather 98
Hell's Hinges 31
Hepburn, Katharine 48, 52, 54, 241

Herzberg, Harry 175–176, 237
High Noon 101–103, 116, 135, 141, 168
High Plains Drifter 231
Hinds, Samuel S. 30
Hingle, Pat 41, 162, 179
Holden, William 58
Hombre (novel) 116
Hopkins, Bo 201
Horn, Tom 217–220, 226–227
Horne, Lena 183, 186
Hough, Emerson 18–21
Hughes, Howard 14, 111
Hughes, Mary Beth 45
Hunter, Tab 125
Huston, John 192–196
Huston, Walter 10–11
Hutchinson, Josephine 161
Hymer, Warren 30

I Wake Up Screaming (novel) 78
The Indians Are Coming! 32

Jack Slade 89–91
Jaeckel, Richard 117
Jagger, Dean 165–166, 170, 172, 175
James, Frank 79
James, Jesse 79, 127
James-Younger Gang 108, 114
Jeremiah Johnson 196
Johnny Reno 156–159
Johnson, Ben 179, 231
Johnson, Russell 97
Jolley, I. Stanford 93
Jones, Buck 15–16, 18, 99
Jones, Henry 117, 119–120
Jones, L.Q. 149, 179
Jubal 118
Jubal Troup 118
Juran, Nathan 98

Kansas Raiders 79
Kastner, Elliot 203, 206
Kaufman, Philip 211, 214–215
Kay, Mary Ellen 93
Kazan, Elia 52–53
Keith, Brian 161, 164
Keith, Robert 170
Kelley, DeForest 149
Kelton, Elmer 228
Kennedy, Arthur 160, 167, 172
Kennedy, Burt 64

Ladd, Alan 15–16, 228, 231
The Lady in the Lake (film) 78
Laemmle, Carl 32
L'Amour, Louis 51, 214, 230–231
Lancaster, Burt 134, 143, 151, 188–190
Landau, Martin 160
Langton, Paul 89
Langtry, Lillian (Lily) 38–40
The Last Challenge 171

Last Stand at Saber River 116
The Law at Randado 116
The Law vs. Billy the Kid 127
Lawman 143, 151, 188–192, 236
The Left-Handed Gun 127–134, 180, 192, 203–204, 222
Leigh, Janet 74, 76–78
Leonard, Elmore 115–117, 119
Leslie, Joan 78–83, 104
Lettieri, Al 198, 202
The Life and Times of Judge Roy Bean 126, 192–195
Lloyd, Kathleen 204
Lockwood, Gary 166
London, Julie 136
The Lonely Man 125–126
Lord, Jack 136
Lowery, Robert 156
Lumet, Sidney 186
Lydon, James 112, 183
Lyles, A.C. 155–156, 158–159

Mackenna's Gold (film) 177–178
Mackenna's Gold (novel) 177
MacLane, Barton 89
MacLeod, Robert 203
Maddow, Ben 59–60, 61, 62
The Magnificent Seven 160, 164
Malden, Karl 160
Malone, Dorothy 89, 90, 149
A Man Called Horse 197, 222, 239
The Man from Colorado 56–61, 62, 119, 126
The Man from the Alamo 155
Man of the West (film) 136–140
Mann, Anthony 63, 73–74, 76, 122_124, 126, 135, 137–138, 197
Marin, Edwin L. 64, 66
Marshall, George 29
Marvin, Lee 223
Mauldin, Bill 146
Maynard, Ken 15, 18, 99
Mayo, Virginia 70, 72, 73, 155
McCarthy, Sen. Joseph 98, 103–104, 106, 121
McCoy, Horace 111, 114
McCrea, Joel 11, 13
McDonald, Ian 60
McDowall, Roddy 193
McEveety, Vincent 171
McGuane, Thomas 202–203, 206, 223–224
McIntyre, John 139
McQueen, Steve 99, 160, 163–164, 221–224, 227
Meeker, Ralph 74, 76
Merkel, Una 30, 33
Michaels, Dolores 149
Milius, John 192, 194–196
Miller, Marvin 78
Millican, James 60, 62, 100
The Missouri Breaks 203–208, 223
Mr. Horn (TV movie) 222
Mister Roberts 121

Mitchell, Millard 74
Mitchum, Robert 57
Mix, Tom 15–16, 32, 91
Moore, Clayton 127
Morgan, Harry 45–46
Morris, Wayne 100–101
Murphy, Audie 41, 79, 95, 97–99, 127, 140, 142–144, 146–147, 154, 160, 240

Naish, J. Carrol 111
The Naked Spur 73–78, 138
The Nameless Breed 135
Neal, Patricia 135
Nelson, Lori 97–98
Nevada Smith 160–165, 222, 227
Newman, Paul 41, 127–129, 130_131, 133–134, 192–196, 203, 222
Nicholson, Jack 203–205, 207
Nickell, Willie 219–220, 226
Night Passage (film) 121, 140–141
Night Passage (novel) 141
No Name on the Bullet 98–99, 141–147
North, Sheree 189
North of '36 (film) 20_
North of '36 (novel) 19–20

Oates, Warren 203
O'Connell, Arthur 136
O'Connor, Carroll 183–184
The Oklahoma Kid 24–28
Opatoshu, David 183
Open Range 239–240
Open Range Men 240
The Outlaw 14
The Outlaw Josie Wales (film) 208_211, 213–216, 229, 231
The Outlaw Josie Wales (novel) 211, 213
Overholser, Wayne D. 182
The Ox-Bow Incident (film) 45–48, 55, 77, 121, 178
The Ox-Bow Incident (novel) 17, 42_44

Paine, Lauran 240–241
Palance, Jack 125
Pale Rider 228–232
Palmer, Betsy 122–124
Parker, Robert P. 142, 240
Pasternak, Joe 30
Pat Garrett and Billy the Kid 131, 180, 201, 227
Patten, Lewis B. 182, 186
Payne, John 104, 106
Peckinpah, Sam 131, 196, 201, 203
Penn, Arthur 127, 129–131, 133, 203, 206–207
Peoples, David Webb 232
Peppard, George 159–162
Perkins, Anthony 122–126, 199
Perkins, Kenneth 95–96, 100–101

Perrin, Vic 100–101
Picerni, Paul 100
Pickens, Slim 226
Pinkerton Detective Agency 109–110
Pitts, ZaSu 16
The Plainsman (1936) 18
Pleshette, Suzanne 162
Poe, Sophie 12
Polonsky, Abraham 222
Porter, Charles 240–241
Post, Ted 178
Powers, Mala 111–112
Principal, Victoria 192, 195
Pursued 57
Pyle, Denver 93, 112

Quantrill, William Clarke 78–79, 208_209
The Quick and the Dead 239
The Quiet One 240
Quinn, Anthony 46, 149, 154

Rage at Dawn 111–114
Railroaded 138
Randolph, Jane 138
The Rare Breed 167
Red River (film) 55
Red River (novel) 55
Red Sundown 182
Redford, Robert 196, 222
Remarque, Erich Maria 33–34
Reno Brothers 108–110
Richter, Conrad 49–52
Riding Shotgun 99–103
Ritter, Tex 34
Robbins, Harold 159
Roberts, Marguerette 52, 241
Robson, May 21
Rogers, Roy 95
Roman, Ruth 65
Roosevelt, Pres. Theodore 5
Rubinek, Saul 234
Russell, Jane 155, 158, 159
Russell, John 208, 229
Ryan, Robert 74, 78, 189
Ryan, Sheila 138

Salmi, Albert 188
San Antone 155
Sanders, Hugh 69, 104, 150
Savage, Les, Jr. 182
Saxon, John 184, 203
Schaefer, Jack 230–231
Scheine, G. David 103–104
Schuster, Harold 90
Scorpio 188
Scott, Jacqueline 166, 170–171
Scott, Randolph 10, 20–21, 24, 64, 66–68, 99–100, 135, 163
Scott, Zachary 64, 68
The Sea of Grass (film) 50–54, 241
The Sea of Grass (novel) 48–50
The Searchers (film) 174

Selander, Lesley 155
The Seventh Seal 143, 145
Shalako 148
Shane (film) 228, 231
Shane (novel) 230–231
Shear, Barry 197–198, 202
Short, Luke 64, 114, 182
Shurlock, Geoffrey 120, 160–161
Siegel, Don 160, 183, 185–186, 202, 223
Silver Lode 104–107
Six Black Horses 98
Slade, Jack 83–89
Sloane, Paul 20
Smith, Kent 183
Smith, William 197
Snodgrass, Carrie 238
Springsteen, R.G. 155–156
Stanton, Harry Dean 173, 204, 206
Starrett, Charles 92
Stehli, Edgar 142
Stephens, Harvey 21, 25
Stevens, Inger 166, 179
Stevens, Leslie 127–128, 133
Stevens, Mark 89–90
Stevens, Warren 141
Stewart, James 29–32, 74, 76–78, 121–122, 139–140, 151, 165, 167, 169–170
Sturges, John 178, 197
Swank, Hilary 236
Swenson, Karl 141–142

Tall in the Saddle 190
Taylor, Dub 183
Taylor, Robert 127
Taylor, Rod 197, 200–201
Taylor, Vaughn 149
Teal, Ray 70–71, 112
Terror Train 179
The Texans 21–25
Thaxter, Phyllis 54
Thompson, Jim 203
Thorpe, Jerry 172
3:10 to Yuma (film, 1957) 117–121
3:10 to Yuma (film, 2009) 120
3:10 to Yuma (story) 117
Three Were Renegades 95, 96
A Time for Killing 171

The Tin Star (film) 122–124, 189, 226
The Todd Killings 202
Tom Horn 99, 221–227
Totten, Robert 183, 185, 202
Totter, Audrey 79–83
Track of the Cat (novel) 44
Tracy, Spencer 48, 52–54
A Tree Grows in Brooklyn (film) 53
True Grit (film, 1969) 240–241
True Grit (film, 2011) 240–241
True Grit (novel) 240–241
Trumbo, Dalton 53, 189
Tucker, Forrest 111–112, 241
Tumbleweed 96–99
Tunstall, John 128
Twain, Mark 85
Twelve Angry Men (film) 121
Two-Gun Marshal 100

Ulzana's Raid 191
Unforgiven 215, 232–236, 238
The Unforgiven (film) 143
Urecal, Minerva 78

Valdez Is Coming (film) 191
Valdez Is Coming (novel) 116
Van Cleef, Lee 96, 123–124
Van Sickel, Dale 156
Vega, Isela 199
The Vengeance of Josie Wales (film) 216
The Vengeance of Josie Wales (novel) 216
Vera Cruz 39, 135
Vernon, John 208
Vidal, Gore 127, 129, 134
Vidor, Charles 58–59
Vidor, King 12–13
Vigilante Terror 93–95
The Virginian (film, 1929) 10–13
The Virginian (film, 1946) 13
The Virginian (novel) 7–9
The Virginian (play) 8

Walker, Robert 48, 52–53
Wallace, George (actor) 93, 111
Wallace, Gov. George 212–214
Wallis, Hal B. 27, 69

Walsh, Raoul 71
War and Peace (film) 121
Warlock (film) 46, 126, 148–154, 242
Warlock (novel) 46, 147–148, 153–154
Warner, Jack L. 45, 57, 66, 68, 79, 99, 165
Wayne, John 13, 53, 63, 69, 190, 196, 241
Webster, Mary 122
Weldon, Joan 64, 101
Wellman, Paul I. 118
Wellman, William A. 45, 47–48, 178
The Westerner 38–42
Whelen, Tim 111, 114
Whipper, Leigh 47
White Heat 63–64
Whitman, Stuart 104
Widmark, Richard 149, 151, 154, 170, 183, 186
The Wild Bunch 171, 180, 196, 222
The Wild One 170
Wilke, Robert 136
Wills, Chill 96, 98
Winchester '73 63, 68, 74
Winner, Michael 188–189, 191
Winniger, Charles 30
Wiseman, Joseph 190
Wister, Owen 5–7, 9–10
Witney, William 142
The Woman They Almost Lynched 78–83, 104
Woods, Harry 190
Woodward, Morgan 166, 183
The Wrong Man 121
Wyler, William 38

Yates, Herbert 79
Young, Robert 96
Young Guns 14
Young Fury 156
The Young Lions (film) 148
The Young Lions (novel) 147
Young Man with a Horn 69

Zachariah 187

www.ingramcontent.com/pod-product-compliance
Lightning Source LLC
Chambersburg PA
CBHW060259240426
43661CB00060B/2833